Wildlife Films

Wildlife Films

Derek Bousé

PENN

University of Pennsylvania Press

Philadelphia

Copyright © 2000 University of Pennsylvania Press
All rights reserved
Printed in the United States of America on acid-free paper

10 9 8 7 6 5 4 3 2 1

Published by
University of Pennsylvania Press
Philadelphia, Pennsylvania 19104-4011

Library of Congress Cataloging-in-Publication Data
Bousé, Derek
  Wildlife films / Derek Bousé.
     p.   cm.
  Includes bibliographical references and index
ISBN: 0-8122-3555-X (cloth : alk. paper)
ISBN: 0-8122-1728-4 (pbk. : alk. paper)
1. Wildlife cinematography.   I. Title
TR893.5. B68   2000
778.5′3859—dc21   00-028676

for
Doug Purl,
whose generosity and encouragement
helped start the ball

Contents

Preface   xi

Introduction   1

1. The Problem of Images   4

2. A Brief History of a Neglected Tradition   37

3. Science and Storytelling   84

4. The Classic Model   127

5. Family Values, Social Mores, Behavioral Norms   152

6. Nature Designed and Composed   185

Appendix: Chronological Highlights from the
History of Wildlife and Natural History Films   195

Notes   223

Bibliography   249

Index   267

Acknowledgments   279

The creative writer, depicting an animal's behaviour, is under no greater obligation to keep within the bounds of exact truth than is the painter or the sculptor in shaping an animal's likeness. But all three artists must regard it as their sacred duty to be properly instructed regarding those particulars in which they deviate from the actual facts. They must indeed be even better informed on those details than on others which they render in a manner true to nature. There is no greater sin against the spirit of true art, no more contemptible dilettantism than to use artistic licence as a specious cover for ignorance of fact.

KONRAD LORENZ, 1963

It is our duty, then, to amuse as well as instruct—and what is more capable of achieving this than the cinematograph?

LEONARD DONALDSON, 1912

Preface

When I first began to research the topic of wildlife films, I began by looking in exactly the wrong places: scholarly journals, film and television histories, genre studies, and other academic sources. It was clear that "serious" scholars of film and television had either overlooked wildlife films or simply dismissed them altogether. Soap operas, romance novels, talk radio, cartoons, and advertisements had all become objects of respectable scholarship, but wildlife films, despite their popularity and long history, went virtually unmentioned. Although I found that the papers and talks I gave about them at academic conferences were received with surprising enthusiasm, it was still some years before I crossed paths with anyone else who took a scholarly interest in the subject. Today there is a small and loose network of scholars interested in wildlife and natural history films, who, despite barriers of language and geography, have begun to exchange papers, observations, and ideas. It is woefully late in the history of motion pictures for this work to have begun, but at least it has.

One of the tasks before us is to gain a more global perspective than the one presented here. Regrettably, I have been able to give almost no attention to production history in the non-English speaking world, or even to the traditions in Canada, Australia, and New Zealand. Instead, I have focused on U.S. and British traditions, although the latter, with its rich history of ferment and creativity, has already received a good deal of attention elsewhere. Book-length studies of the BBC Natural History Unit, Survival Anglia, and Oxford Scientific Films already exist, respectively in Christopher Parsons's *True to Nature* (1982), Colin Willock's *The World of Survival* (1978), and P. S. Crowson's *Animals in Focus* (1981). Mary Field's and Percy Smith's *Secrets of Nature* (1939) had earlier chronicled the production of the "Secrets of Nature" series at Gaumont British Instructional Films during the 1920s and '30s. In addition to these institutional histories (all of which, with the exception of Crowson's, were written by industry "insiders" directly involved in the events they describe), there are a number of professional autobiographies and book-length journal-style accounts from individual filmmakers who have also helped build the industry in Britain: Cherry Kearton's *Wild Life Across the World* (1913), Sterling Gillespie's *Celluloid Safari* (1939), Oliver Pike's *Nature and My Cine Camera* (1946), Michaela Denis's *Leopard in My Lap* (1955) and *Ride a Rhino* (1960), Armand Denis's *On Safari* (1964), Des and Jen Bartlett's *Flight of the Snow Geese* (1975), Tom Stobart's *Tiger Trail* (1975), Desmond Morris's *Animal Days* (1979), Dieter Plage's *Wild Horizons* (1980), Cindy Buxton's *Survival in the Wild* (1980) and *Survival: South Atlantic* (1983), Hugh Miles's and Mike Salisbury's *Kingdom of the Ice Bear* (1985), and a number of books by Gerald Durrell. Barry Paine assures me he is working on one of his own, to be called *A Voice for the Wild.* There have also been several anthologies of "insider" essays, such as *The BBC Naturalist* (1957), *The Second BBC Naturalist* (1960), *Focus on Nature* (1981), *Wildlife Through the Camera* (1982), and *The BBC Natural History Unit's Wildlife Specials* (1997). In addition, writer Andrew Langley contributed an excellent book-length study of the production of a BBC "mega-series," entitled *The Making of "The Living Planet"* (1985). Add these up, along with regular features in trade journals, and you have a fairly comprehensive portrait of wildlife film and television production in Britain—one to which an American like myself could hope to add little.

Nothing quite like this body of insider literature exists to chronicle the development of wildlife film in the United States. Fortunately, Marlin Perkins's *My Wild Kingdom* (1982) and Marty Stouffer's *Wild America* (1988) reveal much about the U.S. television industry's ambivalence toward wildlife programs and its reluctance, until recently, to explore their potential. Other insider views have been less revealing. In *Strange Animals I Have Known* (1931), Raymond Ditmars only briefly discusses his considerable pioneering wildlife film work. Martin and Osa Johnson wrote (or signed their names to) a number of books chronicling their experiences, but these are less about wildlife filmmaking than about the Johnsons themselves and their colorful "adventures." Lois Crisler's *Arctic Wild* (1958) also reveals surprisingly little about the process of filming wildlife with her husband Herb in the 1950s. William Koehler's *The Wonderful World of Disney Animals* (1979) tells of his experiences as animal trainer and wrangler for Disney's "True Life Adventures" and other animal films, but offers little beyond cheery reminiscence. Ivan Tors's *My Life in the Wild* (1979) is about his experiences making feature films and television programs with animal actors, such as *Flipper* and *Daktari.*

There has likewise been relatively little written, for either scholarly or popular consumption, by those analyzing the industry from outside. Raymond Lee's *Not So Dumb: The Life and Times of Animal Actors* (1970), as its title suggests, is not about wildlife films, but does contain a whole chapter on Disney's animal films, including the "True Life Adventures." Most of the book-length studies of the Disney empire, such as Richard Schickel's *The Disney Version* (1985), mention the studio's wildlife films only briefly. The early history of wildlife film in North America received its first significant scholarly acknowledgment in Kevin Brownlow's *The War, the West, and the Wilderness* (1979), although, unfortunately, only in the context of the documentary genre. Pascal and Eleanor Imperato's *They Married Adventure* (1992) is a long overdue consideration of the films of Martin and Osa Johnson. Gregg Mitman's *Reel Nature* (1999) is another welcome recent addition to the scholarly literature on the historical development of wildlife film in the North America. Still, beyond a handful of articles in technical and trade journals, there remains a dearth of material addressing contemporary issues in wildlife film and television, and there is relatively little, overall, to bring the study of American wildlife films out of the archives and into the light of day.

Some, perhaps especially some of those in the industry, may feel I have repeated a pattern among scholars of placing too much emphasis on Disney's films. I believe readers will find my attention warranted, given their role in the development of wildlife film storytelling, but I too am eager to move the discourse on from Disney. Given the many recent developments in the wildlife film industry, there is a great deal else to occupy our attention.

Nevertheless, my approach to many contemporary themes and issues in this book is almost inevitably by way of history, and this has subjected me to the historian's temptation to keep looking ever farther into the past in search of influences and origins. Although, clearly, I attach some importance to popular animal stories in the late nineteenth century, which I believe occupied a place for earlier audiences similar to the one wildlife films occupy for today's, I have tried to check the urge to keep going farther back into the cultural past, and to call up the entire history of natural history representation. Whatever their sources and influences, wildlife films are largely a twentieth-century phenomenon, and it is to that century I have devoted the majority of my attention.

A related temptation in historical scholarship is that of "firstism"—that loathsome habit of pointing to this or that occurrence as the "first" in history. I would like to say that I avoided it, but must confess instead that too often I succumbed. To minimize the annoyance, however, I have included a chronology of significant events, or "highlights," from the history of wildlife film, in an Appendix.

I regret that in this book I have really not dealt with films about underwater creatures—cetaceans, crustaceans, fish, and so on. I see underwater films, however, as operating by somewhat different codes and conventions because of the conditions under which they are made, the behavior of underwater creatures themselves, and several other factors. Although I have confined my analysis to "topside" films, I believe a book comparable in scope to this one can and should be written about films dealing with undersea life.

I have also given only scant attention in these pages to another area that otherwise interests me greatly: that of what might be called "environmental documentaries"—films made with the express purpose of addressing environmental or wildlife protection issues and effecting changes in attitudes, behaviors, policies, and the like. In the tradition of Griersonian documentary, these films alert us to problems, propose solutions, and call us to action. It is my contention, however, that wildlife films are not documentaries; in this book I argue that they are primarily narrative entertainments that usually steer clear of real social and environmental issues (which could alienate some viewers, or make it difficult to sell a film overseas, or worst of all, prevent crucial rerun sales by dating the film). Still, wildlife films continue to be seen by many audience members as a form of environmentally committed documentary. I was recently reminded of this when my students in the United States indicated they assumed that wildlife films were produced mainly by environmental and wildlife protection organizations. The experience was repeated when I spoke to a similar group in Spain. In both cases it seemd to come as a surprise to learn that nearly all wildlife films on television are made by run-for-profit production companies with no formal wildlife preservation or conservation agenda.

How effective any form of mass-market nature imagery is as a means of inducing real social or environmental change on its own, and doing so, moreover, by purposeful design, is open to question. So far there has been a great deal of optimistic presumption but a dearth of real evidence about the power of wildlife films to "save" nature. I have not entered into the "effects" or "effectiveness" debate in this book, but it may be worth noting that during the very period of wildlife films' ascendancy on television (since the early 1960s) the state of wildlife and the natural world has, by most measures, worsened alarmingly. Arguments that wildlife films directly help save nature nearly all rest on anecdotal evidence ("it changed *my* life!" or "we received a thousand letters!"), as well as a failure to consider sampling procedures, viewers' predispositions, and the difficulty of actually measuring "effectiveness." With content designed to appeal to tens of millions of diverse viewers worldwide, film and television are not precision implements that can be wielded with predictable results. Some wildlife films may influence some people in some ways under some circumstances some of the time, but there is little to suggest that the genre itself makes a significant contribution to protecting the lives of wild animals, or to preserving species or habitat, in the sort of systematic or predictable ways that would prove it an effective tool. My reading of the research over the years has led me to conclude that film and television tend, if anything, to ratify and legitimize status quo values, and to reflect those values in both their formal and institutional structures, in spite of whatever good intentions there may be on the part of those who fashion the content of individual works.

Still, my own filmmaking experiences have given me the highest regard for the creative and artistic abilities of the people who make wildlife films. Some whose names appear frequently in these pages, such as Attenborough, Parsons, Stouffer, and Willock, may appear to be ongoing targets of criticism, but this owes less to their film and television work than to their published words, for they are among the few who have put their their thoughts and ideas into print, where they can be scrutinized, dissected, excerpted, and reprinted. Although I have ventured criticisms of films and programs involving their work, or that of a number of other people who have been good enough to speak with me, or with whom I have become friendly, let me assure them that my remarks are intended in the spirit of constructive collegiality we have enjoyed over the years at festivals and symposia, and that my purpose in this book is to widen and deepen appreciation of their work, not to diminish it.

The recent films singled out for criticism here are more a sample of convenience than a random selection. Most were broadcast on U.S. television from 1996 to 1999. To the legitimate question of whether a few relatively minor slips in some of them merit intense scrutiny and criticism, my answer is "yes" if they typify larger patterns, or if they contribute to accumulated misunderstanding of something as important as the welfare of wild animals and the natural world. I have tried to limit my targets to demonstrable errors and misrepresentations of scientific fact, and to make clear that I see these not as deliberate attempts to deceive or mislead, but as examples of the "tyranny of formula" in media—that is, of pressures imposed by convention, and by the economics of a competitive, ratings-driven industry.

Lastly, it is my hope that as more scholars turn their attention to wildlife and natural history films they do so not merely as an untapped source of fodder for "theory" at the expense of a thorough engagement with the films themselves. I offer this book as an invitation to such engagements, and to a greater appreciation of wildlife films and the people who make them.

Introduction

It is remarkable, if one stops to consider, how ill-suited film and television are to some of their most important tasks. As vehicles of science popularization they are unequaled, but as means of conveying the experience of nature to those who crave it, or as delegates representing wild animals to those with the power to determine their fates, film and television are unlikely candidates.

The lives of wild animals, like the stillness of open spaces, may simply be unsuited to film and television representation—but not because these media suffer from technological limitations, or because they deal in two-dimensional images. Rather, the real sources of film and television's incompatibility with nature lie in their histories, in their social and cultural environments, and ultimately, in the economic and institutional agendas to which they have been conscripted. How film and television depict the natural world often has far less to do with science or real outdoor experience than with media economics, established production practices, viewers' expectations, and the ways each of these influences the others.

Consider, as an example, the notorious trailer Time-Life ran on American television in the early 1990s to sell its video tapes of the BBC series *The Trials of Life*. As if designed to illustrate the degree of disparity between the natural world and its media representation, the ad was an extended, rapidly cut montage of action long-shots and intense close-ups (of snarling predators), set to exceedingly percussive music to heighten the sense of drama, danger, and unease. As an image of nature it was exotic, artificial, and tendentious. As a piece of film it was exciting, even Eisensteinian. As television, it seemed perfectly designed to capture viewer attention and prevent channel-changing. As an advertisement to promote sales, it was an unqualified success.[1]

Yet the trailer was roundly denounced in wildlife and natural history film circles. Reportedly, *TOL* host/presenter David Attenborough "was so upset by the ads that he considered taking legal action."[2] Significantly, however, complaints against the trailer did not charge that its rapid cutting, its emphasis on speed, action, and excitement, and its breathless, hyperbolic narration had misrepresented nature or wildlife, but only that it had misrepresented the BBC's series. Although its images were all drawn from series episodes, it was the selection of *which* images that drew the angry responses. One producer charged that it "took 13 hours of natural history and went for all the aggressive parts," yet conceded that intense market pressure is largely what drives "fang television" in the United States.[3] It is certainly no secret that the American market demands "higher tempo—much more action,"[4] but the *TOL* trailer was seen as evincing a characteristically American crassness and lack of restraint. Indeed, just as Hollywood films are often helped at the box office by an "R" ("Restricted") rating, the trailer even included its own restrictive caution: "Warning: some scenes may be too intense for younger viewers." Ultimately, then, the real outrage seemed not to be directed at the distorted image of nature, but at the intrusion of American-style capitalism, with its circus-like air, into the hallowed traditions of the BBC Natural History Unit (which nevertheless profited greatly from the Time-Life deal).

The complaints were a bit like those of a professional wrestler screaming and pounding the mat. The ad, after all, had merely condensed to two minutes what regular wildlife programs typically take an hour or so to do. It was shorter, faster, and more intense, but not different in substance.[5] True, it eschewed narrative, but the manner in which it manipulated time and space certainly broke no new ground. Godfrey Reggio's *Anima Mundi* (1992), which is similar in both content and form, has earned high acclaim for its dramatic juxtapositions of unrelated wildlife images. Although lacking voice-over narration, its real differences from the *TOL* trailer were differences of degree, not of kind. Perhaps precisely because it was an extended, nonnarrative montage set to music (by Philip Glass), and because of the absence of narration, *Anima Mundi* was greeted as an *art* film (as well as a paean to wildlife conservation—it bears the seal of the World Wildlife Fund), while the *TOL* trailer is still reviled.

Yet whatever its faults, the trailer helped the BBC series reach more viewers, through video sales, than would otherwise ever have seen it, and did so precisely by the means for which it was criticized—and which, arguably, summarize the wildlife film genre's relationship to nature. For if there remains something troubling about the *TOL* trailer, it may only be that it represents the art of wildlife films taken to extremes. Perhaps it is a caricature of what are already the genre's excesses. Perhaps it holds a mirror up to them and reflects them back in unflinching clarity. If so, negative reactions to the trailer may simply have expressed the shock of recognition.

For whether in two minutes or two hours, in a promotional trailer or a detailed natural history study, in nonnarrative montages or in elaborately plotted dramatic stories, wildlife film and television depict nature close-up, speeded-up, and set to music, with reality's most exciting moments high-lighted, and its "boring" bits cut out.

1
The Problem of Images

Anyone who spends time outdoors has probably realized that most *real* experiences of the natural world, away from cities and development, tend to be experiences of serenity and quietude. This is what has accounted for most notions of nature's regenerative and spiritually redemptive power.

Yet stillness and silence have almost no place in wildlife film, or in film and television generally—not because they are incapable, as media technologies, of conveying these qualities, but because stillness and silence are incompatible with the social and economic functions of film and television, and with the expressive "vocabularies" they have developed in fulfilling those functions. Film and television are about movement, action, and dynamism; nature is generally not. Film and television also have little tolerance for what is normal and usual in life, thriving instead on what is rare and unusual. Spectacular chases and bloody kills are everyday events on film and television, occurring with remarkable regularity and predictability, yet are surprisingly rare occurrences in reality. Relative to the vastness of the natural world and the slow unfolding of time, these things occupy a minute place. Indeed, the natural world may actually be better suited to a television aesthetic of the C-SPAN sort, or to the cable channel that shows those slow, continuous satellite views of the earth, than it is to competitive prime-time television. Nevertheless, the image of nature found in wildlife and natural history television has been molded to fit the medium.

Form and Formula

It should not be surprising that wildlife films resemble their competition in film and television. Vying with mainstream action-adventure stories and family melodramas means competing on *their* terms and appropriating some of *their* devices and themes. Wildlife film may be recognizable as a genre with its own codes and conventions, but even these are largely variations on the familiar themes and patterns common to virtually all film and television genres. Like horror films, westerns, sit-coms, police shows, and others, the success of individual wildlife films depends on their ability to appear unique while at the same time evoking those familiar patterns. The idea is to present audiences with something recognizable, for which they already have conceptual categories; to be consistent with their previous viewing experiences, to fulfill not thwart their expectations, and to do all this by employing already familiar conventions of realism, not by trying to reproduce reality itself.

The "world" created on the screen is one we enjoy for its own sake, on its own terms, and by its own logic, without comparing it to, or judging it by, our experience of reality. So long as it is plausible, we may accept its conditions even if they do not correspond to those we experience in the real world.[1] Wildlife films need not, therefore, give absolutely accurate reflections of the natural world—especially to viewers who may have had little or no direct experience with wild animals and nature and whose expectations may have been shaped more by media images than by real experience. Critic Robert Warshow once observed that a given type of film appeals only faintly, if at all, "to its audience's experience of reality," but rather "to previous experience of the type itself: it creates its own field of reference."[2] Indeed, much of what we think of as reality may have come to us in the first place by way of representation of some kind. We experience the world beyond our own daily lives mainly, as film critic Richard Dyer has put it, through "texts, discourse, [and] images." Yet reality "is always more extensive and complicated than any system of representation can possibly comprehend and we always sense that it is so—representation never "gets" reality, which is why human history has produced so many different and changing ways of trying to get it."[3]

The questions at this point are: Do wildlife films "get" the realities of nature? Do they convey the natural world to us on its terms, or on theirs? Or has their internal "field of reference," the reality of the world they create on the screen, with its market-driven, formulaic emphasis on dramatic narrative and ever-present danger, slowly shaped people's expectations and perceptions of the real natural world? If so, to what extent, and most important, with what consequences? Research in visual communication suggests that viewers often interpret attributes of film form as attributes of content, for example, mistaking *editing* speed for *event speed*.[4] What might be the implications, then, of widespread perceptions of nature and wildlife *in television terms*—that is, as being characterized by nearly incessant motion, action, and dynamism? Might viewers, especially heavy viewers, see the natural world as dangerous, threatening, even hostile? Might there already be a sort of "mean world syndrome" in some of our perceptions of it?[5]

Wildlife films are of course only one part of a larger media picture that may influence perceptions and expectations of the natural world. Similar portrayals can be seen in feature films, children's programs, and advertisements. Consider the techniques of visual intensification used in television advertisements for four-wheel-drive vehicles, or in depictions of skiing, snowboarding, and so-called "extreme" outdoor sports. The effect of the images is nearly always intensified by rapid cutting among sharply contrasting oblique camera angles, as if the worst tendencies of MTV and *Outside* magazine had run amuck. Yet if the contemplative experience of nature (of the sort reflected in landscape paintings, for example) has given way to its perception as merely a spectacular backdrop for rapid, heart-pounding action, for a vicarious "rush," it seems fairly clearly driven by larger commercial forces. As the next chapter will show, the history of wildlife films confirms the relationship between on-screen action, vicarious thrill, and profitability.

Image and Expectation

Given the pervasive media image of nature as a site of action and excitement, it is not surprising that a common complaint heard in national parks is that the animals don't seem to *do* anything; they just lie there. The torpor that characterizes so much of their lives, and that is so plainly evident in the lives of our own domestic cats and dogs, seems always to come as a surprise and a disappointment to tourists viewing animals in their natural habitats. This is also true in zoos, where, as John Berger has noted, animals almost never live up to expectations, and where, especially to children, "they appear, for the most part, unexpectedly lethargic and dull. (As frequent as the calls of animals in a zoo, are the cries of children demanding: Where is he? Why doesn't he move? Is he dead?) And so one might summarise the felt, but not necessarily expressed question of most visitors as: *Why are these animals less than I believed?*" [6] The answer may seem obvious, but Berger did not look for it on television. Others, however, did. A piece in *The Listener* told of a woman who thought that "wildlife films actually discouraged children: they made nature seem so spectacular, and when the children rushed out into the woods burning with enthusiasm, they found there wasn't a bird to be seen." [7]

Still, the extent to which film and television have contributed to inflated expectations and frustrated experiences is difficult to measure and easy to over-estimate. The "effects" (if any) of wildlife film and television may be impossible to separate from those of the rest of film and television, where the same distortions of reality abound, and to which viewers may be even more heavily exposed.

As an illustration of the differences between the purposes of film and television on the one hand, and the realities of nature on the other, consider the example of African lions, who often spend up to twenty hours a day at rest. In a one-hour (fifty-two-minute) wildlife film for television this would amount to about forty-two minutes of relative inactivity—true to nature, perhaps, but anathema to distributors, broadcasters, and advertisers. Such a film would surely induce mass channel-changing even among viewers who might be content to sit and watch the same lions for forty-two minutes from a Kenyan tourist van, but who have come to expect something else entirely from television. A "proportional" representation such as this of the lives of animals, although compressed to an hour, may or may not give us a true feeling for life in the wild, but it would surely be considered "bad television" and therefore bad business. "Bad television" is not merely an aesthetic judgment of the extent to which some program violates established formal conventions, but a marketing and financial judgment of whether that program is likely to attract large audiences for advertisers. A film "about a jungle where nothing happens," Attenborough once noted, "is not really what you turned the television set on to see."[8] Although it might attract some of the people drawn to Andy Warhol's *Empire* (1964) or Michael Snow's *Wavelength* (1967) or those who use their television sets as video fish aquariums or fireplaces, their numbers would be too small to justify broadcasting such a program. As technologies, film and television are perfectly capable of depicting a jungle where nothing happens or animals that rest 80 percent of their time. As social and economic entities, however, neither film nor television exists to reproduce this kind of reality. The point can be made with a few brief images and a line in the narration, then it's on to more exciting scenes.

Film and television do not and cannot convey reality in its fullness, but have become quite adept at *realism*—that is, at giving convincing impressions of reality. As already argued, they needn't be accurate, only plausible. Our willingness to accept images as having some relation to reality, without actually holding them up to reality for comparison, accounts for the success of television advertising, where we tend to accept the world depicted on its own terms. Although it might be argued that we should expect greater fidelity to reality in advertising, or at least accurate reports of a product's attributes, it is clear that we do not, and that we have come to accept it as a kind of entertaining art that operates according to its own rules.

It seems that the same is true of wildlife films. As already mentioned, because we may have little or no experience of the worlds they depict, we may have nothing against which to weigh the images, or by which to assess their fidelity to reality, and may end up simply accepting them, like advertising, on their own terms. As Warshow suggested, they need not even appeal to our experience of reality, but only to our "previous experience of the type itself"—that is, *to other wildlife films.* Wildlife films may be full of scientific facts, but they have largely been freed of the responsibility of looking just like reality. Like advertising, they have become an entertaining art that operates according to its own codes and conventions.

This does not mean I question the accuracy of the photographic images in wildlife films. Let us assume, for the sake of argument, that most of them provide fairly accurate reports of what was before the camera. I am more concerned with how those images are manipulated, intensified, dramatized, and fictionalized by other nonphotographic formal means—not in a single film but systematically over decades. The use of formal artifice such as varying camera angles, continuity editing, montage editing, slow-motion, "impossible" close-ups, voice-over narration, dramatic or ethnic music, and the like should by no means be off limits to wildlife filmmakers, but by the same token we should not avoid critical reflection on the overall image of nature and wildlife that emerges, cumulatively, from the long-term and systematic use of such devices.

The point is not that these are, in themselves, deceptive, but that their widespread use in wildlife films may do less to acquaint us with nature than to alienate us from it, and that repeated exposure to nature and wildlife through a shroud of cinematic conventions may help make us less, not more, sensitive to it. As in Hollywood films, the invisibility of convention is what allows them to convey the impression of reality,[9] but wildlife films are not Hollywood films—at least, not yet. Nevertheless, they may lead us not toward nature, but toward art. This would be an admirable enough project were it announced and understood clearly. Yet as the art of wildlife films becomes more sophisticated, the reliance on artificial formal devices more widespread, and the devices themselves more subtle, viewers may see wildlife films as offering even more scientifically accurate reflections of reality than in decades past.

But what *kind* of reality? Some argue that a wildlife film shows us things we might actually have been able to see in nature, had we been there (in the position of the camera).[10] This may be true, if we are talking only about the content of individual images, which, I have already suggested, offer acceptable enough reproductions of what was in front of the camera. The problem is that although wildlife films may show us things we might really have been able to see, they typically do so in *ways* we could never see them, and in which nobody ever has seen them *directly*, including the people who film them. Obviously, the natural world does not reveal itself to them in the highly contrived and *cinematic* way it appears on the screen.[11]

Even the animals themselves do not experience their lives as they are portrayed on film and television. Condensed into an hour or less, with the boring bits cut out, their lives appear far more busy and event-filled than they really are or ever could be.[12] To maintain a dramatically compelling pace, animals (as well as on-screen presenters) often seem to proceed directly from one thrilling event to the next. A film about prairie dogs, for example, shows one of them confronting a ferret, a coyote, an owl, a badger, a falcon, a bison, a storm, a fire, and a flood, all in direct succession, if not in real time. The narrator remarks, "In nature, breathless moments and narrow escapes are all part of the *daily routine*." Another film repeats the pattern: in only a few minutes of screen time, a single prairie dog is depicted as confronting a pronghorn antelope, a bison, a rattlesnake, a badger, an eagle, and a marsh hawk, again edited together in a way that suggests real time. The narration concludes that "these small dramas of life and death are *typical of any day* on the prairie." In fact, encounters with predators are quite rare for prairie dogs, just as they are for many other "prey species," if only by virtue of the fact that most of them outnumber predators greatly.

Still, wildlife films often follow a formula of successive predator-prey interactions. An episode of the *Wild Kingdom* series once included the following sequence of confrontations in less than half an hour: a fox chasing otters, a black bear cub nosing a porcupine, an otter challenging a fox and later a duck, an otter chasing a fawn, an otter battling a bobcat, a bobcat killing a gray squirrel, a fox chasing a woodchuck, a fox killing a ground squirrel, and a skunk spraying a fox—all portrayed as among a single day's encounters in one location.[13] BBC producer Christopher Parsons has rightly noted that some films have "crammed in as many incidents and confrontations with other species as time will allow. It may be argued that these confrontations *can* happen in nature, but it is probable that they occur only very occasionally, even when they are direct predator/prey relationships. Four or five confrontations between species that do not normally have much to do with one another give a hopelessly false impression when they are strung together in twenty minutes of film."[14]

Simulation and Its Discontents

All of this begs another question: when images filmed over a period of weeks or months are edited into a dramatic sequence suggesting a single "event," or series of directly related occurrences, what does it all really represent? That is, to what do the images that make up the on-screen event really refer? Presumably, they must refer to something in the real world, rather than simply represent the imaginative creations of filmmakers. Here are some possible answers, each describing a different type of "event," listed in order of increasing formal intervention, and increasing distance from reality:

1. A specific event that actually occurred, *naturally*, at a single time and place before the camera, as it appears on screen. (Here is what David MacDougall has described as "a cinema of duration," not to mention an illustration of the realist aesthetics of André Bazin.[15])

2. A specific event that actually occurred at a single time and place before the camera—not on its own, however, but as the result of some kind of provocation or staging, as when two animals are placed in an enclosure and filmed as they fight. The behavior may be real, but not actually based on

truth, and might never have occurred otherwise. (According to cameraman Stephen Mills, wildlife filmmakers have a tacit agreement that any scene can be staged provided it depicts "a scientifically observable fact," or, as Attenborough put it, is "faithful to the biological truth." Marty Stouffer has described this as being "true . . . yet not always real."[16] The notion here of "factual re-creation" is common also, of course, to documentary and journalism.)

3. A specific event that actually occurred, *naturally*, at a single time and place, but not as it appears on screen, owing to formal manipulations of time and space by way of editing (especially between multiple camera positions that may distort the spatial and/or temporal continuity of the event), or slow-motion photography that may maintain spatial continuity, but no longer depict real time.

4. A "composite" event constructed through editing from fragments of separate events that actually occurred, either naturally or through provocation, either to the same animal(s) or to different, look-alike animals, but not at one time and place as depicted (Often, for example, if an unusual occurrence is captured on film, actions or scenes that create a complete sequence around it are "back-filmed" later with other animals.)

Some might disagree that slow-motion scenes or back-filmed composite events depicting authenticated biological facts are farther from reality than staged events. Yet such an argument may be a measure of the degree to which we accept wildlife films on their own cinematic terms with little objection, and often even with little awareness. Stories abound of scientists basing conclusions on film sequences in apparent unawareness of the editorial manipulations involved. In one such incident recounted by Attenborough, a scientist had studied a film of his depicting ritual bungee-jumping in New Hebrides in the 1950s. Unaware of the ways in which time and space are manipulated in constructing composite events for the screen, he came up with "all kinds of complex mathematical formulae" regarding the speed and momentum of the jump. "I discovered," writes Attenborough,

that he had actually taken my film and measured the moment from when the man's feet left the platform to when he hit the ground, and had used that as the basis of all these calculations, ignoring the fact that I had actually started with a wide shot which had been taken earlier; I had then gone to a close-up of a man on the top, which belonged to *that* jump; I had cut-away to his mother-in-law, who was at the bottom and looking approving; I had then gone back to a wide shot showing a different jumper altogether, before ending with a final shot which was again somebody else, altogether different.[17]

Although Attenborough saw the scientist as guilty of "ignoring the fact" of editorial manipulation and composite, what the story may really illustrate is the invisibility of cinematic convention, even to "an intelligent and honest man." Attenborough does concede that natural history filmmakers "invoke fiction much more than we imagine," but argues nevertheless that a film-maker "should be allowed to introduce fiction into his natural history film-making," and that "on occasion, *un*natural history is one of the most potent ways of revealing natural history."[18]

This echoes age-old notions of fiction sometimes being more true than fact, or at least able to penetrate to deeper (emotional or psychological) truths not revealed by "mere" facts. Yet the only thing anchoring Atten-borough's paradox to reality is the underlying presumption of the absolute truth of the individual photographic image, and faith that its oneness with reality tolerates any kind of formal manipulation. So long as the ingredi-ents are "real" and "natural," the assumption seems that whatever is made of them must, in the end, also be. If one uses only logs and earth as build-ing materials, then a house in the middle of the forest, however imagina-tive its architecture and complex its construction, must be "natural" too, mustn't it?[19]

What has gone almost completely unquestioned in relation to wildlife films has been the presumption of compatibility between cinematic conven-tion and images of natural events and behavior. In *Making Wildlife Movies* (1971), Parsons articulated what may still be the most widely held view on the matter: "unless the film is of an academic nature and made primarily for a scientific audience, the film-maker's only obligation to his audience is to ensure that his film is true to life, *within the accepted conventions of film-making.*"[20]

Some still argue that even to ask the question of how reliable images of nature can be when all the formal conventions of cinematic art are brought to bear on them is to miss the point. Film and television are creative media, they point out, not transparent windows to reality. Precisely. The question is whether, or to what extent, audience members recognize this. Obviously the scientist above, although "an intelligent and honest man," did not. Atten-borough's solution is an appeal to *sincerity*: "in the end, it's the motive of the film-maker that is crucial."[21] Financial motives notwithstanding, it seems fair to argue that the perceptions of viewers may be at least as important, perhaps more.

Among the few challenges to status quo thinking regarding formal ma-nipulation in wildlife films is a 1986 reflection on the use of slow-motion, written by BBC producer Jeffery Boswall. Received opinion regarding slow-motion is that, because it can reveal details of movement and behavior that might otherwise be impossible to detect, its use therefore serves a scien-tific purpose ("*un*natural history . . . revealing natural history"). This argu-ment, however, seems to apply mainly to ethologists or other serious stu-dents of behavioral detail. In films for popular audiences, the main function of slow-motion is to create dramatic, eye-grabbing images that hold their attention—regardless how unreal the depiction of reality becomes. Boswall recalls being told by one filmmaker that he had filmed sea lions in slow-motion because "it would add grandeur," not science. The problem with this, he argues, is that "the slower an animal moves, the larger it appears," and that this makes the filmmaker's decision not just an aesthetic choice but an ethical one. Why? Because to lead viewers to make a false inference, even if only about an animal's size, is to *mis*lead them, and to mislead viewers is a violation of their trust and of the filmmaker's ethical responsibility to them. Boswall goes on to argue, however, that the slower the motion the more likely it is to be detected by viewers, and therefore the less likely it is to mislead. Until that "threshold of self-evidence" is reached, however, he maintains that slow-motion should be signaled to viewers either by the narrator, or by on-screen labels, or by the use of slowed-down "mush" sound.[22]

Such proposals have not only gone unheeded, but have threatened producers with a Pandora's box of similar arguments that could be made in relation to virtually all the formal devices in the wildlife filmmaker's repertoire: continuity editing (such as described by Attenborough above), dramatic music, ethnic music, sound effects, telephoto close-ups, and blue-screen shots, to name a few. And, indeed, they should. Yet it may now be too late, or too academic, or simply naive and unrealistic to ask the question of whether formal conventions associated with the "invisible" style of Hollywood have any place in films that may be thought by viewers to give scientifically accurate representations of reality. At the very least, however, there need to be more candid and revealing discussions like Attenborough's, and even more thoughtful reflections like Boswall's on technique.

Similar reflections on documentary films, and on their "creative treatment of actuality," have likewise tended to judge the degree of reality based on content more than on form. Bill Nichols has noted that documentary films have also remained largely exempt from "formal or aesthetic debate." He cites an argument that documentaries (like wildlife films) are governed by "an aesthetic of content," and that for audiences, therefore, a documentary (like a wildlife film) is only "as good as its content." Nichols adds that only by more closely examining *how* such films are put together can we avoid the misconception that "documentary-equals-reality, and that the screen is a window rather than a reflecting surface."[23] Although wildlife films are not documentaries, Nichols's argument nevertheless applies. This can be seen in a more lengthy passage, in which I have substituted "wildlife" for "documentary":

[Wildlife] films seldom receive analysis that attempts to describe their structure rigorously, since their content is taken to be of paramount importance. Attention turns to content; and structure and, to an even greater extent, style are usually considered only as evidence of the director's attitude toward his subject matter . . . [or of]

how "faithfully" something has been represented. Assumptions prevail that a certain transparency exists between film (text) and referent (reality), the transparency Eisenstein sought to transcend, Bazin to celebrate.[24]

Given questions of wildlife films' relationship to reality, and of the role of formal conventions in defining that relationship, we might say that depictions of animals and nature in wildlife films today lie somewhere between *representation* and *simulation*. The distinction is Jean Baudrillard's, but it may be useful here insofar as it offers a series of categories (Baudrillard calls them "phases") in which an image does one of four things: (1) reflects a basic reality, (2) masks and perverts a basic reality, (3) masks the *absence* of a basic reality, and finally (4) bears no relation to any reality whatever (and is thus pure *simulacrum*).[25] These roughly correspond to a scale used in introductory film courses as a means of graphically classifying various types of motion pictures[26]:

Realism	*Classicism*	*Formalism*
	realistic fiction	
iconic		symbolic
mimetic		mythic/formulaic
Lumière	Griffith	Méliès
documentary	Hollywood films	avant garde
C-SPAN	Prime-time	ads/MTV
	wildlife film	

The position of each name or item here represents only its most obvious tendencies, not absolute categorizations. On the left is the tendency toward external reference, that is, to refer to a known "outside" world by resembling it; on the right is the tendency toward internal reference, or those things that depend on previous experience of the type itself, or membership in some sort of community "to recognize the restricted nature of its formulae, clichés, and stereotypes."[27]

This may help us situate wildlife film, very generally, in relation to other types of motion pictures and television, but its schematic simplicity clearly limits its usefulness in classifying *individual* films, which may combine elements from different parts of the scale. Wildlife films, in particular, may range more widely across it than might other types of motion pictures. One might even situate the major wildlife film producers at different points. One can imagine where Oxford Scientific Films, the BBC, Survival Anglia, National Geographic, and Disney might all be inserted. Further, some might even see different television networks similarly categorized, although distinctions between the BBC and ITV, or between PBS and the Discovery Channel are fading.

Avant-garde films, music videos, and advertisements may all start from no reality at all, and stay there. Hollywood films may start with only surface reality, and penetrate no deeper. Wildlife films, however, have reality as their foundation and starting point, yet typically proceed through a series of artificial formal interventions, as well as fictionalized, dramatic narratives. We might thus make the spectrum even more relevant to them by adding each of the four types of "events" described earlier, along with Baudrillard's four "phases," and give the model a more linear and dynamic aspect:

Realism	*Classicism*		*Formalism*
	wildlife film		
(1) real, natural events	(2) real but staged events	(3) real events formally altered	(4) composite events
(1) reflect reality	(2) mask and pervert it	(3) mask its absence	(4) bear no relation
$\longrightarrow$	$\longrightarrow$	$\longrightarrow$	

This may help illustrate the way wildlife films can stray from reality toward unreality. Because their content is nature, they may never get all the way to the "pure simulation" of phase 4, yet it seems that in some cases, such as *Anima Mundi*, this may be the only thing keeping them from it. The history of wildlife films corresponds closely to the first two, at least, of Baudrillard's phases, as increased formal and technological sophistication has allowed for greater artfulness and illusion. Mills notes, for example, one way in which reality is masked and perverted:

When we film lions gorging on a bloody zebra in the Serengeti, or a cheetah flat out after a bounding gazelle, we rarely turn the cameras on the dozen or so Hiace vans and land-rovers, packed with tourists sharing the wilderness experience. All over the world, we frame our pictures as carefully as the directors of costume dramas, to exclude telegraph poles and electricity pylons, cars, roads, and people. No such vestige of reality may impinge on the period-piece fantasy of the natural world we wish to purvey.[28]

The type of "period-piece fantasy of the natural world" Mills describes, is often referred to as "blue chip" wildlife film. Definitions vary, but among its chief tendencies are: (1) *the depiction of mega-fauna*—big cats, bears, sharks, crocodiles, elephants, whales, and the like; (2) *visual splendor*—magnificent scenery as a background to the animals, suggesting a still-unspoiled, primeval wilderness; (3) *dramatic storyline*—a compelling narrative, perhaps centering on a single animal, with some sort of dramatic arc intended to capture and hold viewer attention (i.e., not a science lecture); (4) *absence of science*—while perhaps the weakest and most often broken of these "rules," the discourse of science can entail its own narrative of research, with all its attendant technical jargon and seemingly arcane methodologies, which can shift the focus onto scientists and spoil the "period-piece fantasy" of pristine nature; (5) *absence of politics*—little or no reference to controversial issues, which are often seen as "doom and gloom" themes, and no overt Griersonian-style propaganda on behalf of wildlife conservation issues, their causes, or possible solutions, although a brief statement may be included at the film's conclusion; (6) *absence of historical reference points*—"There has to be a sense of timelessness," producer Dione Gilmour has said,[29] suggesting that not only must nature itself appear timeless, but there should also be no clear references that would date the film or ground it in a specific time, and thus prevent future rerun sales; 7) *absence of people*—the presence of humans may also spoil the image of a timeless realm, untouched and uncorrupted by civilization, where predator and prey still interact just as they have for aeons.

For now, let us consider the absence of people—at least, *white* people—from the depiction of nature.[30] It has long been noted by art historians that landscape images could be interpreted according to whether or not they included human figures. Long before blue chip wildlife films offered period-piece fantasies of the natural world, images of uninhabited landscapes portrayed what Barbara Novak has described as "a primal, untouched Eden, existing in a realm of 'mythic time.'"[31] In nature photography the presence of a human figure is thought to remove an image from the realm of "fine arts" to the genre of "science."[32] Ansel Adams, for example, never included human figures in his landscapes, which are today recognized as enduring works of art. During the Depression, however, Adams was criticized for his inattention to people and social issues, and for "photographing rocks" while the "whole world is going to pieces."[33] In effect, the charge was that by excluding images of people Adams was creating art rather than science or socially conscious documentary.[34] His images thus fell into Baudrillard's phase 2, in that they were perceived as masking and perverting reality. The parallel to wildlife films today is worth noting; debate today often centers on a similar opposition between documentary and art, but the tendency to exclude people from the picture of nature is as strong as ever.

Wildlife films may thus be arriving at Baudrillard's phase 3, in which they may actually "mask the absence of a basic reality" by the underrepresentation of people, and overrepresentation of animals that may actually be on the edge of extinction. Of the latter, Attenborough once remarked, "I may go into a forest and spend a month taking fleeting shots of monkeys or birds, which I then join together As a result, people seeing the film are likely to imagine that the forest is pullulating with creatures, whereas in fact they are extremely difficult to find."[35]

That was in 1961. Since then many animal populations have declined significantly in the wild but increased greatly on television. Mills has even suggested that wildlife films *should* avoid revealing the truth of declining wildlife populations in order to avoid depressing, and therefore losing, their audiences. If a filmmaker says too much about the issue, Mills notes, "he loses his audience," but if he does not "he loses his subject."[36] Wildlife filmmakers seem generally to have chosen the latter option, although there need not be any such deliberate avoidance or withholding of information for the decline or absence of a species to be masked. Over the course of a few years, a viewer might see more of some animal on television—pandas, tigers, or gorillas, for example—than actually exist in the wild. It seems feasible to speculate that this appearance of plenty could have a reassuring effect, perhaps over time blunting concern among viewers over species extinction. Regardless of explicit statements about extinction inserted into a film's narration, the overall illusion of plenty is nevertheless reinforced visually and given more screen time.

As in other areas of media, it is not so much what we are told, but what we see, and see *repeatedly*, that is likely to influence what we perceive to be true. News reports, for example, may state that the actual incidence of violent crime is down, but when images of violent crime still pervade film and television content, we may be unlikely to internalize this fact, and may even be more afraid. Research has also shown that viewers' perceptions of minority populations often reflect the patterns of minority representation on television rather than statistical realities.[37]

Phase 3, then, may already have arrived. Time will tell whether wildlife films move on to phase 4. For now, they remain suspended somewhere between representation and simulation of nature—between truth and fiction, science and storytelling.

Nature as Narrative

If the speed and intensity of film and television are noticeably lacking in real experiences of nature, so too are the exciting stories and dramatic adventures into which these media often organize reality. Experiences of nature, like life itself, may be linear, but they are rarely narrative, with coherent beginnings, middles, and ends, as well as dramatic climaxes and satisfying resolutions. The natural world did not evolve respecting such conventions, and it continues to resist them—except on television.

Today the importance of narrative structure to wildlife films—the need for some sort of clear, linear, logical-seeming, and above all engaging story line—is denied by no one in the industry. Neither, unfortunately, is the pervasive reliance on the structuring conventions of mainstream cinema—scenes and sequences constructed from shots of varying camera angles and focal lengths (close-ups, long-shots, etc.), linked by way of continuity editing, often intended to work in conjunction with music and narration. Questions about whether such conventions result in a distorted picture of nature, or whether they are appropriate at all to its representation, and what the implications of all this might be, are virtually never raised in an industry where deadlines, budgets, contracts, sales, and daily occupational demands take precedence.

There has, of course, been a parallel dearth of critical scrutiny among film and television scholars, whose emphasis over the years has been on more mainstream media products. Yet many of the critical-theoretical perspectives they have developed can be applied to wildlife films, which, after all, derive their formal structure from Hollywood's model. In the 1970s, for example, film theorists writing in the British journal *Screen* put forth a comprehensive critique of Hollywood-style filmmaking on grounds that its conventions of realism failed to give, or were at odds with, accurate representations of (social) reality. At one level, the *Screen* critique addressed the ontology of visual images, calling into question the very notion "that film is a simple expression of the real."[38] At another level, the critique was ideological, charging not only that realist cinema failed to reproduce reality accurately, but that its simplification of reality's complexities, its smoothing out of life's contradictions, systematically promoted a kind of false consciousness.[39]

Asserted in this critique was the idea that motion pictures represent reality not just by way of visual images, but through a series of multileveled *fictions* that could be difficult (for the average viewer, not the critic) to recognize as such. According to this perspective, events that are contingent appear inevitable; situations that are contrived appear natural; actions and values that derive from culture appear to derive from nature; society's rules thus appear as "natural laws." What was the true cause of realist cinema's systematic *mis*representation of reality? The *Screen* position seemed to be that the failure to represent reality in all its complexity owed to "one dominant discourse: narrative."[40] Although it was unclear that narrative itself actually deceived anyone, it was true that this "dominant discourse" allowed movies and television programs to represent diffuse, disjunctive, ambiguous reality by way of tightly structured, linear, logical stories in which events are ordered, conflicts are resolved, and in which, above all, things appear to make sense. Nichols has argued that narrative codes and conventions not only govern "the inclusion, exclusion, and arrangement of events," but also amount to "an explanation of situations and events," telling us why one follows another, and even why they occur in the first place.[41] Such logical seeming "explanations" could be made to appear as if having emerged naturally from the events in a narrative, and were therefore seen by the *Screen* critics and others as serving ideological purposes. If artificial events could appear natural, so too could the values and pieties of the dominant culture; the status quo, with its dominance hierarchies, might not only be legitimized, but might be seen as being beyond control and immutable to change.[42]

Although wildlife films were never mentioned in such discussions, one needs no theories or jargon to see that they are just as reliant on the same narrative conventions as mainstream films. They even create suspense by essentially the same means—by raising questions *visually* about what will happen (will an animal be caught or killed? will it find food? a mate?), and then proceeding to answer them visually.[43] Perhaps because wildlife films are about nature rather than about human society, fears of ideological mystification might be thought not to apply. Yet, arguably, the fact that they are about nature might entail an even greater potential for naturalizing ideological values—for example, by "finding" in nature the predominance of the nuclear family, or the values of hard work, industry, and deferred gratification. Indeed, because wildlife films are about nature, there may be an even greater commitment than in Hollywood films to making things appear natural. The images are subject to just as much manipulation, yet the claim to represent "the real" is explicit. Images of unrelated occurrences joined in the editing room can therefore be made to produce not just dramatic scenes, but *natural events.* No matter how artificial, these may be even more difficult to question, to see through, or to resist than similar constructions in overtly fictional films. They have even been supported by the claim that they "depict authenticated facts."

Thus, with a greater claim than mainstream films to an ontological oneness with reality, but with just as much reliance on the narrative and formal artifices of classic realist cinema, wildlife films might provide superior demonstrations of some of the models developed by film theorists. Arguably, they contain the most effectively *naturalized* images anywhere in cinema.[44] The attention of theoretically minded critics remained focused for some years, however, on Hollywood, and on the ideological influences lurking in such clearly artificial and stylized works as those in the *film noir*, where the level of artifice is often so extreme that many of the images can hardly be taken by even the most naive of viewers as representations of reality.[45]

Also difficult to accept was the notion that persisted in film theory for some time that filmic narrative itself is an arbitrary convention and a product of circumstance linked to a unique set of historically conditioned social relations. In his analysis of Hollywood film form, Robert Ray makes the following speculation: "Cinema's apparently natural subjection of style to narration in fact depended on a historical accident: the movies' origins lay in a late nineteenth century whose predominant popular arts were the novel and the theater. Had cinema appeared in the Enlightenment of the Romantic period, it might have assumed the shape of the essay or lyric poem. Instead, it adopted the basic tactic and goal of the realistic novel."[46] Historian Robert Sklar has likewise suggested that under different historical circumstances motion pictures might have become something other than a narrative medium—"instruments of science," for example, "like the microscope."[47] Yet this is almost precisely how motion pictures did, in fact, begin —as a scientific research tool for studying the movements of animals. We all know the rest of the story, but was it the gravitational pull of contemporaneous forms (the realist novel and theater) that changed the course of motion pictures, early in their development, toward storytelling?

History suggests that the first urgings of motion pictures toward narrative may even have occurred before the medium itself was fully formed— not, however, as attempts to emulate literature and theater, but from a simple desire for more information. In the mid-1880s, Eadweard Muybridge had already grown dissatisfied with photographing simple physical movements by themselves and began to arrange for more complex events to occur to test the limits of his camera arrangements. Of particular note was a staged scene in which a tiger attacked and killed a buffalo during the 1884 series at the Philadelphia Zoological Garden. The completeness of this event (or *pseudo-event*) went farther than Muybridge's regular locomotion studies, which had depicted only simple actions (see the discussion in the following chapter). When true "motion pictures" emerged just a decade later, it took only a few short years for them to evolve from the depiction of similar simple events (*Fred Ott's Sneeze*, 1894) to a series of events comprising a relatively complex narrative (*The Great Train Robbery*, 1903). "In motion pictures," argues John Fell, "there surfaced an entire tradition of narrative technique which had been developing unsystematically for a hundred years."[48]

It is difficult to see narrative film as a mere accident of historical circumstance when one considers that the will to narrative may be one of humanity's most enduring, if not inescapable tendencies. In the recorded history of representation there is little evidence to suggest there was ever a time when the will to narrative was not present in some degree. Archaeologists and art historians have even discerned narrative elements in prehistoric cave paintings, arguing that some of them appear to be attempts to tell simple stories in picture form, or, at the very least, to link images in some form of rudimentary, proto-narrative sequence.[49] The urge to convey information in linear form, if not actually in stories,[50] is perhaps as old as human language; it could hardly be expected not to surface in such an expressive and sequential form as motion pictures. Literary theorist Robert Scholes may thus be stating the obvious when he writes, "Given its linear, consecutive character, it is not surprising that film has come to be a predominantly narrative medium"—or, we might add, that wildlife film has become a predominantly narrative form.

Yet it should also not be surprising that wildlife film producers, working in a competitive, commercial setting, have perfected and come to rely upon narrative formulas, if only to systematize production. The regular application of these formulas, along with consistencies of theme and character, give wildlife films the rule-governed coherence of a full-fledged film genre, even if they are not acknowledged as such. As Cawelti notes, "a formulaic pattern will be in existence for a considerable period of time before it is conceived of by its creators and audience as a genre."[51]

Ceci n'est pas une Documentaire

Acknowledging wildlife films as a distinct film and television genre means separating them once and for all from documentary. I have already suggested that blue chip wildlife films, with their avoidance of issues and their construction of period-piece fantasies set in mythic time, move wildlife films away from documentary and into the realm of art. Many inside the industry, however, and many more outside it, continue to refer to blue chip films as wildlife or nature "documentaries." Yet there are also those for whom wildlife films are decidedly not documentaries, and who do not include them in documentary discussions, film festivals, or texts. Yet neither side seems to have articulated the reasons for its positions, or to have questioned its assumptions.

When MTV arrived on the scene, for example, or the *G.I. Joe* cartoon series, critics were quick to ask whether these were TV "programs" at all, or instead a new kind of advertising. Regardless how it was answered (if it was), the question at least got asked. Wildlife films have been around much longer, yet the question of what they *are*, let alone of their relation to documentary form and to the documentary genre, has never really been adequately addressed.

By looking at some notable texts on the documentary genre, we can see that scholars in this area have dealt with wildlife films in three ways. The first has been simply to ignore and avoid them altogether, with the result of their systematic exclusion—one might even say *symbolic annihilation*—from texts on documentary, as well as from virtually all film and television histories, genre studies, narrative studies, "effects" studies, formal analyses, and theoretical treatises. Surprisingly, this has also included studies of the ways powerless *others* are represented by the dominant culture and its image-makers—arguments that apply every bit as much to animals as they do to marginalized or disenfranchised human populations (racial, ethnic, and sexual minorities, etc.).[52] The neglect here might be seen at one level as a reflection of a general commitment to humanism, with its unquestioned assumptions of the superior worth of *homo sapiens* relative to other species ("because that's what *we* are," as a student once explained to me the limits of moral responsibility). Humanist concerns were certainly implicit, at times explicit, throughout John Grierson's writings on documentary.[53] Wildlife films, by contrast, often betray sympathies that lie with animals whose interests may be in conflict with those of humans. There is little doubt that this could be seen by some as incipiently antihumanist, and perhaps therefore unworthy of scholarly attention. The critical neglect of wildlife films could also owe to a notion held by some that wild animals are not an acceptable subject for "respectable" art—just as the working classes were once considered an unsuitable subject for respectable paintings.[54]

The second way of dealing with wildlife and natural history films has been to acknowledge their existence, as some film historians have done, but not to provide them with adequate context or categorization. In *Documentary Film* (1952), Paul Rotha excludes them from the ranks of documentary, but for the wrong reasons. His distinction between documentary and "plain descriptive pictures of everyday life," in which he includes "travel pictures, *nature films*, educationals, and newsreels," seems based on the assumption that "nature films" are a sort of pure reproduction of reality involving no creative intervention. As I have already argued, however, they exhibit, if anything, an overabundance of precisely what Rotha felt was missing from them: the "creative dramatisation of actuality." It is also worth noting that of the nondocumentary categories Rotha lists, including travel pictures, educationals, and newsreels, "nature films" is the only one defined by *content*.[55]

Basil Wright, in his critical overview of film history, *The Long View* (1974), praises the work of Swedish filmmaker Arne Sucksdorff, describing him as a documentarist *and* "maker of nature films," thus separating the two types of film, at least provisionally.[56] He also offers a thoughtful assessment of Disney's "True Life Adventures," having reviewed *The Living Desert* (1953) in *Sight and Sound* at the time of its release.[57] In the intervening twenty years, however, Wright apparently turned a blind eye to his own country's thriving wildlife film industry—at least, he fails even to mention it as a possible context in which Disney's wildlife films might be understood. Instead, they are shoehorned into a chapter entitled "Neo-Realism, Witch Hunts, and Wide Screens," and thus consigned to the 1950s as period curiosities.

The third way in which documentary texts have dealt with wildlife films has been to make halfhearted attempts to bring them under the documentary umbrella—out of the rain, as it were, but still not in from the cold. Lewis Jacobs's collection of essays and reviews, *The Documentary Tradition* (1979) makes some tentative gestures in this direction, but only by including essays by writers whose positions are often ambiguous.[58]

In *The War, the West, and the Wilderness* (1979), Kevin Brownlow gives the most thoughtful consideration to the work of some wildlife film pioneers, including Cherry Kearton and the team of Martin and Osa Johnson, but strictly in the context of documentary. Brownlow appears to lack altogether the category of "wildlife film," despite the genre's popularity on television in the late 1970s when he wrote his book.

Eric Barnouw's *Documentary* (1993), considered by many since its first publication in 1974 to be the standard text on the genre's history, does mention the Johnsons, but only in condemning them for the condescending, ethnocentric attitudes in their films, which often express a barely concealed contempt for tribal peoples and even make light of animals' suffering. He is full of praise for Sucksdorff, whom he classifies among the makers of "poetic documentary." Yet Barnouw categorizes Disney as a documentary "Chronicler." He even compares the "True Life Adventures" to ethnographic film (no doubt to the chagrin of anthropologists) by describing them as a "parallel activity" to John Marshall's *The Hunters* (1958) and Robert Gardner's *Dead Birds* (1963). This is a regrettable lapse, but another example of a film historian up against the limits of conventional categorization.[59]

If, however, wildlife films are merely another type of documentary, do they fit one of the recognized, reigning models or subcategories? One problem is that most of these—for example, direct cinema, ethnographic film, cinéma vérité, and observational cinema—are defined by intent, technique, and approach rather than by content. So too are most of the less celebrated models, such as historical or archival documentary. Might wildlife films be their own subcategory, such as "wildlife documentary" or "nature documentary," and if so, is this a valid subcategory, being defined, unlike any of the others, solely by content?

Conversely, if wildlife films are to be categorically excluded from the documentary ranks, does this determination also rest, as it did for Rotha, on content alone—that is, simply on the fact that their subjects are not human? It shouldn't. The depiction of wild animals, even the careful study of them, should not by itself disqualify a film or program as a documentary. In fact, there have for decades been films about wildlife that could rightly be classified as documentaries. Many of these might well fit into the emerging subcategory of "television science documentary," as seen in the United States on the PBS series *Nova*.[60] Others are clearly Griersonian in their orientation toward social amelioration, although those produced by the CBC for *The Nature of Things* series have fallen into both the science and amelioration/advocacy subcategories. Most of the films and videos produced by environmental advocacy organizations such as the Cousteau Society, the Audubon Society, the Wilderness Society, the National Wildlife Federation, and others clearly fit the Griersonian model. For although these are often filled with images of nature and wildlife, what most of them are really about is the relationship human beings have to the natural world, or their impact on it, and thus about issues of political, economic, and social change—specifically: environmental policy reform, natural resource conservation, and building sustainable societies in closer harmony with nature. In their use of film, video, and television as a "pulpit" and as propaganda, and in their frequent calls for citizen action, these films illustrate Grierson's ideals about socially conscious documentary.[61]

Yet at another level animal subjects may be the *difference that makes a difference.* That is, when the subject of a film is a living, feeling being, yet has no way of comprehending the implications of being filmed or the power of visual images and representation in general; when it never will understand these things in the future, (unlike humans who are filmed as infants); and when there are few, if any ethical prohibitions or assurances that the process does not become abusive, the filmmaker enters into a relationship with that subject that is different from all others. The filmmaking process itself involves a different kind of interaction between filmmaker and subject, a different set of responsibilities on the part of the filmmaker to the subject, and ultimately very different results. This is not to say that all bona-fide documentaries depict subjects who understand the filming process and its implications. Consider, for example, the mentally disabled subjects in Frederick Wiseman's *Titticut Follies* (1967), Ira Wohl's *Best Boy* (1979), or Linda Garmon's *Secrets of the Wild Child* (1994). The point here is that few if any filmmakers feel the sort of obligations to animal subjects they automatically do to human subjects. Conceivably, wildlife films might involve a whole new set of theoretical problems, particularly in relation to filmmakers' ethical responsibilities to their subjects, as well as to their audiences.[62] Consider these points:

1. Since it is unlikely that animals can suffer embarrassment from public display of their likeness, disclosure of their "secrets," or violation of their "privacy," it is generally held that they have no secrets and no privacy.
2. Therefore, they do not enjoy *rights* of privacy—or indeed many rights at all that might protect them from invasive filming practices (Margaret Mead once observed, "The more powerless the subject is, *per se*, the more the question of ethics—and power—is raised"[63]).
3. Therefore, "informed consent," in addition to being difficult to obtain, is considered inapplicable and irrelevant—though there remains no precise means for determining the degree to which wild animals *willingly* consent to participating with filmmakers, or merely tolerate them because they have no choice.
4. Therefore, invasive filming techniques allowing filmmakers to probe, to prod, and to reveal are not discouraged, providing for entirely different kinds of behaviors to be shown (urination, defecation, flatulence,

regurgitation, copulation, birth, and, of course, death—including can-nibalism, infanticide, fratricide, etc.) usually without objection from either the subjects or the audience.[64]

5. Therefore, there often seems a greater need for voice-over narration to interpret behaviors that might otherwise seem foreign or offensive to the cultural sensibilities of many viewers; the subjects themselves have no way of explaining or putting their behaviors in context.

6. Therefore, the rules for presenting strictly factual evidence, or for con-structing narratives and telling fabricated stories are far more vague, and far less inhibiting than in human-centered documentary film-making.

7. Therefore, the rules governing the use of creative editing, or construc-tion of composite actions from disconnected events, or even composite characters from many look-alike animals, are also far more permissive and ill-defined than in documentary.

At the most fundamental level, wildlife films reveal these differences in the undocumentary-like approaches they take to such practical matters as

- *Camera placement*—many wildlife shots are routinely obtained through concealment that might be seen as unethical if dealing with human sub-jects.
- *Camera-to-subject distance*—wild animals are often unapproachable, even at considerable distances.
- *Choice of lenses*—wildlife filmmakers regularly use long telephoto lenses to get close-ups, often resulting in an illusion of close proximity to the subject.
- *Artificial lighting*—thought by many to provoke unnatural behavior in night shooting.
- *Sync-sound*—in part because of the distances at which many wildlife scenes are filmed, most wildlife footage is shot silent with either wild or studio sound added later.
- *Selection of which actions to show and which to exclude* (already discussed above).

In light of these fundamental differences from most documentaries, it seems reasonable to consider that conceptually, technically, procedurally, and formally, if not also thematically, most of the accepted practices in documentary filmmaking simply may not apply to films with wild animals as subjects.

The same is true for some of the leading documentary models. Although *ethnographic film*, for example, is often described in terms that might have some application to wildlife films. David MacDougall has described it as "any film which seeks to reveal one society to another," [65] and cites this definition: "Ethnographic film is film which endeavors to interpret the behavior of people of one culture to persons of another culture by using shots of people doing precisely what they would have been doing if the camera were not there." [66]

Many animals do, after all, live in organized societies with complex social interactions and strict rules of behavior, and some of these groups, especially among primates, display sets of practices unique to them that could be called a *culture*.

Hugo Van Lawick's portrait of chimpanzee society, *People of the Forest* (1989), arguably has the look, feel, and purpose of an ethnographic film of the sort described above; although it is made by a professional filmmaker rather than by an anthropologist or ethologist, it is solidly based on intensive research by Jane Goodall (to whom Van Lawick was married for some years) and does convey the feeling of observing from within. Yet its dramatic, if not epic story, and its use of conventional cinematic scene construction along with quasi-omniscient voice-over narration (spoken by Donald Sutherland), have little place in ethnographic film, but are all staples of wildlife filmmaking.

Closely related to ethnographic film is *Observational cinema*, in which the audience learns about the filmed subjects from observing events played out in their natural duration before the camera rather than being broken into fragments and having their significance defined by narration.[67] Clearly, the common practice in wildlife films of illustrating behavior by way of composite events puts them outside the realm of observational film, with its emphasis on the unbroken duration of events. In addition, most wildlife films are based on a treatment, if not on a script (often as a requirement for obtaining funding commitments), so that wildlife filmmakers usually go into the field with a list of preselected shots and scenes, as well as of actions and behaviors they hope to capture on film. Some wait for weeks until the desired actions occur. In such cases, they are essentially seeking footage to *illustrate* preconceived ideas rather than to discover something new. The long hours of waiting for desired behaviors are not only a constant theme in many of their written accounts, but have even led some impatient filmmakers to resort to provocation and staging in order to capture on film the actions they need to suit their storyline.

Direct cinema also refers to attempts at an observational and revelatory rather than illustrative style of documentary filmmaking. Typically, it involves filming subjects who are, ostensibly, just going about their business as if the camera weren't there. The technique, of course, relies heavily on their habituation to the presence of the camera as well as to the people behind it, who are assumed to achieve a certain fly-on-the-wall invisibility. Richard Leacock has called it "the pretense of our not being there." [68] Other

Dieter Plage with orang-utan from *Orphans of the Forest* (1975). Habituated animals have been more common on camera than viewers realize, and call into question wildlife films' relationship to documentary. Mike Price/Survival Anglia.

notable practitioners include D. A. Pennebaker, the Maysles brothers, and Frederick Wiseman (although the latter has labeled his own films "reality fictions"[69]). What Brian Winston described as the presumption of "Nonintervention, with its promise of unmediated observation"[70] could easily be applied to many wildlife filmmakers. Even those who intervene most invasively (in nests and dens) rely nevertheless on their subjects' habituation to the camera to mask the fact from viewers. Others rely on habituation to an automobile or stationary hide containing the camera. Nearly all assume, if only provisionally, that the behavior before the camera is completely natural and unaffected, assuming with Leacock that because of their supposed unobtrusiveness their subjects "soon forget the presence of the camera and attain surprising naturalness."[71]

David and Carol Hughes's *Lions of the African Night* (1987), for example, or Dereck and Beverly Joubert's *Lions and Hyenas: Eternal Enemies* (1991) seem especially good illustrations of this in the way they are shot and presented. Yet because most animals' lives are spent doing relatively little that is visually arresting (as in the example of lions, earlier), the process of deciding when and what to film, and what to include in the final cut is therefore even *more* selective in wildlife films such as these than in the films of Wiseman and the others.

Direct cinema also relies on a set of formal conventions that stand in marked contrast to those of wildlife films—handheld camera, available sound, long takes, and jump-cuts (in place of continuity editing), all of which signify untainted "evidence" and have become the "dominant documentary style."[72] The use of available sync-sound and *diegetic* speech in place of voice-over narration are especially significant. These can, of course, directly affect editing style. As Barnouw points out, editing silent footage (which would include wildlife film) typically results in the creation of artificial "film time," whereas editing for speech tends to allow "real time" to reassert itself, making it more difficult for filmmakers to cut at will, and also for audiences to accept some manipulations of events.[73] Sync-sound is, after all, among the factors responsible for direct cinema's directness, whereas the fragmented events and behaviors seen in wildlife films are more often interpreted in voice-over narration. For practical reasons (not the least of which is a reliance on telephoto lenses), wildlife films rarely make use of sync-sound; even those that come closest visually to the form of direct cinema still rely on voice-over narration and sound effects, and thus retain added layers of artifice and authorial mediation of the sort direct cinema filmmakers emphatically reject.

It seems that the willing participation of subjects in the filmmaking process that originally defined *cinéma vérité* (at least if one accepts Rouch and Morin's 1961 *Chronique d'un été* as the standard), would automatically disqualify this as an acceptable category for the vast majority of wildlife films, given the widespread commitment to an ethic (or an illusion) of nonintervention. In any case, wild animals' responses to the presence of humans is quite the opposite of knowing participation in a film. One could argue that Rouch's notion that camera consciousness is the royal road to self-revelation[74] might be loosely applied insofar as animals' fight-or-flight reaction to the presence of filmmakers may be an example of authentic "wild" behavior—provocation notwithstanding. Yet many wild animals are largely creatures of habit, and it remains a fact that the presence of humans can disrupt those habits, causing behaviors that become increasingly difficult to classify as authentic or natural. This is also true of habituated animals, who have become accustomed to the close presence of filmmakers. Moreover, because animals do not comprehend that their physical actions acquire *meaning* from being seen or filmed, many of their on-camera behaviors therefore lack the self-consciousness that gives human acts communicative significance of the sort sought by Rouch and Morin.[75]

Lastly, *drama documentaries*, or what are often called *docudramas*, or *fact-*

based dramas, in which real events are reenacted, may provide a parallel to wildlife films—the main difference being that in most cases drama documentaries depict specific historic events, while wildlife films are more likely to depict *typical* events intended to illustrate general biological facts. Yet both forms rely on traditional dramatic devices and storytelling conventions in the belief that audiences find these more engaging than straight documentary form. Jerry Kuehl writes that "The argument derives its force from the commonplace belief that most viewers prefer programs made within the conventions of naturalistic drama; that they identify with dramatic personae, and that such identification can be used to get across points which elude viewers of traditional documentaries."[76]

He notes further that "although drama documentaries invite audiences to accept their portrayals as being truthful accounts of actions" rather than straightforward reports, critics from the realm of traditional documentary have nevertheless "found this procedure illicit, since it obliges audiences to judge matters of truth and falsity by aesthetic criteria"—that is, other than by content.[77] Once again, the implication is that more traditional documentaries somehow represent the absence of formal and aesthetic elements, and the transparency, therefore, of the medium. Although this is clearly exaggerated, it does seem true that those working in traditional documentaries impose upon themselves a number of formal limitations that wildlife filmmakers have seen little reason to accept.

It may be instructive, then, to examine in detail how one particular formal device—the close-up—is used in ways that make clear wildlife films' closer relationship, at their most basic structural level, to dramatic narratives than to documentaries.

False Intimacy

One of the means by which wildlife films show us things we might really be able to see, but in ways we are unlikely to see them in reality, is the close-up. We have become so accustomed to close-ups of wild animals that watching wildlife films without them would no doubt be a dull business and as likely to attract and hold viewers as a film of lions resting for forty-two minutes. Close-ups were not always a part of the formal vocabulary of wildlife films, however. Before the 1920s, when telephoto lenses began to be used in filmmaking, shooting close-ups of wild animals would have required filmmakers to get physically closer to them than was often possible or prudent.

If films of this vintage look different from contemporary wildlife films, it is in part because those today use a great many more close-ups. This, along with the use of sound, has given rise to a different editing structure—one that is similar, if not identical, to that of mainstream narrative films, with look-offs, point-of-view shots, reaction shots, and so forth. If early wildlife films are unsatisfying, it may be not only because they fail to show us the details of content we expect to see, but because they also fail to fulfill our expectations of form and structure, and often appear, therefore, technically amateurish. Ray has written persuasively that as a result of the triumph of Hollywood cinema, a dominant formal paradigm was established, with the result that "different ways of making movies would appear as aberrations from some 'intrinsic essence of cinema' rather than simply as alternatives to a particular form."[78]

In adopting the formal paradigm of Hollywood, wildlife films use close-ups to create characters, to promote feelings of intimacy and involvement with them, and to integrate them into a narrative structure. With regard to creating characters, it matters not that wild animals may not be clearly discernible as individuals in either appearance or behavior. Facial close-ups need only isolate one from among the others, after which the voice-over commentary can complete the process of individualizing and establishing a separate identity for it, often by giving it a name. If the narrator continues to call the animal on screen by that name, we have little way of knowing if it is a composite character, let alone how many "actors" are portraying it. Roy Disney, Jr. once remarked of the film *Perri* (1957) that its title character had been played by "*many* different squirrels."[79] While this may or may not pose ethical dilemmas (depending on the degree of factuality one expects), at the very least it helps differentiate wildlife films from documentaries, and demonstrates their closer link to the cinema of narrative fictions where composite characters are rare, but not unheard of. Biographies covering many years in a character's life routinely combine young and old actors in the role. It is also common practice to use sets of twins as a single character in films featuring infants or small children (e.g., *3 Men and a Baby*, 1987). In a scene in *Terminator 2* (1991) involving a mirror reflection, a character is played by both the lead actress and her twin sister. Most obvious was Bunuel's *That Obscure Object of Desire* (1977), in which two actresses played the same character with no attempt to conceal the differences. It is difficult to imagine any of these scenarios in a documentary, although all are common in wildlife films.

The question of whether film and television close-ups can create feelings of emotional intimacy with wild animals is more complex. Television does have the unique ability to let us see them at "stroking distance," and to do so in the comfort of our living rooms. Such an impression of physical proximity combined with regular exposure to familiar characters can give rise to what has been called a "para-social relationship."[80] Research suggests that viewers often do feel they have a personal relationship with human figures on television; many report a feeling of emotional involvement and personal interaction rather than of merely watching images on a screen.[81] Can this occur with (images of) *animals*? That is, can the formal properties of television that allow viewers to feel psychologically intimate with human characters also work to create similar feelings toward animal characters? Animals may appear on the screen at stroking distance, but would that be desirable in real-world experience? It is unclear whether the "proxemic" zones that govern our interactions with people are the same in real-world dealings with wild animals.[82] It is therefore also unclear whether the same "para-proxemic" conditions that apply in relation to humans on television would apply just as well to images of animals on television.[83] A wildlife close-up, after all, confronts us with a wild animal at a distance approximating our personal, or even intimate space, which we generally reserve for friends and loved ones, or those with whom we feel safe. It's been said that television close-ups of wild animals "leap across centuries of evolution by taking us within the fight or flight distances that normally separate individuals."[84] If this is so, then why do we not react with discomfort at seeing a wild animal so close? One reason might be that we have all experienced other animals up close—cats, dogs, horses, and the like—and because so many of the animals depicted in wildlife films closely resemble these domestic species, often having fur coats similar to those we know from experience are soft to the touch.

It does seem that some people have a desire for physical contact with even some of the wildest of wild animals, as evident in the behavior of tourists at national parks. Their attempts to feed animals by hand suggest that they desire and expect a *personal interaction* with them, perhaps as they do with their own pets, and that they seem to want to shift, in John Caughey's phrase, "from the role of observer to that of participant."[85] While this tendency was noted well before the age of television, it is safe to say that wildlife films have done nothing to diminish this behavior, which by some accounts is more widespread than ever. In Britain, where wildlife films have enjoyed a great deal of popularity over the decades, the problem is well illustrated in this news report:

London housewife Barbara Carter won a "grant a wish" charity contest, and said she wanted to kiss and cuddle a lion. Wednesday night she was in a hospital in shock and with throat wounds. Mrs. Carter, 46, was taken to the lions' compound of the safari park at Bewdley, Wednesday. As she bent forward to stroke the lioness, Suki, it pounced and dragged her to the ground. Wardens later said, "We seem to have made a bad error of judgment. We have always regarded the lioness as perfectly safe."[86]

The desire to kiss and cuddle a wild animal, especially a furry one resembling a house cat, may be an extremely common wish.[87] Making wild animals beautiful and appealing, perhaps in the way that attracted Mrs. Carter's affections, is one of the subtle goals of many wildlife filmmakers. Attenborough has argued that among his primary tasks is "to persuade the public that animals are interesting and beautiful,"[88] because it is widely thought that this is a way of making viewers more concerned with wildlife protection, and thus more susceptible to explicit preservation messages elsewhere. The emotions fostered by wildlife films are therefore seen by many as a first step toward meaningful action by viewers (the belief that showing nature's beauty inevitably leads to direct action is a common one). "It is our job," cameraman David Parer has said, "to make the audience empathize with the animal."[89]

Yet close-ups by themselves are unlikely to produce intense feelings of intimacy, emotional involvement, or empathy, as *Anima Mundi* demonstrates. In most wildlife films, facial close-ups are instead carefully integrated, according to cinematic convention, with other shots that give them a narrative and emotional context, and a perhaps even a "meaning."

This may be especially clear in the use of close-ups depicting animals looking directly at the camera—a common occurrence when filming them in their natural habitats, where they are often intensely aware of disturbances. In Hollywood films, and even in some documentaries and news stories, shots of subjects "accidentally" looking at the camera would be considered unusable. In wildlife films, however, face-on shots are some of the *most usable* and most desirable. According to one account, "One of the most beautiful scenes in *The Living Planet*" involves just such a shot of a polar bear: "Suddenly, the beast turns toward the camera and bares its teeth ferociously: this happened when cameraman Hugh Miles happened to unscrew the cap on a flask of soup; at 30 yards, the bear could smell it. The cap was replaced, and the bear shambled away."[90]

A shot such as this, in which the animal responds to the filmmaker's presence, can then easily be integrated with completely unrelated shots to construct a dramatic scene. When introduced first, the close-up may be used as a glance at something yet unseen, and thus serves as a "look-off" shot inviting a cut. The next shot, whatever it depicts, may thus appear to be a point-of-view shot that answers it, showing us what the animal supposedly saw. Cut back to the close-up and it now appears as a reaction shot.[91] A face-on shot is no longer a reaction to the camera, but a reaction to what is shown in the other shot, and thus it becomes part of a fiction. Such a device can be found in *Puma, Lion of the Andes* (1996). When the cat looks into the camera, Hugh Miles declares in the voice-over that she is instead nervously eyeing a nearby male puma. Cut to the male, and the gap between truth and fiction is, as some theorists would say, *sutured.* With this simple editing combination of two shots, a fictional drama is begun, a narrative set in motion. The device also helps establish the female's point-of-view as the guiding one in the scene, thus aiding our emotional involvement and identification with her.[92] Yet, unlike Hollywood films in which actors knowingly participate in the construction of a fictional story, here the animals become unwitting players in a story constructed by others and projected onto them. A real event is thus subtly, perhaps unnoticeably transformed into a fictional one.

We could say that an instance of *individual behavior*, with no communicative significance, is converted into an act of *social behavior*, which does have communicative significance,[93] or that a "natural event" (the animal's look), requiring no interpretive strategy, becomes part of a constructed "symbolic event" (the fabricated narrative in the film), which is intended to communicate and be interpreted by viewers "in accordance with a shared set of rules of implication and inference."[94] Of course, this is true in any instance in which some sort of individual behavior is filmed candidly and made into a *movie*. The difference is that an animal looking toward the camera does not understand that its image is being captured, that its behavior will be seen and interpreted by others has having some sort of meaning. A simple glance may be endowed with meaning merely by the act of being filmed, but a meaning forced on it by integrating it into conventional editing structures.

Of course, as already indicated, many such shots, no matter how close-up and intimate they may look and sound on screen, are actually filmed with telephoto lenses from considerable distances. It is difficult enough to record sync sound under any conditions in the wild, but it is virtually impossible when using long lenses. As a result, nearly all sound in wildlife films is added later, and much of it is fabricated by technicians in a studio using various props. Attenborough has noted, "When you're filming with a long-focus lens, you can't record the real sounds; many of those horrible bone-crunching noises are actually done by a man in a studio, carefully crunching bones in front of a microphone."[95]

Yet when cutting freely between close-ups and long-shots within a single sequence, sound is often kept continuous and uniform, further concealing the fact that the narrative event is a composite constructed from a number of different actual events shot at different times and places. Like color-balancing, sound works to control the potential for disunity, helping to unify into a conceptual whole shots that may in fact be unrelated to each other, suggesting a spatial and temporal unity that may never have actually existed. This is not, of course, unique to wildlife films. As David Bordwell has pointed out, Hollywood filmmakers learned in the early days of sound that it need not correspond exactly to changes in perceived visual distance.[96] Sound that is either unmodulated or only slightly modulated thus functions to keep viewers from becoming aware that some scenes were actually fabricated in the editing and may even include shots that do not match. As a result, viewers may be unlikely to ask why and how an action on screen that is supposed to be an unstaged, unplanned, spontaneous natural event could have allowed for full coverage of the sort that typically involves extensive planning and control.[97] Thus, even where continuity among shots is difficult to achieve, the use of sound helps mask this by remaining continuous, keeping the emphasis, and viewers' attention, on the action and the narrative.

Symbolic Darwinism

Given the emphasis in wildlife films on narrative, on dramatic action, and on creating animal characters that invite viewers to become involved emotionally, it should not be surprising that one of the chief ways in which they communicate scientific content is by dramatizing it with the actions of individual animals. Even the grand, theoretical abstractions of evolutionary biology, which are virtually impossible for the layperson to witness first-hand (although genetic researchers can track changes in fast-multiplying bacteria, fruit flies, and mice), are illustrated in wildlife films with dramatic vignettes depicting the actions of individuals.

This should come as no surprise; mainstream films routinely deal with abstract notions such as good, evil, love, and hate by symbolizing, personifying, or in some other way quickly and economically illustrating them. Film and television, after all, are visual media in which image makers prefer to *show* us something, and to do so in dramatic terms, rather than merely tell us. In wildlife films the beautiful image is not just for the sake of art, or the dramatic chase for the sake of drama; each is also assumed to be an illustration of scientific facts. This, as we have already seen, is the justification used for staged events: they must depict "a scientifically observable fact" (Mills), be "faithful to the biological truth" (Attenborough), and be "true [even if] not always real" (Stouffer). Thus, for demonstration purposes, the actions of individuals, not the interactions between species and their environments, become the sites at which the "survival of the fittest" is seen as being directly played out in the natural world, as if in one-to-one correspondence to individual lives and events.[98]

Darwinian gospel has been open to interpretation, but it seems today that "fitness" to survive, to the extent the concept even survives, may be best thought of as referring not to the "physical fitness" of an individual, for this may be affected by any number of accidental or environmental circumstances. The idea that a single incident of individual struggle provides a clear illustration of evolutionary "fitness" suggests that context, circumstance, and environmental conditions play no part. The animal that drowns in the flash flood or is hit by lightning is certainly no less "fit" to survive than the one a few meters away who is spared. For individuals and even entire species, good luck can be more important than good genes. Indeed, the world may be populated not by the most "fit," but instead by the "lucky survivors in a game of chance."[99]

It may be more productive to speak of the success of a species than of an individual, and of the degree to which that species adapts to its circumstances and fits into its environment. Either way, however, the key factor is capacity to continue producing offspring.[100] "Evolutionary success," as

Leakey and Lewin point out in their study of human origins, "is the production of as many descendants as possible."[101] Darwin himself wrote of the phrase "struggle for existence" (which he had borrowed from Malthus) that he had used it "in a large and metaphorical sense" to refer ultimately to "success in leaving progeny."[102]

In wildlife films, however, "survival of the fittest" and the "struggle for existence" continue to be illustrated not only by individual acts or incidents, but by individual acts or incidents of *aggression*, or, worse, *predation*, neither of which is appropriate to these concepts. The film *Dressing for Dinner* (1993), a survey of animal feeding behavior, opens with this recitation by narrator Anthony Hopkins: "Survival of the fittest: the strongest, the fastest, the toughest. In evolution's world it is always muscle that survives . . . *always*." It takes little familiarity with evolutionary biology to recognize that this variation on "only the strong survive" is misleading. If it were so, then prey species would all be wiped out and only the most powerful of predator species would survive. But on what—each other? In reality, aggression, strength, and brute force do not always prevail; sometimes it is simple opportunism. "The top male chimpanzee," writes Matt Ridley, "is not necessarily the strongest; instead, it is usually the one best at manipulating social coalitions to his advantage."[103]

Even when survival fitness is more appropriately linked in wildife films to reproduction, it is still likely to be illustrated by dramatic scenes of aggressive competition among males. Similar scenes of violent conflict are also used to illustrate the "struggle to survive," although this too is best understood as the struggle to produce offspring, or even the struggle of those offspring to reach reproductive age. Yet because no "struggle" is clearly visible in images of mating, reproduction, and rearing of the young, at least insofar as we equate struggle with *conflict* (as when two opponents are said to be "locked in struggle"), the "struggle to survive" continues to be portrayed in scenes depicting aggressive battles. Although an individual's physical survival may be at stake in such a conflict, the survival of the species or genotype is not. Such battles simply do not illustrate the evolutionary "struggle to survive." The individual who loses one such conflict is not prevented absolutely from reproducing, and may go on to produce many genetic survivors. Nevertheless, the animal who triumphs in such scenes of battle, whether or not by luck or circumstance (such as slippery footing), is then typically pronounced the one most "fit" to survive—a conclusion closer to social Darwinism than to evolutionary biology.

Even more extreme is an argument expressed in a recent study of animal literature, and heard often in wildlife films: "kill or be killed is the natural law,"[104] another variation on "only the strong survive." Since it is virtually always applied to predator-prey interactions, this too might well be restated as "only predators survive," thus revealing the inherent weakness in notions that "survival of the fittest" is seen in interspecies conflict. For in reality predator species rely utterly on the fact that prey animals not only survive, but outnumber them in geometric proportion. If anything, prey species are affected less by predation than by environmental conditions, while it is the survival of predators that often seems precarious. Moreover, many animals, including elephants, rhinos, hippos, manatees, and gorillas, are neither predator nor prey species, and thus neither kill nor (barring wanton slaughter by humans) are killed. Clearly, notions such as "kill or be killed" and "only the strong survive" are greatly misunderstood, and are dubious interpretations of evolutionary biology, as well as of nature itself, but have nevertheless become mainstays of the wildlife film genre.

In depictions of competition between two similar species for the same resources, such notions might, with caution, be applied; in scenes of inter-specific acts of predation, however, they would be completely misplaced. Konrad Lorenz put it well some years ago: "Darwin's expression, 'the struggle for existence,' is sometimes erroneously interpreted as the struggle between different species. In reality, the struggle Darwin was thinking of and which drives evolution forward is the competition between near relations. . . . What threatens the existence of an animal species is never the 'eating enemy' but the competitor."[105]

Thus, as an example of intraspecific competition, Disney's *Seal Island* (1948) may be forgiven for describing a rank-establishing conflict between two male seals as illustrating the principle that "only the fit may survive." In truth, however, the loser need not actually die. As Darwin pointed out, in competition between males for the possession of the females, the result "is not death to the unsuccessful competitor, but few or no offspring."[106] The loser of such a struggle might even triumph in some future battle for breeding rights, and so pass on his genes after all. The film is perhaps even more careless with Darwinian language in a remark made after a young seal pulls itself free from under a larger one: "Free at last. It's a hard life, this *survival of the fittest.*" If the old bull had rolled over and crushed him, as often happens, would it have proven the pup *unfit* to survive? In Disney's *Water Birds* (1952), evolutionary concepts are still being individualized, although less carelessly. When a young gannet hatches, we are told, "now, the *struggle for survival* begins." Forty-five years later, the phrase is echoed when another hatchling emerges in the National Geographic film *Lords of the Everglades* (1997). This time it is a young alligator who is "just beginning his struggle to survive." Neither example is incorrect, technically. The struggle for survival is, after all, largely the struggle of the young rather than that of adult combatants. Again, however, personifying this complex phenomenon invites misunderstanding by suggesting that its significance lies in the drama of the individual.

Indeed, filmmakers often explain their refusal to intervene to save the life of an individual animal caught in a mud bog, for example, as not wanting to interfere in natural processes—assuming, apparently, that intervention to save a single, individual life might somehow tip the scales in one direction and upset the balance of nature, perhaps even alter the course of evolution.[107] Although filmmakers routinely intervene in animals' lives in a hundred other ways, sometimes quite invasively, their belief in the evolutionary significance of an individual animal's *death* evidently runs deep.

Personification of Darwinian concepts occurs most often in service of narrative, and in this sense is part of a *literary* tradition. The analysis of animal literature cited earlier asserts that a particular dramatic incident from a fictional story, in which one fox kit lives while its sibling dies, is "an apt illustration of Darwinian theory, for it is the better animal that survives."[108] In point of fact, the death of such a fox kit could be a totally random occurrence, and is absolutely *not* an apt illustration of Darwinian theory. Still, it makes for an emotionally compelling and dramatic story, and that is what matters.

As will become clear in the pages that follow, in wildlife films it is nearly always story that matters most.

2
A Brief History of a Neglected Tradition

Like the evolution of species, the history of wildlife film reveals no moment when its subject burst into view fully formed. Rather, it came slowly into focus, the result of various historical developments and accidents, some related, some not.

The term "natural history film," today widely used interchangeably with "wildlife film," began to show up in trade journals around 1913. At first applied mainly to films shot under controlled conditions for "for educational purposes,"[1] it soon expanded to include outdoor scenes of animals in their natural habitats. "Wildlife film" didn't come into use until after the middle of the twentieth century, but by that time it was clear that the phenomenon itself, by whatever name, had emerged as a coherent and distinctive type of film, with its own rules, codes, and conventions.

It was also clear that there was a sizable audience for wildlife content on both the big and small screens, and it didn't take long before a full-blown industry developed to meet the demand and create more of it. Among the larger competitors, specialized production units emerged, some formal (BBC), some informal (Disney), devoted exclusively to wildlife and natural history film and television production. Because television was a live medium in its early years, it initially brought wildlife into the studio, where it was introduced by a host and presenter. By the 1960s, however, the formal conventions unique to the new medium had given way to those of an older one: movies. Wildlife movies overtook wildlife television, imposing the conventions of narrative cinema before wildlife television had much time to develop its own forms. For nearly forty years, television's role was chiefly that of distribution and exhibition outlet for wildlife movies—that is, for wildlife content shaped by cinematic codes.

A pair of "how-to" manuals, *The Technique of Wildlife Cinematography* (1966) and *Making Wildlife Movies* (1971), emerged, in which authors John Warham and Christopher Parsons respectively set out to articulate the genre's formal codes and instruct beginners in how to apply them. In chapters entitled "Editing" and "Build-up Sequences," Parsons made clear that wildlife film codes and conventions owed more to mainstream narrative entertainment than to documentary. Still, there was enough that was unique to announce that wildlife films were an entity unto themselves and could be discussed, analyzed, evaluated, and taught as such.

It wasn't until 1978, however, that the first regular ongoing festival devoted solely to wildlife films was founded. The International Wildlife Film Festival (IWFF), held in Missoula, Montana, further signaled that wildlife films had arrived as a motion picture genre distinct from others—especially documentary. Moreover, it showed that there were plenty of filmmakers working according to the genre's conventions and formal codes, and that these translated into criteria for judging and deciding which films were the most successful executions of the form and the fullest realizations of its potential.

In 1980, members of the wildlife film industry founded a symposium at Bath, England, bringing filmmakers together to discuss issues pertaining to the genre, its development, and its future. Two years later the industry founded its own film festival, called Wildscreen, held in Bristol, followed in 1991 by an American counterpart, the Jackson Hole Wildlife Film Festival. Larger and more commercial than the IWFF, these biennial festivals have brought together hundreds of filmmakers, producers, distributors, and others to make deals, to compare notes, to review new work, to pay tribute to leaders in the field, to celebrate tradition, and to acknowledge their membership in a professional subculture. By the mid-1990s there were also wildlife film festivals or symposia in Italy, France, Germany, Japan, and Sweden. Some of these included courses in wildlife filmmaking; even university degrees were being developed to organize and pass on what was recognized as a coherent body of knowledge and practices, as well as a hundred-year tradition.

Yet even after a century of development, wildlife film was still neither universally acknowledged nor recognized in cinema circles as an "official" film genre. Even within the industry there was still some disagreement as to what wildlife films really were, or should be. As the twentieth century ended, however, there was general agreement on at least one point: a wildlife film should be salable to as large an audience, or as many audiences, as possible. Art, science, and commerce had all been stirred together, and commerce had risen to the top.

"Animated Zoology": Pictures, Motion, and Behavior

The profit motive may or may not have been there from the beginning—depending on where or when the "beginning" of wildlife films was or how it should even be defined. It has been argued broadly, for example, that "the history of animal art," which surely includes wildlife films, "must begin with the beginning of all art,"[2] since some of the earliest acknowledged works of visual art—in the cave paintings at Lascaux, Altamira, Avignon, and elsewhere—include a great many images of animals. Eadweard Muybridge remarked in 1882 that "attempts to depict the attitudes of animals in motion probably originated with art itself, if, indeed, it was not the origin of art."[3]

Early efforts to represent wild animals in visual images were clearly *predecessors* of wildlife films, but were they their *ancestors*? That is, they may have come first, but are they directly related? Can a clear line of descent be shown, or is it merely assumed on the basis of the subject matter? There is no certainty among archaeologists or art historians as to what purpose or significance the earliest images of wild animals were intended to have. It may thus be a feasible enough speculation that both wildlife films and early cave paintings have fulfilled some profound human need to see the surrounding world represented, and that this may stem from an even deeper need to impose control over the world by reducing it to manageable images. A widely used college art history text suggests that since the earliest cave paintings art and science have expressed similar desires for "mastery of the environment" and to "control the world of the beasts."[4]

Yet to link wildlife films directly to cave paintings fifteen thousand years old is to argue mainly, it seems, that an impulse to see the world represented in images has been common among humans since the Paleolithic era—a conclusion that tells us nothing about wildlife films' own historical development, their place in contemporary culture, or the value people put on them. To paint wildlife films with such broad cultural-historical brush strokes would be to miss them for what they are and might even be a way of avoiding having to deal with them directly.

Later animal painting, from the sixteenth century on, may provide more useful compass points. The triumph of European art during the Renaissance, and the advent of techniques for making repeatable prints of visual images (which preceded Gutenberg's development of moveable type),[5] along with advances in natural science, fascination for the unfamiliar animals in the new world, and the increased romanticizing of wild animals in Europe (resulting in part from the movement to enclose lands once used communally, which put many people out of contact with nature and animals), all combined to produce the "distinct pictorial genre" of *natural history illustration*.[6] Works in this mode were used for hundreds of years to study natural history phenomena, which they often depicted quite creatively. They are still used in field guides such as those in the Peterson or National Geographic series. Unlike most other visual forms, however, these illustrations ultimately "took their meaning from adjacent written descriptions."[7] In this sense, they prefigured not only wildlife films' combinations of art and science, but also their heavy reliance on "adjacent" descriptions in the voice-over narration to explain the images.

By the late eighteenth and early nineteenth centuries, images of animals, especially birds, were becoming popular in their own right, apart from their value as textual supplements. The noted Scottish ornithologist Alexander Wilson was drawing and painting American birds during this time, although he was soon overshadowed by John James Audubon, who published his celebrated *Birds of America* in 1826. Dissatisfied with the tradition of working from stuffed models, Audubon continued to use dead specimens he himself killed ("I shot, I drew, I looked upon nature"), but devised ways of arranging them in "action poses" that simulated real behavior. Also, like Wilson, Audubon set the birds in his paintings in their natural habitats. The dramatic combination of realistic behavior and natural settings was largely responsible for the enduring success of his images, and also set the standards for the next generation of image-making naturalists.[8] They, however, would employ the new technology of photography. To Audubon's formula of behavior plus natural setting, they added an even more important element: *life*.

Life, however, was the very thing that both motivated and hindered these efforts. Unlike dead animals, who posed cooperatively, living ones rarely held still for the camera. To obtain action poses that were genuine was a much sought-after photographic goal, but exposure times as long as ten seconds made it virtually impossible. Two of the earliest known efforts to make wildlife photos in the field in Africa (1858 and 1863) both failed to secure a single image of a living animal, and ended up only with images of animals shot to death so their pictures could be taken. Even an attempt to photograph elephants in the London Zoo in 1865 failed to get a clear image.[9] What is possibly the oldest known successful photograph of a wild animal in the field is that of a stork on its nest, taken at the remarkably late-seeming date of 1870. Shortly after this, however, a four-year expedition by the darkroom-equipped HMS *Challenger* (1872–76) brought back revealing images of penguin rookeries and even breeding albatrosses. Here at last were images of real behavior in its natural setting.[10]

The Kearton brothers would later make a specialty of this. Richard Kearton described it as "the art of portraying wild animals in their native haunts . . . going about the everyday business of their lives."[11] Their innovative, often daredevil field techniques for obtaining such images are described and photographically demonstrated in books such as *With Nature and a Camera* (1897) and *Wild Life at Home* (1898). Variations on some of their techniques are still in use by wildlife filmmakers today.

In the 1870s faster processes were developed that increased still photographers' ability to cope with field conditions. Yet no sooner were they given this power to *eliminate* motion from their pictures than attempts were launched elsewhere to merge motion with pictures—or, at least, to create photographic simulations of motion. Ironically, just as still photography was becoming a viable medium for wildlife portrayal and study, motion pictures were already on the way to eclipsing it. It is tempting to propose a variation on the earlier quoted statement that "the history of animal art must begin at the beginning of all art," and to say that *the history of wildlife film must begin at the beginning of all film.* Cinema itself began not just with attempts to bring motion to pictures, but with attempts to use pictures to reveal and study the motions of animals—some of which were, at least to some degree, *wild.* That they were put on film to reveal their patterns of movement, their *behavior,* for purposes of science, curiosity, amusement, and financial gain, suggests that in some ways little has really changed since then.

There were several tentative efforts to bring motion to pictures, and several false starts, but it is widely agreed that the story begins with Eadweard Muybridge. In the spring of 1872 Leland Stanford, seeking to settle a bet, hired Muybridge to make photographs proving that all four of a horse's feet leave the ground at one time when it trots. Muybridge apparently photographed Stanford's racehorse Occident at Palo Alto, California, in 1872 or 1873. Although documentation is in short supply, accounts have it that the images were little more than silhouettes but nevertheless confirmed the thesis. The images themselves have never been found, and accounts of their exact date vary, but an 1873 Currier and Ives lithograph by J. Cameron is believed to be based on them.[12]

Muybridge continued to work for Stanford on and off, and to refine his technique. His 1879 "Studies of Foreshortenings" included images of domestic animals—dogs, mules, pigs, and goats—but also members of wild species such as pigeons and deer, which may have been the first "wildlife" to be captured in any kind of motion picture process, primitive though it was. By 1884 Muybridge had accepted a position at the University of Pennsylvania. At the nearby Philadelphia Zoological Garden, he applied his newly improved system to over a hundred different captive wild animals, including a lion, jaguar, kangaroo, zebra, deer, llama, sloth, eagle, elk, stork, vulture, baboon, horned owl, pine snake, red-tailed hawk, and rhinoceros. Wildlife motion pictures had begun. Although still seen primarily as a *scientific* activity, just twenty years later it would be a different story.

In France, Etienne-Jules Marey learned of Muybridge's work in late 1878, while himself similarly engaged in trying to develop a means for photographing wild birds in motion. Not interested in cinematography for its own sake, Marey, a professor of natural history at the Collège de France, looked forward to a time when "One could see all imaginable animals during their true movements." His concept of "animated zoology" was one of the clearest early precursors of modern wildlife films.[13] In 1882 Marey developed the prototype for a "photographic gun" (later called "Marey's wheel") capable of shooting rapidly sequenced photos from a single lens. Significantly, its development was motivated by the desire to make images of animals in the field, under natural conditions rather than the controlled setups of the sort Muybridge used (although Muybridge subsequently experimented with Marey's design).

Yet because these early efforts have come to be regarded by history almost exclusively as "locomotion studies" rather than as images of animals or studies of their behavior, and because Muybridge also made many similar images of humans that have been of far more interest (perhaps because of the nudity), the connection between the early animal locomotion photos and contemporary wildlife films has become obscured. Nevertheless, fascination with animal movement endured among wildlife filmmakers and viewers alike. In 1935, T. D. A. Cockerell was still amazed by it. "Now, with the aid of the moving picture," patterns of animal behavior could be "repeated at will, and when it is desirable, the motion can be slowed down so that every movement is easily studied."[14] In 1946, when pioneer wildlife filmmaker Oliver Pike looked back on his long career, he could still recall the first film he ever saw, but what stood out in his memory, nearly half a century later, was its revelation of animals' movements: "It all seemed too marvelous to be true. The actual movements of the wild creatures could now be captured. The secrets and all the wonders of nature could be brought to the platform alive. And I was determined to do it."[15]

In 1988, more than a century after Muybridge and Marey, Marty Stouffer suggested that animal movements were still for him the object of an unsatisfied curiosity: "a good deal of what might be called my "style" results from this use of slow motion, which allows people to see the action and the beauty of movements that would be nothing but a blur if viewed at normal speed."[16]

Some of wildlife film's most enduring attributes, and some of the deepest urges compelling those who make them, thus appeared almost at the very beginning of their existence. Yet this also included a morally and ethically regrettable practice that in the 1980s and 1990s would bring shame on the wildlife film industry: that of willfully subjecting animals to harm or death for the purpose of filming it. The practice of setting up an actual killing for the cameras started as early as 1884 when Muybridge arranged at the Philadelphia zoo for a tiger to be set loose on an old buffalo who may even have been tethered. In pioneering the use of "disposable subjects," Muybridge set wildlife film on a path that would help differentiate it from documentary.[17] In the 1920s and 1930s, John Grierson set out to define the moral position of documentary, seeing it as a form concerned with human subjects, human society, and human welfare. Wildlife film's own struggle to stake out a moral and ethical position toward its subjects, however, had begun nearly a half-century earlier, even before the motion picture medium itself had been perfected.

Still photographers had, of course, often killed wild animals in order to get images of them; the Muybridge legacy, however, sanctioned killing them simply for more dramatic images. Nevertheless, a number of quasi-scientific rationalizations and euphemisms have been employed to obscure this fact. The buffalo killed for Muybridge's cameras has been described, for example, as being "sacrificed . . . to the cause of the investigation."[18] Death in service of a "cause," after all, is far easier to accept than killing merely to satisfy morbid curiosity. Death would later be a standard feature in motion pictures in general, as it had been in dramatic forms since the ancient Greeks, but in wildlife films, however much artifice was involved—scripting, editing, composite characters, emotional music, digital image manipulation, and various techniques of fakery—death would remain real. Ever since Muybridge, kill scenes have remained wildlife films' chief guarantor of authenticity, just as the obligatory "cum-shot" has in XXX-rated adult films.

In the 1880s and 1890s, however, photographers, scientists, inventors, and entrepreneurs were still laboring to perfect the basic technology of motion pictures. Whatever focus Muybridge and Marey had put on the revelation of animal behavior soon shifted to the development of motion picture technology for its own sake. Breakthroughs in the development of the new medium soon easily overshadowed those in the old—in particular the efforts to capture images of authentic animal behavior in the wild.

In 1895, for example, Richard and Cherry Kearton were hard at work developing their photographic field methods, and published their book *British Birds' Nests*, while Oliver Pike and R. B. Lodge devised a technique by which wild birds in their natural environments tripped a camera shutter and took their own picture. History, however, remembers that in Berlin that year the first public projection of motion pictures occurred, and that on the program was *Mr. Delaware and the Boxing Kangaroo*, likely the first screening of authentic wild animal behavior in full motion. Although it featured a captive animal removed from its natural environment, the film revealed animal behavior in a way that it had never been depicted before, and that still photographers, no matter how ingenious, could never hope to rival. Significantly, it was intended purely as entertainment, not as behavior study. Commerce already seemed poised to upstage science.

The following year, 1896, George Shiras III pioneered techniques for photographing wild animals at night, when many of them are most active, by using a trip-wire setup similar to that of Pike and Lodge. Meanwhile, in British East Africa, Lord Delemere took a still photographer with him on safari and brought back perhaps the first successful photographs of *living* African animals in the wild, including elephants, giraffes, gazelles, and zebras. Yet history remembers the premiere of a series of short films projected in the Edison Vitagraph process on April 23 at Koster & Bial's Music Hall in New York City. On the program that night was *Rough Sea at Dover*, a thirty-two-second film by Robert Paul and Birt Acres. While not a wildlife film, its dramatic images of crashing waves may have been the first vaguely "natural history" oriented film to be projected to a paying audience. Reviews in the press indicate that it was by far the most popular of all the films shown that evening, demonstrating clearly that *unstaged* nature could be a cinematic crowd-pleaser, even without animals.[19] *Mr. Delaware* and *Rough Sea at Dover* heralded the potential for entertainment and profit in film images of wildlife and natural history, and did so even before the century had turned. Science would never again enjoy the lead.

In 1897 the Keartons published their classic work *With Nature and a Camera*, documenting the careful and painstaking techniques they had developed for still photography of animals in the field. That year, however, the rudiments of wildlife and natural history motion pictures all came together, if only for a few seconds, in *The Sea Lions' Home*, a 25-ft Edison film depicting sea lions entering and leaving the water along a rocky shore. Here it all was at last: moving pictures, wild animals, natural behavior, natural habitat, and no people. Indeed, the absence of people gives *The Sea Lions' Home* an enduring, timeless quality that allows it to look almost like black-and-white outtakes of a film shot only last year. By contrast, images of people have helped other works show their age; *Mr. Delaware* now appears a quaint historical relic and the Keartons' book a Victorian collectible.

As early as 1898, audiences were turning out in large numbers in both Europe and America to see moving pictures—*actualités*—of all sorts, including a number that took advantage of the apparently considerable fascination with animals. Unlike *The Sea Lions' Home*, however, most of these were filmed in zoos or animal parks and tended to be fairly static. The main action often consisted of a human feeding the animals, which meant that whatever animal behavior there was consisted mainly of eating—or begging. *Ostriches Running* (1898) provided at least a bit more visual interest, but the static "feeding" films nevertheless persisted for several years, perhaps reinforcing perceptions of animals as humans' dependents. Titles included *Feeding the Sea Gulls* (1898), *Feeding the Pigeons* (1899), *Feeding the Sea Lions* (1900), and *Feeding the Bear(s) at the Menagerie* (1902). The form seemed to reach its zenith in 1903 with *Feeding the Elephants*, *Feeding the Hippopotamus*, *Feeding the Russian Bear*, and *Feeding the Swans*, followed in 1905 by *Feeding the Otters*. The last of the feeding films may have been *Feeding the Seals at Catalina* in 1910, but by then significant changes had occurred in motion picture form that compelled it irrevocably toward dramatic action. The virtually eventless feeding films thus contained the seeds of their own destruction, and may even have hastened the demand for more action—including violent action.

The earliest films centering on violent confrontations between animals were in many ways part of a tradition of staged confrontations and disposable subjects that extended back to similar spectacles staged in ancient

Rome. Titles included *Fighting Roosters* (1898) and *Fight Between Tarantula and Scorpion* (1900), although for sheer cruelty they were surpassed in 1906 by *Terrier vs. Wildcat,* a particularly grisly piece of animal pornography in which a common housecat is tortured mercilessly for the camera, for the amusement of audiences and, ultimately, for profit. The best-known disposable subject from the period was Topsy, the unfortunate "star" of Edison's *Electrocuting an Elephant* (1903). A Coney Island performer, Topsy was given the death sentence after killing one of her keepers (who, reportedly, had been abusive), and was ceremoniously executed at Luna Park before a paying audience.[20] Because the event wasn't staged solely for the camera, the film record of it may be considered a "documentary" recording of a "historical" event. In any case, virtually all early animal action films depicted staged, single events such as this, filmed in a single shot, and so were essentially just more *actualités* like the feeding films. Yet the public's taste for such simple actions, violent or otherwise, would not last long.

In 1907 London audiences were already accustomed to seeing movies at the end of musical performances in the city's music halls, but when Oliver Pike's *In Birdland* premiered at the Palace Theatre in August, audiences were treated to a wild animal film that went far beyond mere *actualités.* At close to ten minutes in length, it had taken two seasons to film and was hailed as "a bold attempt to bring the hidden beauties and wonders of the Country into London."[21] Yet filming complex events and interesting, dramatic animal behavior was difficult, and could involve more patient waiting and cranking of the camera than most filmmakers at the time were willing to invest.

In America the demand was rising for pictures of animals doing something different and exciting. It was met by a series of "hunting films" that had grown out of simple *actualités* but clearly had greater dramatic potential, and worked hand-in-glove with developments in cinematic form then taking place. Their emergence coincided with that of Edwin S. Porter's landmark films *The Life of an American Fireman* (1902) and *The Great Train Robbery* (1903), which had begun to stake out the rudiments of narrative film form, making it possible to tell a story as a series of linked scenes. Perhaps the first animal hunting film to be distributed internationally was the Pathé Frères picture *Hunting the White Bear* (a.k.a. *Une chasse a l'ours blanc*), which appeared in the United States in 1903. Although it showed no signs of Porter's narrative innovations, it had one important thing in common with *The Great Train Robbery*: it was essentially a *chase* picture. Historian Robert Sklar has written that during this time films with chase scenes of some kind, in which "there were two groups racing, one against the other—or, more precisely, one with a head start and the other trying to catch up," were becoming increasingly popular. They provided "at least twice as much opportunity for more shots, locations, and movement, and after 1904 they became the new fad in motion-picture spectacle."[22]

Not surprisingly, by 1906 animal *actualités* had all but disappeared, and in their place were an increasing number of chase-oriented hunting films. Titles from 1906 included *Stalking and Shooting Caribou, Deer Stalking with a Camera,* and *Moose Hunt in New Brunswick* (the latter two were filmed by Biograph's G. W. "Billy" Bitzer, later to gain fame as D. W. Griffith's cameraman on *Birth of a Nation, Intolerance,* and *Broken Blossoms*). Hunting films quickly grew in length and complexity, however, as shown in 1908's *The Wolf Hunt,* an elaborate chase film lasting some fourteen minutes and showing clearly the influence of Porter's narrative and formal innovations. Col. Selig's *Hunting Big Game in Africa* (a.k.a. *Roosevelt in Africa,* 1909) was less formally ambitious but gained more attention for its supposed depiction of Theodore Roosevelt shooting a lion. The scene was actually staged in Chicago with an actor playing Roosevelt, but the "disposable subject" and his death for the camera (or was it for *art?*) were real.[23]

By 1910 the three major categories of proto-wildlife films—Safari Films, Scientific-Educational Films, and Narrative Adventures—were all coming into focus. Each was largely independent of documentary categories recognized today, each directly contributed to the codification of wildlife film as a distinct genre, and each continues to be reflected in the genre today. Narrative adventures have had the most complex development and have proved the most popular with audiences. Because they also made the greatest contribution to the wildlife genre as we know it today, their story is the stuff of later chapters.

The Rise and Fall of the Safari Film

As hunting films began to catch on, the Arctic region quickly emerged as a popular location in films such as in *Polar Bear Hunt* (1903), *Chasing a Sea Lion in the Arctic* (1909), and *Seal and Walrus Hunting* (1910). Especially successful were the films of "Captain" Frank E. Kleinschmidt, the renowned "Big Game Hunter and Naturalist."[24] In the first of these, *Arctic Hunt* (1911), the tone is set by a scene in which the boat containing the camera pursues a moose attempting to swim across a body of water. It is easily overtaken, then shot from a few feet away, but manages to limp ashore before dying. This scene is repeated with a mother polar bear and her cub; her body is winched on deck and ceremoniously skinned by smiling, happy sailors. This film was followed by *Alaska-Siberian Expedition* (a.k.a. *The Carnegie Museum Alaska-Siberia Expedition,* 1912), and *Captain Kleinschmidt's Arctic Hunt* (1914). *Moving Picture World* reported in early 1914 that Kleinschmidt's pictures were shown "before a full attendance of members of the House of Congress, who were then trying to legislate upon Alaskan affairs." The members weighed the evidence of Kleinschmidt's films, then judiciously declared Alaska "the greatest game preserve in the New World."[25]

Soon, however, it was the equatorial regions, the tropics, especially the "dark continent" of Africa that drew cine-cameras like a magnet. The popularity of Selig's *Hunting Big Game in Africa* may have marked the turning point, but the first wildlife moving pictures actually shot in Africa were probably those in the hunting footage shot by an unknown cameraman accompanying Dr. A. David, of Switzerland, on a safari along the Dinder river in East Africa in 1907.

It was not long, however, before safari cameramen began to point their cameras at wild animals who were not being hunted or shot, but whom audiences (some, at least) found fascinating in their own right as *living* creatures. One writer noted of Cherry Kearton's efforts to film tigers in India, "If you want moving images of a "man eater" you cannot shoot him. The livelier he is, the more determined on taking rather than on 'being taken,' the better the picture and the greater the achievement."[26]

Such images, however, as well as receptive audiences for them, and even men who could make them, would all remain in a minority for some years. More typical was Carl Akeley, who, in 1910, hired members of Kenya's Nandi tribe to stage a ritualistic lion-spearing so he could film it. In later years it was claimed that Akeley was "appalled by the magnitude of the slaughter" of African animals by Europeans and Americans.[27] Nevertheless, over a period of three weeks in 1910, fourteen lions and five leopards were killed so he could get his pictures.[28] Then, because his Urban Bioscope camera proved inadequate to the task, the footage was simply shelved. Although the failure inspired him to develop the famous "Akeley camera," it came at the expense of a good many disposable subjects.

There were still precious few cameramen with the skill and experience, let alone the patience, to capture images of *living* wild animals under rugged and uncertain field conditions. *In Birdland* had shown Oliver Pike's skill in filming birds in their natural habitats, yet his pastoral English settings had a "backyard" feel in comparison to the forests of India or the parched expanses of the African savanna.

The Keartons, of course, were the acknowledged masters of rugged conditions and of observing with "infinite patience and infinite resourcefulness."[29] Yet in 1912, *Paul J. Rainey's African Hunt* proved far more successful with audiences in America than had any of Cherry Kearton's films of wildlife. Rainey's innovation was to use a pack of hounds to hunt African animals. Scenes of these violent chases grabbed audiences' attention and held it for an unprecedented run of fifteen months in New York. The film grossed an astonishing half-million dollars, making it one of the biggest money makers of the decade.[30] Kearton's work had received modest attention in Britain when released in fragmented form under several titles, including *Native Lion Hunt* (1909), *T.R. in Africa* (1909), *African Animals* (1909), *Scenes in Massua* (1910), and *With Roosevelt in Africa* (1910), but in the United

States even his most commercial venture, *Lassoing Wild Animals* (1911), featuring the American C. J. "Buffalo" Jones and a crew of cowboys doing just what the title indicates, failed to generate the sort of sensation that Rainey's film did the following year. By 1913, when Adolph Zukor agreed to distribute Kearton's *Native Lion Hunt* in the United States, not even a spirited introduction by Theodore Roosevelt at its New York premiere could help it compete at the box office with Rainey—although the latter's success was short-lived. Less successful was *Rainey's African Hunt* (1914), which was apparently recycled from the earlier release. Still, it was praised by the *New York Times* as "exciting," the sort of response that continued to elude Kearton.

The greater success of Rainey's likely owed to his emphasis on scenes of trapping, hunting, and killing—and his use of dogs. Although his films might be described today as "downmarket," they were, as the *Times* suggested, more exciting than Kearton's, and therefore had greater popular appeal. A few years later there was no denying among producers, distributors, and exhibitors that wildlife films "devoid of thrills and entertainment would not succeed economically."[31] In any case, Rainey's films were among the early demonstrations that a faster-moving and more sensational American style had already emerged. In the 1912 film a rhino is shot, and Rainey's camera is moved in close to record the last gaspings of its slow, agonizing death. Later Rainey's dogs chase a lioness into some tangled brush; after exhausting it with their taunting, they appear to pile on and kill it. A showman of superb taste, Rainey then holds its lifeless head up by the ears for a close-up. Accounts vary of the actual death toll: Rainey may have killed 27 lions in 35 days, or 9 lions in 35 minutes, or both, and a total of 74 lions on the entire trip.[32] In any case, the success with audiences of these on-camera killings allowed similar scenes to persist for several more decades side-by-side with straight wildlife footage.

Still, it was straight wildlife footage, with its revelation of natural behavior, its potential as raw material for creative stories, and its seeming detachment from events of history, that began to separate safari films from expeditionary documentaries. The latter typically depicted historically distinct, indeed, *historical* events. Ernest Palmer's film document of his 1909 trek across China, for example, typified the expedition film of the day. So too Herbert Ponting's *90° South*, which depicts Scott's Antarctic expedition of 1910–13.[33] This one, in fact, even included some straight wildlife scenes depicting penguins, orcas, etc. In contrast to his expeditionary footage, these were more behaviorally typical than historically specific. The noncooperation of the animals, however, proved vexing to Ponting (he was attacked by skua gulls while attempting to film them), and further set these scenes apart from his carefully composed images of Scott's ship and crew.

The same differences can be seen in Cherry Kearton's *T.R. in Africa* (the title that now adheres to some of his 1909 footage). The straight wildlife scenes have a raw, uncomposed, disorganized feel, while the scenes of Theodore Roosevelt, which technically document "historic" events, are more planned and organized. Kearton's journal gives some indication of this: "August 27. We were out early with the camera, but, at first, the light was not very satisfactory. I took the camp and the ex-President with his tent. We then went up on the bank and got Mr. Roosevelt on horseback. From here we rushed on in advance of his safari, until we found the ford of the river where the caravan was to cross. Here we placed the camera, in midstream, and took the party crossing." [34] The carefully composed scene does, in fact, show the caravan crossing the river at the appointed spot, passing just by Kearton's waiting camera.

Also standing in sharp contrast to the spontaneity of his straight wildlife footage were his semistaged scenes of Buffalo Jones and his cowboys in *Lassoing Wild Animals*. As in so many later safari films, these depict *pseudo-events* rather than actual historical events. Years later, as wildlife films developed as a genre, the tendencies would be ironically reversed: many of the makers of human-centered documentaries would strain to capture and preserve the integrity of only real events, while wildlife filmmakers would increasingly resort to controlled shooting and fabrication. When, in the 1960s, "direct cinema" was seen as epitomizing the pursuit of raw, spontaneous, and unmediated reality, wildlife films were at the same time perfecting facsimiles of reality using classical Hollywood techniques.

During their early years, however, despite the outbreak of war in Europe, safari films continued as a sort of cottage industry, and even an apparent indulgence for some, as in *Lady MacKenzie's Big Game Pictures* (a.k.a. *Heart of Africa*, 1915). It featured the requisite combination of hunting and straight wildlife footage of zebras, buffalo, giraffes, elephants, rhinos, hyenas, and baboons. Lady Grace MacKenzie herself is seen on camera shooting two lions and a rhino, all apparently goaded into charging. Also filming African wildlife during the war years, 1914–18, was Harry Eustace, although *With Eustace in Africa* was not released until 1922. Significantly, it was billed not as a safari film but as "a natural history study of animals in their own wild nature habitat."

By that time, however, Martin and Osa Johnson, the first of many married wildlife filmmaking teams, had already arrived on the scene with the feature films *Jungle Adventures* (1921) and *Trailing African Wild Animals* (1923). There would be several more features, including *Simba* (1928), *Across the World with Mr. and Mrs. Martin Johnson* (1930), *Congorilla* (1932), *Baboona* (1935), *Borneo* (1937), and a host of short films about "exotic" places and peoples. The Johnsons were undoubtedly the greatest popularizers of the safari film, even if they weren't its greatest practitioners. Although their films included hunting scenes, and often looked like exploratory expeditions, they were classic safari films depicting pseudo-events arranged and undertaken in order to be filmed. "The Johnson formula," a critic noted, "was irresistible; mount an elaborate safari, improvise various situations as you go along and film them on the spot."[35]

Much has been written about the Johnsons, a good deal of it by the Johnsons themselves, although several of their books were in fact ghostwritten by others. In any case, little of what has been written by or about them has been in connection with motion picture history or tradition, where discussions of them rightfully belong. Instead, they have inhabited the pages of journals such as *Smithsonian, Natural History, Explorer's Journal,* and *Scientific American,*[36] where they have little place, considering that their contributions to science, natural history, and exploration are virtually nil. Yet the fact that they show up repeatedly in such journals, as well as in dozens of newspaper articles, indicates the extent to which they were seen as newsmaking expeditionary explorers rather than as creative filmmakers—let alone as creative wildlife filmmakers. In the years since, wildlife filmmaking couples have been disregarded and/or disowned by *both* the exploration and cinematic communities.

Whether because of their colorful careers on the margins of Hollywood, or their cinematic mish-mashes of fiction and pseudo-documentary, the Johnsons have become important parts of film history—in particular, of course, wildlife film history. Pascal and Eleanor Imperato's impressive study of the Johnsons and their work entitled *They Married Adventure* (1992), is a detailed piece of scholarship that leaves no stone unturned and to which almost nothing can be added. Yet it may have been Kevin Brownlow, in his study of silent film *The War, the West, and the Wilderness* (1979), who made the first significant gesture toward recognizing the Johnsons' contributions to cinema. The Johnsons themselves were skilled and prolific self-promoters, publishing dozens of books and articles touting their exploits, but Brownlow takes their films and filmmaking skills on their own merits, and finds enough that is praiseworthy apart from the hooplah. "Johnson was probably the best cameraman of all the African explorers," notes Brownlow (still using "explorer" instead of "filmmaker").[37]

Significantly, it seems that of all the wildlife photographers and filmmakers that preceded him, Martin Johnson's greatest admiration was reserved for the most sensationalistic of them, Paul J. Rainey. Johnson "wanted very much to follow in Rainey's footsteps . . . in capturing his personal adventures and a genuine picture of Africa on film."[38] Brownlow notes that both the Johnsons "were obsessed by adventure . . . and aimed exclusively for thrills,"[39] yet the emphasis was, indeed, clearly on *personal* adventures. Eric Barnouw declared flatly that "Self-glorification was the keynote" in their films, noting that both Johnsons "were constantly on camera in sequences demonstrating their courage or wit, or both."[40] Lacking the category of wildlife film, however, and trying instead to include them in his discussion of documentary, Barnouw finds little, from a documentary stand-point, to praise about the Johnsons. Whereas Brownlow ventures only to criticize the Johnsons for having "no scruples about authenticity," Barnouw catalogues a series of their offenses, and implicitly measures them against the ethical standards of documentary:

Unabashed condescension and amusement marked their attitude toward natives. . . . In a forest clearing we see them recruiting forty "black boys" as carriers. When one gives his name, it sounds like "coffee pot" to Mrs. Osa Johnson, so his name is written down as Coffee Pot. Johnson's narration speaks of "funny little savages," "happiest little savages on earth." His idea of humor was to give a pygmy a cigar and wait for him to get sick; to give another a balloon to blow up and watch his reaction when it bursts; to give a monkey beer and watch the result.[41]

Perhaps because the victims were nonhumans, Barnouw manages to over-look what was arguably the Johnsons' worst offense: their tendency to pro-voke animals into a filmable reaction, often goading them into charging toward the camera before shooting them in "self-defense." Osa later argued that, because telephoto lenses resulted in shaky images and blurred fore-grounds, she and Martin were forced to work "within shorter and shorter ranges," disingenuously suggesting it was their dedication to craft that put them in harm's way.[42] In one such confrontation with a lion in *Simba*, a title card reads: "We *wanted* to run for our lives—but we *had to stay* for the pic-tures." A few minutes later they got the picture they wanted when a lion "came charging down upon *us*, a roaring storm of fury." Osa fires twice, and the beast goes down just a few feet away (although the intercutting suggests the events were filmed separately).

Elsewhere in her book *Four Years in Paradise* (1944), which recounts the years between 1923 and 1928, she admits they were also well aware that "there was always a danger" when filming elephants, and that "often as not there would be a charge." Nevertheless, she writes, "as we became bolder we went nearer and nearer to the elephants, for we wanted sharp, clear pictures and in our eagerness to get them we were apt to minimize the risks."[43]

A few sentences later comes the revelation that they did, in fact, delib-erately provoke animals in order to get a reaction. The preferred reaction was, of course, a dramatic charge toward the camera—and a bullet: "Martin turned to me and said, 'I'll go out and get a little action, Osa; you take the camera.' He took his double-barreled .470 express rifle, and crept up until he was within seventy feet of the leading elephant. The elephant saw him and charged furiously. Martin took careful aim . . . and let him have a hard-nosed bullet."[44] Through it all, Osa adds, "I stuck to the camera, and kept turning the crank," in accordance with their "solemn pact" to keep film-ing no matter what happened. The elephant, however, kept coming. She describes in detail Martin's efforts at self-induced self-defense. He tried to pump more slugs into "the vital spot just below the center of the head" of the deliberately provoked and now mortally wounded elephant. It is finally Osa who finishes him off, after which they have a celebration. The event can be seen, with added cutaways and reaction shots, in their 1923 film *Trailing African Wild Animals*. At the film's opening, the preserved head of the elephant was displayed in the theater lobby.[45]

In recounting such events, however, Osa Johnson reveals that she and Martin repeatedly used the same technique for getting dramatic shots. In another incident just a few pages later, Martin is at the camera, but the charge is still part of the game: "Sometimes, when Martin took the chances he did in getting much too close to elephants with his cameras, I wondered if he hadn't forgotten that he wasn't in a zoo and there wasn't anything to protect him from being crushed into a pulp, except luck and the chance that I would shoot straight if the animals charged."[46]

George Eastman, of Kodak fame, visited the Johnsons at their camp in Kenya three years later. In a written account of his trip, he describes an incident in which the same goading-filming-shooting technique was used, this time with Eastman at the camera, and Martin Johnson again doing the shooting. In this case a rhino was the victim—shot to death, but not even "immortalized" on celluloid; Eastman's film was strictly for personal enjoyment.

I decided to get a motion picture of him with a Ciné-Kodak. With Phil Percival and Martin Johnson as my guard, I approached to within about twenty yards of him before he saw us, but he had no sooner made us out than he charged. I started my camera, while Phil and Martin stood by. They let him get to within ten yards, and then Phil fired. Martin followed his example, while I was still busy with the camera. The old fellow kept coming, but he began to crumble, and finally fell just five and a half paces from where I stood.

Eastman then makes it unmistakably clear that this scenario—the charging animal shot within a few feet of the camera, and dying on film—was the *preferred* one: "The affair could not have been more perfect if it had been staged, and I felt that it was the opportunity of lifetime. The picture, too, came out well, and I consider it one of the outstanding 'trophies' of my trip."[47]

As the 1920s gave way to the 1930s, however, the Johnsons faced a threat far different from charging animals. During their "four years in paradise," silent cinema had given way to the talkies, but every foot of film they'd shot during that time was silent. Moreover, the Depression had begun to drive down overall movie attendance in America.[48] Hollywood responded by perfecting the high-gloss escapist fantasies that would soon bring about its "golden age," and the triumph of the studio system. It has been said that between 1929 and 1935 the cinema was virtually "remade," as sound put a premium on spoken dialogue and on human actors who could speak it.[49] With movies largely redefined as a talking medium, it was clear that silent images of animals, no matter how thrilling, would be unable to compete in the mainstream motion picture marketplace.

The Johnsons were quick to improvise a transition to sound, however, and managed to release *Simba* in 1928 in both a silent and a hybrid sound version.[50] The latter proved much more successful, despite the fact that its sound additions consisted only of a musical track and a sync prologue in which the Johnsons awkwardly spoke on camera (strangely prefiguring the studio prologues in television programs in later years).

The following year they began making *Congorilla*, which was completed in 1932 and touted as "the first sound film from darkest Africa."[51] It was a claim to *firstism* that was sustained mainly, if at all, on technicalities.[52] Martin Johnson later wrote of his experiences with sound recording that he had already "mastered 'cinematography' before sound photography was added," and so "merely buckled down and attained a fair understanding of this newer and more complicated business"—although he reveals a few pages later that it took two extra men "to handle the sound apparatus."[53] Yet sound, especially dialogue, seemed to shift the Johnsons' attention away from wildlife and even more toward themselves and their own exploits. This was clear in their next film, *Baboona* (1935), although their awkward, stilted attempts to look and sound natural while reciting rehearsed dialogue are among the film's most conspicuous weaknesses.

Ultimately, although their filmmaking practices could be questionable, their skills limited, their scruples dubious, and their self-indulgence undeniable, the Johnsons themselves were popular and so were their films. They brought more popular acceptance to wildlife films than anyone prior to Disney—and a bit of polish too. Soon after Martin Johnson's death in a plane crash in 1937, Lowell Thomas praised him for having shot "some of the best wild animal footage that had ever been seen up to that time." Thomas also reveals that near the end Johnson was told by studio executives that he and Osa had "exhausted the entertainment possibilities of Africa."[54] Whether set in Africa or elsewhere, it seemed that the safari film had, in fact, gone about as far as it could go, and went into decline in the mid-1930s.

Yet it may be more accurate to say that the form had entered its decadence, and that this may even have begun soon after the arrival of sound, as evident in a slew of downmarket productions that emerged in the early 1930s: *Africa Speaks* (1930), *Ingagi* (1930), *Ubangi* (1931), *Matto Grosso* (1933), *Taming the Jungle* (1933), *Untamed Africa* (1933), *Beyond Bengal* (1934), and *Devil Tiger* (1934), most of which received a needed boost from the addition of hyperbolic voice-over narration.

The worst of the lot was probably *Ingagi*, a Congo Pictures "production" (if one can call it that). Scenes apparently shot at different times, in different locations, by different people, on different stocks, ranging from authentic African wildlife footage to backlot scenes of a man in a gorilla suit, were thrown together with little attempt to wrestle continuity from them. Equally random is the slaughter of animals—although all these films included scenes of animals being shot to death. Although these scenes were real, there was enough that was faked in *Ingagi* to earn it a ban from the Hays office not long after its release.[55]

A less lethal variation on the safari film during this time came from one of the originators of the form, Cherry Kearton, who had moved competently into sound films. *Dassan* (1930) is named for the island off the coast of South Africa where the Jackass Penguins, so called for their donkey-like braying, once lived amid crowded and boisterous gatherings (they later disappeared from the island). Kearton is seen throughout the film in traditional, safari-style topee pith helmet. Near the end, standing atop a large boulder surrounded by tens, perhaps hundreds of thousands of penguins, he proclaims: "I have learned a great deal from the penguins—about human nature." The remark is perhaps less funny than it is revealing of Kearton's actual knowledge and understanding of the penguins. Still, *Dassan* was produced and sold as a satirical wildlife comedy, a self-proclaimed "adventure in search of laughter featuring Nature's greatest little comedians." To Kearton, the penguins looked like a million "tiny Charlie Chaplins." What makes *Dassan* significant, however, and what ultimately magnifies its failures, is the fact that it was the work of one of the legendary pioneers of wildlife film, its patron saint in Britain.

Yet the safari film's decadence may have been nowhere more clear than in a trio of phony "capture" films by the Barnumesque American Frank Buck: *Bring 'em Back Alive* (1932), *Wild Cargo* (1934), and *Fang and Claw* (1935). The prologue to *Wild Cargo* spells out the fictitious premise behind Buck's films:

Frank Buck's life work is to dare death. It is his business to penetrate the darkest depths of poisonous jungles to procure the rare and dangerous beasts which fill our circuses and zoos. His self-appointed task is to "bring 'em back alive."

This picture is an authentic and official record of his last expedition into the perils of the Malayan jungles. He had received an order for an entire WILD CARGO of fierce and unusual animals. In photography and in Frank Buck's own voice, the following episodes depict exactly how he went after that WILD CARGO—*and got it!*

A devoted adherent of the vulgar-Darwinist notion that animals live in a state of constant interspecies war, Buck specialized in putting animals of different types together in small enclosures and provoking them to fight on camera. These staged confrontations call to mind the bread-and-circus spectacles of a decaying Rome—except that Buck's animals fought it out in enclosures somewhat less glorious than the Colosseum. *Bring 'em Back Alive* is punctuated at regular intervals by the following staged conflicts:

(1) spotted leopard versus python, (2) black leopard versus crocodile, (3) black leopard versus tiger, (4) tiger versus buffalo, (5) tiger versus crocodile, (6) bear cub versus python, (7) python versus crocodile, and (8) tiger versus python.

Buck's voice-over comments during each of these struggles are too inane to repeat, but are exceeded in their stupidity by the sound effects, which consist solely of men making growling and hissing noises in a hollow-sounding studio, all of which sound alike no matter what combination of creatures are on the screen.[56] The fact that the same animals appear to have been used more than once, and that nearly every fight was filmed from above, as if staged in a pit, seems to confirm observations made by Armand Denis, who directed *Wild Cargo*:

Buck's camp, which I had imagined to be somewhere in the heart of the jungle . . . was a hundred yards or so off the main road . . . conveniently near to the Raffles Hotel, the race track and the other amenities of Singapore, but it was not even faintly reminiscent of a jungle. It consisted mainly of a few cages containing a variety of despondent-looking animals, and of a number of enclosures more or less ingeniously camouflaged and in which obviously the animals were to be placed for various scenes to be photographed. With a sinking heart I began to realize what was expected of me.[57]

According to Denis, the conflicts were staged using animals bought or rented from local people in Singapore, and thrown together in battles that, however unlikely in reality, would be very real for the contestants. Viewing the films confirms the ferocity—and cruelty—of these forced confrontations. The python, wrapping its coils around the tiger's neck (staged conflict 8, above) produces a suffocating, eye-bulging effort by the terrified cat to free itself. It is difficult to watch, but is made all the more gruesome by the knowledge that it was staged in a pit with captive animals solely for cheap matinee entertainment. As such, the scene exemplifies the worst kind of voyeuristic animal pornography. Denis recounts Buck's plan for another such incident that reveals his commitment to the idea of interspecies conflict, his penchant for sensationalism, and the depths of his insensitivity. "Now," he asked Denis, "how's about a fight to the death between a tiger and an orang-utan?" Denis recalls his reaction:

"Well," I said cautiously, "orang-utan occurs in Borneo and Sumatra; there are tigers also in Sumatra, so it is not inconceivable that an orang-utan and a tiger could meet—but surely if they did, they'd just avoid each other. Animals don't normally fight to the death for nothing."

"Don't they, eh?" replied Buck. "When I'm around they do."[58]

Although Buck's efforts to "capture" the same animals could be just as cruel, on one such occasion he failed to bring it back alive. The scene called for him to wrestle a tiger supposedly caught in a pit-trap. Denis describes it as "a large, placid old tiger specially hired from a local animal dealer" in Sumatra. When the pit flooded overnight, quietly drowning the tiger, Buck was undeterred, and gave the order to roll film. As Denis recounts it, "He advanced toward his adversary, and for breathless minutes he did battle with the corpse of the drowned tiger. When I saw the finished film on the screen back in New York a few months later, I was surprised to find the battle with the tiger remarkably convincing."[59]

We see Buck approach the pit, pistol drawn. "I never stepped more carefully," he comments. "I knew now that the pit wasn't quite deep enough . . . he could have come straight out at us." Buck lowers a rope lasso down to ensnare the carcass, and then goes down a ladder into the pit, a large knife clenched in his teeth, to do battle. After the "struggle," the tiger is hoisted out. Its lifeless legs and tail dangle limply from the top of the frame—the only indications of its true state. The phony growls persist as the limp body is lowered into a cage. "He was in the cage, growling and snarling," Buck lies, "but he was mine; he had killed his last human being, and I had kept my promise to capture a real man-eating tiger, one that had actually tasted human flesh."

Like the Johnsons, Buck was clearly the dynamic and dramatic center of his films; his career also went into decline at about the same time as theirs (after *Fang and Claw*, 1935). *Jungle Cavalcade* (1941) was simply RKO's recycling of footage from Buck's earlier films. He returned in one last attempt, entitled *Jacare, Killer of the Amazon* (1943), but by then the entire safari film subgenre had been driven into the ground. Also, there was a war on. His final screen appearance was a bit part in the Abbott and Costello farce *Africa Screams* (1949). Yet, in retrospect, it seems fair to categorize his films among the early efforts to stake out the wildlife genre. Variations on his model have certainly been put to use by others over the years. Stan Brock's and Jim Fowler's often gratuitous animal-wrestling scenes in the *Wild Kingdom* series during the 1960s and 1970s (some of which reportedly involved captive and/or tame animals) certainly call to mind Buck's adventures, as do Steve Irwin's antics in *The Ten Deadliest Snakes* (1996), *Deadly Crocodiles* (1998), and in the popular *Crocodile Hunter* TV series of the 1990s.

After the debacle of *Wild Cargo*, Armand Denis went on to a highly successful career in television on the BBC, but not until he had made some of the last attempts to revive the safari film as a cinematic feature. *Savage Splendor* was released internationally by RKO in 1949, but its travelogue structures and scenes of setup captures were clearly throwbacks to earlier times. Film historians have always tended to link such films to "expedition" documentaries, but from Selig to Rainey to the Johnsons to Buck and beyond, safari films had involved a good deal of staging, acting, dramatic storytelling, and fabricating of events. By the early 1950s the safari form had been in relative dormancy for over a decade, but was quietly undergoing a metamorphosis. Denis's next film, *Below the Sahara* (1953), with its greater emphasis on wildlife,[60] showed evidence of this, but the safari film's true reemergence would come in a whole new medium.

Scientific-Educational Films

The animal *actualités* in the early years of cinema had also given rise to another type of proto-wildlife film far different from hunting and safari pictures. Scientific-educational films began to be made almost as soon as the film medium was perfected, and were part of a larger effort, perhaps inspired by Muybridge and Marey, to use motion pictures, as Leonard Donaldson put it, to "unravel the manifold mysteries of life." In his 1912 book *The Cinematograph and Natural Science*, Donaldson makes a case for "the achievements and possibilities of cinematography as an aid to scientific research."[61] He even cites what may be the first English language use of the term "documentary" in relation to film, taken from a 1908 lecture on surgical practices by a Dr. Doyen, who argued at a Madrid conference that the "cinematograph will also allow of the preservation *in documentary form* of the operations of the older surgeons."[62] The use of "natural history film" as a broad, inclusive category, appears not to have come into use until the year after Donaldson's book, 1913, when it began showing up in trade journals. The fact that its recognition as an entity unto itself still preceded most of the currently accepted ideas of when "documentary" first emerged suggests, at the very least, that documentary did not give birth to wildlife and natural history film, as suggested in some film history texts.

That same year Thomas Edison announced a plan "to utilize the motion pictures to teach all sorts of elementary facts." Interestingly, his films were all tried out on focus-groups of young students, and then further refined "until a satisfactory film on each subject has been prepared." The subjects were "natural phenomena" such as the larval development of houseflies and butterflies.[63] Yet fully a decade earlier Charles Urban had launched the "Unseen World" series of "micro-bioscopic" films in Britain, which included F. Martin Duncan's *Circulation of Blood in a Frog* and *Cheese Mites*, both in 1903. The latter was so revealing (at least to some eyes) that it was banned because of protests from the cheese industry. Today, residing in the vaults of the British Film Institute, it plays more like abstract art or animation. A more accessible effort of this experimental sort was Percy Smith's early time-lapse study *The Birth of a Flower* (1910), followed by his *The Strength and Agility of Insects* (1911), which, although simple, is still revealing and entertaining. Although shown in several other countries, none of these efforts, however, were significant popular successes.

In the United States, Raymond L. Ditmars would soon find a way to take similar material and make it popular. Curator of Reptiles at the New York Zoological Park (the Bronx Zoo), Ditmars had just published *Reptiles of the World* (1910), and was lecturing widely on the subject, when he suddenly "got the idea of presenting animals to the public by means of motion pictures." It was hardly a novel idea, but he planned a "systematic, educational series of zoological films showing members of the main branches of the animal kingdom going about their daily lives." On a "tiny improvised stage" at the Reptile House in the Bronx, he began shooting close-ups of spiders, lizards, frogs, and other creatures,[64] but somehow managed to inject enough humor into the footage to earn the description of "first class entertainment out of what might otherwise appear to be a rather dry and severe course of study."[65] The finished film, *The Book of Nature* (1914), concludes with a sequence called the "Jungle Circus Company," which takes some of Smith's ideas in *The Strength and Agility of Insects* to greater lengths. Ditmars had jerboas jumping hurdles, tree toads climbing ropes, a fly juggling a tiny barbell, and an audience of toads appearing to watch the show.[66] *Moving Picture World* announced that "A New Star Blazes on the Horizon of Educational Kinematography." It praised Ditmars's "gift of humor," and his "talent of imparting knowledge through the medium of the screen." The article continued, "it would seem as if we had the right man to give the world a wonderful course of zoology in motion pictures."[67] E. J. Marey was dead, but his dream of "animated zoology" was still alive. But could or should it be *funny*? *Moving Picture World* thought it should: "It is easy to make entertaining pictures educational, but to make educational pictures entertaining is a more difficult problem. Professor Ditmars has solved the problem absolutely. . . . We look and laugh and learn in one process."[68]

It was not all laughs, however. Ditmars may have been a man of science, but he had also become a popularizer, an entertainer, or, as he noted, a "movie director."[69] Already staging actions on artificial sets, it was probably inevitable that he began to provoke interactions between animals, and eventually to stage deadly confrontations using disposable subjects purchased from a dealer in London who had evidently *brought them back alive*. One such fight-to-the-death involved a mongoose and a cobra. "We tamed the mongoose," Ditmars later wrote, then, when all was ready, "the cobra was cautiously started up through a chute from beneath the stage." The mongoose attacked and killed it so quickly, however, that only a few seconds of film were exposed. A cable was sent to London for another cobra, which arrived a month later. This time, the mongoose was introduced into the enclosure where the cobra already lay. Sounding much more like a filmmaker than a zoologist or curator, Ditmars remarked: "The resulting fight was fine—the mongoose winning, but with much more caution and delay than in the first battle."[70] His transition to "movie director" was complete.

A short time later, in Britain, another attempt to marry education and entertainment took place at British Instructional Films when Percy Smith, Mary Field, and producer Bruce Woolfe launched the "Secrets of Nature" series (1922–33). Each of the "Secrets" dealt with some aspect of natural history—usually wildlife. Some were filmed in zoos, some in a studio, and some in underwater tanks. At eight to ten minutes, however, they were technically known as "shorts," which, Field noted, "are not popular in the film world. . . . The distributor regards them as a nuisance . . . [and] the cinema-going public uses the time when a 'short' is being projected as a chance to rest the eyes, finish the conversation, or powder the nose. 'Shorts' are never advertised outside theaters . . . or in newspapers, and consequently are hardly ever noticed by critics."[71]

The "Secrets" were noticed by John Grierson, however, just long enough for him to dismiss them as mere "lecture films." He added that it was unlikely "they will make any considerable contribution to the fuller art of documentary." In this he was right, but not for the reason he asserted, which was that they "do not dramatize," but only describe.[72] This was unfair and untrue. Field and Smith were working in an industry where dramatic feature films were the main course in everyone's cinematic diet, and they clearly knew on which side their bread was buttered. Just as Ditmars had, they dramatized actuality by combining science with audience-pleasing entertainment values. They noted that even though the "Secrets" had been "hailed as outstanding educational films," this did not "prevent their main object from being entertainment."[73] Their book about the series reveals at several points their concern with the relative entertainment value of various animal species—which of the animals had "star" qualities and so forth. Yet they also argue that the series revealed a great many previously unknown facts, and therefore contributed to scientific research. They even refer to some of the situations they constructed for the films as "experiments." To this day they are generally thought of as "scientific-educational films."

Yet the way the "Secrets" team negotiated the transition to sound in the late 1920s reveals the degree to which they remained committed to entertaining and popularizing. The impetus for the move into sound production came, in fact, from American producers eager for a talking "Secret" to appear on the same bill with the Douglas Fairbanks-Mary Pickford version of Shakespeare's *The Taming of the Shrew*. The result was 1929's *Peas and Cues*.[74] After they had mastered the ability to accompany their films with prerecorded music, however, the "Secrets" team set out to take advantage of the popularity of Disney's cartoons by trying "to reproduce the Walt Disney technique with real animals instead of cartoons."[75] The pair of films that resulted, *Daily Dozen at the Zoo* and *Playtime at the Zoo* (1930), involved synchronizing animals' on-screen movements to music, as if they were keeping time with it. These included "Daisy, the bear who does slimming exercises," an otter who "turned somersaults through the water in waltz-time," and a kangaroo "hopping to the tune of 'Pop Goes the Weasel.'"[76] That same year, in fact, Cherry Kearton had fashioned a montage of penguin eggs hatching to the same tune in *Dassan*, along with a scene of penguins running down a beach accompanied by the sound of honking automobile horns. Although it is unknown if Kearton also took his cue from Disney, it is clear that Disneyesque devices began showing up in wildlife films, British wildlife films, moreover, well before they did in Disney's own (the celebrated scorpion square-dance scene in *The Living Desert*, 1953, was still more than two decades away). The "Secrets" producers later expressed regrets for having detoured in this direction, although they admitted that "the two pictures proved so popular that they were worth all the worry and trouble they had caused."[77]

Perhaps inspired by the "Secrets" series, but in a country that had already shown a greater tendency toward wildlife images with dramatic, even violent conflicts, American documentary cameraman Stacy Woodard set out in the early 1930s on his own project of merging science and entertainment in a series of close-up studies of insects filmed in controlled settings.[78] Whereas Ditmars had called his efforts in this area *The Book of Nature*, Woodard gave his film series the Darwinian sounding title, "The Struggle for Life," and even went so far as to report his "findings" in the journal *Scientific American*.[79] That, however, was where all similarity to science ended, and where popular cinema took over. Entitled "Insect Warriors Battle for the Movies," Woodard's article described a number of by now familiar manipulations of disposable subjects in forced interspecies battles. By pitting them against each other in small enclosures, often in unlikely or unnatural combinations, for the sole purpose of creating dramatic entertainment, Woodard was reenacting in miniature what Frank Buck was doing at the very same time with much larger animals, and what Ditmars had done nearly two decades earlier. The practice has, of course, persisted well into our own time, and is echoed in every bogus claim that in the animal world "it's kill or be killed," and that "only the strongest survive."

What makes Woodard's efforts noteworthy, however, is not only the grandiose presumption of scientific revelation, but the imprimatur of a scientific journal that helped legitimize the pseudo-Darwinian interpretations of his staged events. Yet in such scenes the history of wildlife film is told in microcosm: an artificial construct becomes "real" when run through the naturalizing process of cinema. Drama thus passes for nature, fiction for fact, realism for reality. The entire scale for measuring such things shifts one notch toward artifice, while retaining the categories associated with truth.

Clearly, the veneer of science did not prevent Woodard from projecting his own values onto nature, and from drawing his conclusions from staged actions with little external validity. Not surprisingly, his camera proved the natural world to be a site of "constant," indeed, "*eternal* struggle" between animals of different species. By placing a cricket and a wasp together in a small space and forcing them into confrontation, Woodard saw himself as merely assisting them in "carrying out nature's brutal process" of perpetual interspecies conflict.[80] Yet more important than his denial of his own role in creating such outcomes was his recording of them in a medium then considered to have nearly unimpeachable evidentiary value, and in a form thought to provide "documentary" images equal to Truth itself. It seems essential, then, to detach wildlife films from documentary, but this has still not completely come about.

There were, fortunately, a number of more thoughtful uses of film in relation to wildlife and natural history during this time, but more *filming* than actual films. In 1935 Cornell University professor Arthur Allen successfully filmed the ivory-billed woodpecker, which was already precipitously close to extinction. His footage is considered the only existing film record of the now extinct species, but was not put into commercial distribution. Among similar films that were distributed and exhibited during these years, few revealed a gift for popularization such as that of Ditmars, or Field and Smith. The most significant exception was Alexander Korda's production, *The Private Life of the Gannet*, which was produced in Britain 1934 and went on to win an Academy Award in 1937—the first wildlife film to do so.[81] As the decade closed, G. K. Noble's *The Social Behavior of the Laughing Gull* (1940) was shown at the annual meeting of the American Ornithologists' Union, but was not seen by a popular audience. That same year, however, Hans Hass's *Pirsch unter Wasser* (1940) became one of the first underwater natural history films to gain recognition worldwide.[82] Yet when the war interrupted production, as well as a good deal of research, it was still debatable as to whether or not thoughtful, scientifically informed films about wildlife and natural history could achieve regular critical and popular success. Clearly, there was no formula—yet.

Documentary, Education, or Entertainment?

World War II had thrown the economies of the combatant nations into turmoil, or at least had preoccupied them enough that little in the way of wildlife and natural history film was being made. In neutral Sweden, however, Arne Sucksdorff produced beautiful and innovative films such as *A Summer's Tale* (1941), *Reindeer Time* (1943), and *Gull!* (1944), all of which dealt with wild animals but dispensed with voice-over narration and scientific information in favor of dramatic narrative communicated visually. Barnouw has argued that Sucksdorff's films "seemed perfect for a wartime neutral" in that their content was unlikely to provoke Nazi ire or invite intervention. Although he is full of praise for Sucksdorff's "rare rhythmic sense," for photography "rich in texture," and for "close-ups of animal eyes and fur that are full of sensuous excitement," Barnouw still lacks the category "wildlife film," and so damns Sucksdorff's films with faint praise, effectively dismissing them for their apparent avoidance of social meaning (although he does note that the egg stealing scenes in *Gull!* were seen by some as a parable of Nazism). The real problem, however, is that they don't fit comfortably into familiar documentary categories.[83] Of course, wildlife films had been developing for several decades along lines other than those of documentary.

After the war, the loosely scattered themes, motifs, techniques, and patterns unique to films about wild animals began to come together. This was nowhere more clear than in Disney's series of "True Life Adventures" produced between 1948 and 1960. These films united the disparate elements of wildlife filmmaking up to that time, consolidated them in a unified but still flexible form, and above all popularized them as never before. In so doing, the series brought these elements into focus *as conventions,* and thus as the distinctive features marking a discrete and recognizable cinematic form.

Yet even if the "True Lifes" were helping wildlife films come into their own as a motion picture genre, it was one that still borrowed from other genres—documentary, travelogue, melodrama, musical, even cartoons—in addition to pulling together its own already familiar elements. In fact, few if any of the individual ingredients that made up the "True Life" films were particularly new in themselves. There had already been considerable progress, for example, in technical areas such as micro-cinematography, slow-motion and time-lapse photography, filming underwater, filming with telephoto lenses, and recording sound in the field. Techniques had been developed for capturing revealing images of animal behavior under controlled studio setups as well as under rugged field conditions. Animal storytelling had also advanced considerably; the stories of "literary naturalists" had helped put in place much of what would become the basic wildlife film story model. Elements of it had already shown up in small, B-grade Hollywood films. Moreover, models of narrative and character that would be perfected in the "True Lifes" had even been tested in Disney's own animated features, such as *Dumbo* (1940) and *Bambi* (1942).

What was new about the "True Life Adventures," however, was the way they effectively integrated elements from so many sources, managing at once to link scientific-educational films, safari films, animal adventure stories, fanciful animated features, a bit of comedy, and even elements from legends, tales, and myths. Like the "Secrets of Nature" series, the "True Life" films could include revealing, close-up studies of behavior filmed in laboratory-like studios. Yet, like safari and exploration films, they could also be expansive, surveying broad geographic regions, exploring remote and little-known places, and showing a variety of wild animals in their natural habitats. Like animal adventure stories, they could link sequences together in dramatic narratives of individual struggles, dangers, and even moments of intimacy and togetherness. Like Sucksdorff's films, they could be lyrical, or fantastic and full of wonder. Like Buck's, they could be sensational, condescending, even cruel. Like Ditmars's *The Book of Nature* or Kearton's *Dassan*, they could add comical contrivances to first-rate cinematography. Like Disney's own cartoon features, they could be whimsical, sentimental, and, of course, anthropomorphic. The "True Lifes" were the product not of inspiration or genius, but of history, convention, experience, observation, and shrewd business sense.

Yet there were differences from the earlier types of wild animal films, and these may even have been more significant than the similarities. Where the "Secrets of Nature" films were brief essays of 8–10 minutes, the "True Lifes" started at a half-hour and soon expanded to feature length (70+ minutes). Thus, where the "Secrets" had little room for plot and character development, the "True Lifes" indulged them, developed them in mini-dramas within each film. Where animal adventure stories had excluded factual information, the "True Lifes" included a good deal of it, however superficial. Where safari films had focused on the exploits of human "stars" such as Buck or the Johnsons who provided the point-of-view, the "True Lifes" did away with people (as well as social context) altogether, and were thus in the tradition of today's blue chip wildlife films.

Emerging soon after the second world war, the "True Lifes" came about to some extent as a result of it. Disney had already experimented with live action production in 1941s *The Reluctant Dragon*, and by 1942 the studio was busy, like several others, producing live action films for the government in support of the war effort. When the smoke had cleared, Disney continued in live action production in *The Three Caballeros* (1945) and *Song of the South* (1946), although each included far more generous helpings of animation. Yet the war had also shown that nonfiction films, such as Wyler's *Memphis Belle* (1945), could be nearly as engaging to audiences as the escapist fare Hollywood studios had been making. They could be as strong on action, drama, exciting narratives and engaging characters, and, with far lower productions costs, could be nearly as profitable.

The "True Life Adventures" were thus in keeping with the direction Disney had been moving, but were to be its first *fully* live action films, and thus posed significant risks—particularly because they were live action films *without actors*. This was a distinction Roy Disney, Sr., who managed the company's finances, was quick to make. He had been nudging the studio in the direction of live action productions, but doubted the marketability of pictures that lacked actors and characters, and feared that films featuring only wild animals would be of little interest to distributors or viewers. In fact, Howard Hughes did refuse, initially, to commit RKO to distributing the first of the "True Lifes," *Seal Island*, forcing Walt Disney himself to arrange for a theater in Pasadena to exhibit it—conveniently in time for Academy

Award consideration. The film proved a success with audiences and members of the Motion Picture Academy, however, and on the strength of its award for "Best Two-Reel Short Subject" RKO relented, and distributed the film along with a publicity campaign touting its award (with an image of the Oscar® symbol strategically situated on the promotional one-sheet between the words "Walt" and "Disney").[84] *Seal Island* was so successful, in fact, that it helped secure the Disney studio's much needed bank loans for 1949.[85] Wildlife films were far cheaper to produce than anything else Disney was making, but *Seal Island*, viewed today, shows no sign of cheapness; it is neither primitive nor experimental, but instead shows the Disney formula and style already fully worked out. The revelation, however, that it contained a model capable of securing investment capital as well as profits proved an irresistible motivation to continue exploiting it in film after film.[86]

Seal Island was filmed in Alaska's Pribiloff Islands by Al and Elma Milotte, but the exact circumstances and events that led up to it are unclear. By some accounts, Al Milotte had a camera store in Alaska where Walt Disney walked in one day and asked if he'd like to "make some pictures" about "the development of Alaska."[87] Another account repeats the camera shop story, and adds that "Disney invited them [the Milottes] to shoot material on any aspect of Alaskan life."[88] Walt Disney himself, however, in a 1954 interview, placed the Milottes in the state of Washington: "we looked around for a photographer, heard about Al Milotte up in Seattle, and sent him north to look around and see what he could get."[89] In a 1985 Disney-produced documentary retrospective, Elma Milotte tells yet another story. In this one she and Al lived near Seattle but spent summers in Alaska. After sending Disney some seal footage they had shot, he commissioned them to shoot more. A 1963 profile of Disney in *National Geographic* reported that the Milottes sent back "miles of film," and that later, in viewing it all, it was Walt Disney himself who "stumbled upon one of the great stories of nature: the saga of the fur seals."[90]

The historical record may be forever obscured on the matter of precisely where and how the idea for *Seal Island*, and the "True Life" series came about. Walt Disney maintained that it had all happened much earlier. In 1954 he wrote that the "live animal drama" had been born around 1940 as a result of "using wild creatures as models for study by the animators in cartoon tales, especially *Bambi*."[91] By 1963 he was claiming sole credit: "In *Bambi*, we had to get closer to nature. So we had to train our artists in animal locomotion and anatomy. . . . So we sent the artists out to zoos, and all we got were animals in captivity. Finally, I sent out some naturalist-cameramen to photograph the animals in their natural environment. We captured a lot of interesting things and I said, 'Gee, if we give these boys a chance, I might get something unique!' "[92]

Here Disney suggests that the plan to produce wildlife films was in place in the early 1940s, but was delayed only because the war intervened. Desmond Morris has even argued that the inspiration to produce the "True Life" films came from Julian Huxley's early film work, in particular 1934's *The Private Life of the Gannet.*[93] In his biography of Walt Disney, Marc Eliot argues that the "True Life" series came about because Disney had "lost interest in animation" in the 1940s, when it was not earning much money, and that he was looking for new ventures and ways of diversifying the company's faltering finances.[94] Live action wildlife pictures were relatively cheap to produce, after all, and if given the same distribution and exhibition as the studio's other products could offer higher profit margins.

Perhaps more important than when or where the germ of the idea emerged is what the original motivations and intentions behind it were, but here only more confusion arises. Walt Disney wrote in May 1954 of the "close kinship" between real and cartoon animals, and that not only had the "True Lifes" grown out of pre-war cartoon work, but their purpose was decidedly *not* "education in natural sciences." Rather, it was "to bring interesting and delightful entertainment into the theater."[95]

In July, however, just two months later, an interview appeared in which he gave a much different account. Now the "True Lifes" were a postwar afterthought: "we thought we might stay in the 16-millimeter field after the war," he explains, "and do short educational films"—not, however, for theatrical distribution, but "for school groups, for churches, for clubs."[96] It seems unlikely, given the company's financial problems at the time, that it would have committed any of its resources to such an obviously unprofitable, indeed, *philanthropic* venture. By the following month, August, Disney was voicing disenchantment with the idea of educational films: "We were busy with technicians and educators. . . . Before too long I realized that we weren't going to be able to work with them. "You can't do this," one said, or "you mustn't do that," from another—until I decided that we'd have to do the films our way or not at all."[97]

In another account he is quoted as having been opposed to the idea of educational films from the very start, reportedly having told his associates at the outset that the real purpose of the "True Life" films was "to entertain," and that they "must not teach."[98] This may explain why there were rarely technical or scientific advisors listed in their credits, and why many facts about wild animals seem simply to have been ignored. Schickel has maintained that "Disney had two criteria he always insisted upon. He wanted facts and more facts in the narration."[99] Yet even a casual viewing of these films suggests that any faith in this assurance of factuality is probably misplaced (the bogus lemming "suicide" sequence in 1958's *White Wilderness* is perhaps the most notorious illustration). That Disney found it impossible to work with educators and scientists may very likely have been because of their concern with holding the "True Lifes" to the facts, and thereby limiting their dramatic license. The same discomfort can still be readily heard, even today, at wildlife film festivals, where scientists are often seen as seeking to enforce constraints on creativity. Disney's solution to the problem was to call his cinematographers "naturalists" who were "familiar by study, experience, and close observation with living nature." He praised them as both "scientists and as craftsmen." [100] With such highly credentialed people operating the cameras, there seemed little need for scientific advisors.

In yet another account of the original idea for the "True Life" series, *Seal Island* cinematographer Al Milotte recalled the instructions Disney gave him at the beginning as having been related not to education, but to documentary filmmaking: "I said, 'What kind of pictures?' He [Disney] said vaguely, 'I don't know—just pictures. Movies. You know—mining, fishing, building roads, the development of Alaska. I guess it will be a *documentary* or something—you know.' " [101]

Not surprisingly, Disney is also quoted elsewhere expressing the opposite sentiments, suggesting that his intentions actually bore little connection to documentary. "Anything carrying the Disney name," he proclaimed, "was going to mean entertainment—this I insisted upon. We'd have authenticity, of course, but we'd also have drama and laughs and music." [102] Sinyard has attempted to resolve the confusion in Disney's favor, emphatically maintaining a tenuous connection between the "True Lifes" and documentary: "The documentary was there of course for information and wonder, but what was wrong in bringing to it a bit of entertainment and emotion? His approach to the documentary was not that of a natural scientist or objective observer and analyst, but that of an entertainer." [103]

Ultimately, whether documentary, education, entertainment, or all three, the "True Life Adventures" were launched in 1948 as a series of high-gloss, lavishly scored, full-color wildlife motion pictures, distributed for international theatrical exhibition. If there was a "first" or an innovation with which Disney could be credited, it was this. The studio even formed its own "natural history unit" of sorts, and at any time in the early 1950s might have several wildlife camera teams at work in the field or in the studio, and nearly as many wildlife films in postproduction if not already in distribution. [104] By 1953 it had moved from producing wildlife shorts to features, several of which won more Academy Awards.

In many of these films the Disney formula is more easily heard than seen. Watched without sound, the photography often contains little to set it apart from other wildlife films made in the years since, except that the editing is less slick. In the early shorts the transitions are often choppy and the continuity rough; after *Beaver Valley* (1949) most of the "True Lifes" also included awkwardly edited (and usually "comical") montages, usually depicting behavioral quirks members of some species exhibit regularly or repeatedly (the "joke" seemed to lie in their repetition).

Yet most of what distinguishes them today as "Disney films" came with the addition of animated introductions, insistent musical scores, and breezy narration—the latter often singlehandedly creating animal characters by assigning them names and describing their personalities. Film footage shot in the field was essentially a platform on which the Disney team could go to work, applying the conventions and formulas they had already developed in making animated films.

By insisting that "anything carrying the Disney name" would have to include "drama, laughs, and music," Walt Disney guaranteed that the "True Life" films would bear the familiar Disney stylistic stamp.[105] Still, the "laughs" he promised could be problematic, for, as Ditmars and Kearton had shown, comedy was hardly there waiting to be found among wild animals, but had to be projected onto them. Disney maintained, however, that nature always "casts her characters to type," and among them, fortunately, happened to be a number of "natural comedians."[106] In response to *Beaver Valley* (1949), the second film in the "True Life" series, and the first to feature a comical-musical montage, one reviewer wrote that it carried a full dose of characteristic "Disney whimsy," and, as in the cartoons, the music "enhances all the effects—but chiefly the comic ones."[107]

When the "True Life" unit produced its first feature-length film, *The Living Desert* (1953), objections to the musical comedy elements grew louder. In *The Nation* Manny Farber noted that too many animals seemed to move to the "dance rhythms of a Hollywood musical."[108] Basil Wright, in *Sight & Sound,* pointed to "what might be called the Bathetic Fallacy—the attachment of irrelevant human comment, often in terms of music" (a practice today deeply institutionalized and unquestioned). Wright was simply "not impressed" by the film's portrayals of animals, especially its "attempts to make their activities comic."[109] *Time* found its factual content to be "vitiated by cuteness . . . reducing the picture sometimes to the level of recent Donald Duck cartoons."[110] *Variety* likewise described one of the squirrels in the film as "exhibiting all of the charm of a Disney cartoon character."[111] *Newsweek* also saw a good deal of the cartoon-style "cuteness to be expected from the Disney office."[112] In the *New York Times* Bosley Crowther remarked that "the Disney boys are as playful with nature pictures as they are with cartoons," adding that it was "all very humorous and beguiling. But it isn't true to life."[113] When the second feature-length "True Life," *The Vanishing Prairie* (1954), was released, the forced comedy was again the subject of attention—in particular, Winston Hibler's "humorous commentary."[114] Crowther described the film as being in "the daffy Disney style," and the entire "True Life" series as Disney's "new type of animated films."[115]

It was not all fun and games, however. Several critics also perceived a new level of screen violence in the "True Life" films. Crowther pointed to the "repetition of incidents of violence and death" in *The Living Desert.*[116]

Farber saw "enough terror stuff to unnerve any city-bred animal lover."[117] The *New Yorker*'s John McCarten saw the film as a "Technicolor nightmare" and warned viewers they would need "a good strong stomach."[118] Wright remarked of the film's animals that "nearly all of them [are] locked in combat, fighting (for survival) to the death."[119] *Time* noted that alongside the film's cuteness was a streak of violence: "The very strength of the destructive images is one of the film's weaknesses. More information could have been presented in a more gracious flow of frames if the editors has not felt obliged to juice it up at every turn with violence."[120] Of *The Vanishing Prairie* the following year, the *New Yorker* said that the film displayed "a certain relish for cruelty."[121]

Cruelty and comedy, drama and laughs, cuteness, music—it was a formula, and whatever its shortcomings, it worked.[122] It gave the "True Life Adventures," and in turn, wildlife films as a whole, the coherence they needed to be recognized as an entity unto themselves. This would become clearer in the years after the "True Life" series, when the basic elements of the formula were further refined in Disney's series of hybrid animal narrative adventures. Television would provide the laboratory environment necessary for experimenting with elements of the formula, for applying, adapting, expanding, and developing them, and for seeing the results quickly (in the form of ratings numbers). There would be many deviations and innovations, and a number of alternative models, but the basic "True Life" formula was a winning one, and nothing is imitated like success.[123]

The real Disney legacy to wildlife films, however, was not a prescriptive formula but the revelation that moving images of wild animals could be thoroughly integrated with narrative conventions from mainstream Hollywood films—formal devices, plots structures, situations, themes, motifs, and character types—with which filmmakers, distributors and audiences were already familiar and comfortable. The "True Lifes" thus proved the viability, and the applicability to wildlife, of the very models of form and structure Parsons would later prescribe in his book, *Making Wildlife Movies*, even while trying to distance his from Disney's. In demonstrating the mainstream potential of wildlife films, the "True Lifes" offered examples and models that more scientifically astute filmmakers could borrow and appropriate for their own purposes—which have almost always included entertaining.

Ironically, later distribution for use in schools helped turn the "True Lifes" into educational films by default, as well as making them popular with new generations of audiences, not only increasing their longevity but further institutionalizing the Disney view of nature. According to Schickel, Disney's Buena Vista distribution subsidiary began renting 16mm prints to schools as early as 1952, including 35mm filmstrips licensed by Encyclopaedia Britannica.[124] DeRoos claimed in 1963 that the "True Lifes" had already become "a solid part of the curriculum for thousands of school children, not only in the United States, but abroad—including countries under communist control."[125] It is possible that for a time Disney's wildlife films reached and perhaps influenced more viewers globally than any other nature-oriented media.

Today one can only speculate as to the influence of the "True Life Adventures" on the perceptions and expectations of audiences from the 1950s to the 1970s, and on the sensibilities of other wildlife filmmakers seeking to emulate their success. Stouffer describes an occurrence in which the influence of "True Lifes" became clear to him in a sort of epiphany while shooting a film of his own. "Suddenly," he writes, "something deeper, flashed through my memory. I remembered being six years old, perched on the edge of my seat in a darkened movie theater, staring up . . . as two bighorn rams reared up and lunged toward each other on the screen in front of me. The name of the film was Walt Disney's *Vanishing Prairie* and it had affected me powerfully at the time. . . . Now I realized that the effect of watching that scene so many years ago had been a driving force propelling me to this moment."[126] Although he set out to make a different kind of wildlife film from Disney's, Stouffer nevertheless hints at the difficulty he had in breaking out of the Disney mold: "Most Americans of my generation had grown up with the Disney wildlife films, which probably opened their eyes for the first time to the beauty and enchantment of nature. But I felt the time was ripe for a more realistic portrayal of wildlife in America. *It was a difficult decision to make.*"[127]

Part of the difficulty, he explains, came from the fact that American television executives had become slaves to the tyranny of the Disney formula, and were conditioned to seeking only Disneyesque sorts of films about wild animals. Clearly, though, for whatever reasons, Stouffer seems repeatedly disposed in his book toward defining his endeavors, and himself, professionally, *against* Disney—or at least against Disney's example and style of wildlife filmmaking. The anxiety of influence in such accounts is almost palpable.

Yet there were others, to be sure, making important contributions to the wildlife film genre's development during the heyday of the "True Lifes." Sucksdorff produced what is arguably his masterpiece, *The Divided World*, in 1948; Denis's *Savage Splendor* was released internationally the following year, followed in 1953 by his *Below the Sahara*. In 1951 Hans Hass's *Under the Red Sea* won first prize for feature-length documentary at the Venice film festival, and in 1952 RKO scored again when Irwin Allen's production of *The Sea Around Us*, loosely based on Rachel Carson's book, won the Academy Award for "Best Documentary Feature."

It was Disney's first two feature-length "True Lifes," however—*The Living Desert* and *The Vanishing Prairie*—that won the same award the following two years. Moreover, "True Life" films also won in the category of "Best

Two Reel Short Subject" for four out of five years between 1948 and 1953. Disney's factory system and production values, combined with brand loyalty among viewers (the Disney name was already being marketed), as well as a bit of Academy naiveté, gave the "True Life Adventures" the exposure, popularity, and clout they needed to shape perceptions of what wildlife film was, and perhaps should be. Owing to such successes, the "True Life" films did more to codify the wildlife film genre than any other single entity had up to that time, and arguably, has since.

The Genre Expands, the Screen Contracts

No sooner had the process of codification begun than wildlife film started to be redefined as a television genre. In the United States the way to television was paved as early as 1945 by Marlin Perkins, a zoo director in Chicago with a penchant for popularizing. Perkins writes of the founding incident: "The lifeblood of a zoo is publicity and promotion; so in 1945 when I met a director of the experimental television station in Chicago, WBKB, and was invited to come to the studio with some animals from the zoo and give a talk about them, I jumped at the chance. Television seemed the perfect medium for the Lincoln Park Zoo."[128]

The first transmission that year was sent out to just three hundred receivers in the Chicago area. Ironically, just as wildlife film had begun to take shape before the motion picture medium was perfected, so too was wildlife television getting underway before that medium was fully established. After the NBC television network was founded, it put Perkins's program into national syndication in 1950, with the title *Zooparade*, live from the basement of the reptile house. The atmosphere was friendly and intimate, like that of so many in-studio wildlife programs in Britain in the 1950s and 60s. Yet even though they were transmitted live, each *Zooparade* broadcast was carefully scripted and rehearsed. More important, from a historical standpoint, was the fact that many of them included 16mm film inserts of wildlife scenes shot by NBC camera teams. It was already clear to Perkins that wildlife movies such as these would be a necessary part of wildlife television. Perkins and producer Don Meier "hit on the idea of going into the field and photographing nature in the wild. Don suggested this to NBC. He proposed a trip to Africa, where a film crew would take sync-sound 16mm movies on location, and we would build shows as we moved from place to place in East Africa."[129]

The safari film was reborn. In African national parks such as Nairobi, Kruger, and Amboseli, its conventions were combined by Perkins's team with those of weekly-episode television, resulting in a series of ten half-hour mini-safari films, each devoted to a different animal or topic. American wildlife television was under way, but it looked awfully much like wildlife *film*. Just so, when Disney premiered the *Disneyland* series on ABC in 1954, it

Marlin Perkins pioneered wildlife television in the 1940s, almost before there was television. His *Wild Kingdom* series, which liberally mixed fact and fiction, ran for nearly twenty years (1963–82). Courtesy of Jeffery Boswall.

often broadcast the "True Life" films it already had in the can, further embedding cinematic formal features in wildlife television, and further shaping audiences' expectations in the new medium just as it had in the old.

After Disney's wildlife film unit produced its last theatrical "True Life Adventure," *Jungle Cat* (1960), it quickly moved into production of animal narrative adventures for television, but still with most of the same production values of the theatrical releases. These aired on the new Disney television program on NBC, retitled *Walt Disney's Wonderful World of Color*. The first was *Chico, the Misunderstood Coyote* (1961), followed by a progression of others centering on sympathetic (i.e., humanized) animal protagonists. Although produced for television in the United States, their theatrical production values allowed them to be released by the Buena Vista distribution subsidiary to theaters overseas, where Disney had no television outlets.

In 1963 NBC also premiered Marlin Perkins's and Don Meier's new series, *Wild Kingdom*, which remained in production until 1982. Although the first few shows were set in a studio with zoo animals, the series quickly moved outdoors and evolved toward film. Each show became a short dramatic movie filmed on location, featuring Perkins and Jim Fowler and/or Stan Brock. Brief studio bits were inserted to introduce each film, just as Walt Disney was doing on his weekly series. The convention of hosts appearing on-camera (or "in-vision") continued for decades in the United States, from Perkins and Disney to Bill Burrud, John Forsythe, Lorne Greene, George Page, and Marty Stouffer, but their purpose was little more than to provide a frame for 16mm wildlife movies.

Also in 1963, the National Geographic Society announced the founding of a new series of films that would carry to television the Society's mission of increasing and diffusing geographic knowledge. In December of 1965, CBS television carried the first film in the series to deal with wildlife, *Miss Jane Goodall and the Wild Chimpanzees*, filmed by Hugo Van Lawick.[130] Although the films in the series used well-known actors as narrators, there were no studio introductions or on-camera hosts. Essentially, they were television broadcasts of documentary films (although many would later take on the formal characteristics of classical Hollywood cinema, emphasizing dramatic, often fabricated narratives). In 1968 *The Undersea World of Jacques Cousteau* premiered on ABC television, but, with Rod Serling as off-camera narrator, it was also essentially a series of completed documentary films the network merely broadcast.[131] What all this adds up to is the effective colonization of wildlife television in the United States by wildlife movies, the failure to develop a true wildlife television form or aesthetic, and ultimately the abdication of television to cinema.

Perhaps only in the 1990s did this become clear, after cable television had allowed niche markets to be explored long enough for new forms to emerge. Combined with attempts to lure younger audiences who favored styles more like that of MTV than the BBC, these new wildlife programs at last abandoned cinematic conventions and instead took advantage of the potential offered by television itself, where the formal codes unique to the medium had barely been explored in relation to wildlife content. The most notable trends included presenter-led programs such as *All Bird TV, Crocodile Hunter,*

Buck Staghorn's Animal Bites, and *Kratt's Creatures*, and a spate of "docu-soap" style programs, including *Animal Rescues*, *Animal ER*, *Wildlife Emergency*, and *Animal Court*, in which "people get caught up in the drama" of animals' welfare or survival.[132] Other innovations included *Wild Things!* and, for younger audiences, *Jaws and Claws*. The common denominators in all these were (1) an expanded human presence, or increased interaction between people and animals, (2) dynamic editorial approaches, and (3) low costs and quick turnarounds. By the old cinematic (blue chip) standards, these new programs were low-budget and downmarket. Some were careless in their presentation of nature, as a result of being "[human] character driven, not animal behavior driven."[133] Still, they had an undeniable immediacy, and could often be much more engaging than traditional blue chip pictures shot on film and carefully edited and scored over a period of months, at great expense.

In Britain the situation had been different from the start. A rich wildlife film tradition had existed when television emerged, but did not eclipse more distinctly *televisual* forms. The first attempts to bring wildlife content to television came somewhat later than in the United States, but with greater intensity. Where the development of American wildlife film and television in the early 1950s was piecemeal, the work largely of individual entrepreneurs, Britain quickly saw the development of a full-scale industry. David Attenborough would later argue that, considering the British "passion for the natural world, it should not come as a total surprise that the world's biggest group of film-makers and broadcasters, devoted solely to the job of making natural history programmes for radio and television, should be found in Britain; nor that the British public should greet such programmes so enthusiastically that they are among the most successful of all broadcasts in this country."[134]

The BBC broadcast its first wildlife television programs in 1953 in a monthly series hosted by Peter Scott, who returned in 1954 in the pioneering and long-running series *Look*.[135] After this, the pace of program development quickened considerably. Although *Look* soon began to include film sequence inserts, as Perkins had in his programs a few years earlier, it retained a strong studio component for many years longer. In fact, British wildlife television was much slower than its American counterpart to merge formally with wildlife movies. There were significant differences between the institutional structures of the two broadcasting systems, of course, but a key factor was the BBC's long tradition of radio, and the fact that the earliest wildlife programs in Britain were radio programs. The first of these was *The Naturalist*, developed by Desmond Hawkins in 1946, followed in rapid succession by several others, including the long-running *Birds of Britain* (1951–63), and many more in the years since (even today the BBC Natu-

Pioneer broadcaster Desmond Hawkins, whose radio program *The Naturalist* led to the creation of the BBC Natural History Unit. Here he is honored with a life-achievement award at Wildscreen '98. Derek Bousé.

ral History Unit continues radio programming, and maintains modern, digital radio facilities at Bristol). With precedents having been established by radio rather than by televised movies, a more purely broadcast-oriented tradition emerged in which the capabilities (and limitations) of the television medium were more thoroughly explored. From a cinematic perspective, the programs were chatty and studio-bound. One critic has argued that their main purpose seemed to be calling forth reactions such as: "Good heavens really! Who'd have thought it?"[136]

One reason, however, that film was not rapidly absorbed into program form was the fact that the BBC's Bristol studios were technologically unable in the early years to transmit film images, and so were forced to rely on other formats.[137] The problem had long been solved by 1955, however, when Heinz Sielmann's celebrated and technically innovative film *Woodpeck-*

The author is counseled by longtime BBC producer and former on-air-personality Jeffery Boswall. Like others in the early years of the BBC-NHU, Boswall came from radio, not film production. Wiltraud Engländer.

ers (a.k.a. *Carpenters of the Forest*, 1954) was aired to much acclaim. Yet even by this time many of those working on the BBC's wildlife television programs were still, officially, *radio staff*.[138]

Since the BBC Natural History Unit was formally established in 1957, its Bristol studios have remained a laboratory where an astonishing number of wildlife and natural history television series have been created, including

The World About Us, Private Lives, Wildlife on One, and *The Natural World.* In the 1970s there were attempts to recapture the spontaneity and immediacy of live television with innovative series such as *Badgerwatch* (1977), *Foxwatch* (1978), and *Birdwatch* (1980), which covered events as a news team might, often using a mobile remote unit.[139] Two decades later, *Big Cat Diary* (1996) marked another attempt to explore the properties of television that set it apart from film in a "docu-soap" wildlife mini-series. Over the years the BBC-NHU has also assembled more talented people under one roof than any other wildlife film company, and has kept alive the tradition of the on-camera host/presenter, which has declined in America. At century's end, the BBC was still trying new formats and introducing new faces.[140] Clearly, it had come a long way since the days when Peter Scott sat casually smoking on a living room set at Lime Grove studios.

Anglia Television's *Survival* series, developed by Aubrey Buxton and Colin Willock, premiered on Independent Television (ITV) in 1961, and was intended to differ from its then staid BBC competition by cultivating what Willock described as a "get-up-and-go image." There was to be more energy, more movement, and more excitement, with an emphasis on action-packed scenes filmed in outdoor locations rather than on clinical discussions filmed in studios. According to Willock, "Survival had deliberately set out to capture the widest possible audience, leaving the specialized wood-notes-wild viewers to the BBC. Aubrey Buxton had declared from the outset that we intended to present wildlife as entertainment."[141]

The key difference, Willock explained, was that the *Look* series was "essentially a chat show with film clips, whereas *Survival* favoured 'pure' film."[142] The BBC's Jeffery Boswall, apparently uneasy with the absorption of adventure-movie conventions into natural history representation, glibly described *Survival* as "Pop. Nat. Hist."[143] Yet it was precisely that "get-up-and-go" image that was closer in spirit to American traditions and tastes, and which, along with the emphasis on "pure film" as opposed to studio-chat, made Survival, not the BBC, the first British wildlife and natural history producer to break into the huge and lucrative American market. This was achieved with the help of the J. Walter Thompson company, with whom Survival Anglia Limited had entered into partnership to help sell its films overseas. In fact, the financial benefits of American sales alone were, according to Willock, "the most important thing ever to happen to Survival."[144] The film that started it was *Enchanted Isles*, shot by Alan Root in the Galapagos Islands, and even given a royal premiere in 1967 before being exported to America in 1968.

Two years later, Des and Jen Bartlett's *The World of the Beaver* (1970), with its recognizable American locations (Jackson Hole, Wyoming), and its decidedly Disneyesque story and narration (written by Willock and given a folksy reading by Henry Fonda) performed even better with American audi-

Prince Philip greets Joan and Alan Root at the royal premiere of *Enchanted Isles* (1967), the first British natural history film to break into the huge and lucrative American television market. Survival Anglia.

Des Bartlett improvising during filming of *Flight of the Snow Geese* (1971). Another early success in reaching American audiences, the film won two Emmy awards. Des and Jen Bartlett/Survival Anglia.

ences, as did *Flight of the Snow Geese* two years after that. Willock's account of the former's production further attests to the tyranny of the Disney formula both on the expectations of American network executives, as well as on the creative energies of writers and producers like himself. He writes that the first signs appeared when he set out to prepare the script. "I then did something," he recalls, "which has made me shudder ever since. I gave the two main beaver characters names." After that, the entire narrative structure built around them seemed to take on a Disneyesque quality, as the film's cinematographer, Des Bartlett, was quick to note. After reviewing a draft he told Willock, "you have written a perfect Disney script: you could not have done better if you had been working for Disney for twenty years."[145]

It was not the last time a program following such a model would come out of the Survival factory during Willock's tenure there. *The Leopard That Changed Its Spots* (1978), filmed by Dieter Plage, is one of the most irresistibly

The Leopard That Changed Its Spots (1978). The film's charm came in part from its endearing title character and familiar story elements. Here the orphan "Harriet" is returned to the wild to start her own family. Dieter Plage/Survival Anglia.

charming wildlife films produced by Survival, or by anyone else, for that matter, but its charm may come precisely from the careful construction of its endearing title character, "Harriet," and perhaps more important, from its subtle retelling of a familiar story, or at least its appropriation of a familiar set of story elements: the cyclical plot, the orphan theme, the journey motif, and so forth.

Yet securing the American market required more than a Disneyesque script. According to Willock, it also took the presence of "a big-name narrator," primarily because a well-known name helps "make it promotable."[146] The choice of Fonda, one of America's screen icons and most dignified actors, to narrate the American version of the beaver film was made by J. Walter Thompson and sponsor Quaker Oats. The film's American version was also aided by wall-to-wall music and a good deal of narrative "jeopardy" (animals in tense, dangerous situations), all calculated to appeal specifically to American tastes and viewing habits. Just as today, intense competition and fear of channel-changing determined the form of films aimed at the American market. On the role of wall-to-wall music in maintaining viewer attention, Willock notes, "US audiences have so many channels to choose from and so many commercial break points in each show at which to change their station that continuous sound is thought essential to hold the viewer's attention." [147]

Buxton and Willock recognized that diversity in both style and content would be important to sustain interest in their product internationally. To this end, Survival contracted with the recently formed Oxford Scientific Films to supply it with specialized, although by some standards "academic" material. OSF had, in fact, been formed by a group of Oxford academics, but the demand for "rigorously scientific films" aimed at a "market of class-room students willing to concentrate on tough stretches of exposition" proved disappointingly small, and OSF soon found itself, like Survival, and like so many others in subsequent years, seeking an *entre* to the American market. [148]

That market opened wider in 1970 as a result of a Federal Communications Commission (FCC) decree that at least an hour of each evening's prime-time broadcasting had to be allotted to local TV stations for non-network programming. What happened, however, was that many of these slots went to syndicated programs purchased from independent producers, and many of these were wildlife programs. By 1974, fully *eleven* wildlife and natural history programs were being aired nationally in the United States. [149] Survival's was one of them. With the help of J. Walter Thompson, it put together a half-hour American version of its British series, called *The World of Survival*. Again, a well-known name and voice was added to help make it promotable: American actor John Forsythe narrated the series, and appeared as on-camera host, often on location.

Yet although wildlife programs remained popular in Britain throughout the 1970s, they had difficulty keeping up in the ratings competition in the United States, and so became as vulnerable as any other form of prime-time television to the tyranny of formula. Marty Stouffer recalls a series of encounters in the mid-1970s in which this was revealed to him. Network executives at NBC, which had for many years been airing Disney's weekly program, as well as *Wild Kingdom*, told him that "what they wanted as a final program was, in their words, 'an animal cops and robbers show.' They wanted to see a lot of animals chasing other animals and killing them, but without any actual bloodshed." [150] When he tried to pitch a series to CBS, the tyranny of formula was just as much in evidence. They wanted "a program packed full of drama, comedy, suspenseful cliff-hangers, and happy endings—'warmth and jeopardy,' as they put it." [151] As for ABC, "They weren't interested in the day-to-day lives of wild animals going through their court-ship rituals or bringing food to the nest. . . . They wanted to see more babies barely escape the jaws of villainous predators while the mother risked her life to rescue her young." [152]

In such a formula-obsessed and ratings-driven market, it eventually proved difficult for wildlife films to compete with other prime-time fare. Nature writer Peter Steinhart observed that by 1976 "game shows and re-runs of old comedies were knocking [wildlife films] out of the early evening time slots." [153] By 1980 much of the wildlife programming that had come about in the early 1970s had already disappeared from national television in America. A few programs survived in syndication in various local and regional markets—primarily the larger ones. [154] Still, Steinhart wondered if "there may be fewer wildlife filmmakers in the future. And fewer of the spec-tacular wildlife films we have grown used to." He lamented what appeared to be the "demise of wildlife fare" on American television, and concluded: "Given the precarious plight of wild creatures all over the world, that is a grim prospect to consider." [155]

Neither Steinhart nor anyone else could have predicted what happened next. In 1981 the BBC "mega-series" *Life on Earth* (produced in 1979) aired on American public television and proved a resounding success. PBS shrewdly followed up in the fall of 1982 when it launched the *Nature* series as a weekly forum for one-hour blue chip wildlife and natural history films of the very sort typified by *Life on Earth*. It also contracted with Stouffer to air his half-hour "homegrown" series (and labor of love) *Wild America*. Stouf-fer's films were made on much smaller budgets, and, in what he describes as "an overzealous attempt to make the series a smash hit," included a good deal more "action-packed footage." [156] Although a new era of wildlife tele-vision had begun in the United States, there were still fears at the time, like Stouffer's, that American audiences were not really ready for slower, more studious wildlife films. *Nature* executives worried that their series, with its slowly paced British fare, would not sustain American audiences' attention. Series host George Page later recalled: "We were very nervous before *Nature* went on the air in 1982 as an anthology of natural history films unlike any others offered regularly on American television. They were slowly paced and sparsely narrated, and the sounds of nature dominated the occasional music. . . . *Nature* was not faced-paced or action-filled." [157]

Despite differences in approach, both *Nature* and *Wild America* drew audi-ences of around 3.5 million in their first year, and continued for some years to be among the most popular and successful programs on PBS. As has often been the case, American audiences proved to be more open-minded, tol-erant, and mature than producers and network executives had given them credit for being. Nevertheless, the "Big Three" networks had got out of the

Marty Stouffer. Perseverance got him his own series and helped make him the leading figure among American wildlife filmmakers, but *Wild America* ended amid controversy. Marty Stouffer Productions.

wildlife business before ever committing to it, leaving the market potential of commercial (as opposed to public) television of nationally broadcast, high-end wildlife programs still largely unexplored.

In 1985 the gap was partially filled when The Discovery Channel was launched on American cable systems, followed in 1986 by the *National Geographic Explorer* series on the TBS cable network. By the time Discovery's sister network Animal Planet ("all animals, all the time") was launched in 1996, the American market had already been cracked wide open, providing multiple outlets for wildlife films from around the world. Producers had more access than ever before to the American market, and American viewers had more access to wildlife on television than viewers in any other nation.

Wildlife film production had boomed internationally. Although Britain remained the single largest producer, and America the most powerful and coveted audience, the expanding number of new television outlets worldwide, along with new film festivals, symposia, and production partnerships, also meant an expanding international scope. An international style could even be seen emerging, the result of multinational coproductions designed for distribution to multiple markets, and therefore without noticeable cultural differences. Yet coproduction deals, along with joint ventures (BBC and Discovery), acquisitions (Disney and Devillier-Donegan), and mergers

(Survival and Partridge) began to herald the sort of industry concentration that had been occurring among larger, more mainstream media firms, as seen in Disney's acquisition of CapCities/ABC, or the Time-Warner-Turner merger (both in 1995). At century's end the styles in wildlife films may have been international, but the economies of scale pointed to the triumph of American-style capitalism.

3
Science and Storytelling

It was probably inevitable that as wildlife films began to carve out a larger slice of the television pie in the 1980s and 1990s they began to attract the attention of those eager to expose their contradictions. While academicians averted their gaze, critics and journalists began to look closely at wildlife films—so too did environmentalists, broadcast industry watchers, and investors. What they saw were films balanced precariously on a tightrope between two poles: science and storytelling. Wildlife films often included accurate scientific information, but were nevertheless highly *cinematic* in their treatment of it, in their use of techniques of classical narrative cinema that did not so much illustrate facts as dramatize them. The tension was not only between realism and formalism, but also between information and drama, reason and emotion. It was the same set of oppositions that had often been used to make distinctions between "worthy" and "unworthy" products of culture, between "pure" forms (art, education, and journalism) and debased or "polluted" variations (television, advertising, and tabloids).[1]

The techniques for smooth editing continuity, and seamless narrative construction in wildlife films had long been studiously avoided by filmmakers working more squarely in the "pure" documentary tradition, where slickness suggested artifice and deception. Wildlife films, however, were rarely about specific historical circumstances or events; their depiction of scientific facts often meant showing *typical* occurrences. So long as the facts were correct, many saw no reason why the events illustrating them could not be dramatic, even constructed or staged.[2] As already recounted, however, such approaches had a rather dubious history.

Yet in retrospect it seems strange not to have expected wildlife films to borrow their formal style from Hollywood. There were a number of parallels between mainstream cinema's attempt to portray the human condition in commercial and formulaic terms, and that of wildlife films to portray the condition of nature, while adhering to many of the same industrial and economic constraints. In both cases, whatever truths there were to tell were told by dramatizing them, often by way of familiar narrative structures that fulfilled rather than challenged audiences' expectations. The degree of dramatic fictionalizing in wildlife films could vary, but it came with the formal style, which had been developed in the earliest years of cinema for the express purpose of storytelling.[3] If wildlife films displayed a greater degree of realism than classical cinema, it began to appear that the difference was one only of degree. Realism, after all, was not reality itself, but a well-crafted likeness or impression of reality.[4] Whatever it was, it was plain to see that in wildlife films it had gotten better.

This may have been enough in itself to raise suspicions. Scientific content and dramatic mimesis had long been seen as incompatible;[5] yet there they were side by side, if not thoroughly interwoven, in wildlife programs. In the mid-1980s the CBC documentary exposé *Cruel Camera* emerged as the first hard, investigative look at the genre, and at some of the means by which it created its dramatic stories. Seen by many as an indictment of the entire wildlife film industry, *Cruel Camera* contained documented evidence that animals had often been mistreated in the production of wildlife films, especially in scenes that appeared real but had in fact been staged.[6] Although this was usually done to illustrate actual scientific principles, or "authenticated facts," as the FCC disclaimer once stipulated, the evidence nevertheless suggested that staging, manipulation, and fakery were widespread, and that wildlife films may not have been as true to nature, or to science, as they appeared. Perhaps worse, the evidence also suggested that audiences had for some time been systematically deceived, their sympathies manipulated, their faith betrayed. In both British and American presses, critics began calling attention to the artifice and stagecraft in wildlife films.[7] Television reviewers, even when praising wildlife programs, began acknowledging openly that they were, in fact, calculated constructions and deliberate illusions.[8] Others began to reflect with new sobriety on the limitations of the wildlife film genre, if not of the whole natural history film enterprise.[9]

Yet the viewing public itself showed little sign of alarm at the apparent "outing" of wildlife films. Viewership continued to grow, and interest in the controversy even suggested there was an audience eager to learn more about the behind-the-scenes techniques used in making realistic wildlife dramas. The wildlife film industry began to realize what had long been known to mainstream show biz publicists: that there was profit in confession, and image control in the carefully administered revelation of secrets.[10] This would, of course, require an admission that wildlife films were entertaining fictions rather than documentaries—an admission some were loathe to make in public.[11]

In the mid-1990s it was again the issue of cruelty to animals that forced wildlife films and filmmakers under the lights for interrogation; again, lurking just in the shadows was the spectre of deception. The allegations sur-

Alan Root setting up a remote control camera in a tortoise shell to film wildebeest migration. A wildlife filmmaker "must be a naturalist first, and then a film-maker." Martin Bell/Survival Anglia.

faced in early 1996 when a pair of *Denver Post* reporters uncovered evidence suggesting that Colorado's own Marty Stouffer had committed several ethical violations in the production of his PBS series *Wild America*.[12] Again, however, the questions quickly turned from the issue of cruelty to that of staging and faking. The PBS affiliation, moreover, gave this round of investigation the appearance of greater significance, for it seemed to link the allegations of wrongdoing to the idea that PBS member donations, made in good faith, might in some way have been abused or misspent. There was little substance in this, of course, but coupled with the even more unlikely notion that tax dollars allotted to the Corporation for Public Broadcasting were in some way implicated, the whole matter quickly took on an air of scandal, and seemed an even greater violation of the public trust. This, in turn, gave more emotional resonance to the issues of audience deception and *nature faking* than had any of the revelations a decade earlier. There seemed to be widespread suspicion that behind the mask of innocence (perhaps nowhere

Alan and Joan Root show how they filmed a spitting cobra in a scene from *Two in the Bush* (1982). Audiences responded favorably to such behind-the-scenes revelations, proving the value of carefully managed self-promotion. Martin Bell/Survival Anglia.

better represented than in the genial countenance of Stouffer) was an industry with a Janus face. Again, a wave of critical indignation began to swell in the print media. Starting with other writers at the *Denver Post*,[13] it soon washed across North America[14] and was still rippling on both sides of the Atlantic over a year later.[15]

Observers had raised a number of questions. If the events unfolding on the screen hadn't happened in the way they were shown, was it possible that some of them hadn't really happened at all? However disillusioning, this one could surely be answered in the affirmative. The follow-up question, however, was more difficult: *how much* staging and faking had there been? It seemed that only the tip of the iceberg was visible. Other questions promised further disillusionment: was the purpose of wildlife films to inform and educate, or were they intended merely to distract, to amuse, and to sell audiences to advertisers? If the latter, how great could their commitment to truth really be? Should audiences expect factual reports of reality from them, or marvel at they way they constructed convincing impressions of reality, as in mainstream cinema? In a word, were wildlife films information or drama, fact or fiction, science or storytelling? The answer was, of course, "both," but it was an answer that few outside the industry would find satisfying. It seemed we were left to wonder just how much of what we thought we knew about nature from television we really knew at all.

There was also the lingering question whether or not wildlife films were documentaries. If so, what did this imply about documentaries in general? The documentary genre's own relationship to reality was not wanting for scholarly and critical investigation, but the closest that scholars in this area had come to considering the fictive conventions of wildlife and natural history film had been in the small body of literature on "television science documentary."[16] This subgenre had betrayed a number of conventions and covert structuring devices for molding reality into dramatic narratives, but scholars had not included wildlife programs in their analyses, or even made reference to them. It is possible that some believed a separate analysis of wildlife films to be redundant (implicitly categorizing them as a type of TV science documentary). It may also have been that some simply saw the storytelling aspects of wildlife films to be self-evident, and therefore unworthy of separate scholarly investigation (although this had clearly not prevented intensive study of other film and television genres). There had been a few attempts to stake out the underlying narrative conventions and structuring devices specific to wildlife films, but these had provided no answers to the question of what audiences had a right to expect from them.[17]

The new round of controversy suggested that what had long been taken for granted by those in the wildlife film industry was something with which viewers seemed not to have fully come to terms: that wildlife films were entertaining blends of fact and fiction, that their appeal lay in the stories they told, and that many of these were, in fact, composites or fabrications. Yet the outrage expressed had not really been that of the viewing public in the first place; their attitudes and expectations regarding wildlife film were (and still are) largely unknown.[18] Instead it had been primarily that of journalists, apparently disturbed by the prospect of another genre of nonfiction media, a second-cousin to their own profession, being exposed as mere *art*—or at least as impure truth. Implicit in some of the criticisms, therefore, were a number of normative assumptions about what wildlife films should or should not do, and be.

Moreover, the contradictions within wildlife films also reemerged. The tension could be felt as interpreters of scientific facts confronted an audience of nonspecialists and responded by attempting to dramatize those facts, to reshape the complexities of natural history into narratives that would engage the attention of a popular audience, yet somehow remain true to the facts. Wildlife films were not the first form of popular natural history to spark controversy, but there seemed little, if any, awareness of this among the journalists and critics who wrote about them.

In retrospect, the realization that wildlife films often do involve fabricated events and stories might have resulted in less shock and bewilderment had there been greater awareness of the history and tradition behind them—that is, had the cultural memory extended farther back than the days of Walt Disney and Marlin Perkins in the United States, or Peter Scott and Johnny Morris in Britain. It seems, therefore, that before a thorough analysis of wildlife films as a form of natural history storytelling can proceed, what is needed is a look back at how the two seemingly incompatible traditions that gave birth to them—natural history study and animal storytelling—became wed in the first place. The marriage appears to have been consummated in the late nineteenth century in a series of "realistic" animal stories by well-known "literary naturalists," yet these two old and venerable traditions had been acquainted for over two thousand years.

Fact and Fiction

By most accounts, the formal study of natural history began with Aristotle's *Historia animalium*, around 335 B.C., which provided the raw material for Pliny's better known, and more massive, *Historia Naturalis* in A.D. 75. Despite the four hundred years that separated them, these two works had more in common than the fact that they provided the taxonomic basis for the systematic study of natural history.[19] In addition, both liberally mixed observation with fabrication, truth with fiction, fact with fantasy. "What is so extraordinary," writes Alan Jenkins, in a thoughtful reflection on Aristotle's writings, "is that the man who indulged in or repeated such fantasies could at the same time be so perceptive about other aspects of natural history."[20] The same could be said of Pliny, of course, who corrected some of Aristotle's gross exaggerations, yet added a good many more of his own.

An even more sensational brand of natural history emerged in A.D. 200 in the *Physiologus*, said to have been compiled by Claudius Aelianus. Mixing fact with even larger doses of fiction, this early "bestiary" achieved greater popularity than either of its predecessors, and by the early middle ages had become one of the most popular illustrated books in Europe—a sort of "bestseller" of the early Christian period—and was translated into as many as ten languages. The bestiary tradition extended all the way into the seventeenth century, in works such as Edward Topsell's *The Historie of Foure-Footed Beastes* (1607), which in turn influenced natural history writing in the eighteenth century, such as Thomas Bewick's *A General History of Quadrupeds* (1790). Some of these, like Thomas Boreman's *A Description of Three Hundred Animals* (1730), were even intended for children.[21]

These all showed that when fact was generously blended with fiction the result could be an effective formula for making natural history both informative and entertaining. A comment on this mixture appeared in the late eighteenth century in an advertisement for *The Natural History of Beasts* (1793), a work attributed to Stephen Jones. It might just as well have been used to promote a wildlife film in the late twentieth or early twenty-first century: "The study of Natural History is equally useful and agreeable: entertaining while it instructs, it blends the most pleasing ideas with the most valuable discoveries."[22]

The *Physiologus* had thus lit the way for natural history and science popularizers to follow. Yet popularization itself would later be equated with a host of social ills, from lowered intellectual levels to general cultural debasement. Popular newspapers, popular entertainments, and popular education have all been derided by elites and conservatives as threatening to undermine, or to destroy by contamination, the high standards and qualities of excellence thought to be inscribed in "high culture," and in the traditions of the educated elite.[23] This has been no less true in scientific circles, where received opinion holds that there exists (and must exist) a relationship of mutual exclusivity between popular accessibility on the one hand, and scientific integrity, relevance, and reliability on the other. For many, *good* science and *popular* science almost never intersect. Yet enough good scientists, such as Dian Fossey, Jane Goodall, Stephen Jay Gould, Richard Leakey, Konrad Lorenz, Carl Sagan, Lewis Thomas, and E. O. Wilson have successfully written for a popular audience to suggest, at the very least, that there are presentational modes in which science may have popular appeal and still be "good" science.[24]

Perhaps the real questions here, however, have to do with whether or not scientific content can be *dramatized*. That is, can the presentation of scientific facts accommodate dramatic narrative conventions, with their appeals to emotion, or do these taint scientific information and render it unreliable? The problem, it seems, is not just one of science popularization, but the larger matter of elitist distrust of the media in general. This has been based in part on the long-standing presumption of incompatibility between information and story, or between reason and emotion, with the latter in each case presumed to be lower in both class and moral status.[25]

A classic attempt to wed these supposedly incompatible trends is Rachel Carson's monumental book *Silent Spring* (1962). A work of impeccable scientific scholarship, it reads like anything but a scientific monograph and was condemned by many in the scientific community for what they saw as an unholy alliance of science and storytelling, as well as for its "tainting" of scientific evidence with subjectivism and emotion. Nevertheless, it was the application of these traditional dramatic elements that helped make it a bona-fide bestseller, as well as an effective piece of *environmental commu-*

nication. Its first chapter, entitled "A Fable for Tomorrow," opens on a note of make believe: "There was once a town in the heart of America" (p. 1). After a depressing list of the environmental woes suffered by this mythical community, Carson admits to the fiction—at least to having created the town, but not its problems: "This town does not actually exist," she concedes, "but it might easily have a thousand counterparts in America and elsewhere" (p. 3). As in wildlife films, the scene portrayed may have been fabricated, but it was nevertheless *true to the biological facts.* From there, however, *Silent Spring* is a detailed scientific study of the problems facing such places and an impassioned warning against self-wrought ecological disaster. These are combined with a compelling narrative and a complete set of characters, from scientific experts to politicians to the birds, mammals, and insects who are most at risk. Carson showed that story *could* serve science, but left little doubt in most minds that where the two come together, story *should* serve science.[26]

Wildlife and natural history films might be seen as serving purposes similar to those of *Silent Spring*—to make scientific content accessible to the average person, but also to make it interesting and appealing, and perhaps even to transfer this appeal to its subjects in the natural world, making them something worth caring about and protecting. Yet as wildlife films have helped advance the popularization of natural history in the years since Carson, the hierarchy of science and storytelling has been quietly, but effectively reversed. The refrain heard in the wildlife and natural history film industry today is that story is king, and science its servant.

Historia Fabulosus

Given the irresistible power of narrative, it should come as no surprise that there were written works that dealt with wildlife and the natural world in story form well before Aristotle and Pliny. The inhabitants of earlier ages knew several types of animal stories (typically about animals who talked) that had grown out of mythic and folkloric traditions around the world. Today, however, the best known type of these ancient animal stories is the animal fable, or *beast fable.* The form itself was already established by the time it became linked to the name of Aesop in the fifth century B.C. (still a century before Aristotle), and similar stories can be found in Greek literature from the time of Hesiod, in the seventh century B.C.[27] In Medieval times, *Aesop's Fables* were read alongside the stories that became the well known "beast epic" of Re[y]nard the Fox. The fables had undergone many revisions, however, and by the time of the European Renaissance there were several efforts to reassemble and retranslate complete collections, some of which are still read today. Indeed, the fables have "always been in favour," as one study of animal stories notes, and "have been regarded as the right books to give to children, recommended by educationists from Locke onward." Yet there may be a darker side to the tradition of using the fables to educate; as part of so many people's childhood reading the fables are at "the very roots of that kind of humanisation which turns animals into facets of human character."[28]

Through many rounds of translation the fables were frequently reinterpreted according to prevailing sensibilities. Although they are now thought of mainly as didactic stories with terse moral lessons, it has recently been suggested that the fables may have originally been more coarsely humorous, and may even have been intended as crude, ribald jokes more than as satirical aphorisms expressing collected wisdom.[29] In any case, the use of humanized animals to teach moral lessons, or in some other way to confront fundamental human conflicts, shows up in many other types of stories, from myths to fairy tales. Raglan noted that a "prominent feature of every type of traditional narrative is the human being in animal form."[30] Most such animal characters serve to displace human vices (as well as virtues) onto animals so that they can be confronted, examined, and satirized from a safe distance.[31]

Yet the animals in the Aesopic fables are still recognizable *as animals* rather than as people in animal garb. As such, they can be seen as among the earliest written attempts to fathom the behavior of animals, if only by casting it in human terms that made it easier to grasp. Although humanizing animals may actually do little to help us understand their behavior, it is nevertheless an almost automatic human response to try to understand others by way of analogy to ourselves. This involves the application of *self-knowledge* and *role-taking*, which social psychologists have identified as normal parts of our everyday attempts to make sense of the actions of others, and to divine their motivations.[32] Reflecting on this use of self-analogy, Thomas Hobbes noted in 1651: "Given the similitude of the thought and passions of one man to the thoughts and passion of another, whosoever looketh into himself and considereth what he doth when does think, opine, reason, hope, fear, &c., and upon what grounds, he shall thereby read and know what are the thoughts and passions of all other men upon the like occasions."[33]

The humanized characterizations of animals in the fables were often consistent with what was known, or at least believed, at the time about various animal species and their behavioral patterns. This can be seen in their use of common species stereotypes. Barry Lopez has observed, for example, that the wolf in the Aesopic fables is stereotyped as a "base, not very intelligent creature, of ravenous appetite, gullible, impudent, and morally corrupt."[34] The *Physiologus* and Aristotle's *Historia animalium* were certainly no less given to such tendencies. Yet the fables' frequent combinations of animal stereotypes and human attributes in a single character was more subtle and suggestive. The line between anthropomorphism as a literary device and reigning belief about animal behavior was often blurred, so that the human qualities attributed to a given animal species, even where comically portrayed, could be interpreted by readers as among the real attributes of that species.

While it is almost always the case that seeing elements of humanity reflected in the natural world comes from having projected them there in the first place, in the fables this was clearly intentional. Since then, as animal stories have become more closely linked to natural history study, their creators have attempted to present them more realistically and have tended to disavow any humanizing intentions. As a result, such stories have increasingly been presented in the guise of fact. Thus, human attributes, where discernible, appear not so much to have been projected onto the animals as *found* there. At least, it has been a profitable illusion.

From Fable to Commodity

It might be tempting at this point to conclude that we had uncovered an essential truth about wildlife films by putting them in the oldest possible historical contexts, particularly that of the fable. For if they are part of an ancient tradition of animal storytelling, and if the leading type of animal story in that tradition is the fable, then we might conclude, as many have, that wildlife films are merely latter-day fables. We might go on to reason that they must also stem from the same urges, and serve essentially the same purposes as earlier fables did for their audiences. With this, we might assume we had arrived at a "theory" of wildlife films—one that explains their depictions of wild animals and the natural world as being metaphoric, designed to impart some "natural wisdom" to us, or perhaps even to teach us something about ourselves by way of example. Nature essayist Peter Steinhart has argued along this line, suggesting that because the experience of "difference" provided by animals helps us define clearly what it is to be human, animals "tell us who we are," and their images in wildlife films, therefore, "let us see . . . ourselves as we hope to be." [35] This view is not limited to critics looking in from outside. Stouffer has argued that the point of the stories in his films is, ultimately, to help unlock "the greatest mystery of all—ourselves," adding elsewhere that "there is a whole lot more we can learn from [animals] about ourselves than we have ever dreamed." [36] Even Disney once wrote that we "can learn a lot from nature," especially about "the thing. . . we call moral behavior." [37] Writer-producer Barry Clark has offered a more comprehensive analysis: "Whether by design or by default, most of our nature films, in my view, are intended to serve as fables or moral tales, in which animals are employed as surrogate humans, manipulated by the filmmakers to enact contemporary culture myths, which serve the primary purpose of defining and reinforcing social values."[38]

It might be surprising to those outside the industry to learn just how many inside it regard wildlife films as primarily a storytelling form, and as part of a cultural tradition of storytelling. Cultural historians would no doubt also find it satisfying to be able to connect wildlife films by way of an unbroken line to a source two thousand or more years in the cultural past. This, of course, would greatly simplify the task of coming to terms with these hybrids of natural history and storytelling that have long evaded both categorization and adequate definition.

Although a degree of *fableizing* can in fact be found in wildlife films, as the basis for an overview or "theory" of the genre, a strictly fableist view slights the rich history of the subject and betrays a kind of historicist fallacy in which genealogy overshadows social context. Such a view might well cause us to overlook the fact that, whatever their cultural origins, there is a considerable variety of wildlife film models, storylines, and types.[39] More importantly, we might also overlook the fact that all of them are products of a vastly complex, heavily mediated global culture. As such, they can give rise to a number of different "readings," and serve a number of different social functions: scientific research and documentation, education, wildlife conservation advocacy, animal rights advocacy, artistic expression, as well as mass entertainment, advertising, tourism promotion, and other, more overt forms of commerce. Some of these do in fact reinforce dominant social values; others, like advocacy for animals, may challenge dominant values or at least give rise to "oppositional readings."[40]

Either way, the fact that wildlife films are industrialized commodities produced for sale in a competitive global marketplace makes their existence and value *as messages* fundamentally different from that of fables, tales, and myths in earlier social orders, even when their plotlines are similar to traditional narratives and resonate with the familiar mythic elements to which people have responded for centuries. Moreover, it is important to bear in mind that wildlife films are primarily a visual rather than a verbal form (voice-over narration notwithstanding), and that they are seen by most viewers on television. It is worth considering, therefore, some of the ways the experience of television-viewing differs fundamentally from that of reading or of listening to a storyteller.[41]

Still, telling stories remains central to wildlife films. "Storytelling has and always will guide our programme-making," notes Michael Rosenberg,[42] whose Partridge Films has specialized in story-driven wildlife films such as those by Hugo Van Lawick, which are often variations on traditional, protagonist-centered narratives. Similarly, Stouffer has written that his filmmaking efforts over the years "can be wrapped up in a single word: storytelling," which he sees as the key social function of wildlife films and film-makers: ". . . all through history, our most important and lasting messages have been handed down by songsters and storytellers. For me, these have always been special people who . . . come up with meaningful tales that sat-isfy our need to know about the world and about our place in it . . . [and] show us how the puzzle pieces fit together."[43]

Yet however traditional the narrative, there may be reason to doubt that what television programs have to tell us about the world we live in, how it works, our place in it, and perhaps what to do about it any longer reflects the perspective of poets, songsters, or fableists who represent the contempo-rary interests and values of a particular community or society. Media schol-ars have long expressed concern that as television has become our primary storyteller the stories we are now told no longer reflect the values of commu-nities, or even have their origins in communities, but are instead the prod-ucts of a complex process of industrial manufacturing and marketing.[44] It is thus worth noting that Stouffer also acknowledges having been forced into many compromises by television network executives who did not let him tell his stories his own way, and who imposed on him the conventions of industrialized storytelling and ratings-driven formulas. Wildlife films thus illustrate well the concern scholars have with who or what in contempo-rary society has assumed the role of storytellers. Although virtually never mentioned by name in media scholarship, it takes little imagination to see wildlife films implicated in passages like the following: "For the first time in human history, most of the stories about people, life and values are told not by parents, schools, churches, or others in the community who have some-thing to tell, but by a group of distant conglomerates that have something to sell."[45]

However compelling, intimate, and natural they may seem, or however much they may resemble traditional fables, tales, and myths, the stories told by wildlife films are now as subject as all other forms of television to the influence of competition for ratings and sales. As such, they may be a better reflection of the values and perspectives of global media industries and international finance than of human communities—at least in the sense in which "community" has traditionally been understood. It is true that the "community" of wildlife filmmakers, despite its international makeup, exerts some collegial influence on the shape of wildlife films, and on the types of stories that are told. This *secondary audience*, however, is often far removed from the *primary audience* of the viewing public, and may be un-likely to mirror its interests and values.[46] Moreover, as more wildlife films are coproduced by firms from several different countries, and as interna-tional presales become necessary to secure financing, there is a move away from the expression of clearly identifiable regional or national differences. Although at the narrative level wildlife films transcend cultural boundaries, recently the tendency has been even more strongly in the direction of international themes and styles suitable for multiple markets.[47] To earn back their investments, wildlife films must have stories that are easily exportable and able to travel well across cultural borders. The need for such financially safe stories, as Rosenberg argues, "demands a formulaic response. As filmmakers we are all caught up in a ratings game which . . . inevitably leads to producers churning out the same old tried and tested formulas which have proved so popular. . . . How can anyone be brave and original when programme ideas have to be pre-sold with the bottom line of assured, high ratings?"[48] The safest formula may well be one that derives from traditional narratives. This need not be incompatible with ratings-driven television, which has often thrived on some of our most enduring myths and stories. Because wildlife films are produced for a global market that is increasingly insensitive to regional differences, there may even be more pressure than in mainstream programming to seek common denominators—in this case, patterns and formulas shared by many cultures. Nevertheless, despite their similarities to folk tales and myths, wildlife films inescapably remain industrial commodities.

In attempting, therefore, to uncover some of the primary historical influences that shaped wildlife film as a distinct film genre defined largely by its narrative codes, the place to begin may not, after all, be at the beginning—that is, with the Greeks. Instead, it may be more useful to start with the era in the late nineteenth and early twentieth centuries when mass-produced, mass-mediated culture began to assume its modern role in society. It was during this time that a number of cultural, social, scientific, technological, and literary currents began to converge and gain momentum, leading to a reemergence of anthropomorphic animal storytelling. The Darwinian paradigm shift had already altered the psychological and symbolic significance of wild animals in relation to humans. This had led to greater sympathy for animals (at least in some quarters), and a to new interest in "animal psychology"—a broad term encompassing observation of animal behavior (later to become the modern study of *ethology*) as well as theories of animal cognition and reasoning. As speculations increased about what animals think and how they experience the world, it was perhaps inevitable that animal stories reflecting the animal point-of-view should begin appearing. With increasing interest in natural science generally, and the accompanying demand for natural history literature for a popular audience, the animal story thus emerged as one of the most popular literary genres in the United States in the late nineteenth century. Wild animals became the protagonists in a series of "realistic" novels and short stories, written and mass-produced for a modern, literate, largely urban audience. It was under such industrial conditions that narrative formulas and techniques of character development were tested, refined, and perfected. This in turn gave rise to models of narrative and character that would endure into the twentieth century and be easily adapted to filmic storytelling, where an animal's point-of-view could be communicated even more dramatically and convincingly.[49]

The packaging and selling of commodified nature thus became as much a growth industry in the late nineteenth century as it would in the late twentieth. Those who entered the field, whatever their background or qualifications, became important as intermediaries between the public and the natural world. However fit or unfit they were to play the part, their role was to define, explain, and justify the ways of nature to humans. That some of them saw this as a solemn responsibility did not mean that they necessarily understood nature themselves. Still, their interpretations and characterizations of it were thought to have great influence on the perceptions of the public in the late nineteenth century, and this led to growing concern among some critics and nature advocates.

As the twentieth century dawned, questions began to be raised about the representation of nature in popular media, some of which have never been adequately answered. Among them was that of the efficacy of attempting to impose narrative structure on nature (or, worse, presuming to have found it there). For with narrative came dramatic protagonists, and questions as to whether animal *protagonism* was even appropriate as a form of nature discourse. Were there really "heroes" in nature? Was there tragedy? Questions such as these led, of course, to debates over anthropomorphism, and ultimately to charges of fakery and deception similar to those leveled at wildlife films in the 1990s. There were also other concerns that were less literary, yet still more pressing, several of which still have contemporary relevance. Should animal storytelling be the basis for natural history education? That is, should animal stories, whether in books or on film, be used as natural history texts in schools? What, exactly, did they teach? Did they reinforce social values? Did they accurately convey "natural values"? Or did they pervert both? Was the mass-production of engaging, sympathetic animal stories an effective means of enlisting public support for the cause of wildlife protection? If disappearing species, such as the wolf, became ubiquitous in mass-produced stories and images, could it undermine public perceptions of the reality of their dwindling numbers, or of the threats to their existence? In a word, the rise of animal storytelling at the end of the nineteenth century can be seen as a dress rehearsal for the controversies of the 1980s and 1990s, when many of the same sorts of problems, questions, and issues were confronted, but where few, if any, were resolved.

Darwinian Projections

If any one event could be seen as having set in motion the rise of anthropomorphic animal storytelling in the latter half of the nineteenth century, it might well have been the publication of Darwin's *On the Origin of Species* (1859). It introduced readers around the world to the idea that humans and animals had common ancestors, and may even be, as Darwin noted in his journals, "fellow brethren."[50] Yet the idea of evolution was not new, having also, and in some cases earlier, been taken up in varying degrees and contexts by Goethe, Buffon, the botanist Lamarck, the geologist Charles Lyell, the biologist Alfred Russell Wallace, the social and scientific theorist Herbert Spencer, and Darwin's own grandfather Erasmus Darwin.[51] It was Spencer, in fact, who coined the term "survival of the fittest," which soon became so inextricably linked to Darwinian theory that by 1869 Darwin himself incorporated it into all later revisions of his book.[52]

Spencer, however, was concerned with applying the laws of natural evolution to human society (thus paving the way for social Darwinism), whereas Darwin had to some extent done just the opposite—projecting the laws of human society onto nature. Even some of those who greatly admired his theories questioned this aspect of his thinking. Marx, who claimed that *On the Origin of Species* had provided the basis for his own theory of class struggle, and who is said to have at one time planned to dedicate *Das Kapital* to Darwin, nevertheless expressed concern in a letter to Engels (June 8, 1862) that Darwin had projected human competition onto the animal world. Engels echoed this years later in the manuscript of his unfinished *Dialectics of Nature*: "The whole Darwinian theory of the struggle for life is simply the transference from society to organic nature of Hobbes' theory of *bellum omnium contra omnes*, and of the bourgeois economic theory of competition, as well as of the Malthusian theory of population."[53]

Darwin had in fact acknowledged a debt to Malthus, from whom he had borrowed the term "struggle for existence." He described his own use of it as "the doctrine of Malthus applied with manifold force to the whole animal and vegetable kingdoms."[54] Applying Malthusian theory to the natural world, however, meant understanding nature by projecting theoretical models of human behavior and social organization onto it. Casting it in human terms, moreover, made Darwinian theory consistent with the anthropomorphic tendencies that had long characterized both formal studies and popular representations of natural history.[55] The rest of Engels's statement, however, suggests that Darwin's theories even naturalized human intellectual and social systems, if not also social and cultural values: "it is very easy to transfer these theories back again to the history of society, and altogether too naive to maintain that thereby these notions have been proved as eternal *natural laws of society*."[56]

Although no popularizer himself, Darwin succeeded in giving evolution a method—"natural selection"—and in gaining wider acceptance for it than even Spencer's evolutionary metaphysics.[57] There were those who resisted the whole idea, of course; the ranks of dissenters included not just those with religious convictions, but also men of science. The eminent Swiss scientist and teacher Louis Agassiz, for example, who had done so much to promote Americans' appreciation of the natural world, never did embrace Darwinism, and died in 1873 still unpersuaded.[58] Religious dissenters, of course, saw Darwinism as an assault on the Church's teaching that humans were made in the image of God. The rise of liberal theology, however, helped ease the transition toward acceptance of the idea of evolution, even among many of the faithful. In fact, Darwinian ideas were so well received in the United States, and so quickly taken up there, that by 1870 "the age of Agassiz" in the United States had given way to the age of Darwin.[59] By the end of the century the idea that humans and animals were one in kinship not only carried the full weight of scientific authority throughout the western world, but had also captured the imagination of much of the public, especially in the United States. The movement opposing vivisection and cruelty to animals, already well established in Britain, thus found fertile ground in the United States and began to take solid root.[60] Meanwhile, from the same soil, a number of other interests in the natural world were emerging.

"Science Out of School":
Birdwatching and Amateur Nature Study

As the interest many Americans had in their animal "brethren" grew, the fascination with birds burst into full bloom. Birdwatching, or "birding," once a favorite recreation of elites, had become a popular pastime among the rising middle class in America, and as its popularity grew so too did the market for bird-related literature.[61] So much bird material emerged, in fact, that soon after the Ornithologist's Union formed in 1883 it set itself the task of developing a standardized nomenclature for American birds before the profusion of popular publications using folk and regional names led to widespread and irrevocable confusion. In addition to birdwatching's aesthetic satisfactions, however, it had also become infused with humanitarian motives. In 1886 George Bird Grinnell formed the first Audubon Society, which by 1888 had fifty-thousand members, each of whom had signed a pledge not to kill birds (*nongame* birds, at least), not to destroy nests or eggs, and not to wear decorative feathers.

Yet humanitarian concern for animal welfare was still closely tied to, if not dependent on, some degree of anthropomorphism.[62] Sympathy for animal "others" depended then, as now, on being able to see a bit of ourselves reflected in them—even if it meant projecting ourselves there in the first place. This was as true for birds as it was for other species. Among some nineteenth-century birdwatchers, for example, a "Christian ornithology" emerged in which birds were observed for the moral and ethical lessons it was believed they could teach.[63] Some even had spiritual qualities attributed to them.[64] Believers could point to "good" and "bad" species, and even to individuals whose conduct and manners were exemplary. Those birds the nineteenth century judged as good "had pleasant if not musically significant songs and attractive plumage. They ate weed seeds and insects, but not grain. In large part they built handsome and intricate nests. . . . Their habits were at least well-bred, and they displayed virtues which the nature lover admired [including] industry among the nuthatches and woodpeckers, dignity and devotion in the herons, bravery in the kingbird, modesty among thrushes."[65]

"Bad" birds, by contrast, were not just the meat-eating *raptors* who preyed on these helpless good birds, but included those species who robbed their eggs and even those who, like the cowbird and the cuckoo, laid their eggs in the nests of other birds.[66] Negative views of predator species were by no means restricted to birds, of course. Bears, mountain lions, and perhaps especially wolves were even more severely denigrated for centuries, yet the hatred directed at them was often driven by assumptions similar to those typical of Christian ornithology—that is, that their actions could be explained as attributes (or deficits) of individual character rather than as the fixed behaviors of a species. Reducing behavior to the individual level, as in wildlife films, enabled unwelcome actions to be understood as a form of *deviance* for which the individual could be held morally responsible. Although such normative expectations were not new, they showed clearly the extent of anthropomorphic projections in the post-Darwinian age.[67]

Birdwatching itself, however, had to some extent grown out of the larger field of "nature study," which became increasingly fertile after midcentury for amateurs and hobbyists, as well as for scientists and scholars. It was thus a popular avocation as well as an emerging field of academic scholarship, with each one gaining legitimacy from the other. In public schools it assumed the dimensions of a full-scale educational reform movement, implemented across the United States with the intention of putting urban schoolchildren in touch with the natural world of which they had little experience.[68]

Unlike biology and zoology, however, "nature study" was not restricted to the academy. Because its objects could be so easily found, and because its "methodology" consisted mainly of observation, it became the preeminent form of *popular science.* John Burroughs thus aptly characterized it as "science out of school."[69] More recently, it has been noted that "the very term *natural history* . . . had an aura of amateurism and speculation," and later gave way to "soberer, more precise rubrics."[70] In fact, anyone in the late nineteenth century with an interest in nature and wild animals, and a little time to devote to watching and reading about them, could call him- or herself a "student of natural history"—although the preferred designation was "naturalist."[71] The term could encompass "anyone from Darwin to the lowliest Sunday bug-hunter."[72] A century later it is still in use, alongside the similar self-designation "environmentalist."[73] Although using these terms as *titles* remains problematic, there is still no academic certification or formal training required to do so.[74] The term "naturalist," in particular, has always been used vocationally as well as avocationally, often assuming the status of a credential (or quasi-credential) used in professional contexts. A 1902 review in the *Atlantic*, for example, refers in several places to a well-known nature writer as a "naturalist by profession."[75] Originally the province of botanists, geologists, and zoologists, the title of "naturalist" is now claimed by rangers, zookeepers, veterinarians, tour guides, professional hunters, and even proprietors of reptile farms. Theodore Roosevelt, in his book *African Game Trails* (1910), described himself as a "hunter-naturalist." In the years since, image-makers have also adopted the term. Nature photographers and wildlife filmmakers have become "photographer-naturalists" and "naturalist-filmmakers." Alan Root has argued that a wildlife filmmaker "must be naturalist first, and then a film-maker." Tim Liversedge has even described himself as "first of all a naturalist rather than a filmmaker." Of course, Disney had also insisted that the same was true of his cameramen, but just what it takes or even means to be a "naturalist" in today's world is unclear.[76]

The Rise of the Literary Naturalist

As the number of nineteenth-century "naturalists" grew, so too did the market for natural history literature. Nature writing of all sorts became popular—though even in this early phase of modern mass media, "popular" had already come to mean *commercially successful*. There was money to be made and, just as in the case of wildlife films a few decades later, many entered the field to seek their fortune, some of whom knew little or nothing about nature or wild animals. Those who did were typically not scientists, but *naturalists* whose formal training, if any, was in other areas—art, religion, journalism, education, photography, and in later years film and television. The early "literary naturalists" in the United States—Henry David Thoreau, Thomas Starr King, George Perkins Marsh, Susan Cooper, John Burroughs, and others—were not scientists, but popularizers of natural history who observed nature closely, as a scientist might, but rendered their observations in combination with subjective reflection and interpretation. Burroughs described their style and purpose in terms that might well be applied to wildlife films today, claiming that their purpose was to "to give us the truth in a way to touch our emotions, and in some degree satisfy the enjoyment we have in the living reality." He explained their relationship to science this way: "The literary artist is just as much in love with the fact as is his scientific brother, only he makes a different use of the fact, and his interest in it is often of a non-scientific character. His method is synthetic rather than analytic."[77]

Burroughs's writing in particular looked forward to wildlife films, epitomizing the style that entertained as well as informed. Henry James claimed that Burroughs possessed a "real genius for observation of natural things" and described him as "a more humorous, more available, and more social Thoreau."[78] Yet, like that of Thoreau, the work of this self-described "essay-naturalist" was taken quite seriously, even though he did not write scientific monographs or journalistic reports. His stylized interpretations of the natural world, often held together by a loose narrative of sorts, might be described as *creative treatments of actuality*—the definition that is today widely applied to documentary film, and is surely broad enough to apply also to wildlife film. It was precisely this combination of observation and engaging interpretation of nature that made such nineteenth-century natural history essays one of their generation's equivalents of the late twentieth-century wildlife film, and one of its important precursors. Stouffer has even referred to his films "pictorial essays."[79]

Yet, like the market for natural history films in the late twentieth and early twenty-first centuries, the demand for natural history literature in the late nineteenth century was by no means limited to interpretive, non-fiction essays. Then, as now, narrative exerted a powerful attraction, and audiences for natural history essays also welcomed dramatic stories about engaging animal characters. In many cases these too were based on the writers' own careful observations of the natural world, and had a surface realism that made them difficult for some readers to distinguish from factual accounts. As the twentieth century approached, animal stories and nature essays began appearing side-by-side in such widely read magazines as *Harper's*, *McClure's*, *Scribner's*, *Everybody's*, *The Century*, and *Ladies Home Journal*. By the turn of the century many popular magazines featured an animal story or essay in every issue."[80] It may be difficult, over a hundred years later, to appreciate fully the significance of this, but it might be likened to seeing wildlife films as regular features in the nightly prime-time lineups of all of today's major American television networks.

Also growing at the end of the nineteenth century was the market for full-length novels about animals. The American Human Education Society spotted the trend early. Seeing an opportunity to promote its message of humane treatment of animals to a broad audience, in 1890 it issued an American version of Anna Sewell's *Black Beauty*, which had been published in England in 1877. Dubbed "The Uncle Tom's Cabin of the Horse" for its evocation of compassion and sympathy, it was sold cheap, at twelve cents per copy, in hopes that its anti-cruelty message would find its way into the working classes where horses were used to make a daily living, and where they were also often severely beaten and abused.[81] Significantly, the story unfolded from the horse's point-of-view, a technique for evoking sympathy and gaining greater audience involvement that would soon become the norm for animal stories, and for many wildlife films a few decades later. In 1894 Kipling's *The Jungle Book* was published in the United States, and although the story of Mowgli and friends was clearly fantastic rather than realistic, it nevertheless contributed further to the popularity of novels featuring appealing animal characters. Freud included it on a list of ten "good" books he recommended in 1907 to his publisher, Hugo Heller. Peter Gay has written that Freud's liking for the book may have been because it "could be read as an imaginative protest against the artificiality of modern civilization," but it might just as well have been the anthropomorphic displacement of human conflicts onto nature that appealed to him.[82] In any case, fifty years before Disney began making wildlife films that provoked widespread discussion of anthropomorphism, turn-of-the-century readers began to notice a rising tide of novels and short stories featuring animal characters who were, as Lisa Mighetto has noted, "becoming more amicable and virtuous than many humans."[83]

The leading figures in this literary "movement," and the writers generally credited with having inaugurated it, were two Canadians—Ernest Thompson Seton and Charles G. D. Roberts. Among the others whose names became well known as writers of animal stories were the Americans Gene Stratton Porter and the Rev. William J. Long, as well as Jack London.[84] As a collective attempt to marry natural history with narrative and character, their work must not be underestimated. In the post-Darwinian era of modern mass media, it was these writers who carved out the cultural niche that wildlife films would later fill.

Anthropomorphic Realism

Assessing the value of these animal stories and their place in literary and cultural history has led to disagreement among critics and historians. In the view of some, they were essentially a new form of nature writing: the "realistic" animal story, specifically tailored for a post-Darwinian audience.[85] Others, however, have seen them as little more than a collective recrudescence of the Aesopic fable, spruced up a bit for a new generation of readers, but with nothing particularly realistic beyond a bit of surface detail.[86] Their defenders have countered that, although much of their realism lay at a deeper level, the absence of explicit humanizing clearly distinguished them from traditional animal fables. Roberts's biographer, for example, has written:

In the earlier stories, no attempt is made in the direction of realism or accuracy. The animals are, as it were, human beings dressed up; they speak and think like human beings, and are created with the specific intention of providing didactic comment on human actions and attitudes. The originality of the new form consisted in its shifting of the main focus from the human to the animal world. Now the animals are interesting because they are animals . . . [and we are given] a view of the animal world presented either objectively or from the animal's point of view.[87]

For one thing, the animals in the new generation of stories did not *talk*.[88] They had thoughts, feelings, and emotions, but these were communicated almost solely by means of an omniscient narrator. As in wildlife films today, the narrators functioned not just to describe animal behavior, but to *explain* it, for whereas the meaning of human behavior can often be inferred by way of analogy to ourselves,[89] animal behavior can be incomprehensible to the untutored human eye, and easily misinterpreted. In the absence of an authoritative voice or other information, we often have only self-analogy with which to make sense of the actions of animals, and it is in this sense that anthropomorphism is seen by some as all but inescapable when we try to understand the behavior of animals.[90] Thus, whatever humanizing of animals there was in the stories of Seton, Roberts, Long, and the others would likely have seemed plausible to many readers at the time, especially when, as in wildlife films, it was explained by an all-knowing narrator. Whether in prose or in images, the wholly objective portrayal of actions and events—that is, without commentary—would likely not be enough in itself to convey the individual personality of an animal character, and might even fail to engage audiences' sympathies.[91] Seton, however, had not always relied solely on the narration of events to convey the individuality of his animal characters. Some of his earliest stories had involved talking animals, yet he abandoned this approach and later described it as an "archaic method."[92]

Ultimately the comparison to Aesopic fables could not be sustained at the levels of action and character. The animals in the new generation of "realistic" stories lived the lives of wild, not humanized, creatures; they faced the sorts of survival struggles that real wild animals face: hunger, predation, reproduction, and the ever-present dangers posed by humans. It has been argued, for example, that the animals in Roberts's stories are almost completely preoccupied with the search for food, and that, although this may be realistic, it prevented Roberts from further developing the animal story form.[93] Nevertheless, such realism in the portrayal of the animals' experiences was seen as revealing less about the human condition than about the animal condition—at least, insofar as it was then understood. As portrayals of the emotional experiences of wild animals, these stories were attempts to convey what it would be like to *be* a wild animal—albeit one that is self-aware and capable of divining the significance of events and situations. This degree of self-consciousness in the characters, combined with attempts to tell the stories from their point of view, helped audiences identify with them and become emotionally involved with their struggles, but also left the stories open to the inevitable charges of being unduly anthropomorphic.

Nevertheless, some have seen the "realistic" animal stories of the late nineteenth century as having helped popularize the Darwinian view of the natural world in which the guiding hand of God, represented by order, harmony, and purpose, seemed no longer discernible in nature. The German poet Heine lamented, "Gone is the authority of law and the prophets." In their place seemed to be only conflict, violence, and chaos, which many incorrectly heard in the catchphrases of Darwinism—"struggle for existence" and "survival of the fittest." The stories of Seton, Roberts, and the others, however, can be viewed as having shown to a late nineteenth-century readership that predation, killing, and death did not necessarily reveal a natural world mired in meaningless violence. Instead, their stories suggested that these things, while often tragic-seeming, were part of some design, however abstract, and therefore ultimately served some greater end. It has been argued that their stories "allowed people to accept evolution and struggle without losing the vision of nature as an ordered realm."[94] Although they may have contributed to misinterpretations of the "struggle for existence" in nature, they nevertheless put it on bookshelves and nightstands across America, bringing it into the home and making it seem familiar—just as wildlife television programs would a few decades later.

If the works of these writers reflected the Darwinian worldview, however, it was refracted through the prism of more traditional Victorian sensibilities. Seton's version of Darwinism was one in which the animals that survived and triumphed tended to be those individuals who exhibited elements of *virtue*—courage, sacrifice, fidelity, and so forth. The Darwinian language of "struggle for survival" would again be combined with moralistic judgment when Walt Disney would declare that every animal "must *earn* his right to live and survive by his own efforts and the thing which in human relations is called *moral behavior*."[95] Although such sentiments may have helped make both Seton's and Disney's animal adventures popular with audiences, it was also the very sort of thing that provoked comparisons to fables.

Roberts's stories seemed to some to be more Darwinian than Seton's, but this often resulted in accusations that they were too violent and put too much emphasis on killing. It was a charge that would often be leveled at wildlife films in later years, including Disney's, although among the nature writers there was not the sort of competition for ratings that is claimed to motivate the emphasis on killing and bloodshed in wildlife programs today. It is true that Roberts avoided some of the hallmarks of Setonesque sentimentality, such as giving his animal characters names and presenting them as heroes or moral exemplars, but this did not mean that he eschewed animal protagonism; his stories were, like the others, clearly character-driven.

Yet even Seton, with his oversimplified moral order, avoided projecting good and evil onto animals. Both he and Roberts demonstrated a refreshingly fair-handed treatment of predators, and in this their work did exhibit a kind of Darwinian view of species interrelationships.

The Animal Biography

The contribution of the turn-of-the-century nature writers to the development of contemporary wildlife films lay not only in their realistic portrayals of natural relationships, but also in their methods of narrative exposition and in their creation of realistic animal characters with whom audiences could identify. The result was a type of story in which narrative and character could be virtually impossible to untangle. Whereas stories about human characters can seem implausible if their actions are too far removed from our own experience, stories about wild animals (who are generally believed to act from "instinct") can often seem to be taken straight from nature itself. Moreover, the fact that humans regularly employ self-analogy to understand the behavior and motivations of animals suggests that a bit of humanizing can even make animal characters *more* believable. That is, they can be seen as driven by instincts, but instincts that, fortunately, can be perfectly understood. A 1902 review in the *Atlantic* noted with some irony, therefore, that although Seton's animal characters were far more realistic than those of Aesop or Kipling, "if they were any less human, they would be less popular."[96]

Stories such as those by Seton and Roberts typically follow the adventures of a single animal character over an extended length of time, and thus depict a collection of individual behaviors and adventures that may be seen as cumulatively representing the species. Seton acknowledged his preference for narratives centering on individual animal characters over a more "documentary" approach, and suggested that the character-centered approach was actually the most revealing. He noted in his introduction to *Wild Animals I Have Known,*

I believe that natural history has lost much by the vague general treatment that is so common. What satisfaction would be derived from a ten-page sketch of the habits and customs of Man? How much more profitable it would be to devote that space to the life of some one great man. This is the principle I have endeavored to apply to my animals.[97]

The result was what Seton called the "animal biography," a direct antecedent to the "classic model" of wildlife filmmaking. To construct such a story, Seton, like his filmic descendants, relied heavily on a principle of *composite*— that is, on composite characters and events assembled from observations made of many different ones in the wild. It has been described as a process of "ascribing to one animal the adventures of several," and of combining in that one animal "the traits of many individuals." [98] The result was often individual characters whose lives could seem very *busy*, involving more than their fair share of excitement, danger, and drama. Ordinary lives, after all, make dull stories.

Yet the written word was perhaps even better suited than film to exploring the ordinary, and to elevating minute detail to sublime significance (as perhaps best demonstrated by Proust). It could do this because of its ability to free itself from the constraints of time and to explore at length the details of a moment suspended in time. By contrast, film and television, in which pages of written description can be communicated at a glance, were soon to prove better suited to depicting action than description; the constraints of a fixed running time would make them subject to expectations of something *happening* before that time ran out. The reality of animal life, however, is that there is usually very little action occurring (despite vulgar-Darwinist notions of nature as a place of perpetual conflict). This meant that film and television would eventually become even more dependent on composite events and characters in telling animal stories. Rarely would the life of a real individual animal involve enough drama to make a complete and satisfying film, or, as Seton and his literary contemporaries knew, a good novel or short story.

Seton therefore acknowledged the use of composites, admitting that he had "pieced together some of the characters" in his stories, and adding that this was "made necessary by the fragmentary nature of the records." [99] While this may sound more applicable to film, in which a story is literally pieced together from shot-fragments, what it meant in Seton's case was that if a key narrative event never actually occurred in the life of the individual he was observing for his biographical narrative, or at least not while he happened to be watching, he could simply infer it, and write about it anyway. His readers, of course, had no way of knowing which characters and events he had fabricated and which ones he had actually witnessed. After all, he had given them his assurance of complete authenticity: "These stories are true. Although I have left the strict line of historical truth in many places, the animals in this book were all real characters. They lived the lives I have depicted." [100]

Composites and other fabrications were not, however, invisible in written stories simply because they weren't *visual*. Ironically, they may even have been more conspicuous on the printed page than they would later be on film and television, where far more convincing impressions of reality could be created through the skillful use of camera and editing, later in combination with sound and narration. It was in the earliest years of cinema, in fact, before the medium began its march toward the conquest of culture, but had already begun to colonize epistemological notions of documentation and evidence, that Seton and the others who dealt in written words came under attack for faking nature.

Fabrication and Faking

When the allegations surfaced in 1996 that wildlife filmmakers had misrepresented the natural world and broken faith with their audience, there was little if any realization that history was repeating itself. What few knew was that wildlife filmmakers' literary predecessors had come under similar attack some ninety years earlier. Yet the later conflict involved a relatively minor exchange of fire, whereas the earlier battle lasted for several years.

In the spring of 1903, critical articles began appearing in both literary and popular journals accusing Seton, Roberts, Long, and Jack London of being "Nature Fakers" who had not only misreported the facts of nature, but sacrificed scientific truth on the altar of storytelling, and in the process willfully and systematically deceived the public about animal behavior in the wild. Although the creators of other kinds of fictional stories were given license to invent and fabricate at will, the unfortunate insistence by several of the literary naturalists that their stories were hewn from raw material provided by nature, and were therefore *true*, inevitably meant that they were held to different standards—to what might be seen today as the standards of documentary. Yet the application of truth standards to these stories now appears to have been misguided. A hundred years later it is difficult to see them as anything but purely fictional creations, yet clearly they were not regarded as such in their own time, and apparently not even by some of the writers who created them. As the century of motion pictures dawned, the nature faker controversy suggested that the gulf between literature and truth, between the written word and reality, had widened.

It was at precisely this time that narrative cinema was coming into being, bringing with it a whole new way of telling stories. Edwin S. Porter's *The Life of an American Fireman* emerged in 1902, and has since been widely regarded as the first example of a clear attempt at narrative cinema as a cinema of *cutting* such as we know it today. *The Great Train Robbery* appeared the following year, and announced in no uncertain terms the arrival of a new mode of storytelling that was wholly visual. Given the faith then (and still today) in visual images as carriers of Truth, it is worth remarking that this was also the very year the nature writers came under attack for the artifice in their literary mode of storytelling.

What made this campaign against nature faking different from the one ninety years later, and what elevated it to the level of a *crusade* lasting years, was that the charge was led not by a pack of unknown newspaper writers, but by one of America's most celebrated men of letters—John Burroughs, the grand old man of American nature writing. Although well on in years,

Burroughs was still a formidable figure, whose friends included Walt Whitman, John Muir, Henry Ford, and Thomas Edison. He would eventually be joined in his attack on the nature fakers by an even more powerful and influential friend—Theodore Roosevelt, with whom he had recently spent two weeks traveling in Yellowstone National Park. Roosevelt then held no less a position than President of the United States, and when at last he fired his own broadside at the nature fakers it came straight from the White House.

The first shot in the long war of words, however, was fired by Burroughs in the March 1903 edition of the *Atlantic*. In an article entitled "Real and Sham Natural History," he charged that the animals in Seton's stories, many of which were composites, were so patently false in their character and behavior that his book should have been called "Wild Animals I *Alone* Have Known." Seton's insistence that his stories were written just has he had observed them provoked Burroughs to respond, "This is the old trick of the romancer: he swears his tale is true, because he knows his reader wants assurance; it makes things taste better."[101] Burroughs preferred his nature "unadulterated and unsweetened," adding that "to know a thing is true gives it such a savor! The truth—how we do crave the truth! We cannot feed our minds on simulacra any more than we can our bodies."[102] Burroughs did not object to a nature writer adding his subjective responses and feelings to his observations of nature, but warned: "let him be sure he sees accurately. Let him beware of letting invention take the place of observation."[103] Unrelenting a full two years into the battle, Burroughs wrote:

The nature lover is always tempted . . . to humanize the wild life about him, and to read his own traits and moods into whatever he looks upon. I have never consciously done this myself, at least to the extent of willfully misleading my reader. But some of our later nature writers have been guilty of this fault, and have so grossly exaggerated and misrepresented the every-day wild life of our fields and woods that their example has caused a strong reaction to take place in my own mind, and has led me to set about examining the whole subject of animal life and instinct in a way I have never done before.[104]

The charge of "humanizing" was an old and familiar one, but the charge of "misrepresent[ing] the every-day wild life of our fields and woods" was leveled directly at dramatic storytelling, with its use of composites and its reliance on elements that are actually rare in the everyday life of nature: action, drama, and character. Burroughs's critique would be no less relevant to wildlife films at the close of the twentieth century than it was to animal stories at the beginning of the century.

His main target, and the one for whom he reserved his severest scorn, was the Rev. William J. Long. Although Burroughs regarded Long as little more than a literary charlatan ("the Münchausen of our nature writers"[105]), both men were classic late nineteenth-century *naturalists* who, like Seton,

Muir, and even the Keartons, placed a high premium on patient, careful observation of the details of nature, yet had no formal training in biology, zoology, or in natural science methods. Long even expressed disdain for such intellectual procedures. He not only rejected the academic practice of combining field observation with a thorough study of the existing literature, but openly criticized it. "I have taken infinite pains," he wrote, "to compare my observations not with books, but with the experience of trappers and Indians who know far more of animal ways than the books have ever provided."[106] Long believed that scholarly reading and research would not enhance or sharpen his observations, but would come between him and the direct experience of whatever he was observing and force him into academic categories that did not allow for individual differences among animals. After Burroughs had let go his initial volleys, Long fired back with a detailed response in the *North American Review*:

> The study of nature is a vastly different thing from the study of Science; they are no more alike than Psychology and History. Above and beyond the world of facts and law, with which alone Science concerns itself, is an immense and almost unknown world. . . .
> In a word, the difference between Nature and Science is the difference between a man who loves animals, and so understands them, and the man who studies Zoology.[107]

From a scientific perspective, Long had given himself license to report on animal behavior in narrative accounts based on observations that were neither carried out systematically nor put in a scholarly context linking them to what was already known from legitimate research. When he observed behavior that didn't square with the knowledge collected from scientific study, Long could, with some justification, argue that science, in its search for larger patterns, was not equipped to deal with individual differences among animals. Even today, science's inability to deal with animals as individuals often places it at odds with the goals of wildlife filmmakers who, working in a storytelling medium, often rely as much as the nature writers on audiences' emotional involvement with individual animal characters. In his own way, Long was not only exploring terrain more recently staked out by ethologists and psychologists who have written about individual personalities among animals,[108] but also helping pave the way for wildlife films' acceptance as quasi-scientific "documents" in narrative form. In any case, there was enough truth in Long's critique of science, and of reigning scientific methods, to sustain him through several long years of vituperative debate with Burroughs and Roosevelt.

Charles G. D. Roberts and Gene Stratton Porter got off easier, managing to stay out of the line of fire by avoiding the sort of claims to absolute authenticity and veracity that Seton and Long had made on behalf of their stories.[109] Although Roberts considered himself a "field naturalist," he actually tended to write more from research than from long hours of field observation, and so did not publicly assert that his stories were accurate chronicles of individual animals and events he had actually witnessed in nature. Seton and Long, by contrast, did write from field observation, and so held to their claims that their works were chronicles of this very sort, implying that they therefore had "documentary" value (although the term itself would not actually come into use until some time later). Roberts, although his work was seen as "realistic," was more willing than either Seton or Long to have it accepted as *literature*, and even stated that the animal story "is a psychological romance constructed on a framework of natural science."[110] Similarly, Porter admitted that her stories were nature studies "coated with fiction."[111] Both descriptions fit wildlife films today remarkably well.

In 1907 Theodore Roosevelt formally entered the battle himself in an interview in *Everybody's Magazine*. His chief concern, like that of Burroughs, was with something as old as the Greeks, and no less prominent or problematic today: the tendency in popular natural history toward narrative invention (or projection), and the blurring of the line between fact and fiction. "If the stories of these writers were written in the spirit that inspired [Kipling's] Mowgli . . . we should know that we were getting the very essence of the fable and we should be content to read, enjoy, and accept them as fables. We don't in the least mind impossibilities in avowed fairy tales. . . . But when such fables are written by a make-believe realist, the matter assumes an entirely different complexion" (p. 772).

Yet it was not merely the unwillingness of some of the nature writers to come clean about the degree of fabrication in their works that provoked the angry reactions of Roosevelt and Burroughs. What added fuel to their mutual outrage was the fact that many of these books were used in schools as natural history texts. Roosevelt made clear that high among his concerns was "the matter of giving these books to the children for the purpose of teaching them the facts of natural history." This he called "an outrage." He concluded with a statement that is still as relevant today as it was then: "The preservation of the useful and beautiful animal and bird life of the country depends largely upon creating in the young an interest in the life of the woods and fields. If the child mind is fed with stories that are false to nature, the children will go to the haunts of the animal only to meet with disappointment. The result will be disbelief and the death of interest. The men who misinterpret nature and replace fact with fiction, undo the work of those who in the love of nature interpret it aright" (p. 774).

A few months later, the President spoke out one more time on the subject, writing his own article for the September issue of *Everybody's*. This unofficial presidential proclamation was seen by many as the final word on the subject of nature faking, effectively bringing the long debate to an end. Yet the controversy had raised serious questions that could not be easily resolved. How suitable were popular media, beholden as they were to the commercial pressures of the marketplace, as vehicles for accurately conveying the realities of the natural world? Did these stories about animals make audiences more sensitive to the plight of wildlife? Did they teach? Did they deceive? It seems at the very least that they attested to the power of storytelling combined with close observation and vivid imagery, but they had also revealed weaknesses in this combination of art and science. Perhaps above all, they had pointed to disparities between what was real and what would sell, between scientific accuracy on the one hand, and marketability on the other. It would be for film, some years later, to reveal the ultimate incompatibility of these—although, ironically, in the guise of a heightened realism.

Stories in Pictures

Although the nature faker controversy came to an end in 1907, nature faking in animal storytelling did not. The nature writers' heads were bloodied but unbowed, and they continued to write, and to sell. Even Cherry Kearton would soon take pencil in hand and join their ranks, keeping the tradition alive for several more decades. In 1907, however, Kearton was one of the world's leading wildlife still photographers and was already making the transition to the cine-camera. There, ironically, he would (at least for a few years) resolutely avoid nature faking, and would be praised by Theodore Roosevelt for the "absolute trustworthiness" and "first-rate scientific importance" of his work.[112] When footage from Kearton's African trips premiered in New York in 1913, Roosevelt was on hand to give it an enthusiastic introduction in which he echoed his well-known concern with authenticity in the representation of wildlife: "In moving pictures of wild life there is a great temptation to fake, and the sharpest discrimination must be employed in order to tell the genuine from the spurious. My attention was particularly directed toward Mr. Kearton's work because of its absolute honesty. If he takes a picture it may be guaranteed as straight."[113]

The pictures themselves were, in fact, straight. It was only later, when Kearton attempted to explain the behavioral and social patterns he had observed, that his vision proved skewed. During his first years as a cinematographer he steadfastly resisted going down the Selig-Rainey path of dramatic sensationalism and staged events. Later, however, as both writer and cinematographer, his convictions were less clear. After writing a number of dubious animal stories, he nevertheless appended an "Author's Note" to one of them in which he expressed concern that the evils of nature faking had spread from the printed page to films: "the same thing is true in the world of the cinematograph, where double exposure and many other devices are used to show animals in unnatural situations and to give the effect of their behaving as, in fact, they never behave. The people who try to give us 'sensations' both in films and in books appear to imagine that "art" is needed in that respect to supply the defects of Nature; that the wild life of animals is sadly in need of a little 'gingering up.' "[114]

It was true that Kearton's early films did not employ technical effects that misrepresented animal behavior, but in later years his tendentious use of sound effects, music, and above all commentary managed to mislead and distort as much as any visual means of "gingering up." The man who had pioneered techniques for observing and photographing animals in the wild, whose films fulfilled even Roosevelt's exacting requirements for accurate representation, who was later lionized by the British natural history film establishment and held up as its founding father and patron saint,[115] could thus condemn nature fakers on one page and out-invent, out-fabricate, and out-sentimentalize them on the next. In his films and stories from the 1920s and 1930s Kearton ultimately proved himself a fableist and nature faker of the highest order, despite his expressed disdain for the inaccuracies in the work of his contemporaries.[116]

In the earliest years of the twentieth century, however, their animal stories still faced no real competition from animal films, which had already been around for a decade (since *The Sea Lions' Home* in 1897). Even by 1905 most animal films still consisted mainly of simple and brief *actualités*, with nary a hint of narrative development. The many animal "feeding" films made between 1898 and 1905 were virtually eventless and did not even provide a rudimentary basis for narrative development. Capturing real "events" of animal behavior was difficult, but as motion pictures began generating expectations of movement there could be impatience with nature's languor, with its slowness in giving rise to exciting, filmable events. Provocation, staging, and faking thus seemed born of necessity. It is fair to say that during this time virtually all filmed "events" involving animals were staged, from the feeding films to the execution of Topsy.

When hunting films began to arrive on the scene, with their greater dramatic, and therefore narrative possibilities, feeding was quickly replaced by hunting, stasis by action, and, ultimately, nurturing by killing. Although the earliest of these films were too brief to be considered "narratives" (1903's *Hunting the White Bear* came in at sixty-five feet—less than one minute), and lacked the formal conventions later associated with narrative cinema, they did feature events of the sort that could, with a little imagination, be turned into simple stories. By 1906 they had completely replaced static animal *actualités*, and quickly grew in length and complexity. *Wolf Hunt* (1908), although still crude in its editing, nevertheless sustained a continuous series of events lasting nearly a quarter hour, and showed clearly the influence of Porter's innovation of using editing to form meaningful links between shots and scenes, and thus to construct a simple story from them.

Wild animals, outdoor locations, chases, pursuits, dramatic editing, and rudimentary narrative had all come together; the reign of the "safari film" had begun. Although early hunting and safari films could be genuinely dramatic, sometimes even exhibiting a crude grasp of the basics of narrative film editing, they were still not "animal stories" of the sort to which audiences were accustomed from the books of the nature writers, and so offered little competition to the well-developed narratives and characters on the printed page. Animal films of all sorts were still too brief to sustain the kind of narrative development, conflict resolution, and prolonged involvement with characters that audiences sought from books about animals. With motion picture art still in its infancy, animal storytelling awaited the refinement of the filmic narrative conventions that were then only beginning to take shape. Their application to animals would be slow in developing, although inevitable. D. W. Griffith had only just begun directing films in 1908, and his contributions to the development and refinement of the form of narrative cinema did not take hold immediately.[117] The use of Griffithesque techniques to promote viewers' emotional involvement with animal characters, or to portray an animal's point of view, or even to depict animal subjectivity were still over the horizon—but only just.

The transition of wildlife storytelling from print to celluloid was aided during this period by novelist James Oliver Curwood. Younger than the other literary naturalists, Curwood came of age as a writer well into the era of motion pictures, publishing his first novel in 1908, and his first true work of animal protagonism, *Kazan*, the story of a wolf-dog and his family, in 1914. Today Curwood may best be remembered for his 1916 novel *The Grizzly King*, which later became the basis for Jean-Jacques Annaud's acclaimed film *The Bear* (*L'Ours*, 1988).[118] Although Curwood's story contained some gross behavioral inaccuracies, he nevertheless asserted in Setonesque fashion his claim to veracity, if not to scientific accuracy: "I have scrupulously adhered," he proclaimed, "to the facts as I have found them in the lives of the wild creatures of which I have written." [119] Nevertheless, the novel is a virtual catalogue of wildlife storytelling artifices, several of which may have been conceived with motion pictures in mind. In fact, Curwood began to write for the movies fairly early in his career, dividing his energies between novels and screenplays and reportedly churning out over a hundred of the latter in ten years.[120] It is difficult to imagine, therefore, that his novel writing was not influenced by his interest and experiences in motion pictures.

Curwood even sought to distance himself from his noncinematic literary predecessors, and went so far as to insert satiric jabs at them in *The Grizzly King*.[121] Yet despite his pretensions to a more sophisticated outlook, the novel nevertheless betrays many of the same sorts of humanizing tendencies and anthropomorphic projections that had characterized the high period of nature faking a few years earlier. All of this is woven into the very plot itself, which involves the unlikely situation of an orphaned bear cub being adopted and shown the ways of survival in the wild by an older, more experienced adult male. Despite this improbable scenario, Curwood had refined the narrative of wild animals in a way that brought it closer to filmable form. Stories involving young orphans could be not only more emotionally engaging, but also more visually compelling than stories like those of the earlier nature writers, which often centered on the perpetual search for food by adult animals.[122] Scenes of a young animal separated from its mother and wandering alone in a harsh wilderness needed no commentary to have greater emotional resonance and dramatic impact. There seems little doubt that audiences will tend to root more strongly for a helpless youngster to escape danger than for a capable and experienced adult—almost regardless of the species. It is likely that audiences could be induced to become emotionally involved in this sort of drama even in a clumsily made film. Now a commonplace in wildlife film narratives, it had not been adequately explored prior to Curwood.

Curwood's animal story refinements, along with his wilderness tales about people struggling to live in wild country, thus found a welcome reception not only by audiences, but by a silent film industry hungry for adventure stories that required minimal dialogue and had strong visual appeal. His tales of simple struggles in spectacular wilderness settings were perfect film fodder.[123] It was typical, however, that when his animal-centered stories found their way to the screen the supporting human characters in them were given proportionately larger roles and allowed to carry the story. This was true in Vitagraph's film version of *Baree, Son of Kazan* (1917). Still, there was so much cinematic potential in these stories that not only did Vitagraph film *Baree* a second time (in 1925), but a film production company called Canadian Photoplays Ltd. set up shop in Calgary exclusively to film Curwood's stories in rugged natural locations. Its 1919 production of *Back to God's Country*, based on Curwood's *Wapi the Walrus*, was described by *Photoplay* magazine as having "some of the most remarkable animal stuff every photographed."[124]

The novel *Nomads of the North* (1919) demonstrated once again Curwood's refinement of an animal story formula that could be easily adapted to the screen. A film version of *Nomads* was released in 1920, featuring Lon Chaney and Lewis Stone. Although transformed into a fairly standard romantic melodrama, it nevertheless maintained as a subplot the novel's story of an orphan bear cub and the dog it befriends. Some remarkable animal footage ensues, much of it filmed in rugged outdoor locations, as a number of motifs are rehearsed that would later become standard elements in wild animal films, especially those by Disney (who released a remake of *Nomads* called *Nikki, Wild Dog of the North* in 1961). Many of these elements were seen again the following year, 1921, when *Kazan* was brought to the screen, featuring the celebrated Olympic athlete Jim Thorpe in a lead role.[195] Like *Nomads,* it told a story that included trappers, Mounties, and a last-minute animal rescue, as the wolf-dog protagonist saves a young woman in distress.

Such melodrama would not, of course, continue to be a part of the development of wildlife film. Yet the cycle of wilderness dramas Curwood helped create, in the years before sound film, helped advance the screen depiction of wild animals from exotic curiosities to fully developed characters in well-constructed narratives—indeed, they could even be *heroes.* Wild animals were thus integrated into the formal structures of narrative cinema, from shot/reverse-shot editing to close-ups, that helped individualize them as characters, to point-of-view shots that allowed us to see things from their perspective. Taken in concert, these techniques helped viewers identify emotionally with animal characters, perhaps almost as much as with humans. Significantly, it was the following year, 1922, that Rin Tin Tin became a "star" in Hollywood.[126] Loved by audiences, he received top billing over his human co-stars until his death in 1932 (although the techniques for creating emotional identification with a canine character are used to greater effect in 1943's *Lassie Come Home* as well as in the *Lassie* television series from the 1950s).

The creation of fully rounded animal screen characters, and the application of filmic storytelling conventions to them, were not restricted to wild animals in outdoor settings. Norman O. Dawn's mock melodrama *The Eternal Triangle* (Universal, 1919) featured an all-dog cast in an intentionally cliché-ridden story about "a lovers' configuration between a collie couple" and "a shifty poodle from the big city."[127] Essentially an updated fable with animals in human roles, the film was viewed as little more than an amusing novelty. It is remarkable, however, for demonstrating only four years after *Birth of a Nation* how effectively the formal codes of classical cinema could be applied to animals (and perhaps, therefore, how unnecessary were some of the histrionics characteristic of the acting styles of the day).

Yet, like the domesticated animals in *The Eternal Triangle,* most depictions of wild species, such as those in *Nomads of the North* also depended on individual animals that were tame (in part because telephoto lenses had not yet come into widespread use). Tame or not, the close-up view of animal behavior in *Nomads* (only some of which is staged) is in many ways more compelling than the static, often protracted long-shots that characterized much of the work of Martin and Osa Johnson. The distinction is an important one, for what *Nomads* and films like it did was to find a filmic equivalent to the close-up intimacy with wild animals that had thrilled audiences in the stories of the nature writers. It was this sort of sustained, intimate, close-up view that individualized the animals and made characters of them, in turn making it possible to build narratives around them. By contrast, many of the wild animal and natural history films up to this time, including (if not especially) those of the Johnsons, seemed distant and emotionally unengaging. In truth, the Johnsons' style in the early years may have been in part technologically determined. Although telephoto lenses would have allowed a more intimate approach, Osa Johnson later claimed she and Martin "were dissatisfied with the results because the pictures were unsteady and gave us fuzzy foregrounds."[128] The animal sequences in the Johnsons' films were thus more authentic in some ways than those in animal melodramas, yet were almost never shot for narrative editing, scene construction, or character creation in the way that the animal footage in *Nomads* was, and in the way that virtually all wildlife films are today. The Johnsons' films usually featured rudimentary narratives, and in some cases real drama, yet it was the Johnsons themselves, ultimately, on whom it all hung. By inserting faked reaction shots of themselves into wildlife scenes, it was their point-of-view that dominated, and their experiences, not those of the animals, that gave shape to even their best animal footage. The wildlife drama in virtually all their films thus lay in *their* encounter with the animals, not in the behavior and interactions of the animals themselves. In this sense, the more objectively filmed wildlife scenes in *Nomads*, although staged, are closer than the Johnsons' work, *formally*, to the blue chip wildlife films of today.[129]

At the same time as these developments in the United States, however, the "Secrets of Nature" team in Britain was developing another kind of close-up, intimate view of the natural world. Although the eight- to ten-minute length of these films did not lend them to the sort of narrative and character development found in feature-length films, producer/directors Field and Smith nevertheless set out to find ways of marrying science and storytelling, or at least of conveying science by way of stories. In looking back over the first ten years of work on the series, Field hailed the detailed research and careful attention to scientific procedure that went into making the "Secrets," touting several of them as valuable scientific studies in their own right. She concluded nevertheless that a film "is essentially a story told in pictures," and, in direct contravention of the tenets of scientific research, argued further that making a good "Secret" required having a fairly clear idea of "how the story is to end."[130] In a more comprehensive statement, Field makes clear her commitment to the conventional narrative structure of mainstream feature films: "All films, whether eight-reel features or one-reel 'Secrets of Nature,' ought to be complete works of art. They ought to have a beginning, carefully thought out, from which they should move logically through to a middle, and, with no extraneous material, no clouding or muddling of the issue, they should progress to that end which the beginning demanded, and there stop dead with no anticlimax."[131]

Fields's frequent references to animals as "stars" and "villains" and occasional remarks such as, "sheep and deer have no star value"[132] might be seen as harmless enough conveniences of speech, intended only as mildly ironic metaphors, were it not for some of the more questionable areas of animal storytelling on film of which she and Smith may have been "pioneers." Films such as *Story of Peter the Raven* (1922) and *Brock the Badger* (1933) show that despite their commitment to scientific revelation they were quick to give animals names and to make characters of them, even if the length of their films prevented sustained character development. More revealing, indeed quite startling, is Fields's disclosure that the "Secrets" team had even tried to apply devices from Disney cartoons (creative editing, music, etc.) to real animals. Significantly, it would be several more years before Disney himself would get the idea to Disnify actual wild animals on film.[133]

Drama, Story, Science, and Sound

The early sound years saw developments in wildlife films in both drama and science—or perhaps *pseudo*-science. Cinema had been redefined as a talking medium, freeing films about wildlife and natural history from having to compete with Hollywood completely on its terms (although in some ways they have never stopped doing this), and they continued to feel their way toward the intersection of science and storytelling. The "Secrets of Nature" producers made their brief nod in the direction of Disneyesque science popularization in the early 1930s. Stacy Woodard soon followed with his close-up insect dramas combining the trappings of laboratory science with Hollywood-style drama. Fortunately, Woodard avoided using the term "documentary" to describe his filmic endeavors, but his heavy reliance on terminology borrowed from the theater and from mainstream narrative cinema made clear his dramatic intentions. "We had actors on our stage," he wrote, "insects living the intense drama of nature."[134] Yet merely having one's actors present was not enough. The drama still had to be scripted, staged, and directed: "Frequently it has been necessary to set the stage to reproduce the desert in miniature . . . in order that they [the insects] might conduct their natural amours, seize their natural prey, and fight their battles *under our direction.*"[135]

Unable to find in nature the behavior he needed for his dramatic conception of insect life, and finding it difficult to film naturally occurring behavior in the way he wished to portray it, Woodard opted for the control of the film studio. "Back to Hollywood I went, to the silence of a sound-proof room. There I built a tiny stage, camouflaging it so that it would look to the little actors exactly like their desert home."[136]

The line between the film studio and the scientific laboratory had long been a fairly permeable one, beginning with the efforts of Muybridge and Marey to develop motion picture technology as a scientific research tool. Early works of micro-cinematography like those in Urban's "Unseen World" series, followed by similar close-up studies by Percy Smith, Raymond Ditmars, and others, including the "Secrets of Nature" series, all showed that the film studio and the scientific laboratory had enjoyed a close relationship virtually since the birth of cinema. The way was thus well paved for the emergence in 1968 of Oxford Scientific Films, and later for macro-photographic works such as *The Hellstrom Chronicles* (1971) and *Microcosmos* (1996), *Alien Empire* (1996), and *Beetlemania* (1996).

Yet as Woodard was carrying out his "research" in the early 1930s, and the "Secrets of Nature" series entered its second decade as the "Secrets of Life," most audience members' exposure to film images of animals in the wild still came from hunting and safari pictures. The undisputed leaders in this field remained the Johnsons, who had taken cameras into remote locations, exhibited Keartonesque patience in filming under harsh conditions, and gotten as close to wild animals in their natural habitats as any filmmakers could have. But they could not tell a story.

Ernest B. Schoedsack could. Moreover, he could film under much more difficult physical conditions, make do with far less personnel and materials, and still come up with a solid dramatic story. This had been clear from his collaboration with Merian C. Cooper on the acclaimed documentary *Grass* (1925), which depicted the grueling migration of Bakhtiari tribesfolk over the Zardeh Kuh mountains in Turkey and Persia. Barnouw has complained that "the people in the film remain a mass of strangers to the audience," and that "no individual portrait emerges from them."[137] Yet this was decidedly not the case in Cooper and Schoedsack's next film for Paramount, *Chang* (1927), which centered on a single family in a small village in Siam (Thailand). It featured a simple but compelling story about their struggle to survive frequent confrontations with the wild animals that inhabited the surrounding forests. The wildlife footage in the film was worth remarking. In an essay written years later, in 1941, Richard Griffith, then curator of the Museum of Modern Art Film Library, still found that "the wild animals are uncomfortably close. . . . Even with telescopic lenses and automatic cameras, Schoedsack had to risk life and limb a dozen times to secure these extraordinary shots of charging tigers, pouncing leopards, elephants on the rampage."[138] Considering that *Chang* was made in 1927, its still compelling close-up view of wild animals must be counted as a contribution to the development of the wildlife genre, even if it was not a wildlife film itself.

In truth, however, its dramatic portrayal of marauding animals terrorizing the village is overblown, and is an unfortunate concession both to the ideology of violent subjugation of nature and apparently to studio pressures. Barnouw has also praised the film's "impressive animal sequences," but notes that they were "set in a story framework that must have been part of Hollywood preplanning."[139] William K. Everson has also pointed to the apparent influence of Hollywood in shaping the film's story, and rightly concludes, therefore, that it is "not a documentary," but an "adventure film

without stars." Yet his sensitivity to the film's subtly different levels of artifice brings us closer to the formal differences between wildlife film and
documentary. "Little is really faked," Everson notes, "but it is all very carefully 'arranged' and even staged." The difference between this, however, and
the crude scenes of animals fighting in the films of Frank Buck and others,
lies in Cooper and Schoedsack's meticulous efforts to include "cutaways and
alternate camera angles." [140] Not only did these sorts of devices set narrative
cinema apart formally from documentary (where their strict avoidance is
often a guarantor of authenticity), but they would become essential ingredients in wildlife film as it began to take shape as a narrative genre.

The well-constructed, dramatic animal scenes in *Chang* helped set the
stage for Schoedsack's own project for Paramount a couple of years later, a
solo venture entitled *Rango* (1931). Although it resembles *Chang* in setting
and theme, *Rango* takes a closer and more sympathetic look at the creatures
of the Sumatran forest, especially the orang-utans who are its focus (the
Sumatran tiger is, unfortunately, portrayed as vermin). In this modest little
picture lie not the seeds of modern wildlife film, which had long since been
planted, but arguably, its first real bloom. *Rango* includes patient, close-up
studies of animal behavior and interaction, voice-over narration, a convincing sound-effects track (although it was shot silent), continuity editing, and
above all a coherent story centering on an animal protagonist who engages
our sympathies, and with whom we can identify emotionally. The result may
well be the first fully realized wildlife film, in the modern sense, and the first
feature-length prototype of the classic narrative model that would soon give
definition to wildlife films as a distinct film genre.

Perhaps as a way of making *Rango* seem more of a *talkie*, a scripted studio-
filmed prologue was added in which a man recounts the story of Rango,
the young orang-utan, to his own young son (with obvious parallels). As he
speaks, a series of dissolves takes us visually to the forests of Sumatra, where
the actual story will take place. The camera zooms and tracks forward, and
soon settles on a single orang-utan sitting high in a tree. We are thus introduced to Tua, the father of Rango and himself one of the central figures
in the story. Formally, the sequence is unremarkable—indeed, it is a typical opening for motion pictures of the time. Yet this is an atypical film, for
its main characters are not played by human actors, but are wild animals in
their natural habitat. It is difficult now to appreciate how far ahead of its
time Schoedsack's film was in the straightforward way in which it establishes
animal characters, then proceeds to tell a story that reveals their individual
personalities and explore their intimate lives. Although this was what the
nature writers had attempted to do on the printed page thirty years earlier,
motion pictures had been slow to embrace and develop this kind of animal
storytelling. There had, of course, been some tentative gestures in this di-

rection in films such as *Nomads of the North*, but the films more often thought of as early wildlife films, such as the Johnsons' *Simba*, had failed altogether to accomplish this.

Schoedsack not only had a story to tell, but moved his animal characters to its center and allowed them to carry its weight. It begins and ends with them, and is ultimately their story. If we in the audience are able to identify with the orang-utans as the story's protagonists, it is not because of what the narrator tells us, but because Schoedsack reveals to us their individual personalities in close-up. Here, like in modern wildlife films, his camera patiently captures intimate details of authentic behavior, some of it apparently filmed high off the ground where wild orangs spend most of their lives. Schoedsack's narrative pacing remains leisurely rather than forced, and allows for many more scenes of authentic wild behavior, most of which are filmed in a far more intimate and revealing fashion than almost anything in the Johnsons' entire *oeuvre*. As we watch monkeys feeding, the commentary sounds almost like it was written for George Page or David Attenborough: "These are very happy moments for them. In fact, when there are no tigers or leopards about it's like a holiday." In many ways only its black-and-white photography keeps *Rango* from appearing contemporary alongside more recent films with primate protagonists, such as *Mozu, the Snow Monkey* (1987), *People of the Forest* (1989), *Di Di's Story* (1996), and *Mountain Gorilla: A Shattered Kingdom* (1996).

Having engaged our sympathies for the forest's primates, Schoedsack introduces us to Ali, the tiger hunter in the human village below the forest canopy. He and his young son make up the third father-son relationship in the film, and the one that directly parallels and intersects that of Tua and Rango. The story's real dramatic conflict, however, centers on the tiger, whose loud roar appears (by way of overly-dramatic editing) to send the entire animal population running in terror. The scene is overwrought, but far more convincing, and far more cinematic, than the Johnsons' technique of intercutting close-ups of themselves to convey the tense emotion in a scene. It is also clearly conceived to advance the film's overall narrative rather than merely to create momentary, throwaway dramatic tension. Happily, a sequence of the orang-utans getting into Ali's house and raiding the food stores, while mildly comical, is not staged and played as slapstick in the way that similar scenes are in Disney's *Yellowstone Cubs* (1963), and Stouffer's *Fishers in the Family* (1984). As Tua and Rango wrestle on the floor the scene becomes a study of their behavior and interactions (although another such scene with monkeys raiding the house is set to music clearly intended to make it comical).

The tiger, however, is an ever-present danger to such poignancy—or so we are told in one of the narration's most regrettable excesses: "It must be remembered that any way is a good way to kill tigers. They're a menace to every creature that lives. They're outlaws—ferocious, cunning, greedy, with but one thought: to kill." As this passage illustrates, if *Rango* is lacking in any department, it is in its science and its sensitivity to wildlife preservation issues. What anchors the film in its own historical epoch even more than its black-and-white imagery is precisely this lack of natural history awareness and context. Although Schoedsack shows us a good deal of solid wildlife footage, nearly all of which includes revealing behavior, there is no attempt in the commentary to explain its significance, to put it in context, or to expand our scientific understanding of it.

Some of this footage is so good it needs no commentary. Among the memorable and revealing scenes is one in which the young Rango climbs up a tree and discovers a bird's nest: the amazement and wonder evident in his face (or do we project it there?) tell us all we need to know. The scene was obviously prepared in advance, photographed in close-up, and analytically edited, but the behavior is not forced or provoked; in this sense it illustrates Everson's astute remarks on the differences between being "faked" and "arranged." More important, however, is the fact that this approach to filming wildlife, with its intimate vignette of natural behavior, combined Schoedsack's superb camera work with the gentle inquisitiveness of Pike, the patience of Kearton, and above all the ability of Seton and Curwood to tell stories with three-dimensional animal characters. In this sense *Rango* is not only different from preceding films about wild animals, but also anticipates the style that would characterize the finest blue chip films decades later.

From a storytelling standpoint, however, the film's conclusion, in which the young Rango is caught and killed by the tiger, may be something of a surprise. Schoedsack opted for an ending similar to the animal stories of Charles G. D. Roberts: a life is lost, as happens in the wild, but it is clearly not the life we would expect or wish to see lost. Although the tiger is vanquished, the film nevertheless ends on a note of desolation and despair after Rango's death, rather than celebrating nature's cyclical, regenerative processes. Instead of Rango surviving a rite of passage and beginning his own family, we see old Tua sitting forlornly in a treetop, waiting (we are told) for a son who will never return. Schoedsack had taken wild animal storytelling to the brink of modernity, but in the end did not broaden his story back out to the level of animal species interrelationships. Instead, it remains at the level of individual characters, where every death is tragic. Nevertheless, *Rango* had shown that a character study of an individual animal could also be (or perhaps could not avoid being) an animal behavior study as well, and therefore, ultimately, a profile of an entire species with genuine scientific potential.

Hollywood Takes Over

It was with some irony, then, that a storyline emphasizing nature's eternally recurring cycles did not come from Schoedsack's experiences on location in the fecund rainforests of Sumatra, but from Hollywood itself, from the studios that epitomized Hollywood style and polish on the one hand, and its childlike fantasies on the other: MGM and Disney. Although Paramount had been the most successful of the majors in bringing nonmainstream outdoor adventures to the screen in films like *Grass, Chang*, and Flaherty's *Moana* (1926), MGM was also eyeing the possibilities in such exotic themes and locales. Their versions would, however, be more mainstream, having higher production values, tighter scripting and control, and leaving less to chance. In 1929 MGM sent director W. S. ("Woody") Van Dyke, cameraman Clyde DaVinna (soon to win an Academy Award), and a cast that included Harry Carey and Duncan Renaldo to Africa to begin shooting the early sound film *Trader Horn* (1931). Some of the wildlife footage DaVinna shot there showed up the following year in Van Dyke's *Tarzan the Ape Man* (1932), with Johnny Weismuller, and has since been recycled in many MGM dramas.[141]

In 1933 MGM assigned DaVinna to shoot another outdoor adventure, this one with an even greater emphasis on animals. Called *Sequoia*, it was filmed in Sequoia National Park, high in the Sierra Nevada mountains of California, under the direction of Chester Franklin.[142] The story was based on the novel *Malibu* (1931), by Vance Joseph Hoyt, about two young orphan animals—a mountain lion and a deer. Adopted as infants by a young girl and given the names "Gato" and "Malibu," they are raised together and remain lifelong friends. Although the film differed from *Rango* in that its human characters were given more screen time and dialogue, its real strength, as reviewers were quick to note, was the wildlife footage in which the animals were left alone to interact with each other. Some of it is indeed quite remarkable.

The experiences of making *Trader Horn* and *Tarzan* had acquainted MGM with the difficulties of filming wild animals.[143] For *Sequoia* the studio built an enclosure in which to film the animals. Their scenes could thus be carefully lit and photographed, and made to reflect the MGM gloss. This elaborate compound, and the nearly fifteen months of on-again off-again shooting there, made *Sequoia* one of the biggest and most expensive wildlife filming projects up to that time. Even though it was neither a "pure" wildlife film nor unflawed in its wildlife sequences (Malibu, for example, kept his photogenic antlers all year round), *Sequoia* helped assert the viability of wildlife storytelling on film in the early sound years, and also helped further codify and legitimize the narrative model that would become the classic one for wildlife films. In addition, the MGM imprimatur, the most prestigious in Hollywood, was an undeniably valuable endorsement of wildlife filmmaking. Paramount even considered producing a sequel to *Sequoia*, to be called *Wild Glory*, but later abandoned the plan.[144]

Yet *Sequoia* may seem today like an unusual project for MGM to have undertaken at that time, for not only did it hark back to some of the silent versions of Curwood's stories more than a decade earlier (Hoyt's novel, with its theme of compassion for wild animals, was decidedly Curwoodesque), but it was also a clear departure from the "galaxy of stars" image MGM sought to project. Nevertheless, at the same time as *Sequoia* began production in 1933, MGM also acquired the screen rights to Felix Salten's novel *Bambi*. The property was bought by Sidney Franklin, who was not only one of the top producers and directors at MGM, and a favorite of Irving Thalberg, but also the younger brother of Chester Franklin, *Sequoia*'s director. His intention was not to make an animated feature of *Bambi*, as Disney later would, but to film it, too, as a live action drama—except that the animals would would talk. The plan never materialized, but it is probably no coincidence that Franklin later produced *The Yearling* (1947), another story involving an orphaned deer.

It was probably also no coincidence that the Franklins both found themselves, in 1933–34, working on films about wild deer in the forest. They had made a number of films together during the teens, several with similar nature themes. It seems that what Franklin the younger had in mind for *Bambi* was (save for the voices) something very much like what would become the classic model of wildlife film, and a model for a number of blue chip films many years later in which the story of a single animal is told against a spectacular natural backdrop. The most complete account of the long effort to bring *Bambi* to the screen is undoubtedly the one written by Ollie Johnston and Frank Thomas (1990), who worked on Disney's version of the story and who were in on most of that film's planning. They write that Sidney Franklin saw in Salten's book "poetry, beauty, philosophy," and that his vision of the film was one of "the wind brushing softly against the tall grasses, the warm sun on the meadow, the grandeur of the forest and the majesty of the creatures who lived and died there."[145] He sought for two years to find the right voices for his conception of the story, reportedly testing Victor Jory and Margaret Sullavan, among others, as voice actors. In 1935, shortly after the release of his brother's film *Sequoia* and perhaps even because of it, Sidney Franklin canceled his plans to produce *Bambi*. According to Johnston and Thomas, he decided that "the spirit of the book could never be captured" as a live action wildlife film with voice characterizations added, and so offered the property to Walt Disney, who in turn retained Franklin as a sort of creative consultant on the project.[146]

The original story of *Bambi* is similar to Curwood's *The Grizzly King* in several respects, but the eventual success of Disney's animated version, released in 1942, marked Salten's story as *the* written work responsible for bringing to the screen the narrative of a young animal who is descended from royalty, but who is orphaned at a young age, and whose coming-of-age trials are therefore even more intense and difficult tests of character. Although Disney's animated *Bambi* cannot, of course, be considered a wildlife film, there is little doubt that it set in place some structural supports upon which the studio later built its live action wildlife films. Elements of the basic storyline underlying *Bambi* were honed, refined, perfected, and ultimately institutionalized as conventions of wildlife filmmaking. They formed the central pillars of what was to become the classic narrative model of wildlife film, which, arguably, brought the genre together as a coherent entity.

Coda

At this point it seems useful to take stock of the first half century or so of wildlife film's evolution both as a narrative form and as a coherent film genre—in the United States and Britain, at least. After the early appearance of wildlife images in feeding films, hunting and safari films, and educational documentaries, the dominant cinema was most closely paralleled in the narrative animal adventures that emerged in the late teens, in part growing out of a well-established genre of popular literature. They had adopted the storytelling patterns and animal characterizations of the nature writers, as well as the formal narrative codes of classical cinema, and had brought film images of wildlife into the mainstream. Unlike the other forms, however, where wildlife and the natural world were experienced as objects of curiosity, or as fodder for conquest, in narrative adventures wildlife and nature were individualized, personified, and experienced on a personal, emotional level.

These narrative adventures could, moreover, be divided into two subcategories: those about animals without people (giving rise to the blue chip wildlife films of later years), and those about animals involved with people. The latter type involved more scripting and overall control, and had greater mainstream potential. It could already be seen in the early wild horse dramas *Smoky* (1933) and *King of the Sierras* (1938), and the Norman O. Dawn "northerns," *Tundra* (1936), *Call of the Yukon* (1938—from a Curwood novel), *Orphans of the North* (1940), and *Taku* (1940). Arne Sucksdorff's *August Rhapsody* (1939), *Reindeer Time* (1943), and *The Great Adventure* (1953) are also all in this tradition. In the postwar years the animal-human interaction model could be seen in such thoroughly mainstream films as the much loved *Lassie Come Home* (1943) and its equine reworking *The Gypsy Colt* (1954). Later there would be *Born Free* (1966), its sequel *Living Free* (1972), and eventually Carroll Ballard's *Never Cry Wolf* (1983).[147] During the 1980s and 1990s there would also be dozens of films of this sort aimed at children, with child heroes inserted into wildlife narratives in films such as *Cheetah* (1988) and *The Great Panda Adventure* (1995).

It would still take some time, however, before the thoughts and feelings of animal characters could be effectively communicated on film—at least, without resorting to voice characterizations of the sort Sidney Franklin had planned for *Bambi*, and that would later show up in *Homeward Bound* (1993) and *Babe* (1995). Voice-over commentary could, however, make up for the lack of speaking characters. Just as the nature writers' omniscient narrators had, the film narrator could fill in for us the animals' thoughts and feelings, their appetites and passions, their joys and sorrows. Commentary could not only round out characters and pull together narratives, but also add scientific information that allowed animal stories, framed in the conventions of the classical film style, to serve as illustrations of scientific principles. As science and storytelling came closer together, animal narrative adventures stood poised to absorb, or to co-opt, or perhaps simply to merge with scientific documentaries and safari films. The three types of film did not always mix well, and sometimes remained unmixed, but the currents were nevertheless coming together. Although World War II temporarily absorbed the attentions of filmmakers and the energy and momentum that had gone into the evolution of the wildlife genre, everything was in place for a strong postwar resurgence in production of wildlife and natural history film—and television.

4
The Classic Model

The inevitability of narrative had brought about the eclipse of the nature essay by the animal story, just as the animal *actualité* had given way to action-adventure, hunting, and safari films.[1] Yet personifying and individualizing nature led inexorably to reliance on animal characters with whom audiences could sympathize and even identify emotionally. Arguably, all character-centered stories (which may mean, ultimately, *all stories*) involve some kind of identification. "Unless we are able to relate our feelings and experiences to those of the characters in the fiction," notes Cawelti, "much of the emotional effect will be lost."[2] We have already seen how this is achieved in movies by way of a formal system worked out early in their history, and how it could be applied to animals as easily as to humans. If identifying with animals in wildlife films is complicated by anything, it may not be that they are animals but that wildlife films are combinations of science and storytelling, both mimetic and mythic/formulaic, both an image of reality and of a world defined by dramatic convention projected onto reality.

In mimetic fiction, identification involves recognizing and accepting our emotional involvement with, as Cawelti puts it, "characters, motives, and situations we would not ordinarily choose to imagine ourselves involved in or threatened by."[3] Take, for example, a film that follows the story of a young male lion. Endearing and charming as a cub, graceful and impressive as an adult, we may find it easy to become emotionally involved in the story of his "struggle to survive" in a harsh, unforgiving environment. After he moves into a pride of females, however, and suddenly begins a campaign of systematic infanticide, killing every cub sired by the male(s) he has displaced, we are forced to come to terms with the emotional investment we have made in this character. The challenge posed by a realistic portrayal of this sort is to confront the apparent moral ambiguities of the situation and through them the complexities of life. We must to try to understand rather than simply to condemn or turn away.

In mythic/formulaic stories, however, from myths and legends to modern mass-produced fictions, the protagonists are typically *heroes* whose morally unambiguous adventures offer escape rather than confrontation with difficult questions. Because of their formulaic nature, wildlife films fall just as heavily into this category—but can wild animals be *heroes*? The nineteenth century's "Christian ornithology" had already shown they could be moral exemplars. Well crafted fiction, however, could create strong animal characters who could function even more effectively as idealized embodiments of morally and socially desirable qualities. Realistically rendered, they could be made fully rounded individuals with distinct personalities and personal histories. This was at first more easily achieved on the written page than on film, but as cinematic narrative conventions were adapted to animals, the successes of Rin Tin Tin, Lassie, and others showed how effectively motion pictures could create animal heroes, and how strong could be the emotional bonds audiences felt with them. Perhaps above all, they showed that the drive toward some sort of character-centered, if not overtly *heroic* narrative was difficult to contain, even in films about animals. Of course, a trained dog in a scripted Hollywood picture was one thing; a wild animal filmed in its natural habitat was another. Or was it?

Narrative Tradition

In earlier narrative forms, even animals and humans had often been interchangeable. Traditional narratives (fables, tales, myths[4]) had long cast animals in essentially human dramas. Vladimir Propp, in his well-known study of folk tales, noted that the folk tale form "ascribes with great ease identical actions to persons, objects, and animals."[5] As film and television took over the task of passing on the culture's myths and tales, and of reenacting its ritual dramas, there seemed little reason to expect sharp divisions between the ways images of wild and domestic animals could be put to narrative. What worked for a Hollywood *wonder dog* could, with a few adjustments, work for a wild animal, whether a predator (a wolf, a mountain lion) or a member of prey species (a deer, a rabbit). Narrative standardization made it possible for domestic animals to be cast in wilderness sagas, as in *The Incredible Journey* (1963), or *Milo and Otis* (1986) and, conversely, for wild animals to appear in stories set in the jungle of human society and technology, as in Disney's *Yellowstone Cubs* (1963), Survival's *The Leopard That Changed its Spots* (1978), or Stouffer's *Fishers in the Family* (1984).[6] In each case the story line, motivated by the question, *will they find their way home—and how?* is obviously a variation on the ancient theme of the *quest*, which had already given rise to a kind of standardized narrative that could be traced from the *Odyssey* to *Don Quixote* to the novels of Raymond Chandler.

Film and television's mode of industrialized storytelling was itself a force for narrative standardization through its pressure to exploit saleable formulas. As filmmakers brought up in the dominant storytelling traditions turned their attention to wild animals, and as they competed on the margins of a predominantly narrative industry, there was little reason why accepted storytelling conventions and formulas should be abandoned, so long as they could be made to sell. Moreover, familiar patterns of narrative and character development, dramatic structure, conflict and resolution, and the like were all so deeply embedded in the formal conventions of motion pictures that they were hard to avoid even in films about wild animals. Character development was intensified even further when wildlife films moved to television, which with its smaller screen was a close-up medium given to tight framings promoting greater intimacy (or at least *pseudo*-intimacy) and thus a greater emphasis on character.[7]

Yet although wildlife films continued to be absorbed into the mainstream of media commodities, they could still not function independently of their culture's time-tested storytelling traditions, or be exempt from reenacting its ritual dramas and reinforcing its values. Will Wright has noted that the same is true of westerns, which are "created by specific individuals for popular acceptance," yet are nevertheless "based on a social myth."[8] Wildlife films likewise often consist of traditional narratives that are repackaged for sale to popular audiences rather than passed down through public retellings. As such, they come to us not as organic products of a folk culture but as elements of folk cultural forms that have been appropriated and offered back to us at a price.[9] The industrialization of storytelling has not meant that traditional narratives were scrapped, but that they were adapted to mass-production, distribution, and marketing.

There seemed little reason why, for example, wildlife films should not adopt the familiar narrative of a brave character persevering against overwhelming odds, perhaps even vanquishing foes, and ultimately emerging in triumph.[10] Likewise, there was little reason why wildlife films should not have rising and falling action, dramatic conflicts and resolutions, uplifting endings, perhaps even a little comedy or tragedy. Was there any reason, therefore, why they should not also have heroes, or for that matter villains? There was one: *none of these things are found in nature*. Bravery, heroism, drama, tragedy, comedy, good, evil, and even narrative itself may all be among the categories by which we make sense of the natural world, but we project them onto it just as surely as we look into the stars and see a giant dipper.

Yet the argument that there are no "stories" in nature, no beginnings, middles, or ends, has long been seen as academic hairsplitting; niggling details such as this can be easily overlooked, and generally are.[11] Wildlife films can hardly be expected to succeed, after all, or even to communicate effectively without evoking patterns their audiences would recognize, or without making use of conventions of which audiences had at least some tacit understanding from previous experience. In practice, this meant borrowing from what has been called "the publicly available stock of symbols,"[12] which in this case included familiar plot patterns and character types.

These do not even need to be culturally specific to work; indeed, the more general they are, the more familiar and accessible they are likely to be to more people. Cawelti notes, for example, that "general plot patterns are not necessarily limited to a specific culture or period. Instead, they seem to represent story types that, if not universal in their appeal, have certainly been popular in many different cultures at many different times. In fact, they are examples of what some scholars have called archetypes or patterns that appeal in many different cultures."[13] These include everything from his example of "manuals for aspiring writers that give recipes for twenty-one sure-fire plots" (e.g., boy meets girl, boy loses girl, boy gets girl back)[14] to the archetypal patterns found in older, more traditional narratives around the world. These often reveal fundamental similarities, whether or not they are products of so-called "civilized" or "primitive" cultures.[15] This surprising unanimity among traditional narratives around the world drew the attention of some of the twentieth century's most esteemed thinkers, whose attempts to account for it ranged from speculations about similarities of mind (general traits in the human psyche), to notions of a "collective unconscious," to theories of mythic migration and cultural borrowing.[16] In contemplating the "astounding similarity between myths collected in widely different regions," Lévi-Strauss was left asking, "how are we going to explain the fact that myths throughout the world are so similar?"[17] Joseph Campbell concluded, "it will always be the one, shape-shifting yet marvelously constant story that we find," and that there is "astonishingly little variation in the morphology of the adventure, the character roles involved, the victories gained."[18]

The common patterns in myths and other traditional narratives around the world are so similar in fact, that Campbell distilled from them a "monomyth" (a term first used by Joyce in *Finnegans Wake*), or basic plot model representing the "deep structure" underlying many of the world's mythic systems and storytelling traditions—especially those, like our own, that tend to be devoted to the adventures of a heroic central figure. "The standard path of the mythological adventure of the hero," Campbell observed, "is a magnification of the formula represented in rites of passage: *separation—initiation—return*."[19] In a closely parallel formation, Northrop Frye has described the form of the romance as a less exalted form of myth, but with three similar stages: "the perilous journey . . . the crucial struggle . . . and the exaltation of the hero."[20]

It is precisely on such traditional foundations that the classic model of wildlife film is built. Its archetypal pattern traces the story of an individual animal from birth, through the perils of youth, the trials of adolescence, and finally to the time when he (and in some cases *she*) enters society as an adult, often after a victory of some sort. The nature writers who preceded wildlife films also found that survival adventures alone "proved insufficient material for a worthy plot. The chosen animal must be a hero." [21] Although animal heroes may not be as overtly "heroic" as we have come to expect of our human heroes, they tend nevertheless to earn their hero status through some sort of display of courage, tenacity, or pluck (although ethologists might more accurately describe many of these as "fixed behaviors"), or by in some way embodying certain ideal qualities associated with the species.

Although narrative itself demands that an animal species be individualized, the idea that an individual can symbolize an entire species may be even easier to accept with animals than it is with humans, since it is widely held that there is less individuation among members of nonhuman species. Animals may even be better suited than humans to be characters in standardized narrative adventures, especially those understood to convey general truths. Yet the idea that the truths of the natural world can be understood through empathic identification with individual animal characters, however admirably portrayed, remains problematic, despite the widespread acceptance it gained through the work of the nature writers. It was Seton, with his criticism of the "vague, general treatment" of natural history, who had been most outspoken in promoting a more individual, character-centered approach to nature writing.[22] He had pushed to the foreground the notion that natural history could take the form of *biography*. Problematic or not, by the mid-twentieth century biography had gained wide popular acceptance as a form of nature discourse—not just in print, but in moving pictures as well. By the 1980s it had become so much a part of wildlife filmmaking, in fact, that Marty Stouffer reflected: "I think I will always be more inclined to film programs devoted to the life story of one particular animal. This is the *classic format* for wildlife films, and though I've never been reluctant to break the *rules*, it really is the most satisfying approach for a cinematographer." [23]

With characteristic candor, Stouffer provides an insider's view that there is indeed a "classic" format or model of wildlife film, that it is defined by a set of "rules" of which filmmakers are at least tacitly aware, even if they don't always follow them, and that these rules and conventions often mean having a strong central character and a biographical structure.[24] Moreover, "classicism" in wildlife films, arguably, means Disney, for it was during the period of the "True Life Adventures" that the genre's patterns, themes, and conventions came together and existed in their purest form, if only for a time, before spinning off into the variations we see today.

The Aura of *Fantasia*

It should have come as no surprise to anyone that, at the level of story and character, the "True Lifes" bore distinct similarities to Disney's cartoon films. After all, the studio had a well-oiled and efficient cartoon-making machine already up and running, producing standardized products with a consistent and recognizable style for two decades. In making wildlife films, the Disney factory fell back on the "strategic rituals" of its workplace. It mattered little whether the animals depicted were animated or real: the studio had its content formulas, and it applied them; it had its production routines, and it followed them; it had its creative personnel—seasoned writers, producers, and directors—and it put them to work. Some of those who worked on the "True Lifes" did, in fact, come straight out of cartoon production. As a result, the "True Life" films often had what one reviewer described as an "aura of *Fantasia*."[25]

Indeed, the man who may have been most responsible for the look and feel of that now beloved cartoon classic was a key figure in the production of the "True Life Adventures." Ben Sharpsteen had worked on dozens of animated shorts for Disney in the pre-"True Life" years, and after serving as production supervisor on *Fantasia* (1940) went on to perform the same role on the first "True Life" film, *Seal Island* (1948). After that he alternated easily between animation and "True Life," supervising production of the animated features *The Adventures of Ichabod and Mr. Toad* (1949), *Cinderella* (1950), and *Alice in Wonderland* (1951), as well as the "True Life" films *Beaver Valley* (1949) and *The Olympic Elk* (1952). He even directed *Water Birds* (1952) and served as associate producer on *Bear Country* (1952), *The Living Desert* (1953), and *The Vanishing Prairie* (1954). Increasing his involvement in the series as it became devoted more to feature-length productions, the man who had put the Disney stamp on *Fantasia* went on to be the producer of *The African Lion* (1955), *Secrets of Life* (1956), and *White Wilderness* (1958).

Another link between the "True Lifes" and Disney animation was scriptwriter Ted Sears. He had begun by working on Disney's film adaptations of *Snow White* and *Pinocchio* (1940), then coauthored the screenplays for *The Reluctant Dragon* (1941), *The Three Caballeros* (1945), *Fun & Fancy Free* (1947), *Melody Time*, *Ichabod and Mr. Toad*, *Cinderella*, and *Alice in Wonderland*. Significantly, he co-wrote the "True Life" shorts *Beaver Valley*, *Water Birds*, and *The Olympic Elk*, then in 1953 returned to animated fantasy in *Peter Pan* while also co-writing the feature-length "True Life" film, *The Living Desert*. That was followed by his work over the next two years on *The Vanishing Prairie* and *The African Lion*, before returning to writing for animated features in *Sleeping Beauty* (1959).

In retrospect, Sharpsteen and Sears were not specialists in cartoons or nature films, but were instead company men taking or being assigned to projects when and where needed, and helping bring to each a measure of stylistic and thematic unity.

Even more influential in shaping the "True Lifes" was the man who was their voice: narrator Winston Hibler. A key figure at Disney studios for nearly three decades, Hibler has been noted as one of the handful of producers who "piloted nearly all of the company's product." [26] Yet he was also one of the studio's most important writers. After co-writing *Melody Time*, his script credits closely paralleled those of Sears, in both animated and "True Life" films. In 1956–57 Hibler co-wrote, narrated, and even composed songs for *Perri*, the "True Life *Fantasy*" that pointed the way for Disney's animal films of the 1960s. Even before the "True Life" series ended, Hibler returned briefly to writing for animation with his story contributions to *Sleeping Beauty*, but thereafter confined himself primarily to films featuring animals or outdoor themes, in which he revealed his commitment to the classic model. *Nikki, Wild Dog of the North* (1961), *Charlie the Lonesome Cougar* (1967), and *King of the Grizzlies* (1970) are all formulaic exercises in its application.

Perhaps the central figure in the "True Life" series was James Algar, its house director and one of its chief writers. Algar began his work with Disney by designing characters for *Snow White* and later directed the famed "Sorcerer's Apprentice" sequence in *Fantasia*. Perhaps most significant was his work on *Bambi*. Johnston and Thomas have credited him with having directed the whole first half of it.[27] When the "True Life" series began, Algar not only directed but, along with Hibler and Sears, co-wrote several entries in the series, and was credited as the sole writer on *Bear Country, Secrets of Life, White Wilderness*, and *Jungle Cat* (1960). Like Hibler, his work in later years on such films as *The Legend of Lobo* (1962) and *The Incredible Journey* (1963) also revealed his commitment to the classic narrative model.

What this admittedly lengthy recitation of production credits and *curriculum vitae* shows is that most of the cross-fertilization between the Disney studio's cartoons and its wildlife films occurred at the level of the *writing*, where story and character are conceived.

The similarities were motivated, however, by economic concerns. Audiences so closely identified the Disney name with cartoons that maintaining some recognizable link to them was a way of reducing financial risk as the studio made its first tentative moves into commercial live action films. *The Reluctant Dragon, Saludos Amigos* (1943), *The Three Caballeros, Song of the South* (1946), *Fun & Fancy Free, Melody Time*, and *So Dear to My Heart* (1949) were all contrived, therefore, to include "safe" blends of live action and animated images—although the combination proved anything but safe, as some of these films were significant critical and box-office failures. Nevertheless, the move toward live action had begun; in interviews around the time of *Song of the South*, Walt Disney announced that most of his films from then on would include both animation and live action.[28] Given this pronounce-ment, as well as Roy Disney's initial skepticism about the viability of nature films, it may have been inevitable that *Seal Island*, and all the "True Lifes" that followed, included at least some animated images, if only as tokens. Clearly, the purpose was to avoid alienating loyal audiences, and to reassure them that these supposed "documentaries" were closely related to, if not creative extensions of, the Disney cartoon features they already knew and loved.

To this effect, the "True Lifes" opened with an animated paintbrush that painted in the landscape in each film's establishing shots, allowing the scen-ery to flow onto the screen magically in broad, colorful strokes. In *Secrets of Life* the most "scientific" of the "True Life" films, the magic paintbrush even created the transitions between sequences. If the film's title echoed that of the British series from two decades earlier, its extensive use of animation made clear the differences in intention as well as in general outlook upon the natural world. The "aura of *Fantasia*" was almost palpable. This was even more true later when edited versions of the "True Lifes" aired on Disney's television series, where each film emerged onto the screen through a shower of twinkling, animated fairy dust from Tinker Bell's magic wand. Ultimately, whether in theaters or on television, the films may have been live action, even "true life," but the animated images set the tone of childlike wonder.

Even the titles of individual "True Lifes" could reinforce the feeling of make-believe. They often referred not to real places but to quasi-mythic locales such as "Seal Island," "Beaver Valley," "Bear Country," and "Nature's Half Acre." Although *Seal Island* made no secret of the fact that it was filmed in the Pribiloff Islands in the Bering Sea, its title maintained the Disney buffer between "True Life" and reality. Renaming the Pribiloffs not only helped remove them from reality, but also idealized them, making them set-tings where myth could mediate nature and culture, such that our own so-cial and moral ideals could be reassuringly found among wild animals.

The physical world of these films often seems parallel to our own, but not quite one with it. Events often appear to take place outside of history as we know it. At times they even appear to be set chronologically before the ar-rival of humans, or in places where human civilization has had no effect— even when filmed in carefully managed areas like Yellowstone National Park (as in *Bear Country*). Freud once observed that "in fantasy, man can con-tinue to enjoy a freedom from the grip of the external world." He found an exact parallel in our enjoyment of "reservations and nature parks" that do not betray the presence of humans, and that "maintain the old condition of things . . . reclaimed from the encroaches of the reality-principle."[29] Such idealized portrayals of the natural world are the essence of today's blue chip wildlife films, which, despite their pretense of greater sophistication, typi-cally exclude images that would ground them in the historical present. As wish-fulfilling expressions of the pleasure-principle, their portrayal of the natural world does not differ all that much from the image of nature in the "True Life Adventures," or, for that matter, from the portrayal of the African savanna in *The Lion King* (1994).

The "aura of *Fantasia*" is still pervasive at Disney, where the lines have never been clearly drawn between animation and live action, between fantasy and fact, or, ultimately, between culture and nature. Again, however, nowhere have they allowed for more interpenetration of seeming opposites than in the areas of narrative and character. It is here, rather than in the celebrated visual style, where most of the humanizing of animals takes place, and where the real idealizing and sanitizing of nature occurs, as well as the most effective naturalizing of human values and behaviors. Virtually all Disney's films about animals, whether animated or live action, have made some use of dramatic or comic characterizations and situations familiar to audiences and deeply ingrained in storytelling patterns common to traditional narratives around the world. Although the "True Life" films were not themselves narrative adventures, they had enough of these elements to conform to audiences' expectations, and to echo received notions about the natural world. The results included graphic illustrations of folk beliefs and legends (e.g. that lemmings commit mass suicide), the repetition of cultural stereotypes (such as the innate "nobility" of some animals, e.g. the lion as "king" of beasts), assumptions that nature includes "good" animals (deer, rabbits, and songbirds) and "bad" ones (snakes and scorpions), as well as the notion that "heroes" and "villains" are also found among wild creatures. In this the "True Lifes" seemed at times to place undue emphasis on vulgar-Darwinist ideas about nature as a realm of constant conflict and struggle (while omitting mention of Darwin or evolution altogether). Yet despite the conflict and struggle, the "True Lifes" also reified notions of nature as God's own creation (as was especially evident in *Nature's Half Acre*), and celebrated nature's supposed commitment to idyllic monogamy, nuclear families, and lifelong parent-child relationships. However thick the air of unreality could be at times, it was the unavoidable result of translating into filmic terms the types of stories, situations, and characters representing some of our most enduring myths, cherished values, and deeply held attitudes—not just regarding nature, but also regarding notions of family, community, life, death, and divine creation.

The "Foolproof" Plot

An early Disney film illustrating some of these themes, as well as the basic structure of what would become the classic narrative model of wildlife film, is the 1941 animated feature *Dumbo*. Although widely overlooked as a precursor to the "True Lifes," it nevertheless marks one route by which animals in traditional narratives gained acceptance on the screen. In his book on Disney's films, Maltin refers twice to the simplicity of the story of *Dumbo* and quotes one of the film's animators, Ward Kimball, referring also to its "great simplicity" as well as to its "foolproof plot."[30] Yet what made it seem simple and foolproof was the fact that, like so many wildlife films today, its basic structure was so utterly familiar as to be almost invisible.

The plotting of the story is as follows: the hero is born, is separated from his mother, undergoes trials (initiation rites), proves his abilities, and eventually reenters the society of his own kind, no longer a helpless child. On the surface, it does indeed appear a model of simplicity. Examined more closely, however, the story resonates more deeply than merely at the level of a simple children's story. Its formulaic elements of *separation, initiation,* and *return* (Campbell), or *journey, struggle,* and *exaltation* (Frye), echo from the realms of myth and romance, where such trials and triumphs have traditionally been the stuff of which heroes are made. Even Dumbo's birth is celebrated as a special event at which the entire community of animals gathers, as if coming to pay tribute, suggesting from the start that he may be special in some way. As the plot unfolds, there are even more familiar patterns. Separation from his mother sets him on a symbolic journey from which it is clear that he must eventually return to rejoin his own kind. The trials he experiences along the way are part of the initiation process propelling him out of the helplessness of childhood (although not actually into adulthood), and revealing the ability that elevates him (literally) above the others. At last he is ready to return home in triumph.

Admittedly, this reading of the story emphasizes its mythic and religious parallels (as well as its psychoanalytic implications). Yet if such tales follow a mythic storyline, we shouldn't rush to call their protagonists *mythic heroes.* Campbell explains why:

> Typically, the hero of the fairy tale achieves a domestic, microcosmic triumph, and the hero of myth a world-historical macrocosmic triumph. Whereas the former—the younger or despised child who becomes master of extraordinary powers—prevails over his personal oppressors, the latter brings back from his adventure the means for regeneration of his society as a whole. Popular tales represent the heroic action as physical; the higher religions show the deed to be moral.[31]

The stories we are concerned with in wildlife films are, then, "tales" of "microcosmic triumphs." Like it or not, these are some of the same elements that have accounted for the appeal of another perennially childlike Disney character—Mickey Mouse. In an uncharacteristic aside on pop culture, Erich Fromm once observed that the Mickey cartoons also revealed a clear narrative formula: "the one theme—in so many variations—is this: something little is persecuted and endangered by something overwhelmingly strong, which threatens to kill or swallow the little thing. The little thing runs away and eventually succeeds in escaping or even in harming the enemy."[32] And there we have it: the simple plot formula that became the basis for many of the "mini-narrative" episodes in the "True Life Adventures." Consider Paul Kenworthy's elaborately choreographed scene in which the kangaroo rat escapes the king snake in *The Living Desert*; or the sequence in which the prairie dog escapes jaws and claws both above and below ground in *The Vanishing Prairie*. This pattern is found throughout *Perri*, in which the members of a squirrel colony are relentlessly pursued by a marten. The extent to which the formula was later institutionalized, and the extent, therefore, of Disney's influence in shaping expectations about wildlife, are revealed in the series of incidents recalled in the previous chapter when Marty Stouffer was told by American network executives that they were interested mainly in chases, narrow escapes, mothers risking their lives to save their young, and suspenseful cliffhangers.[33] It is difficult not to see these as variations on the "one theme" described by Fromm. What is significant here, however, is not only the extent to which television imposes such a formula on nature, but that this formula was already visible in Disney's work by 1941, the year Fromm's remarks were published, and the year that *Dumbo*, with its slightly different but nevertheless "foolproof" plot, was released.

What should be clear at this point is that a simple story with a "foolproof" plot is often one firmly grounded in traditional narratives. In wildlife films this is reflected in the focus on the life experiences of a single, endearing character, the *orphan* theme, the *journey* motif, and the overall coming-of-age story with its drama of trial and initiation, separation and return, struggle and exaltation. What *Dumbo* shows is that this narrative formula was fully formed and ready to go by the early 1940s, and was adaptable to widely differing types of animal adventures, from scientifically informed, realistically rendered stories to amusing cartoon fantasies.

Endearing Orphans, Incredible Journeys

Dumbo was not an exclusive Disney creation, but was based on a book by Helen Aberson and Harold Pearl. These literary origins link it even more directly to the tradition of animal storytelling in the works of the earlier nature writers. Curwood had put virtually the same thematic elements and plot structure to use in the more realistic setting of *The Grizzly King* (1916), and they are just as evident in Annaud's film version, *The Bear* (*L'Ours*, 1988). Again, the orphan/absent mother device creates the conditions from which the rest of the story flows. So much does Curwood's story depend on the orphaning of the young cub, in fact, that it is forced into the narrative without explanation. We never do learn how or why Muskwa came to be alone at such a young age, or what actually happened to his mother (although Annaud's film makes up for this weakness by including a scene depicting her death, and even flashes back to it later in a dream sequence). As in *Dumbo*, once the separation from the mother occurs, the young protagonist soon acquires a parental surrogate who shows him the ways of the world. In this case it is an older, more experienced adult male bear named Thor who "adopts" young Muskwa (the gross behavioral inaccuracies in this improbable scenario will be discussed later).

Together they set out on a cross-country journey that challenges the young cub with a number of trials. These include confrontations with other predators, with natural calamities, and with human hunters. His successful negotiation of these marks his coming of age, but such adventures, along with the unlikely pairing of the traveling companions themselves, made the journey in Curwood's story a truly *incredible* one, prefiguring by decades Sheila Burnford's novel *The Incredible Journey* (1961) in which a cat and two dogs embark on a similarly perilous trek. Significantly, the Disney studio found Burnford's animal odyssey so consistent with its own view of life in the wild as to film it *twice*—once in 1963 and again in 1993 under the title *Homeward Bound* (followed by a sequel, *Homeward Bound II*, in 1996).[34]

Journeys are, of course, like orphaned characters and rites-of-passage narratives, central elements in the mythic formula of separation-initiation-return, and in the romantic pattern of journey-struggle-exaltation. Curwood, however, succeeded in bringing these aspects of traditional narratives together with animals in a way that the earlier nature writers had not. Seton, for example, had failed to find a unifying plot device or overarching plot structure; his animal characters have been said to "drift from crisis to unrelated crisis."[35] Roberts supplied a unifying theme and plot structure in his stories about the relentless search for food (with its Darwinian suggestion of struggle for survival), but he, too, "was unable to develop a general repertoire of fresh characters and situations . . . [and] found it difficult to fill up his stories without repetition. The juxtaposition of two or even three parallel searches for food, climaxing in tragedy for at least one, eked out the material for several well-rounded stories, but it did not provide a *pattern* which was repeatedly reusable and fresh."[36]

Curwood found that pattern—*found*, not invented—and by 1916 had brought the animal story closer than it had ever been to filmable form. At the very least, some variation on separation-initiation-return, or journey-struggle-exaltation, gave a motion picture a clearer beginning, middle, and end. Moreover, stories involving young orphans were, and still are, almost certain to be more emotionally engaging than stories centering on the perpetual search for food by adult animals. They are also likely to be more visually compelling, as scenes of a young animal separated from its mother and wandering alone in the wilderness need almost no explanation or voice-over narration to have greater emotional impact. There seems little doubt that audiences will tend to root more strongly for a helpless child to escape danger than for a capable and experienced adult. It is likely that viewers could be induced to become emotionally involved in this sort of drama even in a clumsily made film.

With his precursor to the "foolproof" pattern in focus, Curwood applied it again in *Nomads of the North* (1919). Although the 1920 film version reduced the animals to supporting characters, it nevertheless retained as a subplot the story of Neeva, the orphan bear cub (Neewa in the book), who is adopted by a trapper (after he has killed and eaten its mother). In both the book and the film, the trapper apologizes to the cub for taking its mother's life, and as reparation commits himself to nurturing the young orphan, and thus acting as its surrogate parent. Still, the cub's initiation trials occur when it becomes separated from him after being tossed from a canoe in river rapids along with the trapper's dog Brimstone (Miki in the book). After pulling themselves ashore, they set off together on a cross-country journey described in one of the film's intertitles as an "adventure in the big wilderness." Along the way, they face the obligatory perils, including an aggressive mountain lion, but find their way home in triumph. In Disney's 1961 version, *Nikki, Wild Dog of the North*, this journey in search of home and family takes up much more screen time and is more clearly a series of initiation trials for the two young animals. Still, the earlier version shows that the prototype of the "incredible journey" was already developed by 1920, and was well on its way to becoming a convention in portrayals of wild animals. MGM's *Sequoia*, made just a few years later (1934), thus features a similar sequence that feels almost obligatory. When the orphaned deer and mountain lion, Malibu and Gato, are turned loose in the wilderness by Toni, the young girl who has raised them together, they find themselves, like Curwood's Neewa, orphaned yet a second time. They set out on an initiatory "incredible journey" of their own, during which they brave storms, forest fires, and other hardships together.

Journeys such as this were often undertaken in traditional children's tales by young characters separated from their parents, and therefore at least temporarily orphaned (e.g., Hansel and Gretel). In his book on fairy tales, Bruno Bettelheim describes this as the character's "voyage of finding himself," which often involves an effort to return home, but in any case allows the child to confront challenges, to overcome dangers, and to reap rewards, and to do so all on his or her own.[37] If Curwood and other nature writers were not consciously aware that these were some of the oldest story conventions in literature, especially in children's tales, they must at least have had some awareness that the orphan theme possessed a special dramatic power. Indeed, its appeal is to some of our deepest emotions related to early childhood experiences of attachment and unity, separation and loss. For children, the image of an orphan might well evoke the primal fear of losing their own mothers. Bettelheim suggests that the pervasiveness and power of the orphan theme owes precisely to the fact that children often feel "threatened by complete rejection and desertion." This, he argues, is an expression of the underlying fear of starvation that, especially for infants, is what the loss of the mother ultimately represents.[38]

At attempt to evoke this very fear can be found, in combination with the journey and orphan themes, in the very first of the "True Life Adventures," *Seal Island*. The film's narration describes the key sequence as follows:

And here's one who decided to slip away and see the world on his own—the young explorer. The great adventure is barely under way when he suddenly remembers something he forgot: lunch. Well, there's only one answer to that: mother. . . .

This little fellow will have to keep on looking until he finds the mother he belongs to, or until she finds him—*if* she finds him. And there are some mighty big "ifs" in this world where survival is a daily battle . . . Since no one else will nurse him, let's hope that mother comes home soon, for if anything has happened to her, this pup will surely die . . . Here comes mother at last. . . . Reunion, and a happy ending . . . what a day!

Separation, return, journey, struggle, exaltation—it was all there in 1948 in the first "True Life Adventure," where, as in *Dumbo* seven years earlier, it was set in motion as soon as the mother-child bond was severed. Richard Schickel might well have been describing *Seal Island* when he wrote that the scene in which Dumbo is separated from his mother is potentially terrifying "to small children who tend to have a strong anxiety about separation from their mothers. A matinee audience, dominated by small children, tends to stir very uneasily over this sequence. It is the most overt statement of a theme that is implicit in almost all of the Disney features—the absence of the mother. . . . It is, of course, true that the absence of one or both parents is one of the long-lived conventions of children's literature."[39] The preponderance of parentless "children" (actually animal characters) in Disney stories has also been noted by Dorfmann and Mattelart in *How to Read Donald Duck* (1975). Along with Schickel, they cite the high incidence of "mothers dead at the start, or dying in the course of events," adding that there is "one basic product which is never stocked in the Disney store: parents." They conclude that the world of Disney can be compared to "a nineteenth-century orphanage."[40] In 1942, however, while the ideas behind *Seal Island* were still taking shape, that orphanage would be set in the forest, where among its inhabitants would be a certain large-eyed, spotted fawn.

Freudian Gloom, Filmic Grace

In nearly every respect, including the appropriation of a traditional narrative, the elaboration of a formulaic storyline, the development of character, and the inclusion of mythic resonances surrounding the birth of a "special" child who is tragically orphaned, *Dumbo* was surpassed the following year by *Bambi*. When the "True Life Adventures" came along, few missed their similarities to this story about a lovable little creature in a big forest.

Yet it remains a little known fact among film audiences that America's favorite fawn, and possibly its most beloved wild animal character, was neither conceived at Disney studios nor born in an American forest. He was instead the brainchild of Siegmund Salzmann (a.k.a. Felix Salten), a native of Budapest who lived and wrote in Vienna. Salten's life experiences took place worlds away from the rustic haunts of North American nature writers like Burroughs, Seton, and Curwood, and far from the African veldt that formed the background for several of Kearton's animal stories. Emerging from late nineteenth century café society, and from the intellectual circle known as "Jung Wien," Salten wrote essays, criticism, plays, and short novels, including the erotic story *Die Kleine Veronika*. In 1923, however, at the age of fifty-four, he wrote *Bambi: Eine Lebensgeschichte aus dem Walde*. Translated into English in 1928 by Whittaker Chambers, it became *Bambi: A Life in the Woods* and later just *Bambi*.[41]

It may seem surprising at first that Salten's *Bambi* is consistent in so many ways with the work of the North American nature writers, in particular with Curwood's model, until we consider again how many basic elements are common to storytelling traditions around the world. Salten opens his story with Bambi's birth, and then, at the halfway point (p. 118) makes an orphan of the young protagonist when his mother is killed by hunters. Bambi's father, although absent as a parent, watches over him from a distance, leaving Bambi to form a kind of surrogate family with his friends, who help him through the difficult trials of youth and adolescence. At last, having reached maturity, and having triumphed in a series of initiation rites, the young "Prince" assumes his rightful place in the community with his mate, Faline.

Today's readers may also be surprised to learn that the novel was, like those of Seton and Roberts, originally read as a fairly serious, even somber work intended primarily for adults. Anyone who has read it knows that it lacks the saccharine sweetness of Disney's film treatment, although the latter has no doubt colored many recollections of the original. Johnston and Thomas have described Salten's Bambi in tragic terms as one "who believed Man was his friend, only to be betrayed." They point to grim images in the novel like that of "the last two leaves on a tree contemplating death and the hereafter before the chill wind sent them swirling to the ground."[42] Some have seen the novel as faintly depressing, even morbid. A biographical sketch of Salten notes that the novel contains an "adult interpretation of the hunt and of the hunter," and is "too somber in detail to have been written intentionally for children," for it is too heavily "laden with killings and maimings."[43] A review in London's *Spectator* was downright cautionary: "This is not a book for children alone. . . . Indeed, it may be too heart-breaking for the majority of children."[44] Others have also commented on the novel's heavy death toll. A columnist in *Field & Stream* described the book as "brooding and bloody," arguing that "death is the central theme of *Bambi*" and that something "fears dying, or does die in terrible agony, in almost every chapter."[45] Another has implied that this was a reflection of the *zeitgeist* of post-World War I eastern Europe, arguing that the book was written "in an intellectual atmosphere dominated by Freudian gloom," that it "radiates a cold aura of pessimism," and that Salten's forest setting is a backdrop "in front of which his animal characters suffer, and bleed and limp and die awful deaths," adding that Bambi "staggers through the book watching one after another of his friends and relatives fall to hunters' guns."[46] Salten may have realized over the years that, in America anyway, children made up the largest reading audience for *Bambi*, and this may account for the gentler tone of his 1939 sequel, *Bambis Kinder: Eine Familie im Walde*, which was later translated as *Bambi's Children: The Story of a Forest Family*. Still, the seeming anomaly of all of this in relation to the story of the world's favorite large-eyed fawn is no doubt a measure of the extent to which Salten's original text has become encrusted with a layer of Disney sentimentality.

Yet, in truth, Disney's *Bambi* is not all sweetness and light. It manages to retain some of Salten's sympathy for animals who are subjected to capricious rifle fire, and thus preserves at least some semblance of his justifiable critique of bloodsports. In defense of such rites of masculinity, however, one of the story's severest critics has attempted to draw parallels between the film's conceptual development and the events then taking place in Europe. This compels him to the conclusion that not only were Disney's writers unduly sympathetic to forest creatures, but, in response to Nazi atrocities, had also become increasingly disillusioned with humanity itself, and expressed their pessimism by concocting a script that was, in effect, little more than an antihumanist (read: "antihunting") tract.[47]

Not surprisingly, the actual history of the conception and development of the film reveals no such attempts to indoctrinate viewers with covert, emasculating, pacifist messages, but points instead to a series of day-to-day creative and financial struggles aimed at producing an audience-pleasing picture. The struggle to develop *Bambi* into a cinematically appealing story began soon after Sidney Franklin acquired the rights to Salten's novel in 1933. His subsequent failure to bring to the screen the lush, poetic, live action version he envisioned resulted in his offering the property to Disney in 1935. Disney, of course, had a very different vision of *Bambi* as a film. His idea centered on animals with quirky, amusing personalities, as in his *Silly Symphonies* cartoon series. Having thus far produced only cartoon *shorts* (the studio's first feature-length animated film, *Snow White*, was still in production), Disney's cinema was at that time still one of character more than of story. Despite having Salten's novel to work with, his instructions on *Bambi* were: "We will have to . . . get hold of our characters before we can build the story."[48] For Disney, however, "getting hold" of characters meant finding ways of humanizing them: "the minute you have them say a word, you've got that human parallel established, so I mean in their mannerisms—in their action—it should all be based on certain human things."[49]

It seemed that for Disney all animal characters, if not all real animals, were automatically seen in strictly human terms, if not as character *types*. This is evident in his description of the natural behavior of raccoons: "A raccoon is always washing its food. It washes everything it eats. I saw that animal as a kind of nut . . . the type that wipes off the knife and fork and [is] always wiping out a cup before he pours the tea."[50]

Franklin, however, was less concerned with characterization than with story, and with telling one, just as in wildlife films today, that would engage audiences emotionally for the entire length of a film. His idea for *Bambi* was especially significant for wildlife film storytelling as we now know it. Franklin suggested using the year-in-the-life, or "life-cycle" story line, with its grounding in the cycle of the changing seasons. This had been largely missing from Salten's novel, but had been used earlier in live action films about animal life, such as Ditmars's *The Four Seasons* (1921), as well as in some of the films in the "Secrets of Nature" series. Yet it had still not been effectively combined on screen with a compelling animal story. Franklin's idea was to strengthen the weak closure at the end of Salten's novel by bringing it full circle to another birth, whereas in Salten's ending there is no hint of regeneration and renewal. Franklin suggested that to repeat the circumstances of Bambi's birth would be more pleasing to viewers. He explained to Disney that the audience "loves to feel they have seen a cycle completed, and that they have seen the whole life of a character."[51]

From dramas of character, to stories of animals, to portrayals of the cycles of the natural world itself, there was now a subtle but inevitable continuum in which all were related, and in which all were shaped with virtually the same audience in mind. Today, it is clear that Franklin's instincts regarding story structure were correct; not only has audience response made *Bambi* an enduring "classic," but the seasonal, life-cycle story line has been one of the most serviceable models in wildlife film, and one of the most common means of representing the workings of nature.[52]

If *Bambi* proved a durable model for later wildlife films, the entire Disney pattern of representing nature by way of stories about idealized individuals has probably proven the greater influence. Although the rudiments were there in the stories of the nature writers and in the "Secrets" series, Disney's films improved on them, and were more effective at popularizing the model in which the "story" of an entire species was told by way of the narrative of one character. It was a model that reflected the cycles of nature, yet was also an intimate portrait of an individual, just as its narrative closure was conventional, yet seemed natural. It welded together animal imagery, behavioral revelation, and traditional narrative in a single, unified structure.

Yet *Bambi*'s seasonal, cyclical story line has also earned it criticism. As a result of its suggestion of eternal recurrence, it was alleged that the "prickly uncertainties of Salten's novel are replaced in the film by the crystalline simplicities of myth," with the result that deer biology "is distorted to fit the familiar symbolic cycle of the agricultural year."[53] Although apparently made in ignorance of the use of this story structure in scientific-educational documentaries, and in denial of the fact that the agricultural year is essentially a reproductive cycle similar to that of animals, it may nevertheless be a valid enough interpretation of *Bambi*. At the very least, most of the novel's concern with death is canceled out by the film's birth-to-birth cycle of regeneration and renewal, to which there is indeed a mythic aspect. In myth proper, Campbell has noted, "a continuous 'recurrence of birth'" is needed "to nullify the unremitting recurrences of death."[54]

Yet the producers of the film version of *Bambi* apparently did not consciously set out to mythologize the story.[55] According to Johnston and Thomas, Franklin and Disney's agreement on a seasonal/cyclical plot structure was not motivated by mythic pretensions, but by pragmatic, cinematic, and ultimately financial concerns. Likewise, Disney's own insistence that the death of Bambi's mother be a key scene appears not to have come out of concern with mythmaking, or even myth evoking, but out of simple awareness of the power of the orphan device, and out of a showman's instinct for appealing to the emotions of the widest possible audience. Johnston and Thomas write: "One thing Walt realized early was that Man killing Bambi's mother would be the most powerful and memorable statement ever made in an animated film. No longer philosophical or an important lesson about survival, it spoke directly to the heart."[56]

Film critic Pauline Kael also noted the emotional power of the story: "Bambi's mother is murdered, Dumbo's mother is goaded to madness and separated from Dumbo; those movies really hit children where it counts."[57] Erich Fromm had earlier made the similar point, in his analysis of the Mickey Mouse formula, that people "would not be able to look continually at the many variations of this one theme unless it touched something very close to their own emotional life."[58] The Disney filmmakers had long been successful in promoting audiences' emotional identification with animal characters, as well as in appealing to their unconscious fears and desires. *Bambi*, in particular, revealed a universality of emotion that was hard to deny. The coming-of-age/rites-of-passage story, with its seasonal structure, its reliance on the orphan device (and therefore on the death of the mother to set events in motion), was a broad evocation of traditional narrative patterns common the world over, as well as an intimate story capable of evoking powerful personal emotions. Attempts such as this to find a balance between the big picture and the intimate portrait, between the vision of nature and the vignette of the individual dated at least as far back as the natural history writings of Aristotle. The result, honed over centuries, was a set of conventions for *dramatizing* the ways of nature, for exploring it by way of narrative and character, and thus for finding that balance in which the indifference of the natural world and needs of the individual could be reconciled. It is in this precarious balance where we find both *Bambi* and the "True Life Adventures," although neither, ultimately, could sustain it. It may be that none of Disney's films about the natural world ever did succeed in striking that balance, but nowhere had there been a failed attempt so spectacular or so popular.

The Biography of a Squirrel

If *Bambi* helped plant the seeds from which the "True Lifes" grew, they came to full fruition in *Perri* (1957). Like *Bambi*, this "biography of a squirrel" was based on a novel by Felix Salten,[59] but in many ways stands today as the definitive Disney statement on animal life in the wild. Yet much confusion has surrounded the picture. Some accounts follow the familiar pattern of attributing the work's conception solely to Disney himself. According to one, sometime during the 1950s "Walt Disney laid plans for a new kind of animal picture." Interviewed for the piece, Disney as usual did little to discourage the notion, or to indicate that the film had been primarily the work of Winston Hibler, Paul Kenworthy, and Ralph Wright. Disney stated, simply, "We decided to combine nature's truth with fiction. . . . We would use the documentary material straight from nature, but give it a plot."[60] This was not a new idea, however; "actuality" footage of wild, untrained animals had often been formed into scripted stories, as in *Rango, Sequoia,* and several of Sucksdorff's films. It was not even an entirely new idea at Disney, although many have seen it as such. Maltin, for example, has written, "By making no bones about the "fantasy" angle of the film, it was felt that the Disney nature-film staff could now do what they had tried to hold in check in the bona fide True-Life films—manipulate the documentary footage to their hearts' content and fashion it into a story."[61]

In truth, they had been manipulating "documentary footage" all along in the "True Life" series, and fashioning it into stories—"mini-stories" that did not occupy an entire film, but stories nonetheless. This had been abundantly clear in 1948's *Seal Island*. It is difficult to believe now that the will to narrative was ever held "in check" at Disney, but *Perri* did offer an opportunity to indulge it on a larger scale. The result was the studio's most comprehensive attempt to combine themes, motifs, characterizations, and storytelling devices from the animated films, with the cinematography, editing, and voice-over narration from the live action films.

Yet upon viewing the film today it may still be difficult at first to know what to make of it. Modern terms like "docudrama" are of little help. One writer put it in a category of "Nature Documentaries with a Plot."[62] Another called it "a culminating work of art in the natural science field,"[63] an assessment based on an internal contradiction, but one that no doubt reflected the Disney team's intentions. Hibler himself described it as "a paradox."[64] Stylistically consistent with the "True Life Adventures," its imaginary story and once-upon-a-time narration (written in verse!), ultimately earned it the oxymoronic label of "True Life *Fantasy*." Still, despite its fantasy elements and contrived story, the term that best fits *Perri* is simply "wildlife film," for its differences from countless others made in later years are differences of degree and emphasis, not differences of kind.

The real significance of *Perri* was that it pulled together the narrative and character elements that had been scattered loosely throughout the other "True Life" films, and was thus both their culmination and their death knell. After 1957 only two more feature-length "True Lifes" were produced, *White Wilderness* (1958) and *Jungle Cat* (1960), neither of which contained anything particularly new, suggesting that the series had run its course. It is tempting, therefore, to say that *Perri* marked a new direction in Disney filmmaking, but despite the one-time categorization of "True Life *Fantasy*," it was not an advance into new territory as much as a retreat to the familiar ground of fantasy storytelling. If anything, the "True Life Adventures" had been the new direction at Disney, but by 1960 their production had come to a halt. In looking back at the "True Life" period, Schickel noted a pattern similar to that of Disney's animation, beginning with "relatively modest and unpretentious first efforts," followed by more sophisticated productions, then the move to features, "and then, finally, to bastardization."[65]

Interestingly, the same year *Perri* was released, Disney's Buena Vista subsidiary distributed under the Disney banner a French film called *Niok* (1957), about an orphaned baby elephant (with echoes of *Dumbo*). The familiar story pattern and plot structure are repeated, although, as in *Sequoia*, with the addition of human child as audience surrogate. Like Neewa in *Nomads of the North* and Malibu and Gato in *Sequoia*, Niok is thus orphaned *twice*—once after losing its real parent, and again after being stolen from the young boy who had adopted and taken care of it.[66] Its theft by traders precipitates its "incredible journey," but this forced separation ends with a predictable return in which family unity is restored. The import of *Niok* seems in retrospect to be part of the pattern, begun with *Perri*, of interest at Disney in live action animal films in which narrative and character clearly superseded any pretensions to documentary.

Although the animal adventure films that followed during the 1960s retained the key documentary convention of voice-over narration (with Rex Allen, Jr., eventually replacing Hibler), they nevertheless followed the example of *Perri* in drawing on literary sources for story material. Curwood's *Nomads of the North* was the basis for *Nikki, Wild Dog of the North* (1961); Seton's *Lobo, King of the Currumpaw* became *The Legend of Lobo* (1963), and his *Biography of a Grizzly* was filmed as *King of the Grizzlies* (1970); Sheila Burnford's *The Incredible Journey* and Sally Carrighar's *One Day at Teton Marsh* were also filmed, both under their original titles (in 1963 and 1964 respectively). Even some of the numerous animal adventure shorts produced during this time were drawn from literary sources. *Flash, the Teenage Otter* (1961), a near perfect example of the classic formula, was based on a book by Emile Liers.

Many more of these short films had nonliterary sources, but were by no means exempt from the same storytelling conventions. In most cases they were even more concise exercises in the classic narrative. *Yellowstone Cubs* (1963), for example, is a particularly illustrative case of the orphan and journey themes, and of the formula of *separation, initiation,* and *return,* condensed into thirty minutes. Significantly, the Buena Vista distribution subsidiary made it possible for many such films to be released in Europe as well as in the United States. Even some that premiered on television in the United States, such as *Chico, the Misunderstood Coyote* (1961) and *The Wahoo Bobcat* (1963), were released theatrically overseas where Disney as yet had no television outlets. All in all, these purveyors of the classic model, which betrayed a remarkable narrative standardization, were seen far and wide. Even though the "True Life" series had ended, it was, arguably, the decade of the 1960s that marked the real triumph of Disney animal filmmaking; it was the time when the classic model came most clearly into focus, was most systematically applied, and was most widely seen.

Apotheosis

Elements of the classic narrative model had been showing up sporadically for decades in mainstream Hollywood films, some of which even dealt with domestic rather than wild animals. *Lassie Come Home* (1943) and its equine remake *The Gypsy Colt* (1954) attested to the broad applicability of the story of an individual animal's separation from its original community, and its ultimate return or integration into another. The drama of separation, initiation, and return has come to be accepted by audiences as an appropriate way of depicting not only the lives of animals in the wild, but the "adventures" of household pets as well, as *The Incredible Journey*, *The Adventures of Milo and Otis* (1986), and *Homeward Bound* have all shown. Likewise, it can also be found in films dealing with the domestication of wild animals, including the much loved *Born Free* (1966) and its sequel *Living Free* (1972). Because the classic model makes no distinction between wild and domesticated species, it calls into question the very notion of "wild" and "domesticated" as opposing terms. It suggests that the differences for animals between life in the wild and life in human society are only superficial; behind each lay the same myths reconciling the tensions between individual and community.

Yet during the times when Disney's films were still fresh in memory, applications the of classic model to wild animals were often described as Disneyesque, or as the result of Disnification. *Woody Woodchuck's Adventure* (1960), a short film for children, seems very much in the Disney mold, although produced by Encyclopædia Britannica. It follows the seasonal, year-in-the-life pattern, and includes the orphan and journey themes as little Woody is taken away from the forest and made the prisoner/pet of a young boy, but escapes and returns home in triumph. Thus: separation, initiation, and return, as well as journey, struggle, and exaltation—all in ten minutes. By the end of the decade Colin Willock and Survival got into the act with the Disneyesque *World of the Beaver*, in which Castor, the young hero, is cast out by his parents and embarks on a journey in search of a place to make his own home. After facing several perilous trials, he finds a home and settles in with his new mate Amik, where they reconstitute the family unity and begin the cycle anew. As the 1970s wore on, films as diverse as Disney's *A Tale of Two Critters* (1977), Stouffer's *The Man Who Loved Bears* (1977), Survival's *The Leopard That Changed its Spots* (1978), and the Japanese import *The Glacier Fox* (1979) all revealed how flexible and adaptable the classic model was.

Stouffer's *The Man Who Loved Bears* is of particular interest because of the circumstances surrounding its production as much as for its systematic application of the separation-initiation-return formula. The story begins in spring as Stouffer, playing himself, discovers and adopts an orphaned grizzly cub. As she matures, young Griz journeys too far from home and experiences menacing confrontations with other animals, and even narrowly escapes being shot by a hunter. At the film's conclusion, Griz has grown to maturity and is briefly seen with her own cubs, confirming her return to her wild home and the renewal of the life cycle. Interestingly, Stouffer's account of the film's conception and production indicate that its final form was actually shaped by his attempts to meet a series of escalating demands by CBS executives. Significantly, they wanted "a sentimental human-interest story . . . along the lines of the Walt Disney films." [67] The result, whether intentional on Stouffer's part or not, reworks Disney's *Charlie, the Lonesome Cougar*, with echoes, as well, of *Niok*. The 1980s found Stouffer still applying the classic model on occasion in films such as *Old Man Muskrat* and other entries in his *Wild America* series. *Fishers in the Family* (1984) repeats the pattern of *The Man Who Loved Bears*, and is an equally illustrative case of separation/initiation/return, as Stouffer adopts two orphaned fishers and attempts to teach them lessons in survival in preparation for their return to the wild.

The international appeal of the classic model was evident during the 1980s in a number of films from Japan. Nippon TV's *A Panda's Story* (1984)

The World of the Beaver (1970). The intimate portrait is a genre staple, but named characters and a "classic" storyline pointed to Disney's influence. Des and Jen Bartlett/Survival Anglia.

includes all the requisite themes and situations. Two years later the popular feature *Milo and Otis,* an undisguised rip-off of *The Incredible Journey,* again put the familiar elements to work. Another Nippon TV variation on the classic formula, *Mozu, the Snow Monkey* (1987), was shown on American television, where it became one of the most popular films ever to air on the PBS series *Nature.*

As the 1980s gave way to the 1990s, the classic model could even be found surrounded by BBC documentary trappings in films such as the Bambiesque *Rush, the Fallow Dear* (1990), *Kali the Lion* (1991), or *Aliya the Asian Elephant* (1992), the latter bearing a strong resemblance to *Niok.* Hugo Van Lawick's films for Partridge confirmed his commitment to biographical storytelling, with the separation-initiation-return formula being firmly in evidence in films such as *The Year of the Jackal* (1990), *The Wild Dogs of Africa* (1990), and *Born to Run* (1994), as well as in his 1996 theatrical feature *The Leopard Son.*

During the 1980s and 1990s the classic model could also still be found in animated features, including Disney's *The Fox and the Hound* (1983), the Hungarian film *The Little Fox* (1987), and of course, a few years later, *The Lion King* (1994). Yet at the end of the 1990s, indeed, at the end of the century, nearly perfect examples of it were still plentiful in live action wildlife films. National Geographic's *Yellowstone: Realm of the Coyote* (1996) and *The Last Wolves of Ethiopia* (1997) tell the highly formulaic stories of young canine protagonists, male and female respectively, who are banished from their packs and who embark on similar quests to recover the lost family unity.[68] The CBS/Discovery production *A Meerkat Family Saga* (1997) brings the formula of separation, initiation, return, and exaltation to bear on the story of "Digger":

With his family lost to the conditions of the desert, Digger . . . is forced to leave the safety of his territory and fight to be accepted into another colony of meerkats, hoping to find a mate and start a new family. Ultimately, his courage and persistence pay off. He is accepted into a new family and, having found a mate, starts family of his own. His incredible saga over, it is time for Digger to rejoice.[69]

In *Lords of the Everglades* (1998), writer Allison Argo went a step farther by creating sympathetic characters of otherwise unlovable reptiles in the parallel stories of Ali the alligator and Cleo the crocodile, who set out on cross-country "journeys to adulthood. . . wrought with danger and obstacles."[70] All these films, whether animated or live action, further attest to the classic narrative model's ongoing durability and flexibility, as well as to its continued international marketability.

Yet the extent of Disney's influence has too often been overstated.[71] Ultimately, no single work was responsible for embedding animal storytelling in natural history films, and no one studio or film series for linking wildlife films to other narrative traditions. If they are a part of what Otto Rank once described as "the mass of chiefly biographic hero myths" that makes up our cultural tradition, it is because the forces of tradition have shaped them.[72] The voice telling the story of the animal character does not emanate from an individual or from a single work, but is the voice of a culture talking to itself. It is in the context of cultural tradition that the origins of the classic narrative model of wildlife film are best understood. It is the power of international media markets, however, that has accounted for its longevity.

5
Family Values, Social Mores, Behavioral Norms

The forces of tradition that shaped wildlife films' narrative models have been no less effective in shaping their portrayals of animal behavior. As should already be evident, imposing narrative on nature not only represents the lives of wild animals according to dramatic convention, but also individualizes and psychologizes behavior typical of entire species. Further, attempts to render such behavior intelligible to audiences have often entailed finding simple human analogies for it, which, in turn, have forced it into familiar, moral categories—good, bad, kind, cruel, generous, mean, and so forth. Whether or not it is appropriate to apply such notions to animals has seemed to matter less than that they offer audiences a way of making sense of things, and a vision of a world in which things do make sense—in which each individual life and death has a meaning, a reason for occurring, and an explanation that can be easily understood in terms we already know. What makes popular film and television "popular," after all, is that they do not pose concerted challenges to deeply held values, or to beliefs about the way the world works.

For the viewer's part, deeply embraced cultural values and moral categories may be all he or she has when struggling to make sense of seemingly inexplicable, even shocking acts by wild animals. The indifference of nature to cherished values, as well as to real suffering, can often make it difficult to resist the temptation of moral judgment, even in response to the most neutral of film depictions.

Those who make wildlife films, however, do not come from outside the dominant value systems, and so moralizing of nature finds its way into wildlife films with surprising regularity. This is true even in many of those shot by filmmakers who pride themselves on their thick-skinned ability to avoid making moral judgments of the seemingly brutal events they witness in the wilds. In the process of turning raw footage into stories that engage audiences' emotions, some degree of moralizing of nature is almost inevitable.

Routine acts of predation, for example, become *dramatic conflicts* enlisting all the elements of Aristotelian dramaturgy to engage audiences emotionally. By way of formal devices—close-ups, point-of-view shots, reaction shots, etc, not to mention voice-over narration and dramatic music—we, as audience members, are often "teamed" emotionally with one or the other of the animals involved.[1] Depending on which one, and on the outcome of the chase, the event becomes either a tragedy or a triumph, an occasion for mourning or for celebration. To portray it in completely objective and neutral terms that do not engage viewers' emotions might be the goal of a scientist, but would likely be seen by film and television producers as a waste of an opportunity to do what film and television should do best: grab viewers emotionally. Science may strive to be value-free, but ratings-driven prime-time television cannot afford to be.

The extent to which the wildlife film genre may be something of a vast morality play, in which the virtuous succeed and the strong survive, and in which maintaining social conventions is the surest hedge against an unforgiving environment, is nowhere better illustrated than in the portrayal of animals' family lives and social interactions. Here is where we see that some of the significant occurrences in our own lives—birth, initiation rites, pair-bonding, sexual union, child-rearing, and death—have become the central pillars upon which most wildlife films are built, and make up the "family romance" at the core of the classic narrative model and its variations. For many of us these events are already morally loaded, but when presented by way of tested dramatic and cinematic conventions, they leave little room for either emotional or moral neutrality.

By looking closely at the ways in which animals' family and social lives are portrayed in wildlife films (independent of narrative structure), and at the terms and categories used to describe them, we can see the mechanics by which wildlife films appeal to audiences' emotions and predispositions toward certain values. We can also see how the "big events" in life (see the section Birth, School, Work, Death, later in the chapter) can become vehicles for affirming conventional social mores.

Status Quo Ante

Just as it is difficult for some to countenance the fact that the model of the human nuclear family so widely touted today has actually enjoyed a relatively brief reign historically, so too does the pervasiveness of mating, reproduction, and the rearing of young in wildlife films today make it easy to forget that these were not always mainstays of the genre.[2] In its earliest years they were not even present. Because many of the first wildlife films were shot in zoos, the animals were usually seen doing little more than standing or walking or being fed. Little or nothing was shown of their social behavior, and not much more was known about it. During the years when hunting and chase pictures were popular, or when safari films dominated the scene, the on-screen activities of animals consisted mainly of fleeing, charging, or fighting for their lives—often in staged confrontations. To a large extent, mating, family, and social interactions were simply not among the categories in which wild animals were understood; not surprisingly, during the first two decades of wildlife filming there was relatively little attention to them.

There were a few exceptions, of course, many of which were films about birds. Their nesting behavior had long been of interest to ornithologists, and was certainly an example of animal family life. Oliver Pike's films are exemplary in this regard, including *In Birdland* (1907), *Guillemots* (1908), and *Wild Birds in their Haunts* (1909). Another notable example, entitled *Birds of a Far-Off Sea* (1917), one of the last films to be distributed under the name of Thomas Edison. Shot in the Malagas Islands near South Africa, *Birds of a Far-Off Sea* is one of the best written and photographed of early wildlife films. Its revealing images of behavior are accompanied by understated written commentary that gives clear, if fleeting, attention to mating, reproduction, and raising young. After its opening panoramic shot of a beach thick with ground nesting birds, their mating behavior is given close visual coverage and a title card that reads simply: "A wordless, graceful courtship." Geese, black cormorants, and penguins round out the picture of bird life on the islands. The last title reads: "And here, wet by the flying spray, they raise their young." Total running time: five minutes—shorter even, than Pike's films, but with more of the sort of spectacular scenery that, in combination with close-up behavior study, characterizes the blue chip films of today. Yet despite its graceful handling, *Birds of a Far-Off Sea* set no trends; in the literal as well as the superlative sense, it was exceptional.

During the late teens and early 1920s, depictions of the family and social life of animals began to find their way into a few more films, but these remained tentative gestures for another twenty years, until after hundreds of films about wild animals had already been made. The Johnsons, for example, produced a considerable body of work during the 1920s, but were either inept or uninterested or both when it came to capturing animal behavior on film, and had little, if anything, to say about the social and familial life of the animals they photographed. Neither, for that matter, had Rainey, Selig, Kleinschmidt, Akeley, Ditmars, or, at least in the early years, Kearton. When the family and social lives of animals finally did begin to be explored in any depth on film, it was not even in the sorts films they were making, but instead in fictional adventures such as *Baree, Son of Kazan* (1917, 1925), *Back to God's Country* (1919), *Nomads of the North* (1920), *Kazan* (1921), *Call of the Wild* (1923), and *White Fang* (1925). In these exciting if melodramatic stories animals appeared as characters rather than as fodder. What's more, they had *relationships*—pair bonds, families, even friendships. Even if the animals were not always drawn in a way that was true to nature, they were at least developed in greater depth and with greater sympathy than in more documentary-oriented films, and provided some relief from the seemingly endless parade of anonymous, interchangeable creatures being pursued, prodded, trapped, goaded into charging, and shot.

Throughout the 1920s the alternative to hunting and safari pictures provided by the "Secrets of Nature" produced a more revealing overall portrayal of animal's lives, including, to some extent, their family and social relationships. Yet, hampered by the dearth of research and knowledge in these areas, and by eight-to-ten-minute running lengths, the "Secrets" were unable to explore the subjects in much depth. More significant, historically, may be the fact that mainstream wild animal feature films, with their bigger budgets, longer running times, more extensive distribution, and greater publicity, were simply able to reach larger audiences—as well as, of course, to achieve greater emotional depth. As a result, dramatic narrative became the form in which most audiences encountered wild animals on the screen. In the sound years, animal dramas such as *Rango, Sequoia,* and later *Bambi,* as well as dozens of similar stories about domesticated dogs and horses, helped secure dominance for the view of animals as individuals with unique personalities, who, like humans, enjoyed relationships with friends and family members. It is a view still largely reflected in many blue chip wildlife films today, where it is not at all incompatible with a scientific understanding of the lives and behavior of animals, but where scientific categories often give way to human projections and distinctly moral frameworks.

Following the "Secrets" series, *The Private Life of the Gannets* (1934) held some promise as a solid scientific investigation of animals' family and social structures. Despite the combined forces of Julian Huxley and Alexander Korda, however, it did not deliver. Emblematic of its failure to explore and reveal the gannets' family and social systems is a passage in which Huxley offers a surprisingly careless interpretation (given his advanced knowledge of ritualized bird behavior) of a male gannet's mating display as merely a case of its being "overcome by emotion." His conclusion typifies the capitulation of science to cinematic entertainment in many early wildlife films: "What it means I don't know . . . at any rate, it's a touch of comic relief!" G. K. Noble's *The Social Behavior of the Laughing Gull* (1940) was a step forward in the depiction of animal behavior, but lacked a narration track and, like so many films made by scientists for scientists, was seen by few but scientists. C. R. Carpenter's studies, *Characteristics of Gibbon Behavior* (1942) and *Social Behavior of Rhesus Monkeys* (1947), made some advances in the depiction of family and social interactions among animals, but likewise failed to reach a popular audience, and therefore to influence popular thinking.

Ultimately, then, from the start it was the work of screenwriters and novelists more than of zoologists, biologists, behavioral scientists, or documentary filmmakers that shaped the portrayal of the intimate lives of animals in wildlife films. Today, in an age when the genre is ruled by *story*, the power of writers to shape the image still exceeds that of scientists. This has meant that the social lives of animals have been presented in ways contrived to appeal more to viewers' emotions than to their intellects, or, as one producer put it, "more to their hearts than to their heads."

From Human Analogy to Moral Biology

As discussed earlier, the traditions shaping the classic model of wildlife film narrative have transcended cultural boundaries and reflected deeper, more fundamental patterns of the organization of human thought. Yet where clear cultural differences among humans do exist, as in, for example, the meaning and value attached to the natural environment, the use of warfare and violence, the desire for conquest, the patterns of kinship and social groupings, the role of romantic love in marriage, and the very meaning of marriage and family to society (whether their primary functions are emotional, social, or economic), the views most consistently reflected in wildlife films are those of the countries who produce and export the majority of them, or who have the largest audiences, or both. The idea that they who pay the piper call the tunes may seem easy enough to accept—until it becomes clear that in this case the tunes are those of Christianity, Patriarchy, Capitalism, Colonialism, Social Darwinism, and so on. Wildlife filmmakers are likely to deny that these have any connection to what they do, and to see their application as an overintellectualized interpretation of films that are simply about animals, after all.

Yet just as ethnocentrism is built in to every culture's ways of thinking, so is there little reason to suspect that the cultural biases built in to other genres of industrialized, commodified entertainments do not also find their way into wildlife films—even if they are imperceptible to the people who make them. Few of us, after all, perceive the ideological aspect to maps and globes in which north is "up" and south is "down." These notions have been so thoroughly naturalized that they are part of our very way of thinking about our world. Likewise, western notions of what constitutes "poverty" are so deeply ingrained that characterizations of tribal societies as "underdeveloped" typically go unchallenged. Thus, even if western biases relating to marriage, family, and social structure were difficult to perceive in wildlife films (although they are not), it would still be improbable that such biases could permeate other film and television genres yet fail to penetrate this one.[3] Wildlife filmmakers, moreover, are fairly candid in acknowledging that their films are closer to mainstream entertainments than to science. It would be unrealistic, therefore, to expect wildlife films not to reflect conventional values at some level. Moreover, even when the application of human conventions in areas of family, sex, and social relations to wildlife is contradicted by science, these conventions nevertheless remain expressions of the beliefs and values of the audience that wildlife films are designed to capture. In a ratings-driven industry, producers often argue that it is audiences, ultimately, who both pay the piper and call the tune. And the biggest, most powerful audience, remains that of the United States, where the notion of "family values" has been most thoroughly reified.

At the very least, one might say that the portrayal in wildlife films of animals' family and social relations presents a kind of vast Rorschach pattern in which culturally preferred notions of masculinity, femininity, romantic love, monogamous marriage, responsible parenting, communal spirit, the work ethic, deferred gratification, moral behavior, and the sexual division of labor in marriage can all be read.[4] The difference, of course, is that the inkblots are not haphazard, but instead represent the application of a formula that has relied heavily on human categories and analogies as communicative ingredients. A CBS promotional blurb for *A Meerkat Family Saga* (1997) illustrates the way the complexities of animal behavior are almost automatically reduced to human categories. The meerkats are said to "share a tenderness for one another that is very similar to human love." When a young female's injuries affect the entire family, they display "their very 'human' emotions of sadness."[5] And, of course, the pictures prove it.

Yet of all the parallels and analogies that can be drawn between animals and humans, it may be surprising to learn that those precisely the areas of family bonds, social behavior, displays of affection, and the like are seen by many as the most defensible. Indeed, the meerkat descriptions seem almost to echo Konrad Lorenz's argument that the social behavior of many animals, especially the bonds that hold them together in family and kinship groups, are "analogous with those of man":

In an animal not even belonging to the favored class of mammals we find a behaviour mechanism that keeps certain individuals together for life, and this behavior pattern has become the strongest motive governing all actions; it can overcome all "animal" drives, such as hunger, sexuality, aggression, and fear, and it determines the social order in its species-characteristic form. In all these points this bond is analogous with those human functions that go hand in hand with the emotions of love and friendship.[6]

The sources and motivations of such behavior are still being debated. Lorenz linked them to mechanisms designed to shut off aggression in others, arguing that they exist, therefore, only among animals capable of intra-specific aggression, and not among those who spend their lives peaceably united in flocks.[7] Others have argued that the motivations behind such bonds can, in many cases, be justifiably categorized as *emotion*—that is, as an emotional bond between two animals.[8] Still others have seen close bonds between animals as mere self-serving strategies, often of genetic origin.[9] In any case, behavioral scientists have found that intense personal bonds—*friendships*—do exist between many animals, especially primates.[10]

Creators of animal fictions, whether for print or for the screen, have long assumed these things even in the absence of scientific evidence. Salten's *Bambi*, for decades seen as a realistic portrayal, is essentially a tale of friendship and community in the woods. Curwood's *The Grizzly King* is about the deep friendship between two bears (never mind that the young orphan is a black bear and the old male a grizzly, or that adult male grizzlies have no parental instincts beyond copulation, and that they typically kill cubs likely to have been sired by other males). *Nomads of the North* centers on the equally unlikely friendship and affection between animals of entirely different species—a domestic dog and a wild bear cub. Although upstaged in the 1920 film by a melodramatic subplot, when the story came to the screen the second time as Disney's *Nikki, Wild Dog of the North* (1961) the animals' friendship resumed center stage. "The cub just wanted company," we are told, and as for Nikki, "all he really wanted was a friend." Although the two are at first bound together by a trapper's leather strap, "they would find in friendship a tie far stronger than a leather thong," for beyond Nikki's need for food, "he had a deeper need for companionship." This need even drove him to try to join a pack of wolves, but although "he came in friendship," he was "met with fury," and the next morning was "lonelier than ever."

Some years later, the behavior of a young wolf in *Last Wolves of Ethiopia* (1996) is similarly psychologized. Cast from her pack, she yearns for "a partner to share her days with," and struggles for over a year to recapture the lost unity. Then, one day, "isolation drives [her] to desperate ends. Seeking any kind of companionship, she . . . tries to capture the eye of a herd dog. He's not of her species, but she's spent over a year by herself, [and] it's unclear how much longer she can survive like this." Like Nikki, the young wolf is so lonely that she would "prefer bad company to solitude." Her story ends in triumph, however, when at last she finds fulfillment as alpha female of her own pack. Canines are undeniably social creatures, and are, in fact, driven to form social bonds, but the problem here, as in so many wildlife films, results from dramatizing such facts on an individual level. Inevitably, behavior typical of a whole species is interpreted in terms of individual psychology: the wolf is seen seeking interactions with others—the wolf must therefore *feel lonely*. When behavior patterns are individualized and psychologized in this way, and done so widely and systematically, it seems naive not to think that whatever is gained in the dramatic appeal of one film must come at the expense of accuracy and scientific understanding overall. In any case, it is clear that Disney held no copyright on the poignant drama of a lonely animal who searches for a friend, and who wants, above all, just to belong.

The French scientist Espinas argued in the nineteenth century that "communal life" was not a condition found only among humans and a handful of other "privileged species," but was instead "universal." [11] For those inclined to take them, the mental steps are still short from observing "communal life" to perceiving *communal spirit*, from beholding a gathering of animals (such as penguins or seals) to interpreting it as a *society*; from observing sociability among animals to presuming *dread of solitude*; from observing pair-bonding efforts to seeing them as desperate attempts to stave off a deep and dreaded spiritual loneliness. So, too, is it a short step from observing animals' family life to seeing them as being *family minded*; or from watching them raise their young to seeing them as models of *responsible parenting* and *family values*. Ultimately, then, in the family and social behavior of animals, where so many have seen human parallels, it is a slippery slope from human analogies to moral conclusions. The danger, obviously, is that when moral values are presumed applicable to nature, their universalizing is complete. They become absolute—no longer moral values at all, but moral *truths*.

A recent film on animal families notes, for example, that "caring motherhood" is not something all animals practice, and that another method of reproduction "is to have a lot of offspring and to abandon them." While literally true, the connotations attached to words such as "caring" and "abandon" are at the very least open invitations to moral judgment. When a sea turtle hatchling is then described as "the image of parental abandonment," one can almost hear audience members asking, *But why doesn't the turtle stay and take care of her babies like a good mother?* In fact, infant mortality in the wild is already high even under the most attentive parental care, but filmmakers' routine reliance on the orphan theme to evoke sympathy can suggest not only that abandonment by uncaring parents is the primary danger to young animals, but that human family arrangements and conventional "family values" are the real keys to individual as well as species survival. Judging from the "success" (i.e., overpopulation) of our own species relative to that of sea turtles, one might even conclude that the cultivation of more humanlike "family values" might be the key to avoiding extinction. From such normative ideas it is but a short step to the moral judgment that one animal's young survive because it is a "better" or "more fit" parent than the one whose offspring die or are taken by predators or other natural processes.

In the absence of any explanation that the behavior patterns involved in the reproductive survival strategies of each animal species are the result of long and slow evolutionary processes, and that this has made them *fixed* patterns of behavior, the suggestion that some animals are "uncaring" parents, even when not stated, is often allowed to prevail. Even an animal forced to abandon its young when its own life is threatened is, by such logic, a *bad* parent—although its reproductive value to the species at that point is far greater than that of its offspring, for it is better equipped to survive and can soon produce more of them. From an evolutionary standpoint, abandoning the young under such circumstances makes it a *better* parent.[12]

Although moralizing in wildlife films today usually remains covert, the emphasis on drama can still produce the occasional moralistic hyperbole. One might be too quick to assume that there are no more of the sorts of moral condemnations found in *Rango*'s descriptions of the Sumatran tiger (see Chapter 3), or in the careless remarks Algar and Hibler often inserted into the "True Life" films, as in this particularly (and inexplicably) derisive description of rhinos from *The African Lion* (1955): "This grumpy species goes around with a grudge against everybody. . . . Because they're so un-predictable, they're avoided by most other animals. But this social neglect doesn't phase them; they continue on their way as ill-mannered as ever, and they work off their bad tempers by chasing each other."[13] Similarly, a leop-ard in *Jungle Cat* is described as "a killer both wanton and ruthless, the exe-cutioner of the African plain," who makes a "career of assassination." Today, the notion that predators are "nature's assassins" has, itself, refused to die. Although it seems few would any longer equate predatory killing with ag-gression or hostility, let alone with murder, as recently as 1998, a BBC film on tigers carelessly characterized a cat species from Madagascar as "skilled assassins." In the mid-1990s Time-Life Video, already notorious for its pro-vocative and controversial marketing of the *Trials of Life*, packaged another collection of BBC films under the title *Nature's Assassins*. It might just as well have called them "Nature's Hit-Men" or "Nature's Terrorists." Adver-tisements spoke of "ingenious predator tricks and deceptions. . . strate-gies so diabolically effective, no mere human could have invented them." It even challenged viewers to "Stand your ground on nature's killing fields— if you dare!" For viewers of my generation, the words "killing fields" sum-mon images of Pol Pot's murderous Khmer Rouge. It is a metaphor not to be taken lightly, and one unlikely to endear audiences to the predators de-picted, even though some facing extinction could well use some audience sympathy. The marketing gives little indication as to the real tone and con-tent of the films, but its imagery far exceeds the sort of Disney anthropo-morphism assumed by many to be a thing of the past. Indeed, most of Algar and Hibler's worst excesses pale by comparison.

Even though moralistic hyperbole has declined generally in wildlife films today, animal portrayals rarely escape being run through a moral filter of some kind—usually, however, one that has developed in a specific sociocul-tural context. It is difficult to imagine, for example, that the values of any modern, industrial society or Western nation can be applied broadly to the natural world. What helped build one society and mold its "national charac-ter" is almost assuredly not what is best for wild animals—even if they hap-pen to live within the political boundaries of that nation. To see any human society as a model for widely varying animal species is to assume that we stand atop an evolutionary "ladder," that other animals are climbing up that ladder behind us, and that they must follow our examples if they are to join us on the high rungs.[14]

The subtle way in which moral projection now occurs in hundreds of films is illustrated in a 1995 film about parrots. These birds, we are told, mate for life but often have "affairs on the side." It is an innocuous enough sounding line, and no doubt an economical way of making the point. Yet, left to stand on its own, it is an unfortunate choice of words, for instead of a scientific explanation of what are called "extra-pair copulations," the behavior is reduced to the moral category of marital infidelity. As a result, it is suggested that it is a kind of "cheating" rather than a natural, alternative reproductive strategy.[15] In fact, extra-pair copulations can help a male's reproductive success to rise manyfold, and a female to produce offspring with greater genetic diversity. A female who has lost her mate, moreover, may have no other chance to reproduce unless she can gather an extra-pair copulation from a paired male (a behavior given human emotional resonance at the conclusion of the popular 1983 film *The Big Chill*). Among birds, such alternative reproductive strategies might ultimately serve the survival of the species just as well as the regular pair bond, or might at least be an important natural way of augmenting it. Leaving progeny is, after all, the real measure of success in the "struggle to survive," and the ultimate determinant in the "survival of the fittest." To couch these natural systems in the moral terms of extramarital affairs is to misrepresent the functional dynamics of animal reproduction. Not only might this encourage viewers, who often take such statements at face value, to misunderstand these complex natural systems, but it might even invite them to make a moral judgment of the animals themselves that could, somewhere down the line, affect their welfare.[16] That is to say, if a species were widely perceived as being unfaithful, disloyal, untrustworthy, perhaps even treacherous, would there be popular support for it if it were faced with extinction? Consider the still ongoing effort to extirpate wolves by "predator control" factions in the American west, and the moral language on which they still rely to portray their efforts as a righteous crusade to rid the world of treacherous, murderous, cowardly villains—the "Jeffrey Dahmers of the wilderness."[17]

Wildlife films like the one about parrots have not descended to this level, but, as science popularization, nevertheless routinely seize on human analogies and metaphors as convenient, easily grasped illustrations of elusive and subtle concepts.[18] Scientists themselves sometimes use such terms where no (morally) neutral term exists for a phenomenon or behavior. When a clinical term is coined, however, science popularizers often ignore it in favor of a more familiar but morally resonant human-centered term, which nonspecialist audiences almost inevitably take at face value. Thus, what were intended as aids to understanding become impediments to it. Stripped of their complexities, wiped of their shades of gray, and aimed at the heart rather than the head, human analogies and metaphors too easily give rise to normative implications—especially in areas that some see as parallel to our own notions of sexual politics. In fairness, it must be said that the film in question, *Parrots: Look Who's Talking* (BBC, 1995) is an excellent work, and that small rhetorical liberties such as it includes may be harmless enough on their own. Nevertheless, each adds incrementally to the accumulated misunderstanding that emerges, little by little, from hundreds of films in which similar liberties are taken. The fact that a given film is an otherwise fine work, however, only lends credibility and power to its misstatements.

The American series *All Bird TV* (1997–99), although a fine ornithological series, should perhaps not be compared to a carefully written and more painstakingly produced BBC film, but it demonstrated how less thought and preparation can in some cases lead to more blatant moral pronouncements—and in a package intended for impressionable young audiences. In a program on cowbirds, who, like cuckoos, lay their eggs in the nests of other birds, the series host at first attributes this fixed behavior on the part of an entire species to individual cunning and wile, describing the cowbird as "one of the craftiest, kinkiest" of bird parents. A guest ornithologist in the program doesn't do much better, asserting that cowbirds "hire permanent baby-sitters, but they don't even pay them anything . . . it's crazy!"[19] Although later statements attempt to put the cowbird's actions in a more appropriate behavioral and evolutionary light, the damage is already done. In a youth-oriented program, with an audience unlikely to see through whatever irony might have been intended in such remarks, there is even less room for carelessness, yet typically, more of it.

Even in narrative wildlife films the moral view of nature asserts itself once again by individualizing complex issues and by appeals aimed more at the heart than at the head. A film that has established a strong central character (no matter how many animals actually play the part) such as Perri the squirrel, Kali the lion, Yindi the koala, Inura the dingo, Harriet the leopard, Marty the cheetah, Cleo the crocodile, Echo the elephant, Mozu the snow monkey, or Penny the puma, cannot, as in films such as Hitchcock's *Psycho* or Antonioni's *L'Avventura*, be allowed to die or disappear before the story is finished, or there would be no story. The very fact that she has been singled out to have her story told already suggests she is special (an example of the "status conferral" function of mass media). Yet the real proof that she is a superior individual lies in her survival, at least to the end of the story, while others around her fall by the wayside. In this respect, wildlife films reveal once again their similarities to other narrative entertainment genres. Westerns, detective stories, and other latter-day romances usually center on strong, heroic leading characters who outlive the weaklings that surround them. Even the much revered *Schindler's List* focuses on the experiences of a charismatic hero who survives amidst a host of Jews who do not, and who merely form the background against which his story is told. Narrative films are, after all, typically about the plight or heroics of individuals, not anonymous masses (Eisenstein's *heroless* films notwithstanding). If this tendency to favor charismatic individuals reveals once again the undercurrent of social Darwinism in wildlife films, it may owe less to ideology than to the imposition of conventional film narrative upon nature.

For audiences to follow the life of an individual animal, to care about it, to become emotionally involved with it, and to do so for up to an hour, means that the animal must both engage our sympathies and display what we consider "strengths of character." We must be sympathetic to its plight, but also be able to recognize in it such things as courage, commitment, patience, good judgment, loyalty, fidelity, sacrifice, hard work, devotion to duty and family, and other "virtues." In *A Cheetah Family*, for example, a routine scene in which a cheetah mother feeds her young becomes an exercise in sacrifice and patience that helps solidify the bond between audience and character: "Marty has to look away. She'd like to eat, but the prey she captured was very small, and her first priority is to feed her young cubs. . . . Self-sacrifice is difficult, but it is something that a mother cheetah must do . . . but patience is a virtue; now that her cubs are satiated, Marty can begin to eat." Telling the story of an individual animal thus involves singling-out (and thereby implicitly rewarding) one who displays what we can recognize as *virtues*—even if the behavior in question may actually be innate, stereotyped, or conditioned.

An even more sympathetic example is *Mozu, the Snow Monkey*. One of the most popular films ever shown in the PBS series *Nature*, it deals with a severely birth-defected Japanese macaque. With the odds against her survival seemingly overwhelming, the story is about (or *projects*) the courage, nobility of character, and indomitable spirit that allow Mozu to triumph over adversity. The emotional climax comes when she gives birth to a healthy, normal offspring and proves herself a caring mother like the able-bodied members of her clan. Yet if her disability were the result of a defective gene she carried, it might, arguably, have been better if she had not risked passing on that gene by giving birth, but the film is clearly in sympathy with the happiness of the individual. Scientific questions are silenced by emotionally compelling dramatic narrative.

The lead character in *Last Wolves of Ethiopia* also earns our affection and viewership by her perseverance in the face of suffering, and by "proving an exception to the rule" that in wolf packs "subservient females may bear pups, but they almost always abandon them within a few days to help the dominant female raise her young." By remaining devoted to her own litter, "our" female distinguishes herself as a good and loyal mother, and therefore as a more worthy central character than the selfish-seeming alpha female. From an evolutionary perspective, however, the behavior described could actually make her a "bad" mother by weakening the survival chances of both litters. Yet as an individual character, it ennobles her. Like Marty and Mozu, she earns her happy ending through her noble efforts and humanlike virtues.

Just as Seton's stories in the late nineteenth century individualized Darwinian principles and refracted them through the prism of Victorian mores, wildlife films today still tend to portray individual survival as a reward for effort and virtue. In *Crocodile Territory* (1996), when a croc lunges suddenly to catch a goose we are told that "patience, a virtue crocodiles have mastered, reaps its rewards." This pattern of moralizing survival successes may seem faint, but it is widespread and systematic. Thus, just as the crocodile is rewarded for its supposed patience (something ethologists are unlikely to attribute to it), the goose or wildebeest who is eaten pays for its "failure" to exercise appropriate caution; the squirrel who survives the winter is the one who is the hardest worker, having stored the most food, and demonstrated the greatest commitment to industry and deferred gratification; the family of elephants or the pride of lions that survives drought or hunger is the one with the wisest matriarch or the strongest bonds of affection among them; bonobos thrive because they make love not war; a cheetah's cubs survive because she is a "good" mother, and has taught them well, or because the cubs stick together for a time as adults, and continue to exhibit what one film describes as "an almost inexplicable unselfishness." The animals exhibiting such virtuous behavior are more often than not rewarded in a film's storyline with health and prosperity.

In these ways, Western notions of responsible parenting, filial obligation, obedience by the young, and other categories of proper behavior and personal responsibility are projected onto animals in ways that often make it seem as if life and death are assigned to the deserving—life to the hard working, the selfless, the obedient, the morally upright; death to the selfish, the disobedient, the lazy, the careless. *The Ultimate Guide: Horses* (1998) notes, for example, that a leopard's task in hunting zebras is "singling out the *careless* or weak." It is unclear what a "careless" animal is, or what sort of animal behavior can rightfully be judged as such, but here, as in so many wildlife films, it is punishable by death.

The idea that an animal might be killed through no fault or failure of its own, or that it might be subject to the randomness of an amoral and indifferent nature, to accidents, to chance, to events that can't be explained, too often gives way in wildlife films to a kind of determinism—not a biological determinism, however, but a moral one. The natural world may thus seem to make the sense we think it should, and conform to our notions of how things should be, or how all creatures should behave, but a scientific understanding of nature ultimately gains nothing from imposing a moral order upon it. It may be worth recalling in this context Walt Disney's assertion, cited earlier, that every animal "must *earn* his right to live and survive by his own efforts and the thing which in human relations is called moral behavior."[20] Thus, while nature culls the weak and the sick, televised nature further culls the morally *deviant*. Uncharismatic or unpopular species have long suffered "symbolic annihilation" on television (media theorists' term for their systematic elimination from the screen), but a process of "symbolic selection" (as opposed to natural selection) may be just as pronounced. That is, the patterned way in which some animals live and some animals die on television may be as artificial as it is predictable. The systematic preference for individuals who exhibit socially approved "proper" or "moral" behavior, and the systematic dying-off of those who do not, who are "careless," for example, suggests there may even be a process of "symbolic eugenics," or "symbolic *euselection*" (to borrow Julian Huxley's term) in wildlife television.[21] Few in the industry would deny, in any case, that there are systematic preferences in television for some species over others. In the end, most stories are about these species, and most stories, as we know, have happy endings.

Ironically, the search for "right" behavior in the wild was originally a useful corrective to reigning ignorance that had caused many animals to be feared and destroyed irrationally and unnecessarily for their actions.[22] When the nature writers in the late nineteenth century looked for moral behavior among animals, it was often motivated by concerns that animals were misunderstood or mistreated. Yet the message was not one merely of sympathy and preservation, but that nature itself was a profoundly moral place—sometimes harshly so. It has been said that in Seton's stories "obedience is the primary virtue," and that the author "demonstrated this again and again by showing us the fate of the disobedient, the young lambs who do not come when they are called, and are caught and killed." There is clearly a fabulous element in all this, with the moral being that, like the "careless," the "weak and *the foolish* will not survive."[23]

The ongoing search for moral behavior in nature, however, has in fact been a search for places where morality could be projected, not found. The life of an isolated individual offers a few opportunities, but its interactions with members of its family, community, pride, or pack, provide the real occasions for reading virtue and nobility into animal behavior. In decades past, the growing emphasis on family and community in wildlife films was determined to some extent by the classic narrative model; its pattern of separation and return defined an individual's existence by the presence or absence of attachments. Yet family attachments and communal interactions are the bedrock of existence for many animals, and are unavoidable in any realistic depiction of them. It is difficult to tell the story of a caribou without reference to the herd, for example, or of most wolves without reference to a pack, or of most lions without reference to the pride (although, as will soon be shown, it has been done).[24]

Another factor contributing to the increased emphasis on family in wildlife films has been simple practicality. Species with a unified family life most resembling those of their television audiences are the ones that revolve for weeks or months around a single den or nest site. These are simply easier to film than are nomadic creatures, and to catch on film engaging in family-oriented behavior or related "domestic" activities. This has been especially evident in films about birds. Those species in which a mated pair keep and feed their young in a nest for several weeks (songbirds, birds of prey, etc.) are easier to find and to film than those who do not remain at a nest site, and who instead move about freely with their young in tow (grouse, ducks, geese, wader species, etc.). This was clear enough in 1912 to photographer A. R. Dugmore, who wrote that "the breeding season is the time best suited" to photographing birds, "for then the feathered housekeepers are restricted in their individual range to a comparatively limited area. Having learned the situation of their house, [the photographer] may find them at home when he calls, engaged in attending to their various domestic duties."[25] Four decades later, Heinz Sielmann echoed these observations when he wrote of his experiences with a cine-camera making the groundbreaking film *Woodpeckers* (a.k.a. *Carpenters of the Forest*, 1954), "they had remained faithful to their nesting place, which could not have been more favourably sited for our observations and filming. This meant that we would be able to film the woodpeckers rearing their brood in the same place."[26]

Although no precise count exists, it does seem that the majority of films about birds depict those who fall into the this nesting category, including *Birds of a Far-Off Sea* (1917), *Dassan* (1930), *The Private Life of the Gannets* (1934), *Emperor Penguins* (1955), *The Private Life of the Kingfisher* (1967—followed by a number of programs in the "Private Lives" series in the 1970s), *Secrets of the African Baobab Tree* (1972), *Almost a Dodo* (1975), *Inflight Movie* (1986), *Attenborough in Paradise* (1996), and many others.[27] If it is true that there have been more films about birds with extended nesting times, and that their model of family structure has therefore been put in front of viewers more often, then that model may well have come to be accepted by many viewers as a "norm" of family structure and behavior for all sorts of birds.[28] Because it is also a model in which many already see direct parallels to human nuclear families, viewers may grasp onto those similarities at the expense of equally (if not more) significant differences, and see these patterns of behavior as evidence of moral virtues (i.e. as reflections of their own ideals for human behavior). This had clearly been the case in the nineteenth century when Christian ornithology pronounced the moral judgment that

"good" birds were those who "mated once a year and . . . preserved an appearance of family unity through the nesting season. Their habits were at
least well-bred, and they displayed virtues which the nature lover admired:
domesticity and paternal joy."[29] The same sentiments were echoed a few
years later by Seton. In an essay on snowshoe hares, he argued that most
observers "consider the Hare to be promiscuous or polygamous, but the evidence. . . is in favor of *true* mating." He then added, "among animals a good
father means a good husband."[30]

Among wildlife films, Disney's, of course, are legendary for their similar projections of human family systems and values onto nature. Even when
depicted species bore no resemblance to humans, the "True Life Adventures" could nevertheless reduce their complex social groupings to the sim-
plest of human analogies. *The African Lion*, for example, asserts not only that
lions are "family-minded," but that aside from "occasional squabbles, the
pride is one big, happy family," with the eldest male as undisputed head of
household. From the premise that he is the "King of Beasts," the regal metaphor is pushed to extremes in explaining the structure and functioning of
lion society. Unfortunately, American contempt for royalty is allowed to spill
over onto the lions themselves, and contributes to the already condescending tone: "His Majesty sits on the sidelines and strikes a kingly pose, while
the role of provider is left to the ladies. . . . If only friend husband would do
his part here, things might be easier. A vain hope, however, for the Royal
Spouse still rests on his laurels, and wonders what's holding up lunch."

The regal trappings are still in overuse today, as is evident in titles such
as *Lion: King of Beasts* (1994), *Queen of Beasts* (1989), and in two films with
the title *Lion Queen* (1994 and 1998). More significant in the example above,
however, is the obviously inappropriate use of terms such as "husband" and
"spouse" to describe the relationship of male lions to the pride of females
and cubs. Even in the acclaimed film *Attenborough in Paradise* (1996) the word
"wives" is twice used in reference to mating behavior in birds. The first time
it is to describe birds of paradise, which do form pair-bonds and may therefore justify the metaphor. But when used in relation to bower birds, a species
in which the females live and raise their young alone, it is simply inappropriate and misleading. Whether Attenborough uses "wives" as a term of convenience or with purposeful irony, it reveals how little things have changed in
the half century since Disney's films used terms like "wedding" and "honey-
moon." If marriage metaphors do not seem out of place, then consider how
the following might sound in the same context: *ex-wife, fiancée, lover, old lady,
mistress, tramp, slut, old maid*, or likewise *sugar-daddy, gigolo, wife-beater*, or *stud*.
In the "True Life" films, however, even when not directly mentioned, marriage and sex roles were often projected by the use of names such as "Mrs.
Robin," "Mrs. Tarantula," or "Mr. and Mrs. Kittiwake." Because "Miss" and
"Mrs." tell us much more about marital status than does "Mr.," the result of

using such names is that females are identified and defined by their marital status—that is, in relation to males. It is a problem pointed to by feminists and analysts of women's roles in the media, but one that surely has no place in the representation of nature.[31]

Even the last of the "True Lifes," *Jungle Cat*, released in 1960, persisted in projecting human models of marriage and family onto animals. Its depiction of jaguars in Central America is an image of idyllic monogamy and life-long commitment, as becomes evident when two cats' initial snarling at one another soon shows that "no" means "yes," and that love is a many spotted thing: "what began as an all-out argument has turned into a romantic love spat. It seems these two aren't mad at each other at all. . . . And so, each wooed and won in the proper fashion, the handsome pair agrees to travel through life together." On that road through life, the male will, of course, be the hard-working and even heroic provider for his family. After a lengthy struggle with a gigantic fish called a *pirarucu*, we are assured he will take it home, where it will provide "a fine fish dinner for the jungle cat's family."

Even the most "scientific" of the "True Life" films, *Secrets of Life* (1956), the only one in the series to include a credit for "Consulting Biologists," failed to steer clear of this pitfall. "Usually nature assigns to the male and female separate and well-defined duties," we are told. Fair enough. Then this: "as a rule, father provides, mother protects." It might be more accurately argued that *as a rule, mother provides and father is absent*, but at the very least it is rare that males are the primary providers for young. *Secrets of Life* then points to an exception to its own rule: the case of the stickleback fish, where "nature changes these roles: it's the male who performs the domestic chores."[32] Presented as an exception, it implicitly proves the existence of the "rule" that males are nature's providers.[33]

Another interesting case of male parental behavior is the seahorse. The depiction on film of its unusual mode of reproduction, while very different from that of humans, has nevertheless also been the occasion for recourse to human analogy. Yet reasoning by analogy can lead to conclusions based on analogy, as in this excerpt from a 1988 program entitled *The Tale of the Pregnant Male*: "Seahorse fathers show that it's possible to be both a macho male and a caring parent, though why they in particular have such a tough time remains a bit of a mystery. On the other hand, they are probably the only fathers in the world who can be really certain, one-hundred per-cent, of the paternity of all their offspring."[34] Do seahorses really care about such things? Is the statement seriously meant to imply that they do? Probably not, in both cases. Nevertheless, having been asserted by trusted science popularizer David Attenborough, concern with paternity, like the notion of husbands and wives, takes on the guise of scientific fact regardless of however ironically or rhetorically it was intended.

In *Wild Fathers* (1996), seahorses' concern with paternity is elevated to a quest for "the Holy Grail of certainty," and is portrayed as a near obsession. The female is shown depositing her eggs in the male's pouch, where he will fertilize them, but the commentary is decidedly less matter-of-fact: "He's got them! No other male could have snuk in his alien sperm. They're developing inside him, and they're his, all his. His genes, no one else's. . . . But that still leaves a world full of males that don't know, and they have got to get along somehow." As this excerpt suggests, the preoccupation with paternal certainty may not be that of the seahorse so much as that of the film's human creators—and, ultimately, of the patriarchal culture in which such views originate.[35] For although the reproductive behavior of many animals may give the appearance of concern with genetic certainty, it seems ludicrous even to suggest that animals—especially seahorses—have even the faintest conscious awareness of genes or bloodlines, or that they act from even the most rudimentary concern with such matters. A fixed behavior pattern, developed over countless millennia of natural selection, simply doth not an obsession or anxiety make.

It may be tempting to say that my analysis hinges on too literal a reading of the use of these terms, and that the film's statements are intended as metaphors. Yet flat-out assertions from the same film such as, "It's what every father wants: his own little gene carriers," make it difficult to dismiss it all as poetic license. So does the assertion that in the great "quest for immortality, a female always knows when she's passed on her genes; a male can never be sure, so he suffers from chronic angst and suspicion. . . . Not knowing affects a male's very perception of life, and his behavior." There are few better examples of science popularization's reduction of complex processes to oversimplified formulations, of what should have been metaphors to literal interpretations, and of broad, biological principles to narrow, psychological motives on the part of individuals—in this case, jealousy, consuming desire, angst, suspicion, and other *obsessional neuroses*. However rhetorical the intentions behind such statements, they are nevertheless disappointing in a program carrying the logo of the BBC, from which one might expect a greater effort than, say, Disney, to understand animals in *their* terms, or at least in neutral, more objective terms.[36] Nevertheless, examples such as these show that in confronting members of other species, about whom we know relatively little, even trusted authorities grope hard for human comparisons.

An even more systematic attempt to find analogies between the behavior patterns in human and animal families can be found in the 1995 film entitled simply, *Family*. A charming and entertaining work, *Family*, along with its companion piece, *Ceremony*, was part of a series aimed at revealing the "surprising parallels" between people and animals.[37] Its technique of regular cross-cutting between the staged antics of an extended Victorian family and the activities of animals in the wild provides a consistent set of visual analogies that "prove" the supposed parallels by way of associative juxta-position. The rhythmic regularity of these image juxtapositions recalls, for example, one of the 1984 "Morning in America" advertisements for Ronald Reagan in which images of the President were intercut at regular inter-vals with images of Americans going to work. In the absence of narration, a strong association of jobs and prosperity with Reagan's presidency was accomplished solely at the visual level (even though, in truth, unemploy-ment had increased during his first term in office). The wildlife sequences in *Family* are similarly punctuated with images of the human clan to illustrate the supposed parallels and to foster associations. The addition of voice-over commentary explains and reinforces them, and fills in whatever gaps there may be in the visual evidence. Thus, when a male and female lion are shown withdrawing from the pride to engage in several days of repeated copula-tion, it is said that they are "establishing the pair bond." The scientific tone of the language, however, cannot conceal the projection of monogamy onto a decidedly polygamous species.

The broader phenomenon of family is described in the film as "a *univer-sal system* for taking care of our young and of each other."[38] It is acknowl-edged that there are variations within this "universal system," of course, but "whatever the mating system, some things are common to families every-where." Such as? Well, "boisterous children," for example—although before we have time to reflect on the validity of this, we see images of the human parents annoyed at the rowdiness of their children, and then are quickly told that "when we look into a bird's nest [cut to the nest] we can see the same thing happening." The visual "evidence" suggests that the differences be-tween human and nonhuman animals, and even between different species of nonhuman animals, are mainly superficial. The quest for analogies, then, reveals itself as the ideology of the "melting pot" writ large: *underneath we are all alike.*

But *Family* saves its most normative assertion for last. In a conclusion that might stand generations of zoological and ethological research on their heads (if it were true), the film makes the unabashed claim that the "faithful pair is the basic unit of reproduction." That this is spoken over an image of the human family seems to lend it credence, but the number of nonhuman species that do not fit this universalizing definition is too great even to con-template.

In *Ceremony,* an elaborate human wedding is similarly juxtaposed with images of animals' courtship rituals, mating displays, nest-building, and other social or reproductive behavior. Never mind that in animals these are *fixed* behavior patterns, while in humans they are culturally shaped and constantly subject to changing circumstances (professional concerns, finan-cial hardship, religious or rebellious attitudes, changing fashions, personal preferences, etc.). Once again, cross-cutting between images of humans and nonhumans reinforces the perception of parallels and similarities, and thus projects the model of human monogamous marriage onto the natural world despite the differences described in the spoken narration. Ultimately, both *Family* and *Ceremony*, for all their good intentions, show once again that reasoning by analogy leads to conclusions based on analogy. Yet because of their condensed structuring of archival material, they compact into a few minutes the flaws and questionable assertions that might ordinarily be spread out over many films. Their flaws are, in a way then, not their own but those of the genre.

Kearton's Animal Family

The problem of forcing parallels between animals and humans, and of employing human metaphors and analogies either to simplify for popular consumption, or to conceal ignorance about the facts of animals' family and social lives, began to come into focus soon after the arrival of talking pictures. The use of voice-over narration meant that much more verbal information could be supplied than was possible with title cards, and that behavior could now be explained in detail as it was happening on screen. This, in theory, allowed for more behavior to be shown; along with increasing use of telephoto lenses, it allowed for more depictions of the interactions among animals in family and social groupings. Unfortunately, there was still relatively little known about these areas of animal life, and so films that did attempt to show them may have had a lot to say, but little that was substantive, let alone accurate. The understated written description of a "wordless, graceful courtship" in *Birds of a Far-Off Sea* gave way two decades later to a good deal of what often seemed like open-mike vamping to fill the silence, such as Julian Huxley's remark in *The Private Life of the Gannets*, "It's a touch of comic relief!"

One of the best (or worst) early examples of this, and one of the most spectacular missed opportunities to steer the wildlife genre toward accurate portrayals of the family and social lives of animals, was Cherry Kearton's wildlife "comedy," *Dassan* (1930). Although intended in part as a satire on manners, it failed in this regard by poking fun not at the dominant or the powerful, but at the defenseless. Konrad Lorenz, who found little to laugh at in animals,[39] later cautioned creative artists who, like Kearton, used nature as their canvas, but whose art or comedy was often "a specious cover for ignorance of fact."[40]

Beneath the comedy, *Dassan* betrayed how little Kearton had learned about the penguins themselves, their pair-bonding behavior, and the subtle complexities of their social existence. Although the film might have been excused by its comic intentions, the problems are just as evident in several other noncomical, or less comical films Kearton made in the sound years, including *Mototo* (1932), *African Ambassador: Memoirs of Lady Arabella Ape* (1949), and *Toto's Wife* (1954), as well as in an even greater number of books and stories about animals he wrote during the 1920s and 1930s. In these, Kearton revealed an astonishing, almost willful naiveté regarding the interactions, social organization, and familial bonds of animal species he had been observing and photographing for decades.

Dassan opens with a studio prologue in which Kearton asserts the premise of this and countless other films: that the animals depicted bear a "remarkable resemblance to human beings." On the island, we are introduced to Frank and Flora Flatfeet, a penguin couple whose every behavior is explained solely by human analogy and metaphor. The bride and bridegroom, now husband and wife, move into a house and begin to stock it with furniture—Kearton's terms for describing their layering of an underground nest with grass. Huxley resorted to the same analogy in *The Private Life of the Gannets* when he described a mated pair as looking "like a young couple furnishing a new house." It is difficult today, however, to see anything in their behavior resembling our own notion of private property, although, clearly, it is implied in these interpretations. Setting up housekeeping soon teaches Frank Flatfoot that "marriage was more than a word—it was a *sentence.*" This sort of *schtick* soon gives way to even less sophisticated if more cinematic comedy in a montage of penguin eggs hatching to the tune of "Pop Goes the Weasel." Likewise, a fight between Frank and another male penguin, which Kearton unproblematically attributes to jealousy over their wives, is presented as a comic boxing match with a bell sounding between each "round."

Kearton's projection of the human nuclear family was carried to greater extremes in the book *The Animals Came to Drink* (1933), his professed "counterblast" to nature faking in literature and film. It is precisely in the area of family relations, however, that the counterblast misfires most spectacularly, and that moral biology reasserts itself when the smoke clears. Kearton's portrayal of the social organization of lions, for example, is bereft of anything even resembling scientific accuracy. The word, even the concept of the *pride* does not appear. Instead, the picture Kearton paints is a portrait of the human nuclear family in which two adult lions mate for life, move into a private "lair" to raise their young, and proceed to follow Western conventional standards for the division of labor in marriage. In the chapter entitled "The Lion Cubs," Kearton reveals his adherence to the "rule" that *father provides, mother protects.* He describes the father as leaving the "lair" each day to go out and do the hunting while the mother stays home and watches the cubs. After the father makes a kill, he eats what he can of it, then, as a selfless provider, drags the remainder back to his mate and cubs who have been waiting at home. There is virtually no connection here to real lion behavior. Later, after the young ones are asleep, the adults quietly slip out to hunt together. Even their hunting and stalking techniques reverse the actual sexual division of labor in this area ("Step by step they went forward, the lion a few paces ahead of the lioness . . . the lion stopped and the lioness moved up alongside him"—p. 102). Such stereotyping of family and sex roles is consistent with that of Kearton's Viennese contemporary Felix Salten, yet is far more perplexing, given that Kearton had spent many years not in the *café hauser* of Vienna, but instead out in the wild observing animals in their natural habitats. His humanizing and projection of "family values" does not stop at furry mammals, however, as this passage from chapter 12, entitled "Crocodiles in the Creek," reveals:

the current had soon carried the dead hippopotamus downstream and the giant crocodile, eagerly following it, had found the young female still beside him. He did not mind that. He had resented the coming of three crocodiles to share his feast, yet he felt differently towards one alone, and ready, even, to welcome her companionship. He let her help in dragging the meat below the surface. . . and when, as they swam together towards the end of the pool, she turned aside to enter a narrow creek, he followed her. (p. 111)

Any doubts as to whether they are swimming toward blissful monogamy are soon dispelled: "In that creek the two crocodiles made their home" (p. 112), and "lived in contentment for several weeks" (p. 115).

   In *Island of the Penguins* (1930), the companion book to *Dassan*, Kearton's treatment of animal "marriage" goes a step farther. Chapter 5, entitled, "Family Matters," begins by noting, "The trouble with newly-married peacefulness is that it doesn't last." Then this:

At first it is delightful. Even when, as with the penguins, the husband and wife are so house-proud and so fearful of burglars that they cannot both leave home at once, there is, nevertheless, such delight in the house itself, and in life generally, that hardly seems to matter. . . Mr. Penguin, for instance, goes down to the sea in search of his dinner, leaving his wife drowsily meditating on the perfect bliss of married life. She is very happy, and probably she imagines that if only life will go on just like that, she will never want anything more. Mr. Penguin is just as contented . . . he goes into the hole beside her, caresses her, and embraces with his flippers. How good it is to be home again, feeling so comfortably well fed, and to have such an adorable wife awaiting him! [41]

Here, as in *Dassan*, the resemblance to the commentaries written years later by Hibler and Algar for Disney's "True Life Adventures" is worth remarking, as this excerpt from *Seal Island* (1948) illustrates: "A caress or two, and another bride is added to the harem. Thus, community life in the colony begins. The beachmaster, well pleased with himself, settles down to watch over his new wives, who take their beauty naps, sleeping, heads gracefully up. Ah, what more could one wish? A good home, adoring wives—a peaceful paradise."

The similarities between the two films went beyond their portrayals of romance; both featured juxtapositions of comedy with serious life-and-death events, both subscribed to the myth (discussed below) that animal parents undertake to "educate" their young, and both, ultimately, allow moral biology to flourish in an atmosphere thick with human-animal analogies. Nevertheless, each of these films bucked the trend of hunting and safari pictures that was dominant for so long, and helped establish the precedents and define the conventions that would, ironically, allow later filmmakers to paint a more complete behavioral picture of the social lives of animals. The details of that picture, however, would only gradually be filled in.

Birth, School, Work, Death

The life-cycle story line helped push portrayals of family and social life into the foreground of wildlife films, but it did not take hold immediately, and even when it did there remained significant omissions. Death, always a screen favorite, was there from the start, of course, but sex and birth were for many years taboo. True, Kearton and others had shown eggs hatching, but the birth of mammals on mass-market screens was still some years away from acceptance. Television helped change this; its smaller screen and black-and-white images made for less graphic depictions. Still, after more than fifty years of wild animals on the big screen, Tom McHugh's color footage depicting the birth of a bison calf in Disney's *The Vanishing Prairie* (1954) was considered shocking enough to be banned in New York by the State Board of Censors (although it was later overturned). *Time*'s review of the film began by noting the ban, then exhorted audiences: "Birth, it is clear from this scene, can no more be the subject of prurience than death can. Both are too simple and important. . . . In fact, if the average Hollywood picture had an approach to sex and life as healthy and as honest as Producer Disney shows here, no parent would need think twice about sending his children to the movies."[42] Another reviewer assured readers, "I lived through the scene, and I suspect you will too."[43] Two months later, yet another still saw fit to warn against any further attempts to delete the scene: "Any censors who cut this sequence should themselves be severed from the body politic."[44] Although sermonizing is no longer necessary to justify such a scene (*The Ultimate Guide: Horses*, 1998, includes a graphic birth scene as its opening image), these comments give some indication of how late in the history of wildlife films it was before images of mammalian birth were included, and how incomplete, therefore, was the picture of the lives of animals in earlier films.

Sex, however, was another matter. Like birth, its inclusion in films and television programs depended on the species—on the visibility of the organs, similarities to humans when performing the act, and so forth. The fact that some are still uncomfortable with scenes of copulation may be an indication of the degree to which people continue to identify unconsciously with animals and therefore continue to impose human taboos upon them. In the United States, where immaculate conception seemed more deeply embraced, copulation continued for many more years to be excluded from the media's picture of the lives and behavior of many animals. Survival's *The Family That Lived with Elephants* included a shot of two of the huge beasts in the act, but when it came to American television in a 1974 CBS broadcast sponsored by Kraft Foods, the brief sex scene, although filmed in long-shot, was deleted. Survival's American partner J. Walter Thompson reportedly "deemed it unfit for American eyes."[45] Disney's films, as already shown, simply talked around the matter of sex, following Hollywood's example of alluding to it by way of misleading metaphors of love and romance. Marty Stouffer has written that his depiction of wild boars mating was a television "first" in America. Although it did not meet with resistance from liberal-minded PBS executives, some of the affiliates, in an effort to protect their viewers from unwanted intrusions by reality, nevertheless deleted the scene on their own. Stouffer remarked that "on commercial television, the mating sequence would never have aired," and that "PBS deserves a lot of praise for airing a natural history 'first.'"[46] Congratulations must be tempered by the awareness, however, that this "first" did not come until well into the 1980s. Producer Dennis Kane confirmed this when he remarked in 1992, "Ten years ago, we couldn't show mating at all."[47] In a culture less hampered by sexually repressive attitudes, however, the BBC began to introduce copulation scenes in the late 1950s (although Eric Ashby's depiction of rabbits in the act did generate a few angry letters). More recently, it produced an unabashed look at animal sex and reproduction entitled *The Battle of the Sexes* (1999).[48]

Over the years, however, American audiences proved far more tolerant (and more mature) in such matters than broadcasters had given them credit for being. Even before a Presidential scandal in the late 1990s thrust discussions of human sexuality into American living rooms, prohibitions against graphic scenes of animal sex and reproduction had loosened considerably. Among the most frank depictions of animal sexuality on American television was *The New Chimpanzees* (1995), which, significantly, was broadcast on NBC as one of its high-profile "National Geographic Specials." It begins in familiar territory with the dynastic clan of Gombe chimps well known from so many films based on Jane Goodall's research. Then, just after the half-way point, it shifts to the so-called "pygmy chimps," or bonobos of Zaire, whereupon we learn, "Instead of fighting, bonobos use sex to diffuse aggression. In this genuine make-love-not-war society, bonobos have largely divorced sex from its reproductive role. Sex is used by all bonobos, regardless of gender or age, to form bonds and mitigate tension." We are shown

Scene from *The Family That Lived with Elephants* 1972). A brief elephant copulation scene was cut after being deemed too strong for American audiences. Lee Lyon/ Survival Anglia.

several sexual acts occurring, including *same sex* relations. One between two males, although not graphic in detail, may well have been the first depic- tion of same-sex intercourse between primates, human or nonhuman, ever shown on a major network in prime-time. At this writing, Western civiliza- tion still seems intact. Two years after that broadcast, the half-hour BBC film *Pygmy Chimpanzee: The Last Great Ape* (1997), which dealt solely with bonobos and their unique forms of social interaction, also aired in prime-time in the United States on the *National Geographic Explorer* series (then airing on TBS). By that time it was all rather matter-of-fact.

Many films about chimpanzees over the years have emphasized the acqui- sition of specialized knowledge and skills, such as tool use, by the young. Owing to Goodall's pioneering research, the "termite fishing" behavior of chimps has been well documented on film. It appears from such scenes that the young learn by observation and practice, perhaps even by some degree of imitation. Yet if imitation is involved, it is something of which actually very few other species are capable, and which exists only at "the highest cog- nitive level."[49] The capacity among most species, especially their young, to imitate or mimic behavior is generally not accepted by ethologists or borne out by research. The vast majority of general behavior patterns, even among primates, are simply innate. Nevertheless, imitation is widely attributed in wildlife films to all sorts of species regardless of the absence of scientific sup- port. Received opinion, perhaps owing to no better source than other wild- life films, even finds its way into the respected *Ultimate Guide* series. Its film on horses tells us: "Imitating their parents, foals learn how to be horses," and that they actually "mimic" the behavior of adults. The Japanese film *A Cheetah Family* provides a classic example when it purports to show young cheetahs "imitating their mother's hunting style." If anything, the ability of very young predators to exhibit proto-hunting behavior out of context shows that the behavior is *already present* in their repertoire of innate motor skills, not that they witness it, then recall it later and imitate it movement- for-movement. Because play behavior by young animals consists of rehears- ing, out of context, skills essential to the survival of adults, it is routinely de- scribed in wildlife films as an imitation of *adult behavior.* Yet the fact that the young already possess the behavior shows that it is not the exclusive prov- ince of adults, but is characteristic of the species. Similarly, in the BBC's *Wolf* (a.k.a. *Wild Wolves*, 1998) it is suggested that the one of the most central of in- nate behaviors—begging food from an adult—is learned by the young from the adult female's example when she begs from the male.

Even copulatory behavior, which can be seen in the play of many young mammals, is often described as imitative—although if this were learned only through observation and imitation few species would survive long. This seems an especially clear case of projecting human values (or anxieties). One argument for excluding depictions of sexuality in film and television has stemmed from the fear that children would imitate what they saw. The implication is that sexual behavior is learned visually, that visual conceal-ment of it until adulthood can somehow prevent sexual urges from develop-ing despite the hormonal changes of puberty, and that sex among adults is therefore an imitation of some scene they nevertheless managed to witness anyway. Sex has largely, and problematically, been removed to the realms of culture and politics among humans, but if it were an imitative behavior among animals then, presumably, natural selection would favor the most skilled mimics.

That wildlife films in general continue to assign too much responsibility for the behavior of the young to their parents may be further evidence of the subtlety with which human values are projected onto nature. With re-gard to chimpanzees' termite fishing behavior, there remains only spotty evi-dence that mothers deliberately undertake to pass this skill on to the young, and to instruct them in technique (significantly, chimpanzee mothers do not discipline their young for unruliness, and so apparently have little inter-est in shaping their behavior).[50] Still, animals of all sorts are routinely de-scribed in wildlife films as "passing on" skills and knowledge to their young. *Toothwalkers* (1997), for example, holds that among walruses, knowledge of a particular feeding site "has been passed on from mother to calf for gen-erations." Such intergenerational passing-on occurs in other films, however, with even greater deliberation and purpose. In *Falconeye* (1998), it is said that a mother peregrine falcon must pass on to her young perfect hunting skills so that he can, in turn, pass them on to the next generation.[51] From this ac-count one might conclude that a break in the chain of passing-on could re-sult in the disappearance of the behavior from an entire family line. Each individual thus carries a tremendous responsibility to pass it on, and to pass it on *correctly*, without the sorts of distortion that occur when messages are passed from human to human. Fortunately for falcons, the behavior is actu-ally innate, and is perfected with practice rather than by observation.

The description of behavior as having been "passed on," with its sugges-tion of intentional, purposeful dissemination of knowledge, inevitably im-plies *teaching*. There is a long tradition of "animal education" in wildlife films, as illustrated in countless scenes said to depict adult animals' efforts to "train" their young, and to teach them the skills they will need to sur-vive. Even before being taken up by filmmakers, this was a recurrent theme among nature writers,[52] and was one of the main targets of Burroughs and Roosevelt in their campaign against nature faking. William J. Long's book *School of the Woods* (1902), with its sustained argument that adult animals edu-cate their young ("home schooling" would be the term used today), came under heavy fire from Burroughs: "there is nothing in the dealings of ani-mals with their young that in the remotest way suggests human instruction and discipline. The young of all wild creatures . . . do not have to be taught;

they are taught by nature from the start. . . . Mr. Long would have us believe that the crows teach their young to fly. . . . No bird teaches its young to fly."[53]

Nevertheless, eight decades later the argument could still be heard that a young eagle is, in fact, taught to fly—at least, in such a way as to make it an effective hunter—and done so through systematic and painstaking repeated demonstrations by a parent.[54] Although no one denies the existence and necessity of animal learning, Burroughs had nevertheless made an important distinction between learning and teaching: "To teach is to bring one mind to act upon another mind; it is the result of a conscious effort on the part of both teacher and pupil." Teaching thus implies an agreement between teacher and student that each will play a clear role at an appointed time. But is it clear to the animal student when the lesson begins and when it is over, when it is time to pay attention and when not? From among all the movements and behavior the parent displays through the course of a day or week, does the young student really know which ones are part of the lesson it is supposed to study and which are not? Or should it just observe *all* the parent's movements and behavior, and if so, can this still be called *teaching*? The assumption so often reflected in wildlife films is that if learning occurs, it must be the result of teaching. Although not a formal behavioral scientist, Burroughs offered a conclusion that has withstood a century of behavioral research: "People who think they see . . . animals training their young read their own thoughts or preconceptions into what they see."[55]

Yet the idea of formal education among animals persisted despite Burroughs's protestations. Other writers in addition to Long maintained faith in the existence of ritualized, formal efforts by adult animals to educate and train the young. Curwood's novel *The Grizzly King* (1916) offers an especially vivid illustration in its portrayal of an orphaned cub being carefully and systematically instructed in the ways of survival by an older, more experienced male. Curwood could hardly have been ignorant of the doubts raised during the nature faker controversy regarding the idea of animal education, yet he nevertheless proceeded to build an entire story around it, and it is no less central in Annaud's 1988 film version, *The Bear* (*L'Ours*).

Apparently, among the most important things about which young animals must be schooled, in addition to flight and hunting techniques, are water and swimming. Kearton even described young penguins in *Dassan* as having to be "taught to swim" (presumably, without such teaching they would either drown or remain on land). Organized swimming lessons were mandatory for many animals in Disney's "True Life Adventures." In *Seal Island* we learn that young seals "must learn to swim like any other land mammal," and that "baby seals gather in groups, or pods, for comfort, for safety, and for school—yes, school." Narrator Hibler adds that an "important part of their schooling is learning to breathe for long submersion." In

Irwin Allen's 1952 film version of Rachel Carson's *The Sea Around Us*, it is said of one young fur seal that "Mama teaches him how to swim—and he'd better learn fast, or else." A few years later, in the last of Disney's "True Life" films, *Jungle Cat* (1960), "training" the young in the ways of water is still a concern of parents, as shown when a mother jaguar takes her cubs down to the river, "anxious that her youngsters learn to like it early." Presumably, her anxiety could turn to guilt and self-reproach should one of them drown.

As quaint as these examples from decades ago may seem, the idea of formal animal education has shown little sign of disappearing from wild-life films in the years since. *Family* depicts a group of meerkats in which "a teacher gathers together the youngsters for a feeding lesson," but later shows that, in the case of monkeys, where food is more plentiful the young "don't need so formal an education." A film about horses argues that "a mare must teach her foal what is edible." A film about dolphins includes a scene that purports to show an adult "teaching" a certain feeding technique to a youngster. The next shot "proves" this by showing what is said to be the same young dolphin, some weeks later, practicing the technique and demonstrating thereby that the lesson had been learned. A film in a recent series about wild animal mothers includes a number of similar assertions: a colobus monkey is said to "rely on the lessons it has learned from its mother." A mother serval cat "will train these young servals to hunt one day as expertly as she does." A lion mother "must provide experiences" that will help her cubs learn important skills, and thus, "from their mother, cubs learn the fieldcraft of the hunter." The subsequent film in the series contains even more examples of animal education, suggesting that mothers of virtually all animal species practice a similar brand of home schooling. An adult prairie dog is said to have lived long "mainly because her own mother taught her to look out for danger, and now her pups are taking the same lesson." The pup's plea for food "will not be answered until mother, the teacher, is satisfied that danger has passed, but the pupil has also learned well from mother how to avoid predators." A porcupine teaches its young that melons are edible; young black bears are also said to attend a "feeding lesson." River dolphins are said to "train their young to use sound pulses and echoes for hunting fish." Even "parenting" skills must apparently be taught: a bush baby pup is said to begin her own family only after being "fully trained by her mother."[56] And so on.

Yet rather than delve further into matters best left to ethologists, it is more important here to note that the assumption of animals teaching their young may be followed closely by a moral judgment ready to pronounce the parents of the successful animals better teachers, and therefore better parents than those parents of animals who, for whatever reason, do not survive. The fact that such a moral implication is unspoken does not mean that audiences are unable to hear it. Those animals depicted as dotingly teaching their young are clearly "better," more caring parents, and their species likely the preferred ones—at least, by the human standards audiences bring to such films.

Furthermore, without pushing the school metaphor too far, we might at least consider that its use may entail a number of presumptions about animal behavior in the wild, and projections of human models onto it. Children in school must, after all, pay attention, obey their teachers, practice their lessons, do their homework, and not cut classes. For young animals, failure to learn survival techniques could have fatal results, but as "students" it would nevertheless result from *failure*, even *delinquency*, rather than natural processes. Just as it is the duty of the mother to teach, so is it the duty of the young to pay attention and learn. The doctrine of personal responsibility is asserted once again.

Is it legitimate, however, to claim that animals have any duty or responsibility to behave in a particular way? How often are these notions applied to *fixed behavior patterns?* Duties, responsibilities, and obligations are usually seen in human society as being directed toward others as expressions of a social *contract*, not a social *bond*, and are thus projections onto nature of human social organizations and agreements (which vary greatly from culture to culture). As formalized agreements and expectations, they stand in contrast to "natural behavior," whether animal or human. Among animals, nest building, regurgitating food for the young, even defending them against threats, are largely examples of innate and fixed behavior. Even where such actions may involve some social learning they are not performed out of a sense of social or moral obligation, and should not thus be subject to moral categorization.[57]

The personification and individualization of nature's forces not only gives rise to the idea of responsibilities and obligations among animals, but also makes individual animals into characters, and makes their lives—and deaths —into vehicles of meaning. Their deaths, in particular, are stripped of contingency and made instead to occur in some "meaningful" way in which both life and death can be explained. Our own morbid curiosity about death and dying is also given a justification: in the context of a natural history film it is transmuted from a perverse fascination into an educational experience, and a sacred quest on the part of filmmakers to reveal unexplored truths by the "objective" medium of the camera. While sex and birth remained taboos in mainstream film for many years, happening only off screen, death could be portrayed, for the most part, in full-frontal, graphic depictions—and it didn't even have to be faked. From the unblinking depiction of the execution of Topsy in *Electrocuting an Elephant* (1903), to the countless hunting and safari pictures made over a several decades, animals were regularly seen dying—often being put to death unnecessarily in what now look like so many *snuff* films. Moreover, legitimate scenes of animal predation in the wild were for many years so difficult to capture on film that they too were routinely set up and staged for the camera, beginning as early as 1884 with Muybridge's "sacrifice" of the buffalo to the tiger.

Television, of course, remained for many years more conservative—at least, in the United States. Even into the 1970s, the networks, according to Stouffer, wanted to see chases and predation "without any actual bloodshed."[58] Yet predation scenes, with or without blood, proved to be audience-pleasers and have been as necessary to the success of blue chip films as obligatory sex scenes have to R-rated motion pictures. Indeed, the scene of the big kill can be compared to the obligatory "cum-shot" in XXX-rated films; each serves as a guarantor of authenticity, and thus as a climactic pay-off of a different sort from traditional dramatic climaxes—although the wildlife kill scene could be this as well. It has been the overabundance of such scenes, however, which in part has led to charges of excessive violence and of "eco-porn."[59] We may be told on the voice track that of a certain predator's attempts to catch prey only one in ten ends in a kill, but we certainly do not see nine failures for every one success. The very demands of the medium for drama and climax dictate that kills are greatly overrepresented numerically. To do otherwise might be more true, visually, to natural reality, but it would make bad television. Other genres of "reality television" are just as artificially enhanced and manipulated—a notable exception on American TV being the minimalist C-SPAN, although few would consider it "good television."

In recent years, as wildlife filmmakers have tried to recolonize movie screens with motion pictures such as *The Leopard Son* (1996), and even to move into large formats, such as IMAX, the bloodshed tolerance order has been reversing. On the big screen, a bloody wound (or, for that matter, sex organs) can be several feet wide. This has made television, with its smaller screens and lesser capacity for detail, the more tolerant medium of the two, allowing for more graphic depictions of blood and death as well as sex. As already mentioned, killing scenes have for some years been regarded as necessary to secure audiences, especially American audiences. While serving the same economic purposes as sex and violent action scenes in mainstream film and television, killing and death in wildlife films have been more easily justified and defended than car chases and shootouts on grounds that they are more true to reality, to nature just "nature going about its business," as one commissioning producer put it.[60]

Yet if fighting and dying, killing and being killed, represent the "truth" and the "business" of nature, it is nature conceived in the vulgar-Darwinist terms of *perpetual conflict*, played out, once again, at the level of individuals in interspecific struggles. The degree to which such struggles are expected in wildlife films may be illustrated by a letter some friends of mine received in 1997 from an American producer seeking to buy footage for a "nature series" about "wild animals fighting for survival." The content of the footage, it went on, "should culminate in a struggle between two formidable animals," as well as a little extra "to use before and after the fight." The depiction of nature as a vast gladiatorial arena, where "formidable" animals regularly do battle is sadly pervasive, in part as a result of misguided, exploitative, and generally dubious "nature series" such as this one. The fact that fighting for survival more often means *avoiding* life-threatening conflicts would be unlikely to make for saleable projects, let alone for exciting footage, and so is simply discarded, along with other unphotogenic or inconvenient realities.

Even the animal stories of Charles G. D. Roberts were often criticized in their time for what seemed an overemphasis on fighting, killing, and death. Burroughs noted that the animals in many such stories seemed to live in a perpetual "state of siege" as if in "an enemy's country" from which there was no escape.[61] Ninety years later, the film *Dressing for Dinner* would still maintain that the animal world was one, vast "never-ending arms race" (and provide visual "evidence" in support of the claim). Meanwhile, Time-Life would invoke the image of "killing fields" in its *Nature's Assassins* series. These sorts of interpretations of nature continue to be widespread, such that Roberts's stories, despite charges in their own time of excessive violence, have been "rehabilitated," and are now applauded for the "Darwinian" accuracy of their representations of what are typically called the "harsh realities" of nature. That life in the wild is particularly harsh, however, is a judgment unlikely to be shared by wild animals so well equipped and well adapted by evolution to deal with it. Doubtless they do not experience their own lives as either unduly harsh or as perpetual struggles, let alone as a never-ending arms race.

Nevertheless, everyday life for many individual animals in wildlife films has, somewhat ironically, revolved almost completely around death, or at least deadly struggle. "The syndrome known as Life," wrote Samuel Beckett, "does not admit of palliation." Seton may have had something similar in mind when he asserted in 1898 that "the life of a wild animal always has a tragic end" (a sentiment echoed in John Downer's *Supernatural*, 1999).[62] This has been interpreted to mean that Seton and Roberts had simply refused to evade the supposed "unpleasant fact" that "kill or be killed is the natural law," and that "only the best escaped," and even then only "for a time." [63] In contrast, Jane Goodall noted that even in the midst of plenty a carnivore may simply starve to death rather than be violently killed.[64] Adverse weather conditions are as often the cause of death in the wild as is limited availability of food, especially among the young. Cherry Kearton knew this, and in the midst of *Dassan*'s comedy included a scene of abandoned penguin chicks, "poor little orphans of the storm," as he described them, shown dead in a graphic close-up, the victims of starvation rather than of predatory killing.

In the years since, however, there have been few nonviolent deaths in the dramatic world of wildlife film and television. *Mountain Gorilla: A Shattered Kingdom* (1996) contains a notable exception in a scene in which two young male gorillas awaken one day to find that their aged father has simply passed away in the night. Yet slow or undramatic deaths, even when important to a story such as this one, need not actually be shown on camera, where they take up valuable screen time and detract from dramatic pacing. Unlike dramatic deaths at the jaws of predators, slow, diseased deaths make for bad television. Yet when the death toll in wildlife films is added up, dying is depicted, in the end, as a predominantly violent affair, and the image of killing fields may indeed be the image viewers have of the natural world.

Yet it is still only we humans who kill for "sport"—that is, for the sheer fun and pleasure of killing—despite the assumption of a higher morality and greater value set on life as a result of our commitment to "family values."

6
Nature Designed and Composed

As wildlife films began their second century, they entered a time of bewildering transition unlike any other in their history. The market had undergone a period of unprecedented expansion, but would it go from boom to bust? Wildlife films made for large formats, such as IMAX, had proven successful, but how many such films about whales or wolves would audiences pay to see? Digital and high-definition television were on the horizon, so too was web-based content-on-demand, but to many in the audience their features were still unclear.[1] To many in the industry trying to negotiate the tangle of varying broadcast standards, as well different film and video formats, matters seemed no less uncertain.

The architecture of the industry was also becoming increasingly Byzantine. Although it had assumed an essentially oligopolistic structure, dominated by a few large producer/sellers with significant market share, some of these had already begun forming intricate partnerships and joint-ventures, if not merging outright to form even larger, more powerful organizations. All of this made it increasingly difficult for others to enter and participate. Moreover, the need to sell to global markets, and the fact that budgets had soared beyond the reach of most individual firms, meant that elaborate co-production deals had become the norm. The eight-hour series *Living Europe* (1997) epitomized the new multinational financing. Produced by Green Umbrella (Britain), the partners included SVT (Sweden), NRK (Norway), DR (Denmark), WGBH (United States), WDR (Germany), EO (Netherlands), ORF (Austria), and YLE (Finland). Such productions also relied heavily on international presales. In these ways, costs could be divided and shared, but such deals meant the disappearance of clear national differences in product, and the tendency instead toward an international style. Homogenization could be overcome to some extent by "versioning" for different markets, but having several different versions of a film could make it difficult to talk any longer about a single "work." This still poses problems not only for film critics and historians, but for filmmakers concerned with the integrity of their work, and wishing to be thought of as artists rather than as businesspeople concerned only with markets and sales. Coproduction also created a network of interdependencies in which each organization became more reliant on its competitors for resources. This effectively redefined competition within the industry as a "negotiated struggle" among friendly rivals with mutual interests and complex contractual interrelationships.[2]

Then there was the problem of generational transition among those who actually made the films. The first generation of wildlife filmmakers (Ditmars, Kearton, Kleinschmidt, Pike, Rainey, etc.) had got in early, when there was no competition and no rules. The second generation (Field and Smith, Buck, the Johnsons) had faced an already formed and competitive film industry, to which they responded by developing distinctive styles and market niches. They had also negotiated the transition to sound film. The third generation (Cousteau, Denis, Disney, Grzimek, Hass, Sielmann, etc.) had largely begun in the cinema and then became pioneers of wildlife television. It was with the fourth generation that wildlife film experienced a sort of "baby boom" of producers, on-air personalities, and filmmaker-camerapersons too numerous to name individually. It was this generation that had dominated the scene for over thirty years, but was largely facing retirement at the end of the twentieth century—just as technologies were changing. Many young people stood willing and eager to take their place, but they now faced a far more stratified and capital-intensive industry whose walls were difficult to scale. There were few mechanisms for channeling newcomers into the business, or for assuring that a new generation of wildlife filmmakers could gain the sort of experience that had been available in earlier years when things were more wide open. Hollywood had been aided during this stage in its development by the advent of film schools, the graduates of which went on to dominate the industry. At the century's turn, there were isolated efforts to start specialized wildlife and natural history filmmaking schools, the most ambitious of which combined filmmaking experience with study in biology, ethology, and other areas of science that need more careful consideration in wildlife films. Industry leaders, however, seemed largely indifferent to such efforts.

Viva la . . . Contra-Révolution?

The greatest area of uncertainty was that of impending technological change. Some saw high-definition Television (HDTV) as portending a "revolution" in the industry, and sought to be in its vanguard. Yet, as we have already seen, earlier upheavals in wildlife film form and technology had been relatively bloodless affairs, handled quietly, efficiently, and with little upset. The change from static *actualités* to narrative films had seemed more a natural evolution than a revolution. So too had the transition from silent to sound film, which provides the clearest historical analogy to the fin de siècle technological changes.

The most significant historical change had clearly been the move from the big screen to television, which occurred, ironically, just as wildlife cinematic features were reaching their zenith of popularity. Although television had created many new opportunities and given rise to new talents and personalities, fifty years of cinematic tradition nevertheless weighed heavily on the new medium and distinctly televisual wildlife programs soon gave way to an onslaught of televised wildlife movies. This state of affairs endured for nearly fifty more years, but at last cable and satellite systems opened up niches for televisual (non-blue chip) formats to emerge once again, and to exploit television's unique powers of immediacy and spontaneity.

By contrast, the HD "revolution" seemed in some ways counter-revolutionary. With its promise of large, home-cinema screens, and elevated production costs effectively barring participation by all but the most powerful and established, HD seemed poised to reinforce the dominance of cinematic styles, and to consolidate the power of the old regime, not usher in the new. The balance of power may have fluctuated slightly, but the industry as a whole faced no external revolutionary force threatening to overturn the existing system. The legions of newcomers with their mini-DV-cams and computer editing softwares did not storm the industry's gates, steal its fire, or demand the heads of its leaders. Instead, lacking organization and resources, they stood outside and asked in the most polite way possible to be let in, or short of that, for the leaders' blessings and assistance. It was estimated that from the ranks of aspiring camera people, however, only about of one of them per year was let past the gates.[3]

To many of those already inside, it seemed that HD was not so much a revolution as merely another round of technological and formal adjustments, perhaps like those that had occurred with the arrival of sync-sound. Both involved cumbersome new machinery, decreased camera mobility, more emphasis on postproduction, increased costs, greater need for planning, and the inhibition of creative spontaneity, but all of these could be absorbed with little disruption to business as usual.

Yet sync-sound had seemed to push wildlife films toward greater realism, as well as toward scientific informativeness and accuracy, whereas the technologies that arrived with the twenty-first century, along with the expanding competition and economies of scale in the industry, seemed to herald a move in the opposite direction: toward more drama and spectacle, with less attention to factual exposition (let alone to serious *issues*). The addition of sound had given motion pictures, perhaps especially wildlife films, the ability to mirror reality more accurately, bringing them closer to the Bazinian ideal of "total cinema."[4] Realist schools of film theory have held ever since that faithful representation of reality was the true fulfillment of motion pictures' potential. Wildlife films today, however, are increasingly guided by *formalist* aesthetics, or at least are farther than in the past from the documentary ideal of cinema as a "transparent" medium. Today wildlife filmmakers seem more often to be using the TV screen not as a window to the world, but as a canvas on which to paint dramatic and expressive images of it. The fact that this canvas, in the age of HD and large format (such as IMAX) screens is getting bigger and more visually powerful has not only helped wildlife filmmakers lay a greater claim to the legitimizing mantle of *art*, but has also increased the tendency toward films that are guided by the demands of art, rather than by those of science or ecological concerns.

It has also been argued, moreover, that documentaries addressing specific scientific or environmental issues can, for some time, continue to be made in the old, cheaper-to-produce television formats, on the assumption that they will soon be dated and obsolete anyway. By contrast, blue chip films, with their qualities of spectacular timelessness, are seen as far better suited to HD and large format screens, for they can continue making money for years. The problem in this scenario, obviously, is that the future of natural history television may hold little place for serious environmental documentaries, while welcoming increasingly elaborate and spectacular diversions.

High-Tech Art

As technologies have changed, some filmmakers have adapted and made adjustments in their style and approach. Television, for example, with its small screen, was a more close-up medium than cinema and required more frame-filling images. With HD and large screen formats, however, the possibility of more magnificent scenic panoramas lay open to wildlife and natural history filmmakers in a way that it hadn't in decades. Moreover, with screens that were larger and clearer, it seemed that the need for frame-filling facial close-ups could be reduced, as images of individual animals could be large and clear without having to fill the entire frame. Yet despite less reliance on frame-filling faces, there was no fear in the industry that television's emotional impact would be reduced. Indeed, larger screens were seen by many as being inherently favorable to subjective, visceral experiences rather than to *schoolsey* lecture films about scientific and ecological matters. If this were true, it seemed that wildlife films might be even more likely to appeal, as discussed earlier, to the emotions rather than to the intellect, to the heart rather than to the head, and would thus put greater emphasis on sensation and spectacle than on science. With big screen images thought to be so powerful on their own as to reduce the need for commentary, it seemed a greater proportion of what wildlife films had to communicate would be done so visually, and therefore by dramatic rather than by expository means.

Bigger, clearer, more vivid images seemed inevitably to mean that some kinds of scenes—copulation, birth, and bloody kills, for example—might prove too graphically detailed for many viewers, and might have to be toned down. This, however, could be easily done when dealing with images that were completely digital from shooting to transmission. Graphic bloodshed could be reduced or erased at several stages in postproduction. It could even be done during production, literally in the camera, given the power of digital beta-cams and HD-cams on their own to enhance, decrease, or even eliminate individual colors.[5]

Yet computerized slight-of-hand of this sort was not new. Colors had for some time been digitally corrected in postproduction to compensate for differences among shots filmed at varying times and locations, allowing them to be seamlessly assembled into a single scene or sequence. Sound, moreover, had long been heavily manipulated, if not wholly manufactured. Few in the industry would therefore be likely to see significant discontinuities between new adjustments and already accepted practices. Indeed, even greater manipulation lay in editing practices that were already nearly a century old, and that were designed to serve what was arguably the most subtle and unquestioned artifice of all: storytelling.

With digital technology, however, images that could not be satisfactorily obtained in the field could, conceivably, be created in the computer. Perhaps the empty screen space between a lion and its prey, far out in front of it, could be digitally removed, making them appear closer together on the screen, and making the chase itself appear more dramatic. At the very least, skies could be made more blue, telephone lines and tourist vans deleted, and a few hundred wildebeests or flamingoes added to panoramic shots where needed. The problem of animals' dwindling numbers in the real world could be reduced to one on screen of filling *negative space*. Feature films such as *Terminator 2* (1991) and *Forrest Gump* (1993) had already shown how easy and undetectable digital alterations could be; scholars, in fact, had been voicing concerns since the mid-1980s.[6]

Discipline

There were, arguably, larger issues than image manipulation. New technologies also meant increased costs, and this implied even greater changes in style and technique than those brought about simply by improved picture quality. In fact, changes had already occurred since the 1970s, when it was more common for lone camera teams to spend many months living among their subjects with only a vague outline of an idea, shooting miles of film as they improvised along the way.[7] In the 1980s and 1990s, however, more expensive globe-trotting "mega-series" from *Life on Earth* to *The Life of Birds* showed the hard money value of extensive planning, careful scripting, detailed preparation, meticulous logistical supervision (the *Trials of Life* involved the efforts of some *forty* cameramen), and ultimately, more conspicuous production values.[8] Expanding markets, increased budgets, and changing aesthetics all conspired to introduce greater control into wildlife filmmaking, and thus over the representation of nature.

Yet wildlife filmmaking had been largely a *film*-based practice, and with film stock becoming ever more costly relative to video alternatives, budget controllers sought to reign in what were now seen as indulgences and excesses. Moreover, although super-16mm film, the industry's preferred origination format, could yield adequate results in transfer to high definition, mastering even a single hour of super-16 to HD could add as much as $100,000 to postproduction costs.[9] Some HD enthusiasts advocated shooting on super-35, which boasted greater image quality and image stability in transfer to HD video (owing in part to its three sprocket-holes per frame), but this was an even more costly proposition. Advocates argued, however, that it was the most "future proof" of formats in that it would allow for the even sharper 3,000-line ultra-high definition television that was already anticipated—but in a future that seemed beyond the financial reach of many.

With budgets already soaring, a process had been initiated that was something like the "blockbuster" phenomenon that had been occurring in Hollywood for some years. Mergers and acquisitions made for larger companies able to take on bigger, more costly projects; joint-ventures and coproduction deals also helped make budgets possible that were unheard of just a decade earlier. But pockets were only so deep. New cameras, costly film stocks, expensive HD mastering and other new postproduction charges all took their toll, so that less could be left to chance during production—this, ironically, in an industry that had largely been built on capturing "chance" events on film. No more, it seemed. Shooting ratios had already been cut in half over the decades, from as high as 50:1 to somewhere around 25:1, thought by some to be the minimum necessary for capturing spontaneous, authentic animal behavior in the wild. In the late 1990s, however, amid costly technological changes, there began to be calls from industry executives for even greater "discipline" during shooting, including reductions of ratios to around 10:1 if not lower.[10]

It had long been held in the industry, as we have already seen, that animal behavior could be forgivably provoked or staged, so long as the result on the screen conformed to scientific facts. Yet, as we have also seen, scientific facts have too often proven a weak constraint on creative invention—in particular with regard to projections of human family and moral values onto nature. It seemed unlikely that scientific facts alone would serve as a check on creative digital manipulation. The genie was already out of the bottle.

With production costs and new technologies driving increased reliance on staged events and controlled behavior, it is unclear, in the early stages of wildlife film's second century, how far toward artifice and simulation wildlife films will go. Wildlife filmmakers have increasingly begun, for whatever reasons, to follow Hollywood's example not only in scripting and storyboarding, but also in areas such as camera, lighting, set construction, and overall production design. The concept is not completely new, of course — only the degree of its application. As we have already seen, Disney had earlier negotiated a successful merger of Hollywood style with wildlife content, but with still fairly modest production values. At the end of wildlife films' first century, Hollywood style combined with far greater budgets, resources, and visible production values, to take center stage in works such as the BBC's *Private Life of Plants* and *Alien Empire* series, as well as National Geographic's *Deadly Encounters* and *Nature's Nightmares* series. In these, as in large-format films, there are few shots not carefully planned, set up, lit, and controlled; almost nothing is left to chance.

Looking at the results, one could see the style in such films as evidence of greater sophistication, at least with regard to cinematic technique. One could also see it as a greater refinement of artistic sensibility. Or, one could see it as evidence of greater artifice and manipulation of the material. Indeed, one might do well to see it as the inevitable result of economies of scale in media production. One could not, however, see it as greater naturalness on the part of nature imagery.

Power and Stillness

It seemed at the end of their first century that, although wildlife films had retained nature as their content, they had begun to lose the feel for its dimensions. Its simplicities had been turned into elaborate productions, its stillness to rapidly cut montages, its silences to extended music videos, its intimacies to grand spectacles. Many wildlife films, perhaps especially high-end blue chip films with their production values in full view, seemed to lack a sense of proportion. Some seemed given to tendencies that could very quickly make them as grandiose, as inflated, as bloated, and ultimately as irrelevant to social reality as their Hollywood cousins.

Although the subject of wildlife films has remained nature, one could hear talk at film festivals of "nature designed and composed in advance" — a statement without internal contradiction only if one is God. Indeed, the few cultural critics who have mentioned wildlife films have seemed inclined to view them as attempts to exert a sort of God-like control over nature.[11]

This, however, ignores the institutional demands explored throughout this book that are placed on those in the industry to generate ratings and earn profits. On the whole, the outlook of wildlife film producers toward nature may ultimately be no different from that of society at large: wildlife and the natural world are there as *resources* from which can come enjoyable work, a pleasant living, creature comforts, entertainment, even art.

In the end, no God-like powers exists for filmmakers working in a competitive industry, either over their own images, or over real nature. Whatever control they do have over the representation of nature seems often to be confused by critics, perhaps for rhetorical purposes, with control over nature itself. A filmmaker may "exploit" nature as fodder for a film, but this should not be confused with exploitation of nature in the concrete sense. Manipulation and consumption of images of nature is simply not comparable to manipulation and consumption of nature in the real world, despite attempts to force parallels between them by what are essentially *puns* on words like power, control, consumption, manipulation, and exploitation. Image makers undoubtedly possess a good deal of power in the realm of culture, but the extent to which this translates into actual power over nature, or into political power of the sort that moves mountains, or that saves them from destruction, is unclear, and probably overstated. Despite presumptions about the power of the media to effect social and environmental change, there is little evidence that the state of wildlife and the natural world today is directly related to wildlife film and television.

Still, there may be cause for concern, for it probably remains true that how we see the natural world influences how we treat it. As audiences grow larger, wildlife films become more technically and artistically sophisticated and move farther away from depicting nature on its terms and more toward dramatically recreating it in terms set by visual media. As the twenty-first century finds more and more people removed from direct experience of the natural world, what will be the consequences of an increasing diet of images that distort perceptions of nature by portraying it as a place of incessant drama and action, of sound and fury, or as a place where our own moral and social values can be easily and straightforwardly applied?

The solution, clearly, is *not* to encourage the earth's billions to get out and experience natural areas firsthand. Our numbers alone make this a destructive alternative, and demand that we rely instead ever more heavily on images, such as those in wildlife films, for our experiences of nature. But the closer we look, the more reason we have to doubt that this is what they give us.

As I look at the mountains outside my window, and at the marmot chewing grass under the trees, I cannot help but reflect on how different the scene is from what appears on my TV screen. Instead of sound and fury, the scene is one of stillness and calm—as are, in fact, most people's *real* ex-

periences of the places and animals depicted in wildlife and natural history films on television. It may well be that still photography and painting
are best suited to representing the natural world visually, but, for better or
worse, commercial film and television now bear the bulk of that responsibility. Whether those in the industry sought it or not, the job has fallen to
them, and they have gallantly tackled it using the industrial-strength tools
they have. Whether or not they are the right tools for the task remains open
to question.

Appendix
A Chronology of Highlights from the History of Wildlife and Natural History Films

1858

James Chapman takes wet-plate still photo camera to Africa to photograph zebras and elephants in their natural environments, but brings back only photos of dead animals, shot on the expedition.

1863

Professor G. Fritsch, of Germany, photographs more freshly killed African animals in the field.

1870

Charles Hewins, of Boston, photographs a stork in its nest—one of the oldest surviving photos of a *living* wild animal in its natural environment.

1872 or 73

Eadweard Muybridge thought to have photographed Leland Stanford's racehorse Occident at Palo Alto, California. The image(s) may be counted as the first instance combining photography, motion, and animal behavior. The images themselves have never been found.

1872–76

Photographer C. Newbold, of the Royal Engineers, photographs penguin rookeries and breeding albatrosses during a four-year cruise on HMS *Challenger*.

1876

Muybridge continues his photographic study of Occident's stride, this time more effectively with a faster process.

1878

Muybridge makes more improved animal "motion" photographs at Stanford's estate at Palo Alto.

1879

Muybridge applies his precinematographic technique to horses, dogs, mules, pigs, and goats—also pigeons and deer. The last may have been the first "wildlife" to be captured in any kind of motion picture process. Significantly, photography of animals is seen primarily as a *scientific* activity.

1882

J. B. D. Stillman, a friend an associate of Stanford, publishes *The Horse in Motion*, based largely on the work Muybridge had done at Palo Alto.

Etienne-Jules Marey, professor of zoology at the Collége de France, develops a "photographic gun" (also called "Marey's Wheel") capable of shooting rapidly sequenced photos from a single lens. Significantly, his main interest (and target) was wild birds in flight, as part of his effort to develop what he called "animated zoology."

1884

Muybridge takes his motion-photo process to the Philadelphia Zoological Gardens and "films" a tiger as it attacks and kills a buffalo. The confrontation was staged for the camera, making the buffalo the first "disposable subject" in the history of wildlife filming.

1887

Muybridge completes a report on his work at the University of Pennsylvania (1884–87) entitled *Descriptive Zoopraxography, or the Science of Animal Locomotion.* He also publishes *Animal Locomotion.*

1888

Benjamin Wyles, using a Derwent camera with dry plates, makes still photographs of wild birds (gulls, guillemots, and kittiwakes) in flight, and in their natural environment.

1893

Muybridge lectures and gives Zoopraxograph demonstrations at the Chicago World's Fair. A spectator comments that "flocks of birds fly across the sky with every movement of their wings perceptible."

1894

Marey publishes *La mouvement.*

Cockfight. W. K. L. Dickson, Edison Kinetoscope. Forty-four seconds of feather pulling, but no gore.

1895

Richard and Cherry Kearton publish *British Birds' Nests*, the first natural history book to be illustrated with authentic wildlife photographs.

Oliver Pike and R. B. Lodge develop a technique by which wild birds in their natural environments trip a camera shutter and take their own photograph.

Mr. Delaware and the Boxing Kangaroo is shown in Berlin at the first public projection of motion pictures in Germany. This may be the first wild animal exhibited to the public in a modern motion picture.

Lion, London Zoological Garden. Louis Lumière. A caged lion paces forth and back.
1896
Rough Sea at Dover. Robert Paul and Birt Acres. Among the first Vitascope projected films at Koster & Bial's Music Hall, New York City, on April 23, and possibly the first "natural history" oriented film to be projected to a paying audience. Reviews indicate it was the most popular film shown that evening.
Feeding the Doves. Edison. Shows two little girls feeding chickens and doves, the latter being among earliest wild animals the public watched by way of the new medium.
George Shiras III pioneers techniques for nighttime still photography of wildlife in the field, in some cases using trip wires to trigger the camera.
An unnamed photographer accompanying Lord Delemere's expedition to East Africa photographs elephants, giraffes, gazelles, and zebras.
1897
The Sea Lions' Home. Edison. Depicts sea lions entering and leaving the water in their natural environment. Perhaps the first true wildlife film—or, at least, wildlife film prototype—combining wild animals, natural locations, and natural behavior.
Elephants at the Zoo. British Mutoscope. Filmed in London Zoological Gardens.
The Kearton brothers publish *With Nature and a Camera*, which outlines some of their innovative techniques for photographic animals in their natural habitats.
1898
Richard Kearton publishes *Wild Life at Home*, a "how-to" book for amateur wildlife photographers, and one of the earliest uses of the term "wildlife" in relation to modern visual images.
Feeding the Seagulls. Edison. Single-cam film of gulls fed from the back of a boat in San Francisco bay.
Fighting Roosters; in Florida. American Mutoscope. Waiters at a Tampa Bay hotel stage a cockfight on the lawn (a.k.a. *Cockfight—New Orleans*).
Ostriches Feeding. Edison. Shows twelve grown ostriches feeding. An attendant throws more food.
Ostriches Running, numbers 1 and 2. Edison. Title tells all.
Pelicans at the Zoo. British Mutoscope and Biograph Company. Pelicans being fed at Regent's Park Zoological Gardens, London.
Sea Waves. Edison. Waves breaking on the New Jersey shore.
1899
Elephants in a Circus Parade (a.k.a. *Elephants in a Parade*). American Mutoscope and Biograph. Filmed in Brooklyn.

Feeding the Pigeons. cam: Billy Bitzer. American Mutoscope and Biograph. Shows Massachusetts SPCA's efforts to feed pigeons in Boston.

Pianka and Her Lions. A young woman in a cage with trained lions.

Prof. Paul Boynton Feeding his Sea Lions. American Mutoscope and Biograph. cam: F. S. Armitage. Filmed at Coney Island.

The "Zoological Photographic Club" is founded in Britain.

1900

Feeding Sea Lions. dist: Lubin. Paul Boynton feeding his tame sea lions.

Fight Between Tarantula and Scorpion. British Mutoscope and Biograph Co. Staged confrontation between two animals enclosed in a tin box with a glass front. Filmed in South Africa.

George Shiras III receives the Gold Medal at the Paris World Exhibition for his nighttime photography of wildlife.

1901

Sea Gulls in Central Park. camera: F. S. Armitage. dist: American Mutoscope and Biograph.

Wild Bear in Yellowstone. Edison.

Camera Shots at Big Game, a book written by and illustrated with photographs by the Walihans, one of the first husband and wife teams in to photograph wildlife in the field. Introduction by Theodore Roosevelt.

1902

Deer in Park. American Mutoscope. Filmed in New York City.

Feeding the Bear at the Menagerie. Edison.

Feeding the Bears at the Menagerie.

Sea Gulls Following Fishing Boats. Edison. Filmed in San Francisco bay.

The Elephant's Bath. Deutsche Mutoskope und Biograph. Filmed at the Berlin Zoölogical Gardens.

1903

Carl George Schillings uses "disposable subject"—a tethered donkey—as bait in effort to make still photos of lions "hunting" at night. Schillings's photos, published in two large volumes, are said to have influenced many in England, Germany, and the United States to take up "camera hunting" of wildlife.

John Burroughs's article "Real and Sham Natural History" is published in the March issue of the *Atlantic*—the first shot in the "nature faker" war.

Charles Urban begins his "Bioscope Expeditions" depicting remote areas of the world, including shots of their wildlife inhabitants.

Urban also begins the "Unseen World" series of "micro-bioscopic" films, such as *Cheese Mites*, and *Circulation of Blood in a Frog*, both by F. Martin Duncan.

Electrocuting an Elephant. Edison. Depicts electrocution of "Topsy" at Luna Park, Coney Island, as punishment for killing three men. The film is approximately one minute long, and was shot by either Jacob Blair Smith or Edwin S. Porter. An audience of 1500 watched Topsy, age twenty-eight, receive six-thousand volts.

Feeding the Elephants. dist: Lubin. Shows tame elephant being fed. Promotions indicate that it is fed chunks of *meat.*

Feeding the Hippopotamus. dist: Lubin. Captive animals.

Feeding the Russian Bear. camera: Billy Bitzer. dist: American Mutoscope and Biograph. Filmed in Glen Island, New York.

Feeding the Russian Bear. cam: Billy Bitzer. Shows a man feeding a bear in a cage.

Feeding the Swans. S. Lubin. dist: S. Lubin. Filmed in Philadelphia.

Fighting Rams. Edison. Filmed in India. Two domestic rams butt heads several times with great force.

Hunting the White Bear. Pathé Frères. dist: S. Lubin. (a.k.a. *Une chasse a l'ours blanc; A White Bear Hunt*)

Llamas at Play. cam: Billy Bitzer. Shows llamas running around in a pen, and being fed by a small boy.

North American Elk. dist: S. Lubin. Filmed in a zoo.

North American Grey Wolves. fist: S. Lubin. They are filmed in a cage, being fed. Their "ferocity" was used to promote the film.

Polar Bear Hunt in the Arctic Seas. Pathé Frères. (a.k.a. *Polar Bear Hunt*).

Polar Bears. dist: S. Lubin. Filmed in captivity in the United States.

Unloading the Elephants. S. Lubin. They emerge from boxcars in which they have been transported from New York to Philadelphia.

1904

Elephants at Work in India (a.k.a. *Eléphants au travail aux Indes, Working Elephants in India*). Pathé Frères.

Elephants at Work. Edison. Elephants are shown moving and stacking lumber.

Fox and Rabbits. dist: Pathé Frères (Edison in the United States). Staged event: a fox attacks two rabbits, but is then pounced on by a fox terrier.

Lion and Lioness. Edison.

Lion Tamer. Edison.

Polar Bears at Play with Cubs. Edison.

1905

Bird Rock, Nordland, Norway. Holmes and Depue.

Deer in Wild Park, Goteberg, Sweden. Holmes and Dupue.

Feeding the Otters. Charles Urban Trading Co. dist: Kleine Optical Co.

1906

Deer Stalking with a Camera. cam: Billy Bitzer. American Mutoscope. Filmed in Pinehurst, North Carolina.

Lion Hunt. Charles J. Jones.

Moose Hunt in New Brunswick. cam: Billy Bitzer.

Scene in a Rat Pit. cam: Billy Bitzer. Filmed in New York, it shows a man and a dog in a small room. Another man releases rats from a cage, which the dog quickly kills.

Stalking and Shooting Caribou, Newfoundland. F. A. Dobson. Two caribou approach a small lake. Someone behind the camera shoots one, which runs and tries to swim the lake. Two men in canoes retrieve its body, which is then shown in CU.

Terrier vs. Wildcat. Filmmaker unknown. Depicts a setup fight between a dog and an alley cat. Horribly cruel treatment of a common house cat in staged confrontation.

1907

Dr. Ad. David, of Switzerland, takes professional cameraman on safari along the Dinder River in East Africa. Although the films made were perhaps the first wildlife moving pictures to be shot in Africa, the images themselves were almost all related to hunting.

Stephen Leek films elk migration in Jackson Hole, Wyoming, and later uses his films to arouse public concern for the elk, whom he favored over predator species.

Theodore Roosevelt speaks about against literary nature faking in two articles in *Everybody's Magazine.*

Elephants in India. Pathé Frères, France.

In Birdland, Oliver Pike's film, long held by some in Britain to be the first full-fledged wildlife film to be given a public screening.

Wild Animals. dist: Williams, Brown, and Earle (Britain).

1908

Theodore Roosevelt invites Richard Kearton to the White House to screen films of British birds and mammals for members of the U.S. Biological Survey, in an effort to convince skeptics that wildlife motion pictures could be of value to science. Kearton later screened the films for members of the D.C. chapter of the Audubon Society.

Lion Hunting. dir: Viggo Larsen, Knud Lumbye, Nordisk Films Kopagni.

St. Kilda, Its People and Birds. Oliver Pike for the Williamson Kinematograph Company. Depicts human and bird life on this Scottish island.

The Lion's Bride. dist: Selig Polyscope Co.

The Wolf Hunt. Oklahoma National Mutoscene Company. Depicts men on horseback running down wolves or coyotes.

Toads—Leaping Batrachians. Charles Urban Co. Depicts green tree frogs in all stages of life, from tadpole to adult.

1909

Chasing a Sea Lion in the Arctic. Pathé Frères. (a.k.a. *Chasing Sea Lions in the Arctic; Chasing a Sea Lion*).

Cherry Kearton embarks on his first African safari, to Kenya, with James L. Clark of the American Museum of Natural History. In August he meets and films Theodore Roosevelt at Nyeri. The footage was later released under several titles, including *TR in Africa,* which included good behavior footage of hippos in a lagoon.

Hunting Big Game in Africa. prod: Col. Selig. dir: Otis Turner. cam: Emmett Vincent O'Neill. Includes a *staged* scene of a lion shot on camera (*for* the camera). Filmed in Chicago.

Hunting the Hippopotamus. dist: Pathé Frères. (a.k.a. *Hippopotamus Hunting on the Nile*).

The Lion Tamer. dist: Selig Polyscope Co.

Moderkælighed Blandt Dyrene. Nordisk, Denmark. Shows a variety of young animals being fed and nurtured by their mothers.

Peeps into Nature's Realm. Williamson Kinematograph Co. Depicts curlews, bluetits, and a red-throated loon feeding.

1910

Dr. David returns to East Africa with the same (unnamed) cameraman to film elephant hunts by the Shilluk, Dinka, and Bari peoples along the White Nile.

Cherry Kearton returns to Africa, and films Buffalo Jones lassoing wild African animals.

Carl Akeley hires members of Kenya's Nandi tribe to stage their lion-spearing ritual so he can film it. Over three weeks, fourteen lions and five leopards are killed so that Akeley can get his shots, but his Urban bioscope camera is inadequate to the task, and the footage was never publicly screened. He sets to work designing the Akeley camera.

Feeding Seals at Catalina Isle. Essanay.

Hunting Bats in Sumatra. dist: Pathé Frères.

Hunting Sea Lions in Tasmania. dist: Pathé Frères.

Hunting the Panther. dist: Pathé Frères. (a.k.a. *Tiger Hunting*).

Roosevelt in Africa, Kearton's film, opens in New York to lukewarm reviews.

Seal and Walrus Hunting. Raleigh and Roberts. dist: Film Import and Trading Co. France.

Stephen Leek stages public screenings of films of starving elk in Jackson Hole, Wyoming.

The Birth of a Flower. Percy Smith, for Charles Urban Trading Company. Time-lapse photography shows plant growth.

The History of a Butterfly: Romance of Insect Life Williamson Kinematograph Company. Depicts the life-cycle of butterflies and moths.

Wild Birds in Their Haunts. dist: Pathé Frères (a.k.a *Wild Bird Hunt*).

Wild Duck Hunting on Reel Foot Lake. Lubin Mfg. Co.

1911

J. C. Hemment (later Rainey's cameraman in Africa) makes what may be the first aerial films of wildlife—in this case a flock of wild ducks "in a panic." The flight was eight minutes long.

Arctic Hunt. Capt. Frank E. Kleinschmidt. Could be film from same trip as in *Alaska-Siberian Expedition* (1912).

Lassoing Wild Animals. Kearton's film featuring Buffalo Jones premiers in New York in February, described in the press as "an African hunting picture." Some sources indicate the cameraman was William David Gobbett (Kearton mentions an "assistant photographer" in his memoirs, p. 168). dist: Pathé Frères.

The Strength and Agility of Insects. Percy Smith for Kineto. A study of insects lifting objects many times their size and weight. Reissued in 1918 as *Nature's Acrobats.*

1912

Cherry Kearton travels to North America to film moose in Canada, bears and bison in Yellowstone.

Leonard Donaldson publishes *The Cinematograph and Natural Science,* advocating the use of film in science and natural history education. The first use of the term "documentary" in relation to film appears in this book, in reference to some earlier film efforts from 1908.

Edward B. Clark writes an article entitled "Wild Life in Moving Pictures," A. R. Dugmore publishes *Wild Life and the Camera,* and Cherry Kearton publishes *Wild Life Across the World*—all showing increasing use of the term "wildlife" in relation to visual images—although none yet used it as one word, or used the term 'wildlife film.'

The monthly journal *Wild Life* premiers (January). Edited by Douglas English. Illustrated completely with wildlife photographs.

Alaska-Siberian Expedition. Capt. Frank E. Kleinschmidt's film of a Carnegie expedition to the Arctic. (a.k.a. *The Carnegie Museum Alaska-Siberia Expedition*).

Atop the World in Motion. prod/cam: Beverly B. Dobbs. Depicts life in the Arctic, Siberia, including a walrus hunt.

Paul J. Rainey's African Hunt. cam: J. C. Hemment. Shows safari preparations, unloading of dogs used to hunt animals, trapping and capturing small animals, and straightforward wildlife footage filmed at a waterhole. The film premiered in New York in April, and ran for fifteen months, grossing $500,000. Some scenes may have been from among the footage Rainey bought from Carl Akeley.

1913

The term "Natural History Film" is used in *Moving Picture World* (May 24), indicating that a distinct category was coming to be recognized—this a year before Edward Curtis used the term "documentary" in relation to film.

Gaumont British Instructional Films is founded.

Oliver Pike makes the first film record of a cuckoo hatchling pushing a young reed warbler out of its nest. Still photos taken from the film are published in the May issue of *Wild Life.*

Cherry Kearton's African films are screened in New York in May, released by Adolph Zukor, introduced by Theodore Roosevelt, who assures that Kearton's film are not faked.

Thomas Edison announces his plan for a "revolutionary education" that would "utilize the motion pictures to teach all sorts of elementary facts," with an emphasis on natural history phenomena.

In his "Wild Fox" series, Frank Newman (Britain) adopts the American practice of using "disposable subjects" by releasing trapped rabbits in an enclosure for a fox to kill on camera.

The Beetle's Deception. A supposed "love drama" with an all-insect cast, made by the Russian Loyshki, premiers in London.

1914

Frank Hurley films penguins and elephant seals in Antarctica (on Mawson's failed expedition).

The Book of Nature. dir/cam: Raymond L. Ditmars, curator of Bronx Zoo. Noted for its combination of scientific information and humor. Also includes an early intimation of the "life-cycle" storyline. The last reel features a tiny animal "circus."

Captain Kleinschmidt's Arctic Hunt. Features scenes of Alaskan wild animals being hunted and killed by the trophy hunter (possible recycled footage from his earlier films)

Common Beasts of Africa. Paul J. Rainey. Possibly recycled footage from the 1912 film *Paul J. Rainey's African Hunt.*

The Intelligence of Apes, by Wolfgang Köhler.

Rainey's African Hunt. prod/dir/cam: Rainey. May have been warmed-over, reedited footage from the 1912 film *Paul J. Rainey's African* Hunt, but is nevertheless described in *New York Times* as "exciting."

Terrors of the Deep. Early underwater picture (Williamson bros. for Submarine Pictures Corporation), filmed in the Bahamas.

1915

Lady MacKenzie's Big Game Pictures. cam: Harold Sintzenich. Lady Grace MacKenzie on safari. Shows herds of zebras, buffalo, hartebeests, giraffes, rhinos, and others. She shoots two lions and a rhino, all of which have apparently been goaded into charging. Elephants, rhinos, hyenas, baboons, and others gather around a waterhole. Sources show American financing.

Wild Life of America in Films. prod/cam: Edward A. Salisbury. Wild animals mostly in the western United States. Opened at San Francisco's Tivoli Theater, playing to over 120,000 in two weeks, then in Chicago and New York, although it was originally made for scientific research.

1916

Carl Akeley patents the Akeley camera (which soon saw service in World War I, where Schoedsack first used one, and did again on *Grass* and *Chang*;

Pathé and Fox adopted it for their newsreels; an Akeley was later used by Flaherty to shoot *Nanook of the North*).

James Oliver Curwood publishes *The Grizzly King*, later the basis for Annaud's *The Bear* (*L'Ours*, 1988).

1917

Alaska Wonders in Motion. camera: A.I. Smith. More a travelogue, but with footage of Kodiak bears, walruses, and other animals.

Baree, Son of Kazan. First film version of James Oliver Curwood's novel of a wolf and his family. dir: David Smith. cam: Charles Seeling.

Birds of a Far-Off Sea. Edison/Conquest Pictures. Shows wild gulls, geese, gannets, and penguins on Malagas Island, near South Africa. One of the last pictures to be distributed under Edison's name.

1919

UFA, founded in Germany in 1918, begins producing short documentaries on a number of subjects, including natural history.

Back to God's Country, based on Curwood's *Wapi the Walrus*, is said by *Photoplay* magazine to contain "some of the most remarkable animal stuff ever photographed."

1920

Swedish cameraman Oskar Olson goes to East Africa, filming lions near the Mara river in northern Kenya.

Nomads of the North. Based on Curwood's novel. Although a mainstream outdoor drama, it contains fine animal footage that rehearses the "orphan" and "incredible journey" motifs. These scenes are well received, and make the film a success.

The Gift of Life. American Social Hygiene Association. Portrays principles of reproduction in amoebae, plants, and humans. Uses the evidence to argues for humans' superiority.

The Living World. cam: George E. Stone, associated with University of California, Berkeley. General biology lesson—plants, animals, trees, also microscopic life. Could also be a rerelease or reedited version of *How Life Begins*.

1921

Oliver Pike goes to work for Bruce Woolfe at British Instructional Films

Carl Akeley films gorillas on an AMNH trip with Herbert Bradley. They are the first photos, still or moving, of gorillas in the wild.

Four Seasons. prod/dir: Raymond L. Ditmars. One reel to each season, showing plant and animal life. Early example of "life-cycle" story line, although without narrative.

Jungle Adventures. Martin Johnson. Largely a travelogue, but with wildlife scenes.

Kazan. prod: Col. Selig (featuring Jim Thorpe in a lead role). dir: Bertram

Bracken. cam: Eddie Beesley, Edwin Linden. Based on Curwood's novel about a wolf-dog.

1922

Mary Field, Percy Smith, and Bruce Woolfe inaugurate the "Secrets of Nature" film series at British Instructional Films. The first in the series is *The Cuckoo's Secret*. by Edgar Chance. The series would run until 1933.

J. B. Shackelford, films wild animals in the Gobi desert on an AMNH expedition.

With Eustace in Africa. Harry K. Eustace. Billed as "a natural history study of animals in their own wild nature habitat." Filmed between 1914 and 1918.

Wonders of the Sea. Williamson's Undersea Wonders. prod/dir/wr: J. Ernest Williamson. Exploration documentary depicting undersea plants and animals.

1923

Siegmund Salzmann, a.k.a. Felix Salten, publishes *Bambi: Eine Lebensgeschichte aus dem Walde*.

Call of the Wild. Hall Roach Studios. dir: Fred Jackman. cam: Floyd Jackman. Not a wildlife film, but the wild animal "orphan" theme is developed.

Elephants of Kenya's North Country.

Evolution. Red Seal Pictures. Scientific look at origins of life also shows ways in which humans have controlled their environment.

Hunting Big Game in Africa with Gun and Camera, prod: H. A. Snow and son Sidney Snow. Runs for three months at New York City's Lyric theater. Carl Akeley denounces it for misrepresenting Africa, and for faking some scenes.

Trailing African Wild Animals. dist: Metro. Martin and Osa Johnson. Antelope, buffalo, seven lions, four black rhinos, and one elephant are shot, but, according to press sheet, "only when it was necessary." The elephant is goaded into charging and shot by Osa. The film is endorsed by the AMNH and by Gifford Pinchot, father of the United States Forest Service, then governor of Pennsylvania.

1924

The Johnsons, with AMNH funding, set out to make three films—none of which were completed when they returned in 1928.

Equatorial Africa; Roosevelt's Hunting Grounds. cam: A.J. Klein. Travelogue from Kenya to Uganda to the Nile. Shows zebra, topi, gazelles, impala, lions, waterbucks, rhinos, hippos, baboons, warthogs, antelope, birds, and insects (see *Simba*, below).

1925

Celebrated wildlife still photographer A. R. Dugmore takes up the cine-camera, and films rhinos, giraffes, and zebras at Ngorongoro. He also captured on film an elephant charging to within a few yards of him.

Baree, Son of Kazan. Vitagraph. Remake of the 1917 film version of Curwood's novel.

The True North. dir: Capt. Jack Robertson. A trip through Siberia, showing caribou, bear, the killing of a moose, and so forth.

White Fang. dir: Lawrence Trimble. cam: John Leezer. Western melodrama based on Jack London's book.

Wild Men and Beasts of Borneo. cam: Lou Hutt. Travelogue depicting Hutt and party traveling from Hong Kong to Malaya. An elephant, a leopard, and a python are trapped.

Wonders of the Wild. Burr Nickle Pictures. Travelogue depicting Nickle's travels from Mexico to Japan to Borneo, with seal and sea lion footage.

1926

(June): Carl Akeley joins the Johnsons in Tanganyika to film the lion-spearing ritual that eluded him in 1910.

Alaskan Adventures. dir: Capt. Jack Anderson. dist: Pathé Exchange. Travelogue depicting Alaskan wildlife (bears, salmon, deer, mountain sheep, etc.), plus volcanoes, and other wonders.

Gorilla Hunt. Ben Burgridge leads an attempt to capture gorillas for captivity. An elephant and three lions are shot on camera.

Primeval World of the Forest. August Brückner for UFA, about the Amazon rainforest.

1927

James Oliver Curwood dies.

William Douglas Burden films an expedition to capture Komodo Dragons.

Chang. Paramount/Famous/Lasky Corp. prod/dirs: Merian C. Cooper and Ernest Schoedsack. cam: Schoedscack. Early "docudrama" about human family and their struggle with marauding animals.

The Great Australian Bush, Its Wonders and Mystery. Edward Percy Bailey. Travelogue, with several animals filmed in close-up.

Through Darkest Africa; in Search of White Rhinoceros. dir/cam: Harry K. Eustace. Hunting film.

1928

Dugmore returns to the North America, to film bighorn sheep, mule deer, and elk in the Canadian Rockies.

Bambi: A Life in the Woods, by Felix Salten, is published in English (trans: Whittaker Chambers).

Great Arctic Seal Hunt (a.k.a. *The Swilin' Racket*). Varick Frissell.

Great White North. H. A. Snow. dist: Fox. dir/story: Sydney Snow, H. A. Snow. cam: Sydney Snow. Depicts walrus hunt, capture of a bear in nets, harpooning of a whale, and survey of bird life.

Simba, by the Johnsons, with AMNH funding. Emphasizes dramatic events, provoked behavior, and staged confrontations. Some of the subjects are shot to death on camera. Cobbled together from the three uncompleted films they set out to make four years earlier, *Simba* also includes footage from Alfred J. Klein's *Equatorial Africa: Roosevelt's Hunting Grounds*, which they purchased for $30,000. It also includes the 1926 lion-spearing ritual cofilmed with Carl Akeley, plus nineteen seconds of a similar spearing scene filmed by Klein. A hybrid sound version is also released, with a sync-sound intro by the Johnsons, as presenters, and excerpts from Wagner's *Die Ring des Nibelungen*, plus "How Dry I Am."

1929

The Johnsons, with financial backing from the Fox Film Corporation, set out to film *Congorilla* as a sound film.

Camera Hunting on the Continental Divide, filmed in Glacier National Park is shown as part of a national lecture tour by William Finley. It features scenes of moose, elk, bears, bighorn sheep, etc.

Bathtime at the Zoo, part of the "Secrets of Nature" series, is by some accounts the first film in the series to use sound.

Hunting Tigers in Africa. Produced in conjunction with the AMNH. dir: George M. Dyott, Lee Meehan. cam: Dal Clawson.

Jango. Davenport Quigley Expeditions. Dr. Davenport leads expedition in Africa

Up the Congo. dir: Alice M. O'Brien. cam: Charles Bell. Travelogue.

Wild Heart of Africa. dir: Cub Walker. cam: Kenneth Walker. Exploration documentary of Walker-Arbuthnot African expedition, beginning in Egypt and proceeding into the jungles.

1930

Across the World with Mr. and Mrs. Johnson. dir: J. Leo Meehan. cam: Russell Sheilds. Largely a travelogue, notable for not being filmed by the Johnsons themselves.

Africa Speaks. prod: Paul Hoefler, Colorado Africa Expedition. dist: Columbia. Largely a travelogue focusing on exotic tribal people, with some wildlife footage, and a climactic scene in which a lion appears to kill an African man.

Blizzard on the Equator. Carveth Wells. Contains efforts by Wells to debunk myths of animals' man-eating savagery.

Daily Dozen at the Zoo; Playtime at the Zoo. These entries in the "Secrets of Nature" series are deliberately modeled on Disney cartoons. Animals' movements are synchronized to music to suggest they are keeping time with it, and so on. These films may mark the first documented influence of Disney on the wildlife/natural history genre.

Dassan. Cherry Kearton's film about penguins on the island of Dassan, off the coast of South Africa. Kearton appears and speaks on camera. He also publishes *Island of the Penguins*, featuring several anthropomorphic characterizations.

Auf Tigerjagd in Indien (*Hunting Tigers in India*). Produced by UFA in Germany, it includes some early anthropomorphism in the narration, calling every female elephant "Frau Mama."

Ingagi. Congo Pictures, Ltd., distributed in the United States by RKO. A slapdash, haphazardly edited melánge. Some scenes depict real hunting safaris in Africa; others were shot in a studio and poorly acted. The Hays office banned the film from exhibition because of its blatant fakery.

Peas and Cues (a.k.a. *Sweet Peas*). By some accounts the first film in the "Secrets of Nature" series to use sound. The film was produced in 1929 for release on the same bill as *The Taming of the Shrew,* with Douglas Fairbanks and Mary Pickford.

1931

Rango. Ernest B. Schoedsack's film for Paramount about an orang-utan, pushes the "orphan" and animal family themes into the foreground. May be the first modern wildlife film, because of its combination of protagonism, scripted action, and voice-over narration.

Strange Animals I Have Known. Raymond Ditmars's professional autobiography details his life as early wildlife filmmaker and curator of the New York Zoological Park.

Trader Horn. W. S. Van Dyke's film for MGM includes authentic African safari and wildlife footage shot by Clyde DaVinna, who later shot *Sequoia* (1934). Unfortunately, some scenes of predatory killing were staged using lions that had been starved and then set upon hapless hyenas, monkeys, and deer in a corral. The scenes were shot in Mexico, which, as Brownlow points out, was "beyond the jurisdiction of the SPCA," but spiced up the film for action-hungry American audiences.

Ubangi. "A Davenport-Quigley Adventure," filmed in 1924 on a British medical expedition, by Dr. Louis Neuman.

1932

Bring 'em Back Alive. Frank Buck. Features several staged confrontations between animals of different species.

Congorilla. Martin and Osa Johnson. Touted as the "first sound from darkest Africa." The Hollywood financed film marks their move away from scientific pretensions and toward promoting their own "star" identities. The film includes scenes of the Johnsons capturing and hog-tying a pair of terrified young gorillas, and playing jazz for the Africans.

Jungle Killer. Filmed by Samuel Cummins, edited and narrated by Carveth Wells. An attempt to expose the cruelty of big game hunting. Lawsuits result in footage being removed, and other footage substituted so that Wells's narration no longer matches many of the images. The completed product (with substitute footage) showes so many animals attacking men that it backfires as an antihunting exposé. The footage removed was purloined by Cummins from F. B. Patterson's *Shooting Big Game with a Camera* (19??).

1933

The "Secrets of Nature" series ends when British Instructional Films is taken over by British International Pictures. Woolfe, Field, and Smith move to Gaumont-British Picture Corp., and form Gaumont-British Instructional, where they begin the "Secrets of Life" series.

Sidney Franklin of MGM buys the screen rights to Salten's *Bambi* and plans a live-action production, with actors supplying voices for the animals.

Cherry Kearton publishes *The Animals Came to Drink*, a collection of stories marking an ironic return to "nature faker" type storytelling.

Goona Goona. Armand Denis's first film, shot in Bali, is picked up for limited distribution in France (after failing to find U.S. distribution).

Land und Tiere im Gran Chaco. Eugen Schumacher and Hans Krieg on safari in South America.

Matto Grosso. A filmed safari to Brazil.

Taming the Jungle. Paul D. Wyman's patchwork of safari footage and staging.

Untamed Africa. Wynant G. Hubbard's film record of a family safari, released by Warners.

1934

Stacy Woodard films setup confrontations between insects staged on indoor sets. Woodard writes up the unscientific results in *Scientific American.*

Beyond Bengal. Harry Schenck. dist: Showmen's Pictures. A safari film of sorts, with staged scenes in which Bengalese "extras" risked life and limb by getting into a river inhabited by crocodiles for the benefit of the film. Many crocodiles were then massacred on camera. Critics at the time noted that much of it was staged. The film was revived in 1990 at a "bad taste" film festival ("Festival des geschmacklosen Films") in Berlin.

Devil Tiger. dir: Clyde Elliott. dist: Fox. Docudrama about the hunt for a man-eating tiger. Like Frank Buck's films, this includes many phony conflicts between animals thrown together.

The Private Life of the Gannet. prod: Alexander Korda. narr: Julian Huxley. Some sources credit John Taylor as cameraman; Huxley credits "the brilliant cameraman Osmond Borrodaile," assigned to the project by Korda.

Secrets of Nature. A book written by Mary Field and Percy Smith about the film series by the same name. The series had just been terminated when the book was written, making it thus something of a look back. Although an insider's account of experiences in making films, the book differs from Martin Johnson's ghosted books (e.g. *Camera Trails in Africa*, 1924; *Safari*, 1928; *Lion*, 1929), in that it includes a good deal of valuable technical insights, prescriptions for what to do and not to do, and perhaps most significantly, some intellectual reflections on matters of both form and content. In this sense, it is the first book-length study of the wildlife/natural history genre.

Wild Cargo. A Frank Buck wildlife adventure. Although directed by Armand

Denis, the film features more of Buck's trademark staged confrontations and fake sound effects. Some have written that it contained a fight between a tiger and an orang-utan, staged over objections from the cameraman and animal handler that these two animals would never actually meet in the wild. This scene is not, however, in the Library of Congress print.

Sequoia (aka: *Malibu*). MGM's drama based on novel by Vance J. Hoyt (1931). The story involves an orphaned deer and a mountain lion, raised together as friends. Contains remarkable wildlife footage, which was praised. Its director, Chester Franklin, is the brother of Sidney Franklin.

1935

Arthur Allen, an ornithologist from Cornell, makes what is thought to be the only surviving film record of the now extinct ivory-billed woodpecker.

T. D. A. Cockerell publishes an article in *Science* advocating the use of wildlife films with a more "documentary" orientation in the cause of conservation.

Sidney Franklin abandons his plans to shoot *Bambi* as a live-action wildlife film, and sells the property to Disney.

Fang and Claw. Another Frank Buck adventure.

Baboona. Martin and Osa Johnson. The Johnsons take an "aerial safari" over Kenya in two airplanes, and even "act" in some scenes. Captured animals are put together in a pen so the panic and mayhem can be filmed.

1937

Cinematograph Films (Animals) Act passed in Britain to prevent cruelty to animals in films.

Martin Johnson dies in plane crash near Los Angeles.

African Holiday. Harry Pearson travelogue with wildlife footage.

Ethology of the Greylag Goose, a research film by Konrad Lorenz.

The Private Life of the Gannets, although British, wins the Academy Award in the United States for "Best One Reel Short Subject."

1938

"The Animal Kingdom." A series of six short films made by Britain's Travel and Industrial Development Association (TIDA), in cooperation with the Zoological Society of London, and under the supervision of Julian Huxley, who narrated and appeared in them. Financing appears to have come from the Carnegie Trust.

Strand Film Zoological Productions is formed in Britain. Its first films include *Animal Legends, Animals on Guard, Animal Geography*, and *The Gullible Gull*.

Ethology of the Greylag Goose (Lorenz) is shown to the public in the United States at the American Museum of Natural History.

Dark Rapture. Armand Denis's safari film depicting the Belgian Congo.

The Tough 'Un. A "Secrets of Life" film about dandelions, is shown at the New York World's Fair.

1939

An August Rhapsody. The first of several films by Sweden's Arne Sucksdorff.

Marine Circus, an MGM theatrical short showcasing dolphins and other underwater creatures at Marine Studios in Florida. The temptation to include scenes of young girls in swimsuits, however, proved irresistible.

Tiergarten Südamerika. Eugen Schumacher and Hans Krieg safari in South America.

1940

I Married Adventure. Compilation of the Johnsons' films based on Osa Johnson's ghost-written book.

Pirsch Unter Wasser (a.k.a. *Underwater Stalking*). Hans Hass's film about life in a coral reef is one of the first underwater films to gain wide public attention.

The Social Behavior of the Laughing Gull. G. K. Noble's color silent film, is shown at an annual meeting of American Ornithologists' Union.

1941

Jungle Cavalcade. Compilation of earlier Frank Buck films, reprinted from original negatives, with new narration added.

A Summer's Tale. Arne Sucksdorff.

1942

Bambi, Disney's animated feature, containing many of the character and narrative prototypes for the later, live-action "True Life Adventures."

Characteristics of Gibbon Behavior. Scientific film by C. R. Carpenter.

Men Among Sharks. Hans Hass.

1943

High Over the Borders. National Film Board of Canada.

Jacare, Killer of the Amazon. The last Frank Buck film.

Reindeer Time. Arne Sucksdorff.

1944

The Gull (a.k.a. *Gull!*) Arne Sucksdorff. Filmed in the wild, with no narration added.

1945

Marlin Perkins goes on early TV on WBKB in a series of programs featuring zoo animals that were often tamed for easy on-screen handling. This may be the first wildlife television program anywhere, although it was not distributed nationally.

1946

Desmond Hawkins develops *The Naturalist,* the first natural history radio program (BBC West Region, Bristol).

1947

Social Behavior of Rhesus Monkeys. C. R. Carpenter. Scientific behavioral study film.

The Jackson Hole Wildlife Park, by C.R. Carpenter, features scenes of moose, elk, antelope, etc.

1948

A Divided World. Arne Sucksdorff. Lyrical, dreamlike, "poetic" wildlife film.

Seal Island. Shot by Al and Elma Milotte. Released as the first of Disney's "True Life Adventures." The anthropomorphic tendencies are already well established, including extensive projection of human family & kinship models, as well as the "orphan" and "journey" motifs.

1949

Beaver Valley. The second of Disney's "True Life Adventures."

Savage Splendor. Armand Denis's safari film, is distributed internationally by RKO.

Fishing and Hunting Club. Possibly the first regular wildlife-related show to be distributed across the United States on network television.

Zooparade, Marlin Perkins and Don Meier's program, goes on the air in local markets.

1950

The Royal Society for the Protection of Birds (RSPB), under the direction of Philip E. Brown, begins filming birds as part of its efforts to protect them. The films are silent, and are intended as lecture accompaniments.

Zooparade, Marlin Perkins and Don Meier's program, goes national on the NBC television network (running until 1957).

1951

Marlin Perkins and Don Meier take *Zooparade* out of the studio and on location, shooting on 16mm film with sync sound in Africa, Wyoming, Florida, the Amazon, and elsewhere, thus establishing the model for the later *Wild Kingdom* series.

Jacques-Yves Cousteau begins his career as a broadcaster and film producer, outfitting the *Calypso* with funds from the Direction générale du cinéma français, the French navy, and the ministry of education.

Under the Red Sea. Hans Hass. Wins first prize at Venice for feature-length documentary.

Nature's Half Acre. A Disney True Life Adventure. Academy Award winner for "Best Two-Reel Short Subject."

1952

The Sea Around Us. RKO. prod: Irwin Allen. Nominally based on Rachel Carson's book by the same name, the film is somewhat insensitive to nature. Winner of the Academy Award for "Best Documentary Feature."

Water Birds. Disney "True Life Adventure." Academy Award winner for "Best Two-Reel Short Subject."

1953

Armand and Michaela Denis make their first appearance on television (October).

The RSPB Film Unit is formed consisting solely of George Edwards.

Wild Geese, the first of a series of monthly wildlife programs introduced by Peter Scott, airs on BBC (December).

Adventure premiers on CBS, produced in cooperation with the American Museum of Natural History. Although a general science program, some episodes are about wildlife.

Bear Country. A Disney "True Life Adventure." Academy Award winner for "Best Two-Reel Short Subject." The bears are depicted as lovable, entertaining clowns, who often appear to be keeping time to the film's music.

Below the Sahara. dist: RKO. Armand Denis's late entry in the safari film subgenre.

The Great Adventure (Der Stora Aventyret). Arne Sucksdorff's masterpiece.

The Living Desert. Disney's first feature-length "True Life Adventure." Academy Award for "Best Documentary Feature."

Prowlers of the Everglades. A Disney "True Life Adventure."

1954

Bill Burrud founds his own independent production company specializing in wildlife and "location/adventure" films. Burrud would produce some fourteen syndicated series over the next thirty-five years.

A Kingdom on the Waters. wr/ph/dir: Dr. Istvan Homoki Magy, of Hungary. dist: Artkino. A rare Hungarian film, shot in color. Screened in New York, and favorably reviewed in the *New York Times* by Bosley Crowther as "a mini masterpiece of its kind, and we're not forgetting Mr. Disney's best." It covers some *seventy* different species, with an emphasis on birds.

Caspian Story. dir/ph: Roman Karmen. dist: Artkino. A Soviet film, screened in New York with *A Kingdom on the Waters*, but not reviewed as favorably ("a shrill, blatant tone of triumph").

Disneyland premiers on ABC, featuring reedited versions of "True Life" films.

Filming Wild Animals, with Armand and Michaela Denis, debuts on the BBC (11 November).

The Vanishing Prairie. A Disney "True Life Adventure." Academy Award winner for "Best Documentary Feature."

Woodpeckers (a.k.a. *Carpenters of the Forest*), by Heinz Sielmann, pioneers new filming techniques.

Zoo Quest, with David Attenborough, airs on BBC (December).

1955

The second series of the BBC's *Zoo Quest* programs airs. The programs are filmed in Guiana.

The Mutual of Omaha insurance company takes over sponsorship of *Zooparade.* The partnership with Perkins and Meier would endure throughout the *Wild Kingdom* series.

Konrad Lorenz appears on American television with imprinted ducklings, on a CBS program following the in-studio pattern still dominant in British wildlife television.

The African Lion. A Disney "True-Life Adventure." Filmed by Al and Elma Milotte.

Diving to Adventure, with Hans and Lotte Hass, premiers on BBC.

Emperor Penguins. A Disney "True-Life Adventure." Filmed by Al and Elma Milotte.

Look, a regular wildlife series featuring Peter Scott, premiers in September on the BBC with a program on foxes. The series would run until 1967.

Woodpeckers (a.k.a. *Carpenters of the Forest*), by Heinz Sielmann, is broadcast on the BBC (15 January).

1956

The RSPB premiers *Birds of Britain* at London's Royal Festival Hall. The RFH screenings become an annual event.

Kein Platz für wilde Tiere (*No Place for Wildlife*). Bernard Grzimek's film severely criticizes safari hunting, showing the horrors inflicted on animals, but produces something of a backlash of criticism against Grzimek himself.

Ein Platz für Tiere (*A Place for Animals*), Bernhard Grzimek's live animal TV show, premiers on German TV. Grzimek could be seen sitting at his desk with animals, and would sometimes show film sequences filmed by his son Michael, as well as by Heinz Sielmann and others.

Secrets of Life. A Disney "True Life Adventure" boasting "new" filming techniques—time-lapse filming and the use of macro-lenses. The film is unique in the series in that its credits include "consulting biologists."

The Silent World. prod/dir: Jacques-Yves Cousteau. cam: Louis Malle. Wins first prize at Cannes.

1957

BBC Natural History Unit formally established in Bristol.

Perri. Disney's Bambiesque live-action "biography of a squirrel" marks a new direction in wildlife storytelling. Based on a novel by Felix Salten, who wrote *Bambi.*

Niok. A French film about an orphan elephant, distributed by Disney's Buena Vista subsidiary. The narrative epitomizes the classic model and closely prefigures the BBC's *Aliya the Asian Elephant.*

1958

Grand Canyon. A Disney "True Life Adventure" set to Ferde Groffe's "Grand Canyon Suite." There is no voice-over narration, but a clear day-in-the-life story line. Wins Academy Award for "Best Live Action Short Subject."

On Safari, with Armand and Michaela Denis, premiers on the BBC (89 programs in all).

The Undersea World of Adventure, with Hans and Lotte Hass, premiers on the BBC.

White Wilderness. A Disney "True Life Adventure," features the now legendary faked lemming "suicide" scene. Wins Academy Award for "Best Documentary Feature."

1959

Serengeti Shall Not Die. prod: Bernard Grzimek. Filmed in 35mm by Alan Root. Wins Academy Award in 1960 for "Best Documentary Feature." The Motion Picture Academy reportedly threatened to deny the award unless Grzimek removed two lines from the narration in which he pleas for preservation of nature and wildlife.

The Nature of Things premiers in Canada on CBC.

1960

The BBC and the Council for Nature cosponsor the first "Nature Film Competition."

Jungle Cat. The last "True Life Adventure" feature. Disney then turns to pure animal storytelling in scripted narrative dramas with trained animals and human actors, but which retain a documentary-style voice-over narration.

Countryman, a fifteen minute program featuring Aubrey Buxton, is the germ from which *Survival* springs.

1961

Survival Anglia is established by Colin Willock and Aubrey Buxton. *Survival* premiers on ITV in January. The first program is called "The London Scene," featuring Buxton and his Bentley.

Nikki, Wild Dog of the North. Released by Disney. The second film version of Curwood's novel *Nomads of the North* (1919). Shot by Cangary Ltd. of Canada, but produced by Winston Hibler.

Walt Disney's Wonderful World of Color premiers on NBC. The first wildlife film on the series is *Chico, the Misunderstood Coyote.*

1962

The Legend of Lobo. A Disney story about a wolf, based on Seton's *Lobo, King of the Currumpaw,* mixes fiction with documentary conventions. Cowritten and produced by James Algar.

1963

The National Geographic Society begins its series of films for television (although not with a wildlife film).

Wild Kingdom premiers on NBC in January. Produced by Marlin Perkins and Don Meier, and hosted by Perkins, with Jim Fowler as "associate host." All but one of the program's first year (thirteen episodes) are set in a studio with zoo animals. Captive animals filmed in controlled situations would remain a mainstay of the series during its twenty year run, even when filmed on location.

The Incredible Journey. Disney's film version of Sheila Burnford's novel epitomizes the classic model.

Yellowstone Cubs. A Disney film that curiously blurs the lines between documentary and fiction.

A Place for Birds. Commissioned by the RSPB and filmed by Paddy Carey.

1964

Flash, the Teenage Otter. Disney film that shows the perfection of the classic model. Based on a novel by Emile Liers.

Le jardin extraordinaire premiers on Belgian television. Its half-hour format of wildlife films plus studio discussion would endure for decades.

1965

Miss Jane Goodall and the Wild Chimpanzees, filmed by Hugo Van Lawick, airs on CBS. It is the first National Geographic television program about wildlife. Narrated by Orson Welles.

El mundo maravilloso de los pájaros (theatrical release in Spain). Félix Rodríquez de la Fuente.

1966

Wolfgang Bayer takes charge of production for Bill Burrud's *Animal World* series.

Walt Disney dies in Los Angeles.

Born Free. A feature film based on Joy Adamson's 1960 book.

One Day at Teton Marsh. Disney's film version of Sally Carrighar's novel.

The Undersea World of Jacques Cousteau premiers on the ABC TV network (twelve one-hour films, reportedly contracted for $4.2 million).

1967

The World About Us premiers on BBC2. The first color broadcasts of wildlife films in Britain. The first film in the series is *The Private Life of the Kingfisher,* produced by Jeffery Boswall and filmed by Ron Eastman. Niko Tinbergen praised the film for its combination of behavior revelation and compelling story.

Charlie the Lonesome Cougar. The last wildlife feature from the Disney studios for nearly twenty years. Trained animals and setup conflicts in a scripted fictional story with human actors, and a documentary-style voice-over narration.

1968

Oxford Scientific Films is founded by Gerald Thompson, David Thompson, Peter Parks, John Paling, and Sean Morris.

Enchanted Isles. Alan Root, for Survival. The first British natural history film to air on American television.

Signals for Survival, by Niko Tinbergen, airs on the BBC's *World About Us* series, to great acclaim.

1969

Aventura, a wildlife series developed by Félix Rodríquez de la Fuente, premiers on Spanish television.

1970

October 1: Wildlife film's place on American television is aided when the Federal Communications Commission (FCC) rules that at least an hour of each evening's prime-time broadcasting must be allotted to local TV stations for non-network programming. Unexpectedly, however, the slots were given over to syndicated programming purchased inexpensively from independent producers, many of which were half-hour wildlife programs. By 1974, fully *eleven* of these were being aired nationally, effectively doubling the U.S. audience for wildlife programs.

Private Lives, produced by Jeffery Boswall, premiers in color on BBC1.

King of the Grizzlies. Disney's version of Curwood's *Biography of a Grizzly*, produced by Winston Hibler.

The World of the Beaver. Des and Jen Bartlett for Survival. The film further widens the American television market for British productions. In order to appeal to U.S. audiences, Henry Fonda reads the commentary, and Colin Willock provides a Disneyesque script. Receives high ratings, and is even rebroadcast a few months later.

World of Survival premiers on American TV. The series consists of repackaged ("versioned") films from Survival, hosted and narrated by American actor John Forsythe.

Planeta Azul, a wildlife series on Spanish television, is started by Félix Rodríquez de la Fuente (153 episodes).

Sterns Stunde, a nature program featuring Horst Stern, premieres on German TV. The series takes a critical stand unusual in its day.

1971

Death of a Legend. Bill Mason's film is one of the first to deal with wolves, and to put forth the argument that they are more victims than killers.

1972

Cry of the Wild, Bill Mason's second film about wolves, is released theatrically in Canada and the United States, and earns $4.5 million at the box office.

Jane Goodall and the World of Animal Behavior, on occasional series of two films per year begins a run of several years on the ABC network in the United States. The series was the brainchild of Hugo Van Lawick, but capitalized Goodall's on-screen appeal as a "personality." The films are sponsored by DuPont.

Following the Tundra Wolves. Neil Goodwin's film is one of the first to show wolves hunting and preying on caribou, much of which is shot from the air.

1973

First BKSTS Symposium.

Heinz Sielmann re-shoots *Woodpeckers* in color.

The African Elephant (a.k.a. *King Elephant*) filmed by Simon Trevor in Panavision for theatrical release.

Behavior and Survival, a thirteen-part series produced by Niko Tinbergen and Hugh Falkus, airs on BBC.

The Incredible Flight of the Snow Geese airs on American television, and wins two Emmy awards.

The Vanishing Wilderness. prod: Art Dubbs. cam: Heinz Sielmann. Dubbs shrewdly markets the film to American theaters using "four-wall" booking.

Wild, Wild World of Animals, packaged by Time-Life, premiers on American television. It would run until 1976.

1974

Partridge Films is founded by Michael Rosenberg.

Survival's *Among the Elephants* (a.ka. *The Family that Lived with Elephants,* and *We Live with Elephants,* is broadcast on American TV. A brief copulation scene is removed after J. Walter Thompson executives decided it too strong for American audiences.

El Hombre y la Tierra, a wildlife series on Spanish television, is started by Félix Rodríquez de la Fuente.

1975

Lee Lyon, who had worked as an assistant to Dieter Plage, is killed by elephants in Rwanda while working on her own film for Survival.

David Suzuki takes on the host/presenter role in the CBC series *The Nature of Things.*

1977

Bill Burrud is given a star on Hollywood's "Walk of Fame."

Badger Watch premiers on the BBC, as an attempt to recapture the immediacy of life television.

The Man Who Loved Bears. Marty Stouffer's hour-long film is broadcast on American network TV. It features a fictionalized dramatic narrative, with Stouffer (playing himself) raising an orphan grizzly cub. The story in many ways parallels Disney's *Charlie the Lonesome Cougar.*

Wildlife on One premiers on BBC1.

1978

The International Wildlife Film Festival is founded in Missoula, Montana, by Dr. Charles Jonkel.

1979

Life on Earth. BBC-NHU's first "mega-series" (thirteen parts) premiers on BBC2, and becomes an international success.

Félix Rodríquez de la Fuente dies in a plane crash while filming in Canada.

Survival becomes the first British television company to sell programs to China.

1980

Animals in Action, Survival's wildlife program for young audiences, premiers. It is hosted by wildlife artist Keith Shackleton.

The Bath Wildlife Filmmaker's Symposium is founded.
1981
Life on Earth achieves success on American television.
1982
The first WILDSCREEN festival is held in Bristol.
Scandinature Films is founded by Bo Landin and Hans Ostbom.
The Living Planet, the second BBC-NHU "mega-series" scores another international success.
Nature premiers on PBS, with films produced by BBC-NHU, Partridge, Survival, and other sources around the world. Producer George Page introduces each film and reads the narration.
Wild America, Marty Stouffer's series, debuts on PBS. The series focuses on North American animals. The emphasis in many of the episodes is on storytelling, sometimes involving scripted dramas with Stouffer playing himself.
1983
Ratings figures for the first year of PBS's *Nature* and *Wild America* series suggest audiences of 3.7 and 3.4 million, respectively (compared with the long running *Wild Kingdom*'s 4.5 million).
Marty Stouffer's scene of wild pigs copulating is allowed to remain in an episode of *Wild America*, a sexual first on American TV. Some local affiliates, however, remove the scene anyway.
1984
The Living Planet premiers. It is the second of the BBC-NHU's 'mega series.'
The Natural World premiers.
Cruel Camera. George James, for the CBC program *The 5th Estate.* This documentary exposé reveals systematic cruelty and abuse of animals in both Hollywood features and wildlife films. Several wildlife filmmakers, including Marlin Perkins, are interviewed on camera.
1985
The Discovery Channel premiers on cable and becomes a major outlet for wildlife films by producers from around the world.
1986
Cruel Camera airs on WNYC in New York, and is reviewed in the *New York Times.*
In-Flight Movie. John Downer, for BBC. Heralds an innovative approach to wildlife filming.
National Geographic Explorer premieres on Turner's TBS network, providing another United States outlet for wildlife content.
1988
Heinz Sielmann is given a lifetime achievement award at Wildscreen.
Jean-Jacques Annaud's fictional film *L'Ours* (a.k.a. *The Bear*) earns $100 million in Europe before being released in the United States.

Supersense. John Downer, for BBC.
1989
Peter Scott dies.
Jean-Jacques Annaud's *The Bear* scores a surprising success in American cinemas, and is reviewed in *Film Quarterly.*
1990
Bill Burrud dies in Los Angeles.
The Trials of Life premiers. Time-Life launches its now notorious ad campaign for the video release of the series, emphasizing action, violence, and gore. The campaign is a phenomenal success and sells millions of units.
1991
The Jackson Hole Wildlife Film Festival is founded in Wyoming.
Green Umbrella Productions is founded by Peter Jones and Nigel Ashcroft.
BBC Wildvision, a joint venture between the BBC-NHU and BBC Enterprises, is formed to serve as a commercial arm of the Natural History Unit to take advantage of the its library of film footage and sound recordings to make new programs for commercial sale to advertisers and to other film and television producers, and to generate revenues over and above what the license fee provides.
1993
The Japan Wildlife Film Festival is founded in Toyama.
Dieter Plage dies in an airship accident at the start of a new filming project in the Sumatran rainforest.
1994
Disney's animated feature *The Lion King* achieves international success, in part by reworking some of the key character and narrative devices common to many wildlife films.
1995
National Wildlife Productions, the film and TV production arm of the National Wildlife Federation, is founded by Christopher Palmer, formerly of Audubon Productions.
National Geographic Television is formed as a division separate from its nonprofit parent. NGT will pay taxes and be able to engage in joint-venture production arrangements.
Explore International is formed as a distribution partnership between NGT and Canal+ to help NGT market its products internationally.
1996
The *Wild America* series, produced by Marty Stouffer, ends a fourteen year run on PBS amid controversy.
Animal Planet, the "all animals all the time" cable channel, is launched by DCI. Within two years, 70 per-cent of its schedule would be made up of original programming.

DCI announces a partnership with CBS to bring wildlife films back to that network. They are produced by Discovery Productions, premiered on CBS, and are later shown the Discovery cable channel.

The Leopard Son. Hugo Van Lawick. The first venture into feature films by Discovery Productions fails to recreate the box-office success of Annaud's *The Bear,* and receives only limited distribution in the United States, opening on 100 screens. The film lost $2.5 million in its theatrical run, but was later broadcast on Discovery cable channel.

1997

Animal Planet Europe is launched.

National Geographic Channel (NGC) is launched international, although not in the United States. It is carried on NewsCorp's BSkyB satellite, with plans to be in thirty countries by year 2000.

The "Wildlife Europe" film festival founded in Stockholm.

United Wildlife is formed as a division of United News & Media, effecting a merger of Survival and Partridge Films by means of a takeover among their parent companies.

Southern Star (Australia) gains control of Oxford Scientific Films and Independent Wildlife by acquiring their parent company Circle Communications (Britain).

Buena Vista Television, a Disney subsidiary, announces: "Walt Disney returns to its roots in nature filmmaking with the production start of an extraordinary new documentary series."

Jacques-Yves Cousteau dies.

Wild America, the Stouffer brothers' dramatic feature film (produced by Mark Stouffer) is released to two-thousand theaters.

1998

Disney opens "Animal Kingdom" in Florida, in which parts of Africa are re-created, complete with wild animal species. A concurrent release of a big-budget theatrical film about African wildlife, by Dereck and Beverly Joubert, is planned in conjunction with the event, but fails to come off.

Africa's Elephant Kingdom. An IMAX production by Discovery Channel Pictures (DCP).

Fox enters wildlife television production by acquiring 80 per-cent of the TVNZ Natural History Unit.

The Life of Birds, another BBC "mega-series" with David Attenborough, airs in Britain.

Living Europe premiers in Europe, but differs from the BBC's "mega series" in that it has no on-camera host as a unifying presence. The eight hour series is produced by Green Umbrella, along with at least eight other partners.

George Page steps down, after sixteen years, as narrator and on-screen host of the PBS series *Nature,* although he continues as executive producer.

Desmond Hawkins is given a life achievement award at Wildscreen '98.
1999
Discovery postpones its plans to start a full-time HD channel, but launches a weekly series on DirecTV called *Discovery HD Theater*, half of the programming of which will be natural history.
TBS, the cable "super-station" in the United States, after years as a major venue for wildlife films, ceases broadcasting documentary and nonfiction programming—with the exception of the NWF/Turner co-productions *Wild! Life Adventures*. The long-running *National Geographic Explorer* series moves to the CNBC cable network.
David Attenborough receives a lifetime achievement award at the Jackson Hole Wildlife Film Festival.
The IMAX film *Whales*, produced by National Wildlife Productions, earns nearly $40 million at the box-office, further attesting to the future possibilities for wildlife in large-format productions.
2000
Wildscreen Center opens, marking an effort to bring wildlife television and film (including IMAX) together with more traditional natural history educational and recreational experiences for the public.

Notes

Introduction

1. By 1996, video sales had topped $100 million, attributed largely to the advertising trailer (McElvogue, 1996, 1997; Slade, 1992).

2. McElvogue (1996, 1997).

3. The BBC's Alastair Fothergill, quoted by McElvogue (1996: D14). See also Fry (1996).

4. Landin (1998: 16).

5. The formal structure of the *TOL* trailer was to a great extent re-created in the title sequence of Discovery's flagship wildlife program *Wild Discovery*. Ironically, in 1996 the BBC Natural History Unit entered into partnership with Discovery to air films on this very program, and with this sequence as the lead-in—including *Salmon: Against the Tides* (1996), narrated by Attenborough himself.

Chapter 1. The Problem of Images

1. See Cawelti (1976: 32, 10); Schatz (1981: 10).

2. Warshow (1964: 85).

3. Dyer (1993: 3).

4. See Messaris (1994: 90).

5. On the "mean world" of television, see Gerbner et al. (1980, 1994).

6. Berger (1980: 21, emphasis added).

7. May (1981).

8. Attenborough (1987).

9. See Ray (1985: 32–55); Messaris (1994: 150–54).

10. Cameraman Stephen Mills has argued the opposite: that wildlife films show us things "we could *never* see in real life" (1997: 6, emphasis added).

11. A perceptive article in the British weekly *7DAYS* noted of wildlife programs that "the camera's picture is more exciting than anything the human senses can record" (Brayfield, 1989: 10).

12. See Attenborough (1961), especially the section "Condensing of Time," pp. 98–99.

13. See Ricciuti (1974: 82).

14. Parsons (1971: 16).

15. See MacDougall (1985: 285n); Bazin (1967: 17–40, 1978: 67–82).

16. Mills (1997). Attenborough is quoted by Langley (1985: 60). Stouffer is quoted by Sink (1996). See also Attenborough (1961: 99–100); Parsons (1971: 19–21).

17. Attenborough (1987: 12).

18. Attenborough (1987: 12). Elsewhere, he offers a more complete discussion of the necessity of adopting filmic convention in natural history filmmaking (Attenborough, 1961).

19. For a beaver, the answer is yes. For humans, we might answer no based on the philosophical presupposition that humans stand apart from nature. In the United States, however, ancient Native American pueblo structures are often seen as parts of nature rather than as parts of human cultural history (see Bousé, 1996).

20. Parsons (1971: 14, emphasis in original).

21. Attenborough (1987: 12).

22. Boswall (1986: 560–61).

23. Nichols (1981: 171–72).

24. Ibid. 208.

25. Adapted from Baudrillard (1983: 11). He does not assign the "phases" numbers.

26. Adapted from Giannetti (1990: 2), with elements suggested by Silverstone (1984: 388) and Nichols (1981: 20, 49).

27. Silverstone (1984: 387).

28. Mills (1997: 6).

29. Quoted in "Doing What Comes Naturally . . ." (1996: 35).

30. Blue chip films occasionally include images of tribal peoples living close to the animals, but it seems their image is thought not to shatter the timeless nature idyll. This was true of images of Native Americans in many nineteenth century landscape paintings (see Novak, 1980; Bousé, 1996).

31. Novak (1980: 189).

32. Jussim and Lindquist-Cock (1985: 31).

33. Cartier-Bresson, quoted by Solnit (1989: 43).

34. See Cahn and Ketchum (1981: 133).

35. Attenborough (1961: 98).

36. Mills (1997: 6). The second part of Mills's remark echoes the common misperception that wildlife films can help save species from decline or extirpation. For evidence that wildlife populations have declined significantly during the very years that mark the heyday of wildlife television, see the World Wildlife Fund's *Living Planet Report* (1998).

37. See Gerbner (1993); Gerbner et al. (1980, 1994); Gerbner and Signorielli (1979); Signorielli (1984).

38. McDonnell and Robins (1980: 354).

39. Carroll (1988) has rightly argued against the notion that fictional movie narratives are seen by audiences as "real." My argument here is that a fictional wildlife film might be taken as "true."

40. McDonnell and Robins (1980: 191).

41. Nichols (1981: 212).

42. For an example of the *Screen* position before it was revised, see MacCabe (1974). See also Nichols (1981), Ellis (1982), and for an opposing view, Carroll (1988).

43. Carroll (1985) distinguishes between "micro-questions" and "macro-questions" in film narrative. Wildlife films tend, in my view, to make greater use of the former—that is, to pose narrative questions that are answered by an event or scene that follows almost immediately, rather than later on in a long, complex, overarching narrative.

44. Brian Winston's statement that "Documentary more than any other filmic form 'produces nature as a guarantee of truth'" (the last part borrowed from Stuart Hall), might thus be amended to read, "*Wildlife and natural history film* more than any other filmic form" (Winston, 1993: 55).

45. In her introduction to *Women in Film Noir*, E. Ann Kaplan asserts that realist cinema, or the "classic text," represents the "Truth" by "giving the impression that it gives access to the "real world" (1980: 2). While not literally true (few could mistake film images for reality), surely wildlife films, often regarded as "documents" of nature, might be seen as conveying an even stronger impression of "access to the real world." The world of nature they depict is arguably more real than the world portrayed in Hollywood films.

46. Ray (1985: 34). MacCabe (1974) concurs.

47. Sklar (1975: 3). For another view of the relationship between science and motion pictures, in particular documentary, see Winston (1993).

48. Fell (1974: xv).

49. See, for example, Martineau (1973).

50. The difference between "narrative" and "story" is subtle but significant. "Not every narrative makes a story," writes Scholes, the difference being that a story is "a narration that attains a certain degree of completeness," although he concedes that this closure can be implied rather than actual (Scholes, 1979: 420).

51. Cawelti (1976: 19). See also Schatz (1981: vii–viii)

52. "How we treat others is based on how we see them," writes Richard Dyer (1993: 1), a superb critic, but one who, like so many others, may have a blind spot when it comes to nonhumans.

53. Grierson (1979b).

54. See Nochlin (1971), especially the section entitled "The New Range of Subject-Matter," pp. 33–40.

55. Rotha (1952: 105).

56. Wright (1974: 349).

57. Wright (1954).

58. Elsewhere I have discussed some of these individually (Bousé, 1998).

59. Barnouw (1993: 50–52, 186–90, 210).

60. See Gardner and Young (1981); Underwood (1981); Silverstone (1984); Hornig (1990); Wilson (1992: 117–56).

61. See Grierson (1979b: 11). For an analysis of Griersonian-style documentary films and videos dealing specifically with environmental issues in the United States, see Bousé (1991).

62. The most noted observer and prolific commentor on ethics in wildlife filmmaking is Jeffery Boswall (1962, 1968, 1982, 1986, 1989, 1997).

63. Quoted by Pryluck (1988: 262).

64. The moral judgment implied in taboos against cannibalism, infanticide, and fratricide, if not the very concepts themselves, are cultural constructs and have little place in the study of animal behavior other than as descriptive labels. Where incidents of this sort are observed among animals they are still little understood—but they *are observed* and are not undertaken by the animals in secrecy. This marks a crucial difference between humans and animals as film subjects.

65. MacDougall (1976: 136).

66. Walter Goldschmidt, quoted by MacDougall (1985: 278).

67. See MacDougall (1985: 275).

68. Quoted by Levin (1971: 204).

69. See Benson and Anderson (1989).

70. Winston (1993: 44).

71. Quoted by Winston (1993: 43).

72. Winston (1995: 254).

73. Barnouw (1993: 251).

74. Rouch once said of a subject, "whatever he tries to be [on camera], he is only more himself" (quoted by MacDougall, 1985: 282).

75. See Worth (1981: 134–37).

76. Kuehl (1988: 106).

77. Ibid. 104.

78. Ray (1985: 26).

79. From an interview in *Cruel Camera* (1984). Many of them were thrown to predators so the pursuit and kill could be filmed.

80. Horton and Wohl (1956). Their notion of "para-social relations" was originally postulated exclusively in relation to celebrities seen regularly on TV, and who played *to* the television audience, attempting to draw them in to pseudo-intimacy by direct address.

81. Caughey concludes from such accounts that "to an important extent the flickering images are apprehended *as people*," that is, not just as images (1984: 36).

82. See Hall (1969).

83. As defined by Meyrowitz (1986), "para-proxemics" combines Horton's and Wohl's concept of "para-social relationships" with Hall's notion of "proxemic" spatial relations. The argument is that we respond psychologically to media figures based on the perceived interpersonal distance at which we encounter them on the screen—that is, on the basis of the proxemic zone (intimate, personal, social, or public) in which they *appear* to be located, as determined by their size in relation to the television frame.

84. Steinhart (1988: 13).

85. Caughey (1984: 37).

86. Cited by Berger (1980: 15).

87. Whether it is a "natural" desire is another question. An argument can be made that a fear reaction to such an animal would be a normal one, an evolutionary legacy related to instincts for self-preservation. Interestingly, this reaction is still present in many viewers' responses to film images of snakes and other reptiles.

88. Mills (1997: 6).

89. "Doing What Comes Naturally . . ." (1996: 34).

90. James (1985: 94).

91. See Branigan (1985) and Messaris (1994) for fuller discussions of close-ups and point-of-view shots.

92. In creating dog's-eye-view shots for the film *Benji*, cinematographer Don Reddy noted, "Photographic intimacy with the dog was important to audience involvement in the story" (Reddy, 1974). Research shows, however, that the most complete identification is achieved when these POV shots are integrated with facial close-ups (see Messaris, 1994).

93. See Engländer (1997: 6).

94. Gross (1985: 2). I do not mean to imply here that a look-off followed by a point-of-view shot is an arbitrary convention; on the contrary, it is based on patterns of real-world seeing in which we really do follow the glance of people gazing intently at something.

95. Attenborough continues, "it can be as misleading to put *no* sound effect on . . . it's more distorting not to put anything on than to put on a fabricated sound effect.

If you put nothing on, then it looks as thought the animal is a mysterious thing that moves totally in silence" (quoted in James, 1985: 96).

96. Bordwell writes, "At first they believed that for maximum realism, the microphone should be placed as close to the camera as possible, so that in long shot there would be appropriately distant sound. It soon appeared, however, that more compelling cues would be furnished by a microphone placed fairly close to the players, even when filming long shots. The result was only a slight change in reverberation and volume when cutting from long shot to closer view—certainly nothing as acoustically drastic as the shot change was visually" (1985: 119).

97. "Full coverage" refers to the practice of filming an event from multiple camera angles, allowing the editor a wide range of shots from which to choose in constructing the final scene.

98. In a similar vein, Matt Ridley has written that the first life on earth may have been "atomistic and individual," but since then it has become "a team game, not a contest of loners" (1996: 14). For an argument that the struggle for existence *is* the struggle among individuals, however, see Julian Huxley's introduction to the 1964 edition of *Evolution: The Modern Synthesis*.

99. Leakey and Lewin (1996: 35). See also Raup (1991) for a more complete development of the idea of extinction as the result of bad luck rather than bad genes or lack of "fitness" for survival.

100. Of course, the species most adapted to its particular environment can be the one most vulnerable to extinction if that environment changes. The most specialized organisms are, in a way, then, the most highly evolved, *and* the least likely survivors should change occur—which the earth's geological record suggests is inevitable.

101. Leakey and Lewin (1977: 212).

102. Darwin (1909: 73)

103. Ridley (1996: 157).

104. MacDonald (1998: 226).

105. Lorenz (1963: 20, 21).

106. Darwin (1909: 95).

107. In many places, however, not interfering is dictated by policies that *officially* confuse the fate of an individual with that of a species, or even with the balance of nature. Jane Goodall writes of an incident in which she and Hugo Van Lawick witnessed a severely crippled and starving lion. "The kindest thing would have been to end her suffering," she writes. "But we were in the National Park, where there are strict rules that one must not interfere with the course of nature" (Van Lawick and Goodall, 1971: 39). Whether the lion died at that moment or a few hours later, however, could have had no significant bearing on the "course of nature" in an evolutionary sense.

108. MacDonald (1998: 230).

Chapter 2. A Brief History of a Neglected Tradition

1. Jackson (1913).

2. Klingender (1971: 3). Berger has likewise written, "The first subject matter of painting was animal. Probably the first paint was animal blood" (1980: 5).

3. Muybridge (1982: 3).

4. Gardner (1980: 28).

5. Ivins (1969); Blum (1993: 7–8).

6. Blum (1993: 3–19).

7. Ibid. 7.

8. See Elman (1977: 60–123); Jenkins (1978: 74–87).

9. In 1867 John L. Gihon made an "instantaneous" photograph of a horse in motion, although it is unclear as to his success in freezing the motion of the legs (Haas, 1976: 47).

10. Guggisberg (1977: 13). These dates are considerably earlier than the 1882 photographs of gannets in the Gulf of St. Lawrence, which are elsewhere said to be the earliest successful wildlife photographs taken in the field (Jenkins, 1978: 181).

11. R. Kearton (1898: vii, ix).

12. Haas (1976: 46–49, 83).

13. Reportedly, Marey read of Muybridge's work in an article that appeared in the December 18, 1878, edition of *La Nature*. His "animated zoology" remark was made in a letter he wrote to the editor of the journal in February 1879 asking to be put in touch with Muybridge. See Haas (1976: 114); Mozley (1979: xvii–xviii).

14. Cockerell (1935: 369).

15. Pike (1946: 14).

16. Stouffer (1988: 124).

17. A gray area is suggested by Flaherty's *Nanook of the North* (1922), which includes scenes of animals being killed exclusively for the film—although they were not its main subjects.

18. Mozley (1979: xxix, xxxi).

19. Musser (1990: 118); Baldwin (1995: 273).

20. An image of Topsy receiving 6,000 volts can be seen in *Before Hollywood* (Fell et al., 1987: 109). The film itself (transferred from a paper print) can be seen at the Library of Congress.

21. Pike (1946: 17). His claim here that "Nothing of the kind had ever been seen before," made in 1946, is either naive or uninformed, but seems to have been taken seriously by many Brits, who persist in seeing this as the first public screening of a wildlife and/or natural history film.

22. Sklar (1975: 29).

23. Staging of the shooting is described in "Scientific Nature-Faking" (1909).

24. The oxymoronic description is taken from an advertisement in *Moving Picture World*, February 21, 1914, p. 996. Brownlow credits Kleinschmidt with making "more truly documentary scenes of Eskimo life" than Flaherty's (1979: 476).

25. Bush (1914a: 956).

26. Clark (1912: 520). Reportedly, however, Kearton once asked an Indian Sultan "to shoot a tiger at fifteen yards, while he took the photograph" (Donaldson, 1912: 50).

27. Imperato and Imperato (1992: 93).

28. Bodry-Sanders (1991: 133).

29. Clark (1912: 523).

30. By some accounts, Rainey's film was one of the biggest money-makers of the decade. See "The Paul J. Rainey African Pictures" (1912).

31. Imperato and Imperato (1992: 131).

32. The figure of twenty-seven lions in thirty-five days comes from Imperato and Imperato (1992: 96). The other numbers come from "The Champion Lion-Killer" (1912: 616).

33. See Brownlow (1979: 415–17, 425–34). *90° South* was released on laserdisc in 1992 by Lumivision.

34. C. Kearton (1913: 100–101). Strangely, despite Roosevelt's enthusiasm for Kearton's films and photographs, Kearton is not mentioned in Roosevelt's collected letters (see Morison, 1951). In *African Game Trails* Roosevelt mentions Kearton only once: "Then there was another safari, that of Messrs. Kearton and Clark who were taking some really extraordinary photographs of birds and game" (1910: 329).

35. Houston (1986: 145). Reportedly, even the celebrated Cousteau expeditions during the 1960s and '70s were also "undertaken purely for the purpose of obtaining film footage," according to producer Marshall Flaum (Ricciuti, 1974: 75).

36. See, for example, Akeley (1924); Thomas (1937); Stott (1980); Alden and Stott (1981); Preston (1984); Houston (1986). The word "expedition" and variations on "explore" show up repeatedly in the titles of these pieces.

37. Brownlow (1979: 469).

38. Imperato and Imperato (1992: 97–98).

39. Brownlow (1979: 465).

40. Barnouw (1993: 50).

41. Ibid. 50–51.

42. Osa Johnson (1944: 129). Brownlow, however, reports that the Johnsons did use telephoto lenses (1979: 469).

43. Ibid. 129–30.

44. Ibid. 130–31.

45. Imperato and Imperato (1992: 111).

46. Osa Johnson (1944: 138).

47. Eastman (1927: 536).

48. See Bergman (1971); Brauer (1982).

49. Baxter (1968: 14).

50. Lumivision's 1992 "restored" version of *Simba* on laserdisc unfortunately includes neither the voice-over narration nor the sound effects added in 1928. Instead, it adds a completely new musical score featuring "traditional Kenyan melodies."

51. Barnouw (1993: 50).

52. Paul Hoefler's *Africa Speaks* (1930) contained some sound sequences, but not enough, evidently, to make it a true "sound film." MGM's *Trader Horn* (1931) included some scenes (staged confrontations) shot in Mexico. Frank Buck's *Bring 'em Back Alive* (1932) looked like an African safari picture but was filmed in Malaysia and Sumatra.

53. Martin Johnson (1934: 597).

54. Thomas (1937: 159).

55. "Hays Bars 'Ingagi' Film" (1930).

56. Although Armand Denis directed Buck's 1934 film *Wild Cargo*, he does not mention in his autobiography *On Safari* (1964) the fact that the film was shot silent, and that, apparently, no sound was even collected on location.

57. Denis (1964: 59).

58. Ibid. 58.

59. Ibid. 61.

60. See Crowther (1953a).

61. Donaldson (1912: 3).

62. Quoted by Donaldson (1912: 19, emphasis added). Winston (1988) has argued that Edward Curtis was the first to use the term "documentary" in relation to film in a 1914 article about his own *In the Land of the Head Hunters*. Prior to that, it had long been held that the first use of the term was by John Grierson in a 1926 review of Flaherty's *Moana* (Grierson, 1979a: 25). Winston is probably correct in suggesting that Curtis was the first to use the term "in a clearly Griersonian sense"—that is, as

the "creative treatment of actuality" (Winston, 1995: 9). The earliest use of the term "natural history film" I have found is in a 1913 piece in *Motion Picture World* (Jackson, 1913)—still before Curtis, Flaherty, or Grierson. At the very least, this should make clear that wildlife and natural history film did not emerge as an offshoot of documentary, but had already emerged a recognized form in its own right.

63. "Edison's Revolutionary Education" (1913).

64. Wood (1944: 150, 151).

65. Bush (1914c).

66. Wood (1944: 152). Ditmars was preceded in his efforts, however, by a Russian named Loyshki, who had been training and filming beetles for several years (see Sutcliffe, 1913).

67. Bush (1914b: 1095).

68. Bush (1914c: 769).

69. Ditmars (1931: 118).

70. Ibid. 126–27.

71. Field and Smith (1939: 236).

72. Grierson (1979b: 36). The remark might be explained by what Rachel Low has described as a "considerable coolness," borne of competition, between the "Secrets" team and the Grierson group (1979: 33).

73. Field and Smith (1939: 21).

74. Here some historical confusion emerges. Historian Rachel Low's account differs from that of Fields. Low asserts that the first "Secret" to use sound was *Bathtime at the Zoo*, shown in November 1929 and made by Arthur Woods" (Low, 1979: 20).

75. Field and Smith (1939: 231).

76. Ibid. 231.

77. Ibid. 232.

78. In *Film on the Left*, William Alexander describes Woodard as one of "America's finest cameramen" (1981: 132). After his insect "experiments," Woodard went on to become one of the original cinematographers on Pare Lorentz's film *The River* (1937), although he dropped out before completion.

79. Woodard (1934).

80. Woodard's language bears an uncomfortable resemblance to that of a contemporaneous movement in Europe claiming to be fulfilling the dictates of History, Destiny, and even Nature by destroying the Jewish "vermin" inhabiting the continent—while also filming much of the process. Ironically, Joseph Goebbels himself commented in his journals about his liking for wildlife films, especially the Johnsons' *Simba*, and is said to have found in it a rationalization for his own vulgar-Darwinist ideas about "survival of the fittest."

81. Academy Award nominations had also been given to a pair of films, *Krakatoa* and *The Sea* in 1932–33 for "Best Short Subject" in the "Novelty" category. *Krakatoa* won. Although neither film was about wildlife per se, *Krakatoa* may be the first film about a natural history topic to win an Academy Award.

82. Hass (1959: 267).

83. Barnouw (1993: 186–88). It is unclear why Barnouw chose to include a discussion of Sucksdorff at all in a book so committed to notions of documentary film's mission to reveal the human condition, and its presumed power to help combat injustice and ameliorate suffering. In a 1948 *New York Times* article, Arthur Knight also praises Sucksdorff's films, but also lacks the category of "wildlife film," and so, like Barnouw, does not really know what to do with them (Knight, 1979).

84. The one-sheet is reproduced on p. 122 of Neil Sinyard's book (1988).

85. Eliot (1993: 198–213).

86. See, for example, Watts (1995: 100). See also Glasberg and Schwartz (1983) for a summary of the literature on the power of finance capital ("bank control") in shaping corporate products, with particular relevance to the style and content of media products, an area also explored by Murdock (1982) and Turow (1984).

87. McEvoy (1955: 23); Schickel (1985: 284).

88. Sinyard (1988: 120).

89. Quoted by Jamison (1954: 16).

90. DeRoos (1963: 178).

91. Disney (1954a). This dates the impulse behind the "True Lifes" to the late 1930s or early '40s. Field had earlier written of the "Secrets of Nature" team's idea to apply Disney methods to live animals came about in 1930—well before the idea occurred to Disney or his team.

92. Quoted by DeRoos (1963: 178).

93. Morris (1979: 89). He offers no evidence to support his claim.

94. Eliot (1993: 200).

95. Disney (1954a: 38).

96. Jamison (1954: 16).

97. Ibid. 16.

98. Lee (1970: 193).

99. Schickel (1985: 287).

100. Disney (1954b: 23). The term "naturalist" has long signified amateur status, as opposed to trained scientists steeped in the scholarly literature, but Disney cameraman Tom McHugh did, in fact, have a Ph.D. in biology.

101. Quoted by McEvoy (1955: 23); and Schickel (1985: 284).

102. Jamison (1954: 16).

103. Sinyard (1988: 100).

104. Although it preceded the founding of the BBC Natural History Unit in 1957, the Disney studio was not the first to have its own unit devoted to nature film production. As early as the 1920s, British Instructional Films had its "Secrets of Nature" team, and Germany's UFA had its Decla-Bioscope division, although its mission included producing some cultural films as well as scientific natural history films.

105. Jamison (1954: 16).

106. Disney (1954b: 24, 25). Disney had, of course, been preceded in these sentiments by Kearton, who described the penguins in *Dassan* as "Nature's greatest little comedians."

107. Ganio (1951: 39).

108. Farber (1953).

109. Wright (1954: 35).

110. "The Living Desert," *Time*, November 16, 1953.

111. "The Living Desert," *Variety*, October 7, 1953.

112. "The Living Desert," *Newsweek*, November 23, 1953.

113. Crowther (1953b).

114. Hart (1954: 432). Complaints about condescending, humorous commentary were not new. The "Secrets of Life" team had received criticism for the humorous commentary by E. V. H. Emmett (Low, 1979: 33).

115. Crowther (1954).

116. Crowther (1953b).

117. Farber (1953).

118. McCarten (1953). He describes the animals in the film using terms such as "vermin . . . murderous . . . arrogant . . . [and] livestock."

119. Wright (1954).

120. "The Living Desert," *Time*, p. 108.

121. Hamburger (1954).

122. Rather than "formula," Disney pointed to a "True Life Adventure *method*" that could be adapted and applied elsewhere (Disney, 1954a).

123. Boswall (1973) identifies five different formulaic models of wildlife film. Elsewhere I have added five more (Bousé, 1989), but the grandest typology scheme is that of Nørfelt (1992).

124. Schickel (1985: 21–22).

125. DeRoos (1963: 162).

126. Stouffer (1988: 4–6).

127. Ibid. 164, emphasis added.

128. Perkins (1982: 113).

129. Ibid. 122.

130. *National Geographic* magazine included a companion article in its December 1965 issue (Van Lawick-Goodall, 1965).

131. The Cousteau films were produced for ABC by Metromedia through an arrangement with BBD&O, the advertising agency for the series sponsor, DuPont. See Ricciuti (1974: 75–76).

132. Clark Bunting, quoted by Fry (1999: 32).

133. Amanda Tennison, quoted by Fry (1999: 33).

134. Parsons (1982: 7).

135. See Boswall (1969). *Look* ran from 1954 to 1967.

136. Crowson (1981: 71).

137. Parsons (1982: 30).

138. Ibid. 32, 34.

139. Ibid. 353–61.

140. See McElvogue and Birch (1998).

141. Willock (1978: 27).

142. Ibid. 28, 29.

143. Ibid. 77, 78.

144. Ibid. 76.

145. Ibid. 123–24.

146. Ibid. 124.

147. Ibid. 194–95. See also John Sparks's assessment of Willock's popularizing strategies (Sparks 1981).

148. Crowson (1981: 69–75). The quotation is from p. 75.

149. See Ricciuti (1974).

150. Stouffer (1988: 127).

151. Ibid. 60.

152. Ibid. 183.

153. Steinhart (1980: 43).

154. Despite declining numbers nationally, in 1981 there were several wildlife programs on local television in Los Angeles, including *Safari to Adventure, Last of the Wild, Great Adventure,* and *Wild World of Animals* (Dickson, 1981).

155. Steinhart (1980: 45). Like many others, Steinhart based his arguments on the assumption that the presence of wildlife films on television is somehow directly connected to wildlife conservation and protection—that is, that they are helping save animals by raising consciousness and concern, and perhaps even motivating people to action. There is little real evidence of this, however.

156. Stouffer (1988: 188).

157. In Shreeve (1987: 11).

Chapter 3. Science and Storytelling

1. These oppositions have long been part of debates over culture, especially the "mass culture" debate of recent decades. See Jensen (1990).

2. See Ricciuti (1974); Attenborough (1987); McLaughlin (1997); McPhee and Carrier (1996a).

3. See Ray (1985).

4. The usual term in this context is "illusion" of reality. Carroll (1988) has argued, however, against its use to describe cinematic realism, rightly pointing out that images in mainstream movies do not, and are not intended to, "fool" anyone into thinking they are real at the phenomenal level. In wildlife films, however, the impression of reality is often so convincing that "illusion" may in some ways be applicable—unless we are talking about images on the TV screen fooling audiences into believing there are real animals in their living room.

5. The presumed opposition between science and narrative is central to Lyotard's argument in *The Postmodern Condition* (1984). In contrast to this, Haraway has argued that scientific facts, indeed, science itself, is "a storytelling practice," that biology "is inherently narrative . . . kin to Romantic literature," and that science is made up of "potent fictions" (1989: 4, 5). And, as Noël Carroll has noted, Darwin himself "told what must be one of the grandest narratives ever conceived" (1997: 95).

6. The film aired on the CBC program *The 5th Estate*. Its first half deals with the mistreatment of animals in mainstream Hollywood films, while the second half deals with mistreatment in wildlife films.

7. See James (1985); Tweedie (1985); Corry (1986a); Montgomery (1988).

8. See Webster (1986); Corry (1986b, 1987); Charle (1988).

9. See Attenborough (1987); Steinhart (1988); Northshield (1989).

10. Attempts to exploit this market include: *Two in the Bush* (1982), a self-portrait by Alan Root; *A Breed Apart* (1985), profiling several Survival cameramen; *Wildlife Jubilee* (1982), a celebration of the BBC-NHU's twenty-fifth anniversary; and *Sex, Hot Eruptions, and Chili Peppers* (1982), a salute to the series *The Natural World*. More recently, Partridge and TVNZ collaborated on *Natural Passion* (1995). National Geographic has produced several similar retrospectives and short filmmaker profiles. While all of these behind-the-scenes films reveal some of the techniques used in making wildlife films, they are also carefully constructed self-promotions and exercises in image management.

11. Those working in documentary film proper have so far acknowledged the artifice in their own work mainly in the form of intellectualized gestures of "self-reflexiveness" (Allen, 1977; Ruby, 1988) but have hardly been forthcoming about the decisions that go into molding reality into engaging dramas. "Documentarists have, for years," writes Winston, "obfuscated basic issues so that they could, at one and the same time, claim journalistic/scientific and (contradictory) artistic privileges" (1995: 6). In truth, many documentary filmmakers have, from Grierson on, acknowledged the *need* for a good story, even if they haven't addressed *how* that story is created from the non-narrative raw material of life (see Biskind, 1982: 64).

12. Carrier (1996a, b); McPhee (1996); McPhee and Carrier (1996a, b, c, d).

13. McGuire (1996); Obmsascik (1996); Saile (1996).

14. Foster (1996); Husar (1996); Sink (1996); Tayman (1996).

15. Coward (1997); McLaughlin (1997); Owen (1997); "Wildlife film-makers admit" (1998).

16. Gardner and Young (1981); Silverstone (1984); Hornig (1990); Curtin (1993).

17. See Boswall (1973); Nørfelt (1992); Bousé (1995).

18. Stephen Kellert (1983, 1993) has identified several categories of attitudes toward wildlife (e.g. aesthetic, utilitarian, humanistic, moralistic, etc.) and has made some preliminary attempts to find relationships between these and wildlife television (Kellert et al. 1986). Yet the data show little about viewers' attitudes toward wildlife television itself, and the uses and gratifications they seek and expect from it. Jacquie Burgess (1992) and the Glasgow Media Group (Philo and Henderson 1998) have come closer by using focus groups and informal interviews to elicit viewers' responses to wildlife programs. Larger audience analysis related specifically to wildlife programs was for years limited to a handful of BBC in-house studies carried out in the 1970s (e.g., Shaw, 1973). Recently, the BBC has contracted with Jane Barrett Market Research to carry out focus group studies.

19. See Mayr et al. (1953).

20. Jenkins (1978: 8).

21. See Ritvo (1985).

22. In Ritvo (1985: 76–7).

23. See Rosenberg and White (1957); Jacobs (1961); Gans (1974).

24. Even Darwin was widely read in his own time by a nonscientific audience. Carl Sagan, who rose to fame with the PBS series *Cosmos* (1979), was subsequently dismissed, even shunned by many in the scientific community for his efforts at science popularization. Such elitism in the ranks of scientists was widely noted in eulogies to Sagan after his death in 1996.

25. That media messages should be conduits of accurate and value-free information is largely a journalistic notion. Jensen (1990) casts the opposition between dramatic "story" journalism and neutral, objective, "information" journalism as one of "emotion" versus "reason," and notes Americans' historic distrust of the "polluting" influence of emotion on the purity of reason.

26. While Carson was researching her book in the late 1950s, natural history subjects were experiencing a surge in popularization, finding their way onto movie and television screens in a number of creative new treatments (see the Appendix).

27. Lenaghan (1967).

28. Blount (1975: 26). See also Underwood (1986).

29. See Dijk (1996). See also Temple and Temple's recent translation of Aesop (1998).

30. Raglan (1956: 258).

31. On "displacement," see Freud (1965: 343).

32. On self-knowledge, see Humphrey (1986); on role-taking, see Mead (1934).

33. Humphrey (1986: 72); Kennedy (1992: 21).

34. Lopez (1978: 251).

35. Steinhart (1981: 584).

36. Quoted by McLaughlin (1997: 31).

37. Disney (1954a).

38. Personal correspondence, December 1997.

39. See Boswall (1973), Nørfelt (1992).

40. On distinctions between "dominant," "negotiated," and "oppositional" readings, see Hall (1980).

41. See Blumler and Katz (1974); Bryant and Anderson (1983); Condry (1989); Gerbner (1986); Gerbner et al. (1994); Neuman and de Sola Pool (1986).

42. Rosenberg (1996).

43. Stouffer (1988: 368).

44. See Gerbner (1986). See also MacDonald (1957) and Mills (1956) for elabora-

tions of the argument that mass-produced culture products are called "popular" yet are not actually of popular origin; instead, they are produced and distributed "from above." Raglan concludes that folk tales are also not of popular origin: "the literature of the folk is not their own production, but comes down to them from above" (1956: 140).

45. Gerbner (1993: 1). It is unclear, however, that the profit motive automatically corrupts the information contained in a given media product (see Jensen, 1990: 172).

46. This may correspond to the idea of "oppositional readings" discussed earlier (Hall, 1980). For a discussion of the concepts of "primary" and "secondary" audiences, see Cantor (1971).

47. See Westcott (1997); Bousé (1997).

48. Rosenberg (1996).

49. Although wildlife films abound with examples of attempts to represent the point-of-view of animals, some of the most innovative and visually arresting can be found in *Supersense* (1988), a BBC series exploring animal perception. Its producer described it as depicting "the sensory worlds experienced by other creatures" (Downer, 1988: 9). This was followed by a sequel entitled *Lifesense* (1990), which was "inspired by the belief that the relationship between animals and ourselves could also be viewed afresh from this unique perspective" (Downer, 1991: 7). Part of its purpose was to show how animals see *us*.

50. In *Origin of Species* Darwin deliberately downplayed the idea that humans were related to apes—although this aspect of the book nevertheless drew most of the fire. It was not until years later that he devoted an entire work to the idea in *The Descent of Man* (1871), but by then much of the smoke had cleared.

51. See Millhauser (1959).

52. This first occurred in the 5th revised edition of *On the Origin of Species* (1869), and in all subsequent revised editions, in the heading of Chapter IV: "Natural Selection; Or The Survival of the Fittest."

53. Engels (1940: 208). He also notes that "Darwin did not know what a bitter satire he wrote on mankind, and especially on his countrymen, when he showed that free competition, the struggle for existence, which the economists celebrate as the highest historical achievement, is the normal state of the animal kingdom" (1940: 19).

54. Darwin (1909: 74).

55. Darwin's phrase "struggle for existence" had come from Malthus, but Malthus had supported his arguments about human society with observations of *nature*: "Through the animal and vegetable kingdoms, nature has scattered the seeds of life abroad with the most profuse and liberal hand. She has been comparatively sparing in the room, and the nourishment necessary to rear them. . . The race of plants, and race of animals shrink under this great restrictive law. And the race of man cannot, by any efforts of reason, hope to escape it" (Malthus, 1914: 6).

56. Engels (1940: 208–9). For a more up-to-date consideration of the problems in drawing inferences from animal behavior and social organization to that of humans, see the articles in the collection edited by Von Cranach (1976), especially the one by Crook (pp. 237–68).

57. Although Darwin himself almost never spoke out to promote or defend his theories, the task was energetically taken up in England by zoologist Thomas Huxley ("Darwin's Bulldog"), and in the United States by Harvard botanist Asa Gray, along with John Fiske and Edward Youmans. Spencer was not as reserved as Darwin

in promoting his ideas, but his failure, according to Hofstadter, was that he "did not extend his generalization to the whole animal world, as Darwin did," and therefore "failed to reap the full harvest of his insight" (Hofstadter, 1955: 39).

58. Elman (1977: 124–56). He describes Agassiz's attitude toward Darwinism as "a pious armour of implacable opposition" (p. 125).

59. Darwin's eclipse of Agassiz seems part of the triumph of empiricism over idealism in other areas of culture. "The end of the 'era of Agassiz,'" writes Novak, "roughly coincided with the end of the great era of American landscape painting." She adds that "the demise of Agassiz and the advent of Darwin signaled, as nothing else could, the approaching demise of landscape painting as a major form of spiritual expression in America" (1980: 288, n113).

60. See Singer (1975); Regan (1983); Nash (1989); Mighetto (1991).

61. See Brooks (1980: 133–80).

62. Concern for animal welfare has often been dismissed as misguided anthropomorphism. Dawkins has written, "the conviction that it is possible to draw an analogy between suffering in ourselves and that in other species is probably the basis for people's concern about animal welfare" (1980: 111). More extreme is Kennedy's view that humanitarian compassion for animals is evidence of "an empathically inspired fantasy" (1992: 114, 121).

63. See Schmitt (1989).

64. See Ingersoll (1923).

65. Schmitt (1989: 37–8).

66. The term "raptor," commonly used to refer to birds of prey, even by many ornithologists, is itself a case of anthropomorphic projection onto nature, being derived from the Latin word *rapere*—to seize, rob, kidnap, even rape.

67. The history of humans imposing normative expectations and punishments on animals is recounted by Thomas (1983).

68. See Schmitt (1989); Lutts (1990); Huth (1957).

69. Burroughs (1905: 202).

70. Ritvo (1985: 89).

71. See Allen (1978); Jenkins (1978); especially Barber (1980: 27–44).

72. Barber (1980: 28).

73. A 1994 poll showed that 83 percent of Americans who voted identified themselves as "environmentalists" (Lean, 1997), even though membership in environmental organizations showed significant decline.

74. A more heated debate over titles, credentials, and qualifications has been ongoing in relation to ethnographic film. Filmmakers often go into the field with no background in anthropology or ethnographic method, yet call their work "ethnographic" and themselves "ethnographers."

75. Boynton (1902).

76. "Wildlife Film-Making: A Freelance . . ." (1973: 70). Attenborough has written that wildlife camerapeople must have "such a deep knowledge and empathy with animals that [they] know what one is going to do before it does it" (Scholely, 1997: 8). On the use of "naturalist," see also Rayman (1999: 59); Disney (1954b: 23); DeRoos (1963: 178); Foster (1954).

77. Burroughs (1905: 191).

78. James (1876: 66).

79. McLaughlin (1997: 28).

80. Mighetto (1991: 11).

81. Mighetto (1991: 53); Lutts (1990: 22).

82. Gay (1988: 166).

83. Mighetto (1991: 4).

84. President Ronald Reagan cited Long's *Northern Trails* as one of the most memorable readings from his childhood (Mighetto, 1991: 19). Curwood saw a brief resurgence in popularity in 1989 after his 1916 novel *The Grizzly King* became the basis for the film *The Bear* (see Benabent-Loiseau, 1989; Miller, 1989; Bousé, 1990). Porter's *A Girl of the Limberlost* (1909) was cited by conservationist David Bellamy (1997) as his favorite "natural classic."

85. See Dunlap (1992).

86. See Schmitt (1989).

87. Keith (1969: 88).

88. There are exceptions. Porter's *The Song of the Cardinal* (1903), for example, includes a bird that does seem to speak, yet it is not clear whether its refrain of "Wet year! Wet year!" is to be understood as actual speech or as a projection of the mental experience of the farmer who provides the story's point-of-view.

89. See Humphey (1986, 1987).

90. See Kennedy (1992).

91. There have been wildlife films made in the sound era without voice-over narration. Sucksdorff's *The Gull* (1944) and Annuad's *The Bear* (1988) have shown what is possible, although it was achieved in both cases at the expense of realism, for the absence of the narrator's voice meant more reliance on artificial storytelling devices. In Sucksdorff's film this meant an overabundance of dramatic music combined with tendentious editing, while in Annaud's it meant staged behavior, much of which was unnatural, if not plainly false. Reggio's *Anima Mundi* (1992) also eschews voice-over commentary, but in a nontraditional, non-narrative approach that is part music video, part dialectical montage.

92. The advent of "talkies," of course, brought about the return of talking animals in popular stories—first in animated form (e.g., *Bambi*) and later in live-action settings (as in the series of films featuring Francis the talking mule, or the *Mr. Ed* TV series). It is interesting to note, however, that the technique used more recently in *Homeward Bound* (1993) and *Babe* (1995) was already considered "archaic" nearly a century earlier.

93. Magee (1980).

94. Dunlap (1992: 56).

95. Disney (1954a, emphasis added). Leakey and Lewin also point to "the Western ethos of success through effort" as motivating misinterpretations of evolution by natural selection (1996: 17).

96. Boynton (1902: 136).

97. Seton (1898: 7).

98. Schmitt (1989: 48–49). The principle of "composite" is, of course, an essential element in any kind of *series* fiction revolving around a single character, and is a narrative convenience allowing many different stories to be told without having to introduce audiences to new characters each time. This is somewhat different from the use of composites in wildlife stories and films, in which multiple "actors" are used in the construction of a single character.

99. Seton (1898: 7–8).

100. Ibid. 7.

101. Quoted by Lutts (1990: 40).

102. Burroughs (1952: 8).

103. Ibid. 51.

104. Burroughs (1905: v).

105. Quoted by Brooks (1980: 211).

106. Quoted by Lutts (1990: 54).

107. Long (1903: 687, 688).

108. See Fossey (1983); Goodall (1986, 1988); Masson and McCarthy (1995).

109. Roberts argued in a *New York Times* piece that "the whole question is not one of veracity but of judgment" (see "Defends his Stories," 1907).

110. Roberts (1902: 24).

111. Quoted by Schmitt (1989: 25–26).

112. From Roosevelt's introduction to Kearton's *Wild Life Across the World* (Kearton, 1913: v).

113. From an advertisement in *Moving Picture World*, May 31, 1913, p. 884.

114. Kearton (1933: 110).

115. A 1979 BBC program entitled *The Wildlife Moving Picture Show* (presented by Jeffery Boswall) celebrated Kearton's contributions to the founding of the wildlife and natural history genre.

116. Several of the leading nature writers were in fact Kearton's contemporaries. Seton and Roberts were born in 1860, Long in 1866, Salten in 1869, Kearton in 1871, and Curwood in 1878. All would have come of age during the years when "a late Victorian frame of mind" was was said to be emerging that pointed the way toward the twentieth century, when Kearton, Curwood, and Salten made some of their most significant contributions (Houghton, 1957: xv).

117. See Jacobs (1968).

118. Like Salten's *Bambi*, *The Grizzly King* has also been noted for its antihunting sentiments. Curwood wrote in the preface that the book was intended to "make others feel and understand that the greatest thrill of the hunt is not in killing, but in letting live." He expressed his own feelings of guilt for having once killed four grizzlies in a single day, adding, "In their small way my animal books are the reparation I am now striving to make."

119. Curwood (1989: 4).

120. Schmitt (1989: 151).

121. Almost in the manner of Jean-Luc Godard's "reflexive" films from the 1960s, Curwood's story comes to a halt as two human characters sit and, for four pages, discuss the art of writing animal stories such as the very one in which they are at that moment characters (1989: 59–63).

122. See Magee (1980).

123. This type of plot—white pioneers struggling against the wilderness itself—has been described as a "Northern," distinct from the Western (see Fiedler, 1969). On its use by Curwood, see Miller (1989) and Schmitt (1989: 151).

124. Brownlow (1968: 29). Klepper (1999: 149) lists Shipman-Curwood Productions as the film's producers.

125. *Kazan* was produced by Selig Productions, which had earlier produced *Hunting Big Game in Africa* (a.k.a. *Roosevelt in Africa*). See "Scientific Nature Faking" (1909).

126. Rin Tin Tin (1916–1932), a German shepherd found in a German trench during World War I and brought to Hollywood, appeared in fourteen features and two serials. Several of his scripts were written by Darryl F. Zanuck, then still at Warner's (see Katz, 1994: 1152).

127. Hoffman (1990: 152).

128. Osa Johnson (1944: 130). See also Houston (1986: 154).

129. There have been some fine recent wildife films hinging on the filmmaker's encounter with the animals. Of particular note is Hugh Miles's *Puma: Lion of the Andes* (1997), Des and Jen Bartlett's *Wild Survivors* (1993), Hugo Van Lawick's *Serengeti Diary* (1995), and Simon King and Jonathon Scott's *Big Cat Diary* (1996). Less satisfying is

the recent trend in which well known celebrities, acting as audience surrogates, are taken into the wild for set up encounters with animals.

130. Field and Smith (1939: 188).

131. Ibid. 48–49.

132. Ibid. 50.

133. For those aware that Mickey Mouse made his debut only two years earlier (in the silent *Plane Crazy* and the talking *Steamboat Willie*—both 1928), Fields's remark may seem to suggest that Disney's influence had spread with remarkable speed. In fact, Disney had begun in theatrical cartoons in 1922, the same year as the "Secrets" series premiered, with a series of "Laugh-O-Grams." These were followed in 1925 by the "Alice in Cartoonland" series, and in 1927 by the "Oswald the Lucky Rabbit" series. Disney's brand of animated character creation and his penchant for physical humor had thus been around for some time already, and had built an audience over a length of eight years by the time the "Secrets" team appropriated the Disney style, which was by then highly conventionalized. Disney himself, however, noted years later that his own idea to produce "live animal drama" in the Disney style didn't come about until the late 1930s or early 40s, during production of *Bambi* (see Disney, 1954a).

134. Woodard was preceded by twenty years in his appropriation of dramaturgical terms by the Russian beetle trainer Loyshki, who made a film sometime before 1913 called *A Drama of the Middle Ages*, with an all-insect cast (Sutcliffe, 1913).

135. Woodard (1934: 178, emphasis added).

136. Ibid. 177.

137. Barnouw (1993: 48).

138. Griffith (1979: 23).

139. Barnouw (1993: 50).

140. Everson (1978: 235–36).

141. DaVinna had formerly been official photographer of the U.S. Pacific Fleet. Shortly after leaving for Africa to film *Trader Horn*, he was awarded the 1929 Academy Award for his cinematography in *White Shadows in the South Seas*, which had been "co-directed" by Van Dyke and Robert Flaherty (see Brownlow 1979: 490–499; Wiley and Bona, 1986: 12). Van Dyke, in *Horning into Africa* (1931), describes his experiences on the long and difficult *Trader Horn* shoot, including a few brief accounts of DaVinna's efforts to film some thirty-five species of wild animals. The camera team included Bob Roberts and George Nogle, the latter of whom had made underwater footage of sea creatures for *White Shadows*.

142. Production materials for *Sequoia* show many personnel changes during its drawn-out, sporadic shooting between May 1933 and October 1934. In addition to Franklin, Nick Grindé and Edwin Marin evidently also directed the film at points. DaVinna evidently shared the camera work with Leonard Smith and Chester Lyons, with the final credit going to Lyons.

143. Unfortunately, some of *Trader Horn*'s grislier wildlife scenes, involving bloody fights between animals, were not shot on location in Africa, but staged and filmed by a second unit in Mexico—a fact the studio did not want publicized.

144. This could have been because Paramount went into bankruptcy in late 1932 and operated at a loss during reorganization. MGM was the only studio to hold its market value and continue operating at a profit during the difficult early years of the depression (see Schatz, 1988). This, along with its move to a "unit" (as opposed to a centralized) production system, may have accounted for its ability to take on a somewhat risky picture like *Sequoia* and stay with it despite the disruptions in shooting and personnel.

145. Johnston and Thomas (1990: 106).

146. Ibid. 106–108.

147. *Never Cry Wolf* was based on a story by Farley Mowat. For a lively discussion of the book, the movie, and scientific accuracy in wildlife films, see Jonkel (1985).

Chapter 4. The Classic Model

1. My analysis of narrative structure here is indebted to Propp's structural study of folk tales (1968). Propp, however, argued for a firm, unchanging sequence of basic events, whereas no such absolute sequencing of events exists in wildlife films. Will Wright has noted that Propp's approach "is unnecessarily restricting, for it is easy to recognize a set of essentially similar stories with slightly differing orders of events" (1975: 25). I have therefore declined to lay out an actual sequenced model of numbered events, although readers wishing to see such a model may refer to my earlier study of Disney animal narratives (Bousé, 1995).

2. Cawelti (1976: 18).

3. Ibid. 18.

4. The term "traditional narrative" (Raglan, 1956), may well be interchangeable with "plot type," "formulaic pattern," or "archetypal story pattern" (Cawelti, 1976). Although I have endeavored not to conflate "plot" and "story" (see Tomashevsky, 1965: 66–78), I especially wish to avoid disputes over differences between "myths" and "tales." Psychologist Rollo May argues that tales "can become myths" if they exhibit certain attributes (1991: 196), while Raglan sees an opposing dynamic in which myths (at least some) become folk tales. The term "traditional narrative" provides a way out, but Raglan doesn't leave it at that, arguing that ultimately "all traditional narratives are myths," for they are all "connected with ritual" (1956: 128, 141). Alan Dundes argues that "Culture patterns normally manifest themselves in a variety of cultural materials," and thus are not limited to single categories we impose on them, such as "myth," "tale," or "fable," or, for that matter, "novel," "play," or "comic strip" (in Propp, 1968: xiv–xv).

5. Propp does point out, however, that other scholars have made a distinction between "animal tales" and other types of tales, including "tales with fantastic content" and "tales of everyday life." But, he asks, "Don't tales about animals sometimes contain elements of the fantastic to a very high degree?" And conversely, "Don't animals actually play a large role in fantastic tales?" It is here he concludes that "the tale ascribes with great ease identical actions to persons, objects, and animals." Pursuing the matter into the area of fables, he continues, "the question is then raised as to the difference between a 'pure animal fable' and a 'moral fable.' In what way are the 'pure fables' not moral, and vice versa?" (1968: 5, 7).

6. The story line of a wild animal lost in the human world was employed in a number of Disney adventures from the early 1960s. The desire to see how wild animals cope with human technology is probably as old as human society itself, and is clearly evident in many pre-cinematic circus and carnival acts, such as bicycle-riding bears, piano-playing chickens, and so forth. In film and television this scenario has often been rendered comically, although in some Disney films it could degenerate into a cinema of cruelty as the unwitting "actors" were subjected to a series of plainly dangerous "comic accidents."

7. These very aspects of television have also meant that it came to thrive on "personalities," and so has given rise to many "documentary" style wildlife and natural

history programs in which the "characters" are biologists and other experts photographed in talking-head close-ups.

8. Wright (1975: 25). He also makes the important point that although westerns and folk tales are both traditional narratives, the tales studied by Propp (1968) were "popularized and standardized by many retellings" over centuries, whereas western movies are (like wildlife films) produced by industries rather than by storytellers, and are not subject to standardization through public retelling (1975: 25).

9. See MacDonald (1957).

10. This "heroic" pattern was thought by myth scholars in the early twentieth century to be allegorically related to the rising and falling of the sun. Thus Otto Rank's account of it, written in 1914 (and adapted from Brodbeck's *Zoroaster*, 1893), goes as follows: "The newborn hero is the young sun rising from the waters, first confronted by lowering clouds, but finally triumphing over all obstacles" (Rank, 1959: 6).

11. Recall Mary Field's remarks, quoted earlier, that all films, including wildlife films "ought to have a beginning, carefully thought out, from which they should move logically through to a middle, and . . . should progress to that end which the beginning demanded" (Field and Smith, 1939: 48–49).

12. Carey (1989: 28).

13. Cawelti (1976: 5–6). Compare Cawelti's remarks here on "general plot patterns" to Frye's discussion of "*mythoi*, or generic plots" (1957: 162).

14. Cawelti (1976: 5).

15. The terms "civilized" and "primitive" have fallen into disuse as scholars have become more sensitive to the biases implied in them. Yet "history" and "prehistory" continue to be used in a similar fashion, and with nearly identical implications. In both cases the determining factor is often *literacy*. Lévi-Strauss has recommended the term "without writing" instead of "primitive" (1978: 15). Even though "primitive" is regarded as ethnocentric, or even faintly racist when applied to existing cultures, "prehistoric" has so far not been recognized as an equally discriminatory term, which often has the effect of marginalizing and discrediting the pasts and cultural traditions of some (usually dark-skinned) peoples. For a discussion of how this has been institutionalized and systematically applied, see Bousé (1996).

16. See Rank (1959); Jung (1959); Eliade (1954, 1963); Raglan (1956); Lévi-Strauss (1963); Campbell (1972). Raglan also points to the worldwide similarities in folk and fairy tales, and concludes that there has been so much cross-cultural borrowing as to call into question the "folk" origins of any culture's own supposed folk tales (pp. 130–33).

17. Lévi-Strauss (1963: 208). The question is taken out of context; Lévi-Strauss was in fact among those who saw myth as revealing general traits of the human psyche. He maintained for decades that myth was actually a kind of "objectified thought" (1969: 10–11), and therefore shed light on the conceptual structure of the human mind, which was essentially *binary*.

18. Campbell (1972: 3, 37–38).

19. Campbell (1972: 30, emphasis in original).

20. Frye (1957: 186–87).

21. Magee (1980: 230). He adds, however, that "with heroism enters villainy, moral insight, and active affections."

22. Seton (1898: 7).

23. Stouffer (1988: 219, emphasis added).

24. See also Parsons's chapter on "Scripting," in *Making Wildlife Movies* (1971: 154–59).

25. Ganio (1951: 38).

26. Maltin (1984: 22).

27. Johnston and Thomas (1990: 127).

28. Maltin (1984: 78). In fact, Disney studios faced financial troubles throughout the 1940s, and after the release of *Bambi* in 1942 produced only one *fully* animated feature—1943's *Victory Through Air Power*—until *Cinderella* in 1950. By that time, according to Schickel, Disney had "transformed his operation from one devoted completely to animation to one in which animation was becoming a sideline" (1985: 268).

29. Freud (1971: 381).

30. Maltin (1984: 49–51).

31. Campbell (1972: 38). Note the parallel hierarchy in Frye's description of the hero in myth and romance: "in myth proper he is divine; in romance proper he is human" (1957: 188).

32. Fromm (1969: 153). For a critique of Fromm's "clinical" analysis of Mickey Mouse, see Berland (1982).

33. Stouffer (1988: 127, 183).

34. Disney's first version of *The Incredible Journey* (1963) was actually filmed by the Canadian production company Calgary Ltd., but was nevertheless scripted and co-produced by James Algar, one of the forces behind the "True Life" series.

35. Magee (1980: 230).

36. Ibid. 228, emphasis added).

37. Bettelheim (1976: 164–5).

38. Ibid. 159. The argument here is at odds with the British school of "Object Relations," which derives largely from the work of Melanie Klein. According to this body of theory, the issue is not so much fear of starvation, as Bettelheim argues, but fear of abandonment by the person who occupies the primary position in our early inner life, and who is therefore not only our first *loved other*, but, indeed, our *first other*, and thus the one from whom we derive our earliest sense of self. As such, the issue is not overt fear of being deprived of the nurturing breast, but anxiety over the existence and unity of the self. Either way, the implications for the emotional power of the orphan theme are undiminished.

39. Schickel (1985: 266).

40. Dorfmann and Mattelart (1975: 20, 33, 35).

41. There is some disagreement as to the date of the original German language publication of *Bambi*. It has been set, variously, at 1923 (May and Mork, 1988), 1924 (Cartmill, 1993), and 1926 (Lutts, 1992). Fortunately, all agree on 1928 as the date of Chambers's English translation.

42. Johnston and Thomas (1990: 104–6).

43. May and Mork (1988: 499).

44. Quoted in May and Mork (1988: 498).

45. Reiger (1980: 12, 16). The irony of these remarks was apparently lost on Reiger, considering that his magazine is devoted to hunting and killing animals. It seems fair to say, therefore, that "death is the central theme" of *Field & Stream* as well.

46. Cartmill (1993: 8). The fact that Austria had suffered terribly during World War I may have contributed to the "aura of pessimism," but scapegoating Freud has long been a favorite pastime among American anti-intellectuals.

47. Cartmill (1993: 10). Unfortunately, the opportunity to confront openly and deal with the arguments in a legitimate critique of hunting is evaded here by the implication that its critics (in this case the writers of *Bambi*) are pathologically misanthropic. This kind of ad hominem attack, with its either/or simplicity (one is either for animals or for people) deflects debate over the morality of bloodsports to one

over the sanity of those who would dare criticize hallowed tradition, thus leaving the real moral questions unanswered.

48. Johnston and Thomas (1990: 112).

49. Ibid. 122.

50. Ibid. 114.

51. Ibid. 119. If the idea for ending with a birth was Franklin's, the idea for the birth of *twins* may have come from the Disney shop. Dorfmann and Mattelart have pointed to the great "quantity of twins" among characters in Disney comic books (1975: 34).

52. The effectiveness, or at least the utility of the life-cycle model is discussed by Parsons (1971) and Boswall (1973, 1974b).

53. Cartmill (1993: 10).

54. Campbell (1972: 16).

55. In contrast to *Bambi*, it seems fairly clear that Disney's *The Lion King* (1994) was intentionally conceived as a latter-day myth (see Daly, 1994; Klass, 1994; Maslin, 1994; Sterritt, 1994). In making *Bambi* the filmmakers were working from an original novel, and at the same time feeling their way somewhat blindly in the unexplored realm of feature-length animation. Five decades later, there is little that is exploratory, original, or innovative about *The Lion King*, even though it was not based on an established tale. It thus manages to feel like the rote application of tried and true money-making formulas, conceived by the marketing department more than by real writers (see Bousé, 1995).

56. Johnston and Thomas (1990: 108).

57. Kael (1970: 225).

58. Fromm (1969: 153).

59. Salten (1938).

60. De Roos (1963: 186).

61. Maltin (1984: 142). It is difficult to know whether this is an interpretation or a report based on facts from interviews and documents, although the former seems the most likely.

62. De Roos (1963: 186).

63. Lee (1970: 208).

64. Quoted by De Roos (1963: 188).

65. Schickel (1985: 291).

66. The addition of a human child as a companion to an orphaned animal would become a widely employed convention in animal adventure films in later years, such as *The Journey of Natty Gann* (1983), *Cheetah* (1988), *The Great Panda Adventure* (1995), and many others. This undisguised audience surrogate in the adventure, however, obviously distracts viewers' emotional involvement away from the main animal figure. Still, while such works cannot be considered wildlife films, they nevertheless remain variations on the classic narrative model.

67. Stouffer (1988: 160). CBS later refused to air the program.

68. *The Last Wolves of Ethiopia* was a twenty-minute version of a fifty-two-minute French-German coproduction (Canal + and ZDF) called *Abyssinian Wolf* (1997), which had included a good deal more scientific content, although with a somewhat less coherent structure. *Yellowstone: Realm of the Coyote* was the work of Montana wildlife cinematographer Bob Landis, who told me privately that the story had been imposed on his footage. In both cases the final products were tailored by writer Robert Goldberg for broadcast on *National Geographic Explorer*.

69. From a promotional blurb at the CBS website during the week of 12–18 April 1997.

70. From a synopsis of the film in the 1998 International Wildlife Film Festival catalogue.

71. It has been argued, for example, that that Cousteau films, *National Geographic Explorer,* and even the films on the PBS series *Nature* (many of which are imported from sources around the world) are all mere "offshoots of the Disney formula" (King, 1996: 64). Not only does this greatly oversimplify the case, but it is also made in apparent unawareness of the long-standing and venerable European traditions of wildlife and natural history filmmaking that preceded the "True Lifes."

72. Rank (1959: 14).

Chapter 5. Family Values, Social Mores, Behavioral Norms

1. Meyrowitz (1986) defines "teaming" as an emotional alignment of viewers with characters, achieved by the camera's replication of our personal proxemic orientation to others around us.

2. On historical and cultural variations in human family structures, see Gottlieb (1992), Ridley (1993), and, of course, Engels (1978/1884). There has always been considerable variation among cultures in the ways children are raised, and even the terms "mother" and "father" have different meanings and applications in different cultures (Eisenberg, 1990: 15).

3. Research has shown that mainstream television in America has systematically reflected and reinforced conventional values, perhaps especially in areas of sex roles and family/social structure (see Gerbner, 1993; Gerbner et al., 1994). In American motion pictures, the 1934 Hollywood Production Code, which reigned for thirty years, explicitly prescribed, for example, that "the sanctity of the institution of marriage and the home shall be upheld."

4. This is not to say that there isn't monogamy among mammals (see Kleiman, 1977; Ridley, 1993).

5. From the CBS website for the week of 12–18 April 1997.

6. Lorenz (1963: 211).

7. Ibid. 143, 208–9.

8. Masson and McCarthy (1995: 64–90).

9. See Ridley (1996).

10. See Goodall (1988); Smuts (1985); Harcourt and de Waal (1992); Ridley (1996: 151–54).

11. Quoted by Allee (1958: 11). It has also been shown that fish often "exhibit modes of sociality usually attributed only to higher vertebrates" (McKaye, 1981: 173), and have even been observed to demonstrate "altruistic behavior" (McKaye, 1977). For more accessible reflections, see Lorenz (1963); Masson and McCarthy (1995); Ridley (1996).

12. Many animals may abandon their young rather than risk their lives defending them. This suggests a paradox: as the young mature, surviving the earliest, most severe threats to their survival, their reproductive likelihood increases, and so too does their *reproductive value* (RV) to the species. Yet mammalian mothers' willingness to defend them decreases as they mature, which, oddly, is when their RV is higher. Rodents in particular exhibit this apparently maladaptive trait, yet their numbers can still increase rapidly by way of the reproductive efforts of the adults. For a thorough discussion, see Daly (1990).

13. In this derisive description of rhinos, Algar and Hibler may have been re-

peating opinion received from the Johnsons' films. Compare a title card from *Simba* (1928): "The Rhino is always looking for trouble and hoping for it."

14. Other metaphors for the evolutionary ladder are the mountain and the arrow, with humans at the pinnacle or tip respectively. Either way, the implication is that we are the *most evolved* life form, indeed, the *culmination* of evolution for whom evolution has ended, rather than one highly evolved, and still evolving species among many, each evolving separately along its own line. This had been the view of Darwin's colleague Alfred Russell Wallace, as well as, more recently, Teilhard de Chardin and others (see Leakey and Lewin, 1996: 77–98).

15. The word "cheating" is, in fact, used for convenience in some scientific literature on animal behavior. Emlen (1981), for example, uses it in a discussion of bird behavior, but carefully places quotation marks around it (p. 218). On the subject of animal monogamy, see Kleiman (1977). See also Ridley's readable and engaging discussion in *The Red Queen* (1993).

16. Countless millions of animals have, over the centuries, been flogged, tortured, and even publicly executed for their supposed moral transgressions and criminal offenses (see Thomas, 1983).

17. Dahmer was a notorious mass murderer in the United States who cannibalized his victims. The analogy was made by Ralph Seekins, of the Alaska Wildlife Conservation Association, interviewed on the *CBS Evening News*, 2 December 1994. There is no evidence of cannibalism among wolves, although the grim record of their persecution and slaughter by humans (see Lopez, 1978) may be more deserving of the Dahmer analogy.

18. Even astute texts on the behavior and social lives of animals have not been exempt from spurious analogies to humans. One points to examples of animals who spend the night together, arguing that it is "as though they were engaged in a slumber party" (Allee, 1958: 27). The behavior is more likely a safety measure than a social sleepover.

19. The phenomenon observed in cowbirds and cuckoos, sometimes called "cuckooism" even when observed in other species, is formally known as "interspecific brood care," or "alien brood substitution," and occurs also among ants, wasps, and a long list of fish species, including large-mouthed bass (see McKaye, 1981). One study of cowbirds in Panama has even shown that their "cuckooism" can benefit the survivorship of the host species (Smith, 1968).

20. Disney (1954a, emphasis added).

21. Huxley (1964). The terms "symbolic eugenics" and "symbolic euselection" are my own, although an important analysis of television's "symbolic annihilation" and other means of dealing with social "deviants" can be found in a trio of articles by Larry Gross (1984, 1988, 1991) with unintended relevance to depictions of animal "others."

22. See Thomas (1983).

23. MacDonald (1998: 230–31), emphasis added.

24. The red wolf subspecies, found in the eastern United States, often does live in family groups smaller than the packs of ten or fifteen typical of their cousins in the west. Some even live and hunt alone. Pack behavior mainly serves the purpose of bringing down large prey; where this is not necessary, wolves sometimes adopt alternative strategies, which include living in pairs or even alone. See Crook (1976); Lopez (1978: 32–36); Schaller (1972); Van Lawick and Goodall (1971: 61, 80–86).

25. Dugmore (1912: 6–7).

26. Sielmann (1959: 39). Unfortunately for Sielmann, in this particular instance the woodpeckers' nest was taken over by starlings.

27. Others who have discussed the relative ease of shooting such films, and of constructing the studio sets or altering nests to accommodate a camera and lights, include Field and Smith (1939), Sparks (1988), and Stouffer (1988).

28. Over- and underrepresentation of certain species, behaviors, and models of family structure is a problem, however, requiring extensive and systematic analysis of *aggregate data* of the sort collected in studies of the representation of women and minorities on television (e.g., Gerbner, 1993; Gerbner and Signorielli, 1979; Signorielli, 1984). Such systematic, quantitative content analysis of the representation of nature and wildlife on television has yet to be done.

29. Schmitt (1989: 37–38).

30. Seton (1907: 601).

31. See Underwood (1986).

32. It is unclear whether the film depicts the three-spined stickle back (*Gasterosteus aculeatus*) or the ten-spined stickleback (*Pygosteus pungitius*), which differ in their manner of nest construction, but male brood care is also found in the family *Syngnathidae*, including seahorses, pipefish, and needle fishes (see Box, 1973: 14–17).

33. "Primary *maternal* caregiving is the predominant mode in most animal species," writes Yogman (1990: 462). Male parental care is rare among animals "in which fertilisation occurs within the female's body," such as mammals (including humans), while in "externally fertilizing vertebrates" such as most fishes and amphibia, male care of the young is more common (Daly, 1990: 34; see also Ridley, 1978). Still, the family dynamics of some animals are flexible, and may be significantly altered by captivity. There are also reported examples of captive zoo animals, in particular some cat species, in which the fathers uncharacteristically remained attached to the mother and offspring, and even appeared to take on the role of food bringer (Masson and McCarthy, 1995: 98).

34. This example was first examined in an unpublished paper by Crowther (1992).

35. Rank has written that our embrace of "the father's individual role of begetter of his children" came about relatively recently in human history as a result of the "transition from a primitive group-family (kinsfolk)," to the present-day small family with the father as head of household (1959: 300).

36. It has been argued, for example, that British audiences have come to expect BBC natural history programs "to be based on scientific truth" (Prince, 1998: 61). Yet it might just as well be argued that audiences have come to expect convincing, well-executed, realistic *illusions* of truth, presented in accordance with the conventions of television entertainments.

37. From the catalogue description submitted to Wildscreen '96.

38. "The variety of social organizations in the animal kingdom is considerable," writes Box. "It ranges from simple and transitory associations, to highly complex and permanent systems which demonstrate high levels of co-operation and division of labour among their members." She concludes, "Looking at the spectrum of examples of animal social organization . . . we can see it is extremely difficult to draw general conclusions" (1973: 11, 45).

39. Lorenz (1952: 57–66). "It is seldom that I laugh at animals," Lorenz remarked, "and when I do, I usually find out afterwards that it was at myself . . . that I have laughed" (p. 57).

40. Lorenz (1952: xvii). See his quotation at the start of this book.

41. Kearton (1930: 70–71).

42. "The Vanishing Prairie," *Time*, August 23, 1954.

43. Hamburger (1954).

44. Hart (1954: 432).

45. Ricciuti (1974: 77–78).

46. Stouffer (1988: 217). See also Slade (1992).

47. Quoted by Slade (1992).

48. See Sparks (1999). A recent study by the Glasgow Media Group suggested that some audiences may now prefer scenes of animal sex to those depicting predatory killing (Philo and Henderson, 1998).

49. Maier (1998: 90). The closest thing to imitation among animals may be what is called "visual social learning," although this applies mainly to solving specific problems (which are almost always related to obtaining food).

50. Goodall has written of an incident, however, in which one chimp seems deliberately to have led another to the termite mound, apparently so it could observe the technique. See Goodall (1988: 35–37, 74–75, 161–63).

51. I have not seen *Falconeye* in English, so this is a rough translation from German of both the film's title and the text of its commentary.

52. See Lutts (1990: 40–41, 82–83, 125–26).

53. Burroughs (1903).

54. Tomkies (1987: 136–37).

55. Burroughs (1905: 83–84; see also pp. 88–94). Although learning is studied extensively in animal behavior science, the concept of "teaching" is virtually nonexistent in the literature.

56. Lorenz argued that "maternal instinct" does not exist among animals, and that "Species-preserving behavior toward the young" is instead the function of a number of behavior patterns, reactions, and inhibitions that function as a systemic whole, so that it only appears as if a particular animal "knew what it had to do" (1963: 113). A number of recent studies of nonhuman primates have emphasized the role of learning and experience in mothering. Studies of "motherless mothers" have shown that female monkeys raised without mothers nevertheless learn over time to be effective mothers themselves, and thus do not need to be taught. See Ruppenthal et al. (1976); Coe (1990).

57. The idea that innate and learned behavior are opposing terms is no longer accepted by most of those who study animal behavior. In its place are more complex notions involving combinations of heredity *and* learning. See, for example, Dimond (1970: 32–35), although the idea can be traced back to the work of Konrad Lorenz in the 1930s.

58. Stouffer (1988: 127).

59. See Foster (1996); Kuntz (1998); McElvogue (1996); Sink (1996); Slade (1992); Steinhart (1983). Elsewhere, Steinhart also discusses the "outdoor porn" of animals-versus-people scenarios in films about marauding sharks, grizzlies, mountain lions, and the like (1980: 41).

60. NGT's Keenan Smart, quoted by Slade (1992).

61. Burroughs (1903). Darwin did, however, use the unfortunate phrase "all nature is at war, one organism with another," in an 1858 paper he presented with Alfred Russel Wallace (quoted by Leakey and Lewin, 1996: 34). The metaphor is no longer considered appropriate to evolutionary biology.

62. Seton (1898: 10).

63. MacDonald (1998: 226).

64. Van Lawick and Goodall (1971: 39).

Chapter 6. Nature Designed and Composed

1. See Davies (1998).

2. A press release by United Wildlife (22 September 1997) announced the merger of Survival and Partridge films, describing them as "friendly rivals" that would now be "highly complementary" to each other as partners "working together on new projects," and touts the many new collaborative possibilities and synergies. See also Fry, (1998). For scholarly analyses of such friendly rivalries and mergers, see Glasberg and Schwartz (1983) and Turow (1984).

3. Allen (1998: 21).

4. See Bazin (1967, 1978). See also MacCabe (1974), and Williams (1980) for elaborations of realist arguments. On the relationship of film sound to film form, see Bordwell (1985: 118–20), Bordwell and Thompson (1985), and Salt (1985), as well as most of the other essays in the volume edited by Weis and Belton (1985).

5. See, for example, Dillon (1999).

6. See Bossen (1985); Brand (1985); Harris (1991); Martin (1991); Zelle and Sutton (1991).

7. See Bartlett and Bartlett (1973, 1975); Buxton (1980); Buxton and Price (1983); Plage (1980); Willock (1978, 1981). See also McCrae (1989), and "Wildlife Film-Making: A Freelance Director-Cameraman's Viewpoint" (1973), an interview with Alan Root. In stark contrast, wildlife films shot in expensive large formats, such as IMAX, are even shot by specialized large-format camera operators rather than by seasoned wildlife filmmakers familiar with the intricacies of animal behavior from years of experience in the field.

8. See Langley (1985) for a detailed account of the vast logistical detail in such a production.

9. The figure comes from Jeff Rice, postproduction manager at ABC/Kane in the 1990s (Mrozek, 1998: 28).

10. See Clark (1997, 1998).

11. See, for example, Crowther (1992), Wilson (1992). While not addressing wildlife films per se, Berger (1980) invokes the same themes and ideas in his reflection on zoos. Scholey, however, may be understating the case when he writes that wildlife filmmakers have "little or no control over their subjects and it is the animals themselves that must tell the story" (1997: 10). This echoes the disingenuous prologue to some of the "True Life Adventures" claiming that "nature herself is the dramatist."

Bibliography

Aesop. (1998). *The Complete Fables*. Trans. Robert Temple and Olivia Temple. London: Penguin.

Akeley, Carl E. (1924). "Martin Johnson and His Expedition to Lake Paradise." *Natural History* 24: 284–88.

Alden, Sondra Updike and Kenhelm W. Stott (1981). "Safari Museum: Chanute Memorizalizes Famous Exploring Couple." *Explorer's Journal* 59, 2: 58–63.

Alexander, William. (1981). *Film on the Left: American Documentary Film from 1931 to 1942*. Princeton, N.J.: Princeton University Press.

Allee, W. C. (1958). *The Social Life of Animals*. Rev. ed. Boston: Beacon Press.

Allen, David Elliston. (1978). *The Naturalist in Britain: A Social History*. Harmondsworth: Penguin.

Allen, Doug. (1998). "Getting Started in the Business of Wildlife Camera Work." *Image Technology* 80, 9 (October): 20–21.

Allen, Jeanne. (1977). "Self-Reflexivity and the Documentary Film." *Cine-Tracts* 1 (Summer): 37–43.

Attenborough, David. (1961). "Honesty and Dishonesty in Documentary Film Making." *Photographic Journal* 101, 4 (April): 97–102, 130.

———. (1987). "How Unnatural Is TV Natural History?" *Listener*, May 7: 12.

Baldwin, Neil. (1995). *Edison: Inventing the Century*. New York: Hyperion Press.

Barber, Lynn. (1980). *The Heyday of Natural History: 1820–1870*. Garden City, N. Y.: Doubleday.

Barnouw, Eric. (1993). *Documentary: A History of the Non-Fiction Film*. 2nd rev. ed. New York: Oxford University Press.

Bartlett, Des and Jen Bartlett. (1973). "Beyond the North Wind with the Snow Geese." *National Geographic* 144, 6 (December): 822–47.

———. (1975). *The Flight of the Snow Geese*. New York: Stein and Day.

Baudrillard, Jean. (1983). *Simulations*. Trans. Paul Foss, Paul Patton, and Philip Beitchman. New York: Semiotext(e).

Baxter, John. (1968). *Hollywood in the Thirties*. London: Tantivy Press.

Bazin, André. (1967). *What Is Cinema?* Vol. I. Trans. Hugh Gray. Berkeley: University of California Press.

———. (1978). *Orson Welles: A Critical View*. Trans. Jonathan Rosenbaum. New York: Harper Colophon.

Bell, Elizabeth, Lynda Haas, and Laura Sells, eds. (1995). *From Mouse to Mermaid*. Bloomington: Indiana University Press.

Bellamy, David. (1997). "Natural Classic." *BBC Wildlife* 15, 8 (August): 77.

Benabent-Loiseau. (1989). *The Odyssey of the Bear*. New York: Newmarket Press.

Benson, Thomas W. and Carolyn Anderson. (1989). *Reality Fictions: The Films of Frederick Wiseman*. Carbondale and Edwardsville: Southern Illinois University Press.

Berger, John. (1980). "Why Look at Animals?" In *About Looking*. New York: Pantheon, 1–26.

Bergman, Andrew. (1971) *We're in the Money: Depression America and Its Films*. New York: Harper Colophon.

Berland, David I. (1982). "Disney and Freud: Walt Meets the Id." *Journal of Popular Culture* 15, 4: 93–104.

Bettelheim, Bruno. (1976). *The Uses of Enchantment: The Meaning and Importance of Fairy Tales*. New York: Knopf.

Biskind, Peter. (1982). "Does Documentary Have a Future?" Roundtable discussion. *American Film* 7, 6 (April): 57–64.

Blount, Margaret. (1975). *Animal Land: The Creatures of Children's Fiction*. New York: William Morrow.

Blum, Anne Shelby. (1993). *Picturing Nature: American Nineteenth-Century Zoological Illustration*. Princeton, N.J.: Princeton University Press.

Blumler, Jay and Elihu Katz. (1974). *The Uses of Mass Communications: Current Perspectives on Gratification Research*. Beverly Hills, Calif.: Sage.

Bodry-Sanders, Penelope. (1991). *Carl Akeley: Africa's Collector, Africa's Savior*. New York: Paragon House.

Bordwell, David. (1985). *Narration in the Fiction Film*. Madison: University of Wisconsin Press.

Bordwell, David and Kristin Thompson. (1985). "Fundamental Aesthetics of Sound in the Cinema." In *Film Sound: Theory and Practice*, ed. Elisabeth Weis and John Belton. New York: Columbia University Press, 181–99.

Bossen, Howard. (1985). "Zone V: Photojournalism, Ethics, and the Electronic Age." *Studies in Visual Communication* 11, 3 (Summer): 22–32.

Boswall, Jeffery. (1962). "Filming Wild Nature: Fair Means or Foul?" *Scientific Film* 3: 110–13.

———. (1968). "Right or Wrong? An attempt to Propound a Rational Ethic for Natural History film-makers." *SFTA Journal* 32/33: 53–59.

———, ed. (1969). *Look*. London: BBC.

———. (1973). "Wildlife Filming for the BBC." *Movie Maker* (September): 590–632.

———. (1974a). "New Responsibilities in Wildlife Filmmaking." *BKSTS Journal* 56, 2: 28–32, 42.

———. (1974b). "Private Lives: The Philosophy and Anatomy of Television Wildlife Series." *EBU Review* 25, 6: 37–45.

———. (1982). "The Ethics of Wildlife Filmmaking: A Discussion." *BKSTS Journal* 64, 1: 12–13, 25.

———. (1986). "The Ethics and Aesthetics of Slow Motion in Wildlife Films." *Image Technology* 68, 11 (November): 560–61.

———. (1989). "Animal Stars: The Use of Animals in Film and Television." In *The Status of Animals: Ethics, Education, and Welfare*, ed. David Paterson and Mary Palmer. CAB International.

———. (1997). "The Moral Pivots of Wildlife Filmmaking." *EBU Diffusion* (Summer): 9–12.

Bousé, Derek. (1989). "The History and Tradition of Wildlife Films in America." Unpublished M.A. thesis, Annenberg School for Communication, University of Pennsylvania.

———. (1990). "The Bear." *Film Quarterly* 43, 3 (Spring): 30–34.

———. (1991). "The Wilderness Documentary: Film, Video, and the Visual Rhetoric of American Environmentalism." Unpublished Ph.D. dissertation, University of Pennsylvania.

———. (1995). "True Life Fantasies: Storytelling Traditions in Animated Features and Wildlife Films." *Animation Journal* 3, 2 (Spring): 19–39.

———. (1996). "Culture as Nature: How Native American Cultural Antiquities Became Part of the Natural World." *Public Historian* 18, 4 (Fall): 75–98.

———. (1997). "What is a Wildlife Film?" *EBU Diffusion* (Summer): 2–4.

———. (1998). "Are Wildlife Films Really Nature Documentaries?" *Critical Studies in Mass Communication* 15, 2 (June): 116–40.

Box, Hilary. (1973). *Organisation in Animal Communities.* London: Butterworth.

Boynton, H. W. (1902). "Books New and Old: Nature and Human Nature." *Atlantic Monthly* 89 (January): 134–41.

Brand, Stewart et al. (1985). "Digital Retouching," *Whole Earth Review* (July): 42–49.

Branigan, Edward. (1985). "The Point-of-View Shot." In *Movies and Methods*, Vol. I2, ed. Bill Nichols. Berkeley: University of California Press, 672–91.

Brauer, Ralph. (1982). "When the Lights Went Out—Hollywood, the Depression, and the Thirties." In *Movies as Artifacts: Cultural Criticism of Popular Film*, ed. Michael T. Marsden, John G. Nachbar, and Sam L. Grogg. Chicago: Nelson-Hall, 25–43.

Brayfield, Cecilia. (1989). "Deafened by the Call of the Wild." *7DAYS* (December 10): 10.

Brooks, Paul. (1980). *Speaking for Nature: How Literary Naturalists from Henry Thoreau to Rachel Carson Have Shaped America.* Boston: Houghton Mifflin.

Brownlow, Kevin. (1968). *The Parade's Gone By . . .* New York: Bonanza.

———. (1979). *The War, the West, and the Wilderness.* London: Secker and Warburg.

Bruneau, Marie-Agnés and Sarah Walker. (1998). "A Natural New Order." *Television Business International* (July/August): 22–25.

Bryant, Jennings and Daniel R. Anderson. (1983). *Children's Understanding of Television: Research on Attention and Comprehension.* New York: Academic Press.

Burgess, Jacquie. (1992). "The Nature of the Box." *BBC Wildlife* 10, 10 (October): 52–53.

Burnford, Sheila. (1961). *The Incredible Journey.* New York: Bantam.

Burroughs, John. (1903). "Real and Sham Natural History." *Atlantic Monthly* 91 (March): 298–309.

———. (1905). *Ways of Nature.* Boston and New York: Houghton Mifflin.

———. (1952). *John Burroughs' America: Selections from the Writings of the Hudson River Naturalist*, ed. Farida A. Wiley. New York: Devlin-Adair.

Bush, W. Stephen. (1914a). "Arctic Hunts." *Moving Picture World* (February 21): 956.

———. (1914b). "A New Star." *Moving Picture World* (February 28): 1095.

———. (1914c). "The Book of Nature." *Moving Picture World* (November 7): 769

Buxton, Cindy. (1980). *Survival in the Wild.* London: Collins.

Buxton, Cindy, and Annie Price. (1983). *Survival: South Atlantic.* London: Granada.

Cahn, Robert and Robert G. Ketchum. (1981). *American Photographers and the National Parks.* New York: Viking Press.

Campbell, Joseph. (1972). *The Hero with a Thousand Faces.* Princeton, N.J.: Princeton University Press.

Cantor, Muriel G. (1971). *The Hollywood TV Producer, His Work, and His Audience.* New York: Basic Books.

Carey, James. (1989). *Communication as Culture: Essays on Media and Society.* Boston: Unwin Hyman.

Carrier, Jim. (1996a). "Activists Demand End to Staging of Scenes in Wildlife Programs." *Denver Post,* February 15: 23A.

———. (1996b). "Stouffer sought Klondike, Snow." *Denver Post,* February 16: 1A, 12A.

Carroll, Noël. (1985). "The Power of Movies." *Daedalus* 114, 4 (Fall): 79–103.

———. (1988). *Mystifying Movies: Fads and Fallacies in Contemporary Film Theory.* New York: Columbia University Press.

———. (1997). "The Concept of Postmodernism from a Philosophical Perspective." In *International Postmodernism: Theory and Practice,* ed. Hans Bertens and Douwe Fokkema. Amsterdam and Philadelphia: Benjamins, 89–102.

Carson, Rachel. (1962). *Silent Spring.* Boston and New York: Houghton Mifflin.

Cartmill, Matt. (1993). "The Bambi Syndrome." *Natural History* 102, 6 (June): 6–12.

Caughey, John. (1984). *Imaginary Social Worlds.* Lincoln: University of Nebraska Press.

Cawelti, John. (1976). *Adventure, Mystery, and Romance.* Chicago and London: University of Chicago Press.

"The Champion Lion-Killer." (1912). *Literary Digest* 44, 12 (March 23): 616–17.

Charle, Suzanne. (1988). "Hunting Wildlife with a Movie Camera." *New York Times,* March 13: 31, 39.

Clark, Barry. (1997). "Vive la révolution!" *EBU Diffusion* (Summer): 37–41.

———. (1998). "New Media for the New Millennium." *Image Technology* 80, 9 (October): 18–19.

Clark, Edward B. (1907). "Roosevelt on the Nature Fakirs" (interview). *Everybody's Magazine* 16, 6 (June): 770–74.

———. (1912). "Wild Life in Moving Pictures." *Technical World Magazine* 16 (January): 519–26.

Cockerell, T. D. A. (1935). "Zoology and the Moving Picture." *Science* 82, 2128 (October 18): 369–70.

Coe, Christopher L. (1990). "Psychobiology of Maternal Behavior in Nonhuman Primates." In *Mammalian Parenting: Biochemical, Neurobiological, and Behavioral Determinants,* ed. Norman A. Krasnegor and Robert S. Bridges. New York: Oxford University Press, 157–83.

Condry, John. (1989). *The Psychology of Television.* Hillsdale, N.J.: Erlbaum.

Corry, John. (1986a). "*Cruel Camera,* About Animal Abuse." *New York Times,* March 24: C18.

———. (1986b). "Where the Driver Ants and the Drill Baboon Dwell." *New York Times,* April 27: H27.

———. (1987). "Best of *WILD AMERICA:* 'The Babies.'" *New York Times,* March 17: C18.

Coward, Ros. (1997). "Wild Shots." *Guardian Weekend,* December 6: 34–43.

Crisler, Lois. (1956). *Arctic Wild.* New York: Harper.

Crook, John H. (1976). "Problems of Inference in the Comparison of Animal and Human Social Organizations." In *Methods of Inference from Animal to Human Behavior,* ed. Mario Von Cranach. Chicago: Aldine, 237–68.

Crowson, Paul S. (1981). *Animals in Focus: The Business Life of a Natural History Film Unit.* Horsham, Sussex: Caliban Books.

Crowther, Barbara. (1992, January). "Towards a Feminist Critique of Television Natural History Programmes." Presented at the Feminist Methodologies Conference, London University Institute of Romance Studies.

Crowther, Bosley. (1953a). "Below the Sahara." *New York Times,* September 2: 20.

———. (1953b). "The Living Desert." *New York Times,* November 10: L38.

———. (1954). "The Vanishing Prairie." *New York Times,* August 17: L17.

Curtin, Michael. (1993). "Packaging Reality: The Influence of Fictional Forms on Early Television Documentary." *Journalism and Communication Monographs* 137 (February).

Curwood, James Oliver. (1914). *Kazan.* New York: Grosset and Dunlap.

———. (1919). *Nomads of the North: A Story of Romance and Adventure Under the Open Stars.* Garden City, N.Y.: Doubleday.

———. (1989). *The Bear* (originally published as *The Grizzly King,* 1916). New York: Newmarket Press.

Daly, Martin. (1990). "Evolutionary Theory and Parental Motives." In *Mammalian Parenting: Biochemical, Neurobiological, and Behavioral Determinants,* ed. Norman A. Krasnegor and Robert S. Bridges. New York: Oxford University Press, 25–39.

Daly, Steve. (1994). "Mane Attraction." *Entertainment Weekly,* July 8: 18–25.

Darwin, Charles. (1909). *The Origin of Species.* Reprinted from the 6th ed., 1872. New York: P. F. Collier & Son.

Davies, Ashley. (1998). "Public Still in the Dark on Digital, Say Surveys." *Broadcast* (October 9): 8.

Dawkins, Marian Stamp. (1980). *Animal Suffering: The Science of Animal Welfare.* London: Chapman and Hall.

"Defends His Stories." (1907). *New York Times,* June 14: 6.

Denis, Armand. (1964). *On Safari.* London: Companion Book Club.

De Roos, Robert. (1963). "The Magic Worlds of Walt Disney." *National Geographic* 124, 2 (August): 159–207.

Dickson, Robert G. (1981). "Natural History Programmes on American Television — a Sampling." *BKSTS Journal* 63, 9 (September): 559–63.

Dijk, J. G. M. van. (1996). "The Function of Fable in Greco-Roman Romance." *Mnemosyne* 49, 5 (November): 513–42.

Dillon, Mark. (1999). "Field Technology: The Gear for Out There." *RealScreen* 2, 12: 38–45.

Dimond, Stuart J. (1970). *The Social Behavior of Animals.* New York: Harper and Row.

Disney, Walt. (1953). "What I've Learned from Animals." *American* 155: 106–9.

———. (1954a). "Why I Like Making Nature Films." *Women's Home Companion* (May): 38.

———. (1954b). "The Lurking Camera." *Atlantic Monthly* 194, 2 (August): 23–27.

Ditmars, Raymond L. (1931). *Strange Animals I Have Known.* New York: Blue Ribbon Books, Inc.

"Doing What Comes Naturally . . ." (1996). *incamera* (Spring): 34–35.

Donaldson, Leonard. (1912). *The Cinematograph and Natural Science.* London: Ganes.

Dorfmann, Ariel and Armand Mattelart. (1975). *How to Read Donald Duck: Imperialist Ideology in the Disney Comic.* Trans. David Kunzle. New York: International General.

Downer, John. (1988). *Supersense: Perception in the Animal World.* London: BBC Books.

———. (1991). *Lifesense: Our Lives Through Animal Eyes.* London: BBC Books.

Dugmore, A. Radclyffe. (1912). *Wild Life and the Camera.* Philadelphia: Lippincott.

Dunlap, Thomas R. (1992). "The Realistic Animal Story: Ernest Thompson Seton, Charles Roberts, and Darwinism." *Forest & Conservation History* 36, 2 (April): 56–62.

Dyer, Richard. (1993). *The Matter of Images: Essays on Representations.* London and New York: Routledge.

Eastman, George. (1927). "A Safari in Africa." *Natural History* 27, 2: 533–38.

"Edison's Revolutionary Education." (1913). *Literary Digest* 47, 14 (October 14): 576–77.

Eisenberg, Leon. (1990). "The Biosocial Context of Parenting in Human Families."

In *Mammalian Parenting: Biochemical, Neurobiological, and Behavioral Determinants*, ed. Norman A. Krasnegor and Robert S. Bridges. New York: Oxford University Press, 9–24.

Eliade, Mircea. (1954). *The Myth of the Eternal Return, or, Cosmos and History*, Trans. Willard R. Trask. Princeton, N.J.: Princeton University Press.

———. (1963). *Myth and Reality*. Trans. Willard R. Trask. New York: Harper and Row.

Eliot, Marc. (1993). *Walt Disney: Hollywood's Dark Prince*. Secaucus, N.J.: Carol Publishing Group.

Ellis, John. (1982). *Visible Fictions: Cinema, TV, Video*. London: Routledge and Kegan Paul.

Elman, Robert. (1977). *First in the Field: America's Pioneering Naturalists*. New York: Mason/Charter.

Emlen, Stephen T. (1981). "Altruism, Kinship, and Reciprocity in the White-Fronted Bee-Eater." In *Natural Selection and Social Behavior: Recent Research and Theory*, ed. Richard D. Alexander and Donald W. Tinkle. New York Concord: Chiron Press, 217–30.

Engels, Frederick. (1940). *Dialectics of Nature*. Trans. Clemens Dutt. New York: International Publishers.

———. (1978/1884). *The Origins of the Family, Private Property, and the State*. Peking: Foreign Languages Press.

Engländer, Wiltraud. (1997). "Some Reflections by a Student of Animal Behaviour." *EBU Diffusion* (Summer): 5–8.

Everson, William K. (1978). *American Silent Film*. New York: Oxford University Press.

Farber, Manny. (1953). "Films." *Nation* 177, 26 (December 26): 574.

Fell, John. (1974). *Film and the Narrative Tradition*. Norman: University of Oklahoma Press.

Fell, John et al. eds. (1987). *Before Hollywood: Turn-of-the-Century American Film*. New York: Hudson Hills Press.

Fiedler, Leslie. (1969). *Return of the Vanishing American*. New York: Stein and Day.

Field, Mary and Percy Smith. (1939). *Secrets of Nature*. London: Scientific Book Club.

Fisher, John Andrew. (1991). "Disambiguating Anthropomorphism: An Interdisciplinary Review." In *Human Understanding and Animal Awareness*, ed. P. P. G. Bateson and Peter H. Klopfer. Perspectives in Ethology 9. New York and London: Plenum Press, 49–85.

Fisher, Ronald Aylmer. (1930). *The Genetical Theory of Natural Selection*. London and New York: Oxford University Press.

Fossey, Dian. (1983). *Gorillas in the Mist*. Boston: Houghton Mifflin.

Foster, David. (1996). "Unnatural Practices." *Broadcast* (October 11): 26.

Foster, Frederick. (1954). "Walt Disney's Naturalist-Cinematographers." *American Cinematographer* (February): 74–74, 104–5, 109.

Freud, Sigmund. (1965). *The Interpretation of Dreams*. Trans. James Strachey. New York: Avon.

———. (1971). "Twenty-Third Lecture: The Paths of Symptom Formation." *A General Introduction to Psychoanalysis*. Trans. Joan Riviere. New York: Pocket Books.

Fromm, Erich. (1969). *Escape from Freedom*. New York: Avon.

Fry, Andy. (1996). "Fur Starts Flying." *Broadcast* (October 11): 25.

———. (1998). "Prodution: New Game, New Players." *RealScreen* 1, 12: 12–14.

———. (1999). "How Low Can You Go?: Cost-Conscious Natural History." *RealScreen* 2, 12: 30–35.

Frye, Northrop. (1957). *Anatomay of Criticism*. Princeton, N.J.: Princeton University Press.

Ganio, Alma. (1951). "Disney's Nature Films." *Films in Review* 2 (November): 37–39.

Gans, Herbert J. (1974). *Popular Culture and High Culture: An Analysis and Evaluation of Taste*. New York: Basic Books.

Gardner, Helen (1980). *Gardner's Art Through the Ages*. 7th ed. Rev. Horst de la Croix and Richard G. Tansey. New York: Harcourt Brace Jovanovich.

Gardner, Carl and Robert Young. (1981). "Science on TV: A Critique." In *Popular Television and Film: A Reader*, ed. Tony Bennett et al. London: BFI, 171–93.

Gay, Peter. (1988). *Freud: A Life for Our Time*. New York and London: W.W. Norton.

Gerbner, George. (1986). "The Symbolic Context of Action and Communication." In *Contextualism and Understanding in Behavioral Science*, ed. Ralph L. Rosnow and Marianthi Georgoudi. New York: Praeger, 251–68.

———. (1993, June). "Women and Minorities on Television: A Study in Casting and Fate." Report to the Screen Actors Guild and the American Federation of Radio and Television Artists.

Gerbner, George, Larry Gross, Michael Morgan, and Nancy Signorielli. (1980). "The 'Mainstreaming' of America: Violence Profile no. 11." *Journal of Communication* 30, 3: 10–29.

———. (1994). "Growing Up with Television: The Cultivation Perspective." In *Media Effects: Advances in Theory and Research*, ed. Jennings Bryant and Dolf Zillman. Hillsdale, N.J.: Lawrence Erlbaum, 17–42.

Gerbner, George and Nancy Signorielli. (1979). *Women and Minorities in Television Drama, 1969–1978*. Philadelphia: Annenberg School of Communications, University of Pennsylvania.

Giannetti, Louis. (1990). *Understanding Movies*. 5th ed. Englewood Cliffs, N.J.: Prentice-Hall.

Glasberg, Davita Silfen and Michael Schwartz. (1983). "Ownership and Control of Corporations." *Annual Review of Sociology* 9: 311–32.

Goodall, Jane. (1986). *The Chimpanzees of Gombe: Patterns of Behavior*. Cambridge, Mass., and London: Harvard University Press.

———. (1988). *In the Shadow of Man*. Rev. ed. Boston: Houghton Mifflin.

Gottlieb, Beatrice. (1992). *The Family in the Western World: From the Black Death to the Industrial Age*. New York and Oxford: Oxford University Press.

Gould, James L. and Carol Grant Gould. (1989). *Sexual Selection*. New York: Scientific American Library.

Grierson, John. (1979a). "Flaherty's Poetic *Moana*." In *The Documentary Tradition*, 2nd ed., ed. Lewis Jacobs. New York and London: W.W. Norton, 25–26.

———. (1979b). *Grierson on Documentary*. Rev. ed., ed. Forsyth Hardy. Boston and London: Faber and Faber.

Griffith, Richard. (1979). "*Grass* and *Chang*." In *The Documentary Tradition*, 2nd ed., ed. Lewis Jacobs. New York: W.W. Norton, 22–24.

Gross, Larry P. (1984). "The Cultivation of Intolerance: Television, Blacks, and Gays." In *Cultural Indicators: An International Symposium*, ed. G. Melischek, Karl Erik Rosengren, and J. Stapper. Wien (Vienna): Verlag der Österreichischen Akademie der Wissenschaften (Austrian Academy of Science), 345–63.

———. (1985). "Life vs. Art: The Interpretation of Visual Narratives." *Studies in Visual Communication* 11, 4 (Fall): 2–11.

———. (1988). "The Ethics of (Mis)Representation." In *Image Ethics: The Moral Rights of Subjects in Photographs, Film, and Television*, ed. Larry Gross, John Katz, and Jay Ruby. New York: Oxford University Press, 188–202.

———. (1991). "Out of the Mainstream: Sexual Minorities and the Mass Media." In

Gay People, Sex, and the Media, ed. Michelle A. Wolf and Alfred P. Kielwasser. New York: Haworth Press, 19–46.

Guggisberg, Charles A. W. (1977). *Early Wildlife Photographers*. New York: Taplinger.

Haas, Robert Bartlett. (1976). *Muybridge: Man in Motion*. Berkeley: University of California Press.

Hall, Edward T. (1969). *The Hidden Dimension*. Garden City, N.Y.: Anchor Books.

Hall, Stuart. (1980). "Encoding/Decoding." In *Culture, Media, Language: Working Papers in Cultural Studies, 1972–79*, ed. Stuart Hall et al. London: Hutchinson, 129–38.

Hamburger, Philip. (1954). "Where the Deer and the Antelope Play." *New Yorker* 30, 27 (August 21): 60.

Haraway, Donna. (1989). *Primate Visions: Gender, Race, and Nature in the World of Modern Science*. New York and London: Routledge.

Harcourt, Alexander H. and Frans B. M. de Waal, eds. (1992). *Coalitions and Alliances in Humans and Other Animals*. Oxford: Oxford University Press.

Harris, Christopher. (1991). "Digitilization and Manipulation of News Photographs," *Journal of Mass Media Ethics* 6, 3: 164–74.

Hart, Elspeth. (1954). "The Vanishing Prairie." *Films in Review* 5, 8: 432–33.

Hass, Hans. (1959). *We Come from the Sea*. Trans. Alan Houghton Brodrick. Garden City, N.Y.: Doubleday & Company.

Hawkins, Desmond, ed. (1960). *The Second BBC Naturalist*. London: Adprint.

"Hays Bars 'Ingagi' Film." (1930). *New York Times*, June 12: 30.

Heller, Agnes. (1984). "Can Cultures Be Compared?" *Dialectical Anthropologist* 8 (April): 269–74.

Hoffman, Judith L. (1990). "Norman O. Dawn and the Discourse of Special Effects Cinematography." M.A. thesis, University of Texas, Austin.

Hofstadter, Richard. (1955). *Social Darwinism in American Thought*. Rev. ed. Boston: Beacon Press.

Hornig, Susanna. (1990). "Television's *NOVA* and the Construction of Scientific Truth." *Critical Studies in Mass Communication* 7, 1 (March): 11–23.

Horton, Donald and Richard Wohl. (1956). "Mass Communication and Para-Social Interaction: Observations on Intimacy at a Distance." *Psychiatry* 19, 3 (August): 215–29.

Houghton, Walter E. (1957). *The Victorian Frame of Mind, 1830–1870*. New Haven, Conn.: Yale University Press.

Houston, Dick. (1986). "The Boy and Girl Next Door Made Movies Far Away." *Smithsonian* 17, 8 (November): 144–55.

Hoyt, Vance Joseph. (1931). *Malibu*. New York: Grosset and Dunlap.

Hughes, Nancy. (1998). "Disney Television." *RealScreen* (special ed.) 1, 12: 34.

Humphrey, N. K. (1986). *The Inner Eye*. London: Faber and Faber.

———. (1987). "The Inner Eye of Consciousness." In *Mindwaves: Thoughts on Intelligence, Identity, and Consciousness*, ed. Colin Blakemore and Susan Greenfield. Oxford: Basil Blackwell, 377–81.

Husar, J. (1996). "Sage Advice for Those with 'Staged' Fright: That's Entertainment." *Chicago Tribune*, February 14, 4: 4.

Huston, Aletha C. et al. (1992). *Big World, Small Screen: The Role of Television in Society*. Lincoln and London: University of Nebraska Press.

Huth, Hans. (1957). *Nature and the American: Three Centuries of Changing Attitudes*. Lincoln and London: University of Nebraska Press.

Huxley, Julian. (1964). *Evolution: The Modern Synthesis*. New York: John Wiley.

Imperato, Pascal James and Eleanor M. Imperato. (1992). *They Married Adventure: The*

Wandering Lives of Martin and Osa Johnson. New Brunswick, N.J.: Rutgers University Press.

Ingersoll, Ernest. (1923). *Birds in Legend: Fable and Folklore.* New York: Longmans, Green.

Ivins, Charles. (1969). *Prints and Visual Communication.* Cambridge, Mass.: MIT Press.

Jackson, W. H. (1913). "How Natural History Pictures Are Taken." *Moving Picture World* (May 24): 795.

Jacobs, Lewis. (1968). *The Rise of the American Film: A Critical History.* New York: Teachers College Press.

———, ed. (1979) *The Documentary Tradition.* 2nd ed. New York and London: W.W. Norton.

Jacobs, Norman, ed. (1961). *Culture for the Millions.* Princeton, N.J.: Van Nostrand.

James, Henry. (1876). "John Burroughs." *Nation* 33 (January 27): 66.

James, Jamie. (1985). "Art and Artifice in Wildlife Films." *Discover* (September): 91–97.

Jamison, Barbara Berch. (1954). "Amazing Scripts by Animals." *New York Times Magazine,* July 18: 16–17.

Jensen, Joli. (1990). *Redeeming Modernity: Contradictions in Media Criticism.* Newbury Park, Calif., and London: Sage.

Jenkins, Alan C. (1978). *The Naturalists: Pioneers of Natural History.* New York: Mayflower.

Johnson, Martin. (1929). *Lion: African Adventure with the King of Beasts.* New York and London: G. P. Putnam's Sons/Knickerbocker Press.

———. (1934). "Wings over Africa," *Natural History* 34 (November): 596–611.

Johnson, Osa. (1944). *Four Years in Paradise.* Garden City, N.Y.: Halcyon House.

Johnston, Ollie and Frank Thomas. (1990). *Walt Disney's Bambi: The Story and the Film.* New York: Stewart, Tabori, and Chang.

Jonkel, Charles. (1985). "Never Cry Farley: A Treatise on Wildlife Fact and Fancy in Film and Novel." *BKSTS Journal* 67, 3 (March): 104–6.

Jung, Carl Gustav. (1959). *The Archetypes and the Collective Unconscious.* Trans. R. F. C. Hull. Collected Works, vol. 9, part I. Princeton, N.J.: Princeton University Press.

Jussim, Estelle and Elizabeth Lindquist-Cock. (1985). *Landscape as Photograph.* New Haven and London: Yale University Press.

Kael, Pauline. (1970). "Current Cinema." *New Yorker.*

Kaminsky, Stuart M. (1974). *American Film Genres.* New York: Dell.

Kaplan, E. Ann, ed. (1980). *Women in Film Noir.* Rev. ed. London: BFI.

Katz, Ephraim. (1994). *The Film Encyclopedia.* 2nd ed. New York: HarperCollins.

Keith, W. J. (1969). *Charles G. D. Roberts.* Toronto: Copp Clark.

Kearton, Cherry. (1913). *Wild Life Across the World.* London, New York, Toronto: Hodder and Stoughton.

———. (1930). *Island of the Penguins.* London: Longmans, Green.

———. (1933). *The Animals Came to Drink* New York: Robert M. McBride.

Kearton, Richard. (1898). *Wild Life at Home: How to Study and Photograph It.* New York: Funk and Wagnalls.

Kellert, Stephen R. (1983). "Affective, Cognitive, and Evaluative Perceptions of Animals." In *Behavior and the Natural Environment,* ed. Irwin Altman and Joachim F. Wolhill. New York and London: Plenum Press, 241–67.

———. (1993). "Attitudes, Knowledge, and Behavior Toward Wildlife Among the Industrial Superpowers: United States, Japan, and Germany." *Journal of Social Issues* 49, 1 (Spring): 53–69.

Kellert, Stephen R., Catherine A. McConnell, Sharon Hamby, and Victoria Dompka.

(1986). "Wildlife and Film: A Relationship in Search of Understanding." *BKSTS Journal* 68, 1 (January): 38–43.

Kennedy, John S. (1992). *The New Anthropomorphism.* Cambridge: Cambridge University Press.

King, Margaret J. (1996). "The Audience in the Wilderness: the Disney Nature Films." *Journal of Popular Culture* 24, 2 (Summer): 60–69.

Klass, Perri. (1994). "A 'Bambi' for the 90's, via Shakespeare." *New York Times,* June 19, 2: 1.

Kleiman, Devra. (1977). "Monogamy in Mammals." *Quarterly Review of Biology* 52, 1 (March): 39–69.

Klepper, Robert K. (1999). *Silent Films, 1877–1999.* Jefferson, N.C. and London: McFarland.

Klingender, Francis Donald. (1971). *Animals in Art and Thought.* London: Routledge and Kegan Paul.

Knight, Arthur. (1979/1948). "Sweden's Arne Sucksdorff." In *The Documentary Tradition,* 2nd ed., ed. Lewis Jacobs. New York and London: W.W. Norton, 233–35.

Kuehl, Jerry. (1988). "Truth Claims." In *New Challenges for Documentary,* ed. Alan Rosenthal. Berkeley: University of California Press, 103–9.

Kuntz, Tom. (1998). "Television's Most Violent: It's Payback Time." *New York Times,* January 18, wk 7.

Landin, Bo. (1998). "Scandinature Films: Truth & Consequences." *RealScreen* (special edition) 1, 12: 16–20.

Langley, Andrew. (1985). *The Making of the Living Planet.* Boston and Toronto: Little, Brown.

Leakey, Richard and Roger Lewin. (1977). *Origins.* New York: E. P. Dutton.

———. (1996). *The Sixth Extinction: Biodiversity and Its Survival.* London: Phoenix.

Lean, Geoffrey. (1997). "The Great Environment Debate." *BBC Wildlife* 15, 4 (April): 24–28.

Lee, Raymond. (1970). *Not So Dumb: The Life and Times of Animal Actors.* New York: A. S. Barnes.

Lenaghan, R. T., ed. (1967). *Caxton's Aesop.* Cambridge, Mass.: Harvard University Press.

Levin, G. Roy. (1971). *Documentary Explorations: 15 Interviews with Filmmakers.* Garden City, N.Y.: Anchor Press, Doubleday.

Lévi-Strauss, Claude. (1963). "The Structural Study of Myth." In *Structural Anthropology.* Trans. Claire Jacobson and Brooke Grundfest Schoepf. New York: Basic Books, 206–31.

———. (1969). *The Raw and the Cooked.* Trans. John Weightman and Doreen Weightman. New York: Harper and Row.

———. (1978). *Myth and Meaning: Cracking the Code of Culture.* New York: Schocken Books.

"The Living Desert." (1953). *Variety,* October 7: 6.

"The Living Desert." (1953). *Time,* November 16: 107–8.

"The Living Desert." (1953). *Newsweek,* November 23: 100

Living Planet Report. (1998). World Wide Fund for Nature.

Long, William J. (1902). *School of the Woods.* Boston: Ginn.

———. (1903). "The Modern School of Nature-Study and Its Critics." *North American Review* 176 (May): 687–98.

Lopez, Barry. (1978). *Of Wolves and Men.* New York: Charles Scribner's Sons.

Lorenz, Konrad. (1952). *King Solomon's Ring: New Light on Animal Ways.* New York: Thomas Crowell.

————. (1963). *On Aggression.* Trans. Marjorie Kerr Wilson. New York: Bantam.

Low, Rachel. (1979). *Documentary and Educational Films of the 1930s.* London: Allen and Unwin.

Lutts, Ralph H. (1990). *The Nature Fakers: Wildlife, Science, and Sentiment.* Golden, Colo.: Fulcrum.

————. (1992). "The Trouble with Bambi: Walt Disney's *Bambi* and the American Vision of Nature." *Forest & Conservation History* 36, 4 (October): 160–71.

Lyotard, Jean-François. (1984). *The Postmodern Condition: A Report on Knowledge.* Minneapolis: University of Minnesota Press.

MacCabe, Colin. (1974). "Realism and the Cinema: Notes on Some Brechtian Theses." *Screen* 15, 2 (Summer): 7–27.

MacDonald, Dwight. (1957). "A Theory of Mass Culture." In *Mass Culture: The Popular Arts in* America, ed. Bernard Rosenberg and David Manning White. Glencoe, Ill.: Free Press, 59–73.

MacDonald, Robert H. (1998). "The Revolt Against Instinct." In *The Wild Animal Story,* ed. Ralph H. Lutts. Philadelphia: Temple University Press, 224–36.

MacDougall, David. (1976). "Prospects of the Ethnographic Film." In *Movies and Methods,* ed. Bill Nichols. Berkeley: University of California Press, 135–50.

————. (1985). "Beyond Observational Cinema." In *Movies and Methods II,* ed. Bill Nichols. Berkeley: University of California Press, 274–87.

Magee, William H. (1980). "The Animal Story: A Challenge in Technique." In *Only Connect: Readings on Children's Literature,* ed. Sheila Egoff, G. T. Stubbs, and L. F. Ashley. Toronto and New York: Oxford University Press, 221–32.

Maier, Richard. (1998). *Comparative Animal Behavior: An Evolutionary and Ecological Approach.* Boston and London: Allyn and Bacon.

Malthus, Thomas R. (1914). *An Essay on Population,* vol. 1. London and Toronto: J. M. Dent.

Maltin, Leonard. (1984). *The Disney Films.* Rev. ed. New York: Crown.

Martin, Edwin. (1991). "On Photographic Manipulation." *Journal of Mass Media Ethics* 6, 3: 156–63.

Martineau, LaVan. (1973). *The Rocks Begin to Speak.* Las Vegas, Nev.: KC Publications.

Maslin, Janet. (1994). "The Hero Within the Child Within." *New York Times,* June 15: B-1.

Masson, Jeffery and Susan McCarthy. (1995). *When Elephants Weep: The Emotional Lives of Animals.* New York: Delta.

May, Derwent. (1981). "Nature on the Screen: Should Wildlife Cameramen Contribute to Horror Movies?" *The Listener,* October 1: 364.

May, Jill P. and Gordon R. Mork. (1988). "Felix Salten." In *Writers for Children: Critical Studies of Major Authors Since the Seventeenth Century,* ed. Jane M. Bingham. New York: Charles Scribner's Sons, 497–501.

May, Rollo. (1991). *The Cry for Myth.* New York: W.W. Norton.

Mayr, Ernst, E. Gorton Linsley, and Robert L. Usinger. (1953). *Methods and Principles of Systematic Zoology.* New York: McGraw-Hill.

McCarten, John. (1953). "Beasts, Birds, and Vermin." *New Yorker* 29, 39 (November 14): 135–36.

McConnell, Catherine A. (1984). "Wildlife on Television: Its Significance, History, and Potential." Unpublished paper, School of Forestry and Environmental Studies, Yale University.

McCrae, Michael. (1989). "Presenting Crazy Alan Root." *International Wildlife* 19, 6 (November/December): 30–34.

McDonnell, Kevin and Kevin Robin. (1980). "Marxist Cultural Theory: The Althusserian Smokescreen." In Simon Clarke et al., *One-Dimensional Marxism: Althusser and the Politics of Culture*. London and New York: Allison and Busby, 157–231.

McElvogue, Louise. (1996). "Running Wild." *Los Angeles Times*, February 14, D1: 3, 14.

———. (1997). "Jaws, Claws and Cash: Show Biz Jungle of Wildlife." *New York Times*, September 29, B1: 5.

McElvogue, Louise and Jane Birch. (1998). "Wild Ambition." *Television Business International* (July/August): 16–20.

McEvoy, J. P. (1955). "McEvoy in Disneyland." *Reader's Digest* 66, 394 (February): 19–26.

McGuire, Jerry L. (1996). "Shoot to Thrill." *Denver Post*, January 21: 12–13.

McKaye, Kenneth R. (1977). "Defense of a Predator's Young by a Herbivorous Fish: An Unusual Strategy. *American Naturalist* 111: 301–15.

———. (1981). "Natural Selection and the Evolution of Interspecific Brood Care in Fishes." In *Natural Selection and Social Behavior: Recent Research and Theory*, ed. Richard D. Alexander and Donald W. Tinkle. New York and Concord: Chiron Press, 173–83.

McLaughlin, Kerry. (1997). "Marty Stouffer: White Hunter, Black Heart" (interview). *Bunnyhop* 7: 27–31.

McPhee, Mike. (1996). "Ch. 12 drops 'Wild America.' " *Denver Post*, February 14: 1A, 13A.

McPhee, Mike and Jim Carrier. (1996a). "Wild Photos Called Staged." *Denver Post*, February 9: 1A, 22A.

———. (1996b). "Fate of Wildlife Show in Doubt." *Denver Post*, February 10: 1A, 16A.

———. (1996c). "Unnatural Selection?" *Denver Post*, February 11: 1A, 22–23A.

———. (1996d). "Filmmaker Would Use Disclaimer." *Denver Post*, February 20: 1A, 9A.

Mead, George Herbert. (1934). *Mind, Self, and Society*. Chicago: University of Chicago Press.

Messaris, Paul. (1994). *Visual "Literacy": Image, Mind, and Reality*. Boulder, Colo.: Westview Press.

———. (1997). *Visual Persuasion: The Role of Images in Advertising*. Thousand Oaks, Calif., and London: Sage.

Meyrowitz, Joshua. (1986). "Television and Interpersonal Behavior: Codes of Perception and Response." In *Inter/Media: Interpersonal Communication in a Media World*, 3rd ed., ed. Gary Gumpert and Robert Cathcart. New York and Oxford: Oxford University Press, 253–72.

Mighetto, Lisa. (1991). *Wild Animals and American Environmental Ethics*. Tuscon: University of Arizona Press.

Miles, Hugh and Mike Salisbury. (1985). *Kingdom of the Ice Bear: A Portrait of the Arctic*. Austin: University of Texas Press.

Miller, Ron. (1989). "An Author Who Forsook the Hunt." *Philadelphia Inquirer*, December 3: 2F.

Millhauser, Milton. (1959). *Just Before Darwin*. Middletown, Conn.: Wesleyan University Press.

Mills, C. Wright. (1956). *The Power Elite*. New York and Oxford: Oxford University Press.

Mills, Stephen. (1997). "Pocket Tigers: The Sad Unseen Reality Behind the Wildlife Film." *Times Literary Supplement*, February 21: 6.

Montgomery, M. R. (1988). "TV's Nature Lessons." *Boston Globe*, October 31: 17.

Morison, Elting E., ed. (1951). *The Letters of Theodore Roosevelt.* Cambridge, Mass.: Harvard University Press.

Morris, Desmond. (1979). *Animal Days.* London: Book Club Associates.

Mozley, Anita Ventura. (1979). Introduction to *Muybridge's Complete Human and Animal Locomotion,* by Eadweard Muybridge. New York: Dover.

Mrozek, Carl. (1998). "Nature in High Def: Perils and Payoffs." *RealScreen* 1 (12): 26–30.

Murdock, Graham. (1982). "Large Corporations and the Control of the Communications Industries." In *Culture, Society, and the Media,* ed. Michael Gurevitch, T. Bennett, J. Curran, and J. Woolacott. London: Methuen, 118–50.

Musser, Charles. (1990). *The Emergence of Cinema: The American Screen to 1907.* New York: Scribner.

Muybridge, Eadweard. (1982). "The Attitudes of Animals in Motion." In *The Movies in Our Midst,* ed. Gerald Mast. Chicago: University of Chicago Press, 3–7.

Nash, Roderick. (1989). *The Rights of Nature: A History of Environmental Ethics.* Madison: University of Wisconsin Press.

Neuman, W. Russell and Ithiel de Sola Pool. (1986). "The Flow of Communications into the Home." In *Media, Audience, and Social Structure,* ed. Sandra Ball-Rokeach and Muriel G. Cantor. Beverly Hills, Calif.: Sage, 71–86.

Nichols, Bill. (1981). *Ideology and the Image.* Bloomington: Indiana University Press.

Nochlin, Linda. (1971). *Realism.* New York: Penguin.

Nørfelt, Thomas Fibiger. (1992). "Naturbilleder." Unpublished thesis, Institut for Film, TV, og Massekommunicakation, Københavns Universetet (Copenhagen University).

Northshield, Robert. (1989). "All Those Critters Look Cute, but . . ." *New York Times,* February 12: 31H.

Novak, Barbara. (1980). *Nature and Culture: American Landscape Painting, 1825–1875.* New York and Toronto: Oxford University Press.

Obmsascik, M. (1996). "There Really Is a Wild Part to 'Wild America,' " *Denver Post,* February 17: 1B.

"The Olympic Elk." (1953). *Natural History* 61, 4 (April): 190–91.

Owen, Jonathan. (1997). "Filming: How Far Do You Go?" *BBC Wildlife* 15, 7 (July): 32–34.

Parsons, Christopher. (1971). *Making Wildlife Films: A Beginner's Guide.* Harrisburg: Stackpole Books.

———. (1982). *True to Nature.* Cambridge: Patrick Stephens.

"The Paul J. Rainey African Pictures." (1912). *Moving Picture World,* April 20: 214–15.

Perkins, Marlin. (1982). *My Wild Kingdom.* New York: E. P. Dutton.

Peterson, Dale and Jane Goodall. (1993). *Visions of Caliban: On Chimpanzees and People.* Boston and New York: Houghton Mifflin.

Philo, Greg and Lesley Henderson. (1998). *What The Audience Thinks: Focus Group Research Into the Likes and Dislikes of UK Wildlife Viewers.* A study by the Glasgow Media Group, commissioned by Wildscreen.

Pike, Oliver G. (1946). *Nature and My Cine Camera.* London and New York: Focal Press.

Plage, Dieter. (1980). *Wild Horizons: A Cameraman in Africa.* London: Collins.

Porter, Gene Stratton. (1903). *Song of the Cardinal.* Indianapolis: Bobbs-Merrill.

Preston, Douglas J. (1984). "Shooting in Paradise." *Natural History* 93, 12 (December): 14, 16, 18, 20.

Prince, R. A. (1998). "The Development of Natural History Programming Within the BBC Natural History Unit in Bristol." Unpublished graduate thesis, University of West England.

Propp, Vladimir. (1968). *Morphology of the Folk Tale.* 2nd ed. Trans. Laurence Scott, intro. Alan Dundes. Austin: University of Texas Press.

Pryluck, Calvin. (1988). "Ultimately We Are All Outsiders: The Ethics of Documentary Filmmaking." In *New Challenges for Documentary,* ed. Alan Rosenthal. Berkeley: University of California Press, pp. 255–68.

Raglan, Fitzroy Richard Somerset IV, Baron. (1956). *The Hero: A Study in Tradition, Myth, and Drama.* New York: Knopf.

Rank, Otto. (1959). "Forms of Kinship and the Individual's Role." In *The Myth of the Birth of the Hero, and Other Writings,* ed. Philip Freund. New York: Knopf, 296–315.

Raup, David M. (1991). *Extinction: Bad Genes or Bad Luck?* New York: W.W. Norton.

Ray, Robert. (1985). *A Certain Tendency of the Hollywood Cinema, 1930–1980.* Princeton, N.J.: Princeton University Press.

Rayman, Susan. (1999). "African Producers Have the Inside Edge." *RealScreen* 2, 12: 59–62.

Reddy, Don. (1974). "Putting a Dog's Point of View on Film." *American Cinematographer* (October): 1180–81.

Regan, Tom. (1983). *The Case for Animal Rights.* Berkeley: University of California Press.

Reiger, George. (1980). "The Truth About Bambi." *Field & Stream* 84 (May): 12, 16–17.

Ricciuti, Edward R. (1974). "Indiscreet Elephants, Maladjusted Raccoons, Romantic Beavers, Insane Sharks, Frolicsome Morays, Lumber-Eating Seals, Courageous Octopuses, Drowning Jaguars, Waiting Lovers and Other Wonders of Televised Nature." *Audubon* 76, 6 (November): 68–102.

Ridley, Mark. (1978). "Paternal Care." *Animal Behavior* 26, 3 (August): 904–32.

Ridley, Matt. (1993). *The Red Queen: Sex and the Evolution of Human Nature.* London: Penguin.

———. (1996). *The Origins of Virtue: Human Instincts and the Evolution of Cooperation.* London: Penguin.

Ritvo, Harriet. (1985). "Learning from Animals: Natural History for Children in the Eighteenth and Nineteenth Centuries." *Annual of the Modern Languages Association Division on Children's Literature and the Children's Literature Association* 13. New Haven, Conn.: Yale University Press, 72–93.

Roberts, Charles G. D. (1902). *The Kindred of the Wild: A Book of Animal Life.* Boston: L. C. Page.

Robertson, David. (1984). *West of Eden: A History of the Art and Literature of Yosemite.* San Francisco: Yosemite Natural History Press and Wilderness Press.

Roosevelt, Theodore. (1907). "Nature Fakers." *Everybody's Magazine* 17, 3 (September): 427–30.

———. (1910). *African Game Trails: An Account of the African Wanderings of an American Hunter-Naturalist.* New York: Scribner.

Rosenberg, Bernard and David Manning White, eds. (1957). *Mass Culture: The Popular Arts in America.* Glencoe, Ill: Free Press.

Rosenberg, Michael. (1996). "Evolution Theory." *Broadcast,* October 11: 29.

Rotha, Paul, (1952). *Documentary Film.* London: Faber and Faber.

Rowland, Beryl. (1973). *Animals with Human Faces: A Guide to Animal Symbolism.* Knoxville: University of Tennessee Press.

Ruby, Jay. (1988). "The Image Mirrored: Reflexivity and the Documentary Film." In

New Challenges for Documentary, ed. Alan Rosenthal. Berkeley: University of California Press, 64–77.

Ruppenthal, G. C., G. L. Arling, H. F. Harlow, G. P. Sackett, and S. J. Suomi. (1976). "A 10-Year Perspective of Motherless-Mother Monkey Behavior." *Journal of Abnormal Psychology* 85: 341–49.

Saile, Bob. (1996). "Seeing May Not Be Believing." *Denver Post*, February 20: 8D.

Salt, Barry. (1985). "Film Style and Technology in the Thirties: Sound." In *Film Sound: Theory and Practice*, ed. Elisabeth Weis and John Belton. New York: Columbia University Press, 37–43.

Salten, Felix. (1928). *Bambi: A Life in the Woods*. Trans. Whittaker Chambers. New York: Simon and Schuster.

———. (1938). *Perri: The Youth of a Squirrel.* Trans. Barrows Mussey. New York: Bobbs-Merrill.

Schaller, George B. (1972). *Serengeti: A Kindom of Predators*. New York: Knopf.

Schatz, Thomas. (1981). *Hollywood Genres: Formulas, Filmmaking, and the Studio System.* New York: Random House.

———. (1988). *The Genius of the System: Hollywood Filmmaking in the Studio Era*. New York: Pantheon.

Schickel, Richard. (1985). *The Disney Version*. Rev. ed. New York: Simon and Schuster.

Schmitt, Peter J. (1989). *Back to Nature: The Arcadian Myth in Urban America*. Baltimore and London: Johns Hopkins University Press.

Scholes, Robert. (1979). "Narration and Narrativity in Film." In *Film Theory and Criticism*, 2nd ed., ed. Gerald Mast and Marshall Cohen. New York and Oxford: Oxford University Press, 417–33.

Scholely, Keith, ed. (1997). *The BBC Natural History Unit's WILDLIFE SPECIALS*. Foreword by David Attenborough. London: Trident Press.

"Scientific Nature Faking: The Roosevelt African Expedition as It was Staged and Photographed." (1909). *Collier's* 43 (July 3): 13.

Seton, Ernest Thompson. (1898). *Wild Animals I Have Known*. New York: Scribner.

———. (1958). *Biography of a Grizzly*. New York: Grosset and Dunlap.

———. (1907). "The Snow-Shoe Rabbit." *Everybody's Magazine* 16, 5 (May): 599–608.

Shaw, Irene. (1973). "Wildlife Programmes on British Television: a Research Report." *EBU Review* 24: 6, 49–55.

Shreeve, James. (1987). *Nature: The Other Earthlings*. New York: Macmillan.

Sielmann, Heinz. (1959). *Windows in the Woods*. Trans. Sidney Lightman. New York: Harper and Brothers.

Signorielli, Nancy. (1984). "The Demography of the Television World." In *Cultural Indicators: An International Symposium*, ed. Gabriele Melischeck, Karl Rosengren, and James Stapper. Wien (Vienna): Verlag der Österreichischen (Austrian Academy of Science), 137–57.

Silverstone, Roger. (1984). "Narrative Strategies in Television Science—A Case Study." *Media, Culture and Society* 6, 4 (October): 377–410.

Singer, Peter. (1975). *Animal Liberation*. New York: Avon Books.

Sink, Mindy. (1996). "The Call of the Wildlife Show." *New York Times*, April 15: C7(N), D9(L), col 1.

Sinyard, Neil. (1988). *The Best of Disney*. New York: Portland House.

Sklar, Robert. (1975). *Movie-Made America*. New York: Vintage.

Slade, Margot. (1992). "Killers in the Mist: TV Nature Shows Grow Nastier." *New York Times*, June 14: 6E.

Smith, N. G. (1968). "The Advantage of Being Parasitized." *Nature* 219: 690–94.

Smuts, Barbara B. (1985). *Sex and Friendship in Baboons.* New York: Aldine de Gruyter.

Solnit, Rebecca. (1989). "Uncommon Perceptions." *Sierra* 74, 4 (July/August): 43–50.

Sparks, John. (1981). "The World of Survival." *BKSTS Journal* 63, 9 (September): 603–4.

———. (1986), (February). "Violence on Television: the NHU Perspective." A contribution to the Wyatt Committee. Unpublished paper.

———. (1988). "Filming What Comes Naturally." *New Scientist* 24/31 (December): 41–45.

———. (1999). *The Battle of the Sexes.* London: BBC.

Steinhart, Peter. (1980). "Wildlife Films: End of an Era?" *National Wildlife* 18, 1 (December/January): 36–45.

———. (1981). *BKSTS Journal* 63, 9 (September): 578–84.

———. (1983). "Ecoporn." *Audubon* 85, 3 (May): 22–25.

———. (1988). "Electronic Intimacies." *Audubon* 90, 6 (November): 10–13.

Sterritt, David. (1994). "Disney studio roars with 'The Lion King.'" *Christian Science Monitor* 86, 141 (June 5): 12.

Stott, Kenhelm W., Jr. (1980). "Martin and Osa Johnson: Exploration Was Their Way of Life." *Explorer's Journal* 58, 3: 106–9.

Stouffer, Marty. (1988). *Wild America.* New York: Times Books.

Sutcliffe, J. B. (1913). "Educated Insects." *Moving Picture World,* May 24: 795.

Taft, Robert. (1938). *Photography and the American Scene.* New York: Dover.

Tayman, J. (1996). "Marty Stouffer's Apocryphal America," *Outside* (June): 26.

Thomas, Keith. (1983). *Man and the Natural World: A History of the Modern Sensibility.* New York: Pantheon.

Thomas, Lowell. (1937). "The Story of Martin Johnson." *Natural History* 39, 3: 154–67.

Tomashevsky, Boris. (1965). "Thematics." In *Russian Formalist Criticism: Four Essays,* ed. Lee T. Lemon and Marion J. Reis. Lincoln: University of Nebraska Press, 61–98.

Tomkies, M. (1987). *On Wing and Wild Water.* London: Jonathon Cape.

Trivers, R. L. (1972). "Parental Investment and Sexual Selection. In *Sexual Selection and the Descent of Man, 1871–1971,* ed. B. Campbell. Chicago: Aldine, 249–64.

Tuchman, Gaye. (1978). "Introduction: The Symbolic Annihilation of Women by the Mass Media." In *Hearth and Home: Images of Women in the Mass Media,* ed. Gaye Tuchman et al. New York and Oxford: Oxford University Press, 3–38.

Turow, Joseph. (1984). *Media Industries: The Production of News and Entertainment.* New York: Longman.

Tweedie, Tony. (1985). "Secrets of the Not-So-Wild Life: Attenborough Defends Use of Captive Animals." *Sunday Independent,* March 24.

Underwood, Caroline. (1981). "Images of Nature on Television: A Modern Bestiary." Unpublished M.A. thesis, York University, Ontario, Canada.

———. (1986). "Ought Mickey Mouse to Have Been Born?" *BKSTS Journal* 68, 1 (January): 22–25.

"United Wildlife: A New Giant in Wildlife Filmmaking." (1997). Press release (September 22).

Van Dyke, W. S. (1931). *Horning into Africa.* California: Graphic Press.

Van Lawick, Hugo and Jane Van Lawick-Goodall. (1971). *Innocent Killers.* Boston: Houghton Mifflin.

Van Lawick-Goodall, Jane. (1965). "New Discoveries Among Africa's Chimpanzees." *National Geographic* 128, 6 (December): 802–30.

"The Vanishing Prairie." (1954). *Time*, August 23, 72.

Von Cranach, Mario, ed. (1976). *Methods of Inference from Animal to Human Behavior*. Chicago: Aldine.

Warham, John. (1966). *The Technique of Wildlife Cinematography*. London: Focal Press.

Warshow, Robert. (1964). "The Gangster as Tragic Hero." In *The Immediate Experience*. Garden City, N.Y.: Anchor Books, 83–88.

Watts, Steven. (1995). "Walt Disney: Art and Politics in the American Century." *Journal of American History* 82, 1: 84–110.

Webster, Bayard. (1986). "On the Trail of Cougars, Crocodiles, and Gooney Birds." *New York Times*, May 11, Sec. 2: 33–34.

Weis, Elisabeth and John Belton, eds. (1985). *Film Sound: Theory and Practice*. New York: Columbia University Press.

Westcott, Tim. (1997). "Call of the Wild." *Television Business International* (July/August): 18–20.

"Wildlife Film-Makers Admit to Using Captive Animals as Stars." (1998). *Sunday Times*, August 9: 1–2.

"Wildlife Film-Making: A Freelance Director-Cameraman's Viewpoint." (1973). (interview with Alan Root) *EBU Review* (November): 70–71.

Wiley, Mason and Damien Bona. (1986). *Inside Oscar: The Unofficial History of the Academy Awards*. New York: Ballantine.

Williams, Christopher, ed. (1980). *Realism and the Cinema: A Reader*. London: Routledge and Kegan Paul.

Willock, Colin. (1978). *The World of Survival: The Inside Story of the Famous TV Wildlife Series*. London: Andre Deutsch.

———. (1981). "The Background of 'Survival' and the Making of Wildlife Programmes for Television." *BKSTS Journal* 63, 9 (September): 540–43.

Wilson, Alexander. (1992). *The Culture of Nature*. Cambridge, Mass.: Blackwell.

Winston, Brian. (1988). "Before Flaherty, Before Grierson: The Documentary Film in 1914." *Sight and Sound* 57, 4 (Autumn): 277–79.

———. (1993). "The Documentary Film as Scientific Inscription." In *Theorizing Documentary*, ed. Michael Renov. New York: Routledge, 37–57.

———. (1995). *Claiming the Real: The Griersonian Documentary and Its Legitimations*. London: BFI.

Wood, L. N. (1944). *Raymond L. Ditmars: His Exciting Career with Reptiles, Animals and Insects*. New York: Junior Literary Guild and Julian Messner.

Woodard, Stacy. (1934). "Insect Warriors Do Battle for the Movies." *Scientific American* 150 (April): 178–79.

Worth, Sol. (1981). "Symbolic Strategies" (with Larry Gross). In Worth, *Studying Visual Communication*, ed. Larry Gross. Philadelphia: University of Pennsylvania Press, 132–47.

Wright, Basil. (1954). "The Living Desert." *Sight & Sound* 24, 1 (July-September): 35.

———. (1974). *The Long View*. New York: Knopf.

Wright, Will. (1975). *Sixguns and Society: A Structural Study of the Western*. Berkeley: University of California Press.

Yogman, Michael W. (1990). "Male Parental Behavior in Human and Nonhuman Primates." In *Mammalian Parenting: Biochemical, Neurobiological, and Behavioral Determinants*, ed. N. Krasnegor and R. S. Bridges. New York: Oxford University Press, 461–81.

Zelle, Ann and Ronald Sutton. (1991). "Image Manipulation: The Zelig Phenomenon." *Journal Visual Literacy* 11, 1: 10–37.

Index

Italicized page numbers indicate illustrations.

ABC television network, 70, 72, 80, 83, 213, 216, 217, 232n.131
ABC/Kane, 248n.9
Aberson, Helen, 137
Academy Awards, 66, 69, 210, 212, 213, 215, 230n.81
Across the World with Mr. and Mrs. Martin Johnson, 49
actualités, 44, 45, 113, 127, 186
Adams, Ansel, 15
Adventures of Ichabod and Mr. Toad, The, 132
Adventures of Milo and Otis, The, 128, 147, 150
advertising: as cultural debasement, 84; similarities to wildlife films, 6, 7, 14, 20, 87, 94, 170; of individual wildlife films, 1–2, 59, 160, 220; the TV "world" created by, 7
advertisers, 7, 87, 220
Aesop's Fables, 91, 92, 103, 106
Africa Screams, 56
Africa Speaks, 53, 207, 229n.52
African Ambassador: Memoirs of Lady Arabella Ape, 172
African Animals, 47
African Elephant (a.k.a. *King Elephant*), 217
African Game Trails, 101, 229n.34
African Lion, The, 132, 167
Agassiz, Louis, 99, 236n.58, 59
Akeley, Carl, 47, 154, 201, 202, 203, 204, 206
Alaska-Siberian Expedition, 46, 202
Algar, James, 133, 160, 173, 215, 242n.34, 244n.13
Alice in Wonderland, 132
Alien Empire, 119, 191

Aliya the Asian Elephant, 150, 214
All Bird TV, 72, 162
Allen, Arthur, 61, 210
Allen, Irwin, 180, 212
Allen, Rex Jr., 146
Almost a Dodo, 166
American Human Education Society, 102
American market: for early wildlife films, 44–48; influence on wildlife film form and content, 2, 45, 47, 69, 76, 78–82, 137, 175, 182, 208, 217, 218, 219, 220; lure of to foreign producers, 76, 78–80, 217
American Ornithologists' Union, 61
American style (of wildlife film and television), 48, 69, 70, 73, 76, 78–81, 137, 182–83, 203
Anglia Television, 76
Anima Mundi, 2, 14, 31, 237n.91
Animal Court, 73
animal biography, 106–8, 131, 145
animal education, 174, 177–81, 247n.55
Animal ER, 73
Animal Planet, 82, 220
Animal Rescues, 73
Animals Came to Drink, 172, 209
animated zoology, 38, 41, 58, 196, 228n.13
Annaud, Jean-Jacques, 114, 179, 204, 219, 220, 221, 237n.91
anthropomorphism, 63, 92, 96–100, 103–5, 114, 160, 207, 208, 212, 236n.62. *See also* humanizing animals; morality; and nuclear family
Antonioni, Michelangelo, 162
Arctic Hunt, 46, 202

Argo, Allison, 150
Aristotle, 89, 91, 145
Ashby, Eric, 175
Atlantic, The, 109
Attenborough, David, 1, 7, 10, 11, 12, 15, 30,
32, 33, 73, 121, 167, 213, 221, 222, 223n.5,
224n.16, 226n.95, 236n.76
Attenborough in Paradise, 166, 167
audiences: attempts to lure, 1, 2, 15, 28,
76, 80, 81, 87, 143, 156, 157; deception
of, 12, 26, 32, 85–88, 142, 175; demands
and expectations of, 1, 5, 7, 12, 16, 20, 28,
37, 45, 47, 68, 69, 71, 72, 80, 81, 85, 87,
88, 143, 246n.36; filmmakers' obligations
to, 11, 22–23, 85; emotional involvement
of (with animal characters), 29, 31, 33,
103, 114, 116, 121, 139,153, 163, 226n.92;
interpretation of images by, 5, 8, 11, 12,
16–18, 20, 25, 27–29, 32, 88, 152, 161, 162,
166; primary and secondary, 95, 235n.46;
scientific vs. popular, 11, 88, 90; tastes of
American, 45, 46, 47, 48, 59, 63, 64, 81,
143
Audubon Society, 22, 99
Audubon, John J., 40
August Rhapsody, 125, 211

Babe, 126, 237n.92
Baboona, 49, 53, 210
Back to God's Country, 154, 204
back-filming, 10
Badgerwatch, 76
Ballard, Carroll, 126
Bambi (film), 62, 64, 124, 125–26, 141–45,
155, 209, 210, 211, 237n.92, 242nn.28, 47,
243n.55
Bambi (novel), 124, 125, 141–45, 158, 205,
206, 209, 238n.118, 242n.41
Baree, Son of Kazan, 115, 154, 204, 206
Barnouw, Eric, 22, 50, 51, 61, 62, 230n.83
Bartlett, Des and Jen, 76, *78*, 217, 238n.129
Battle of the Sexes, 175
Baudrillard, Jean 13–15
Bayer, Wolfgang, 216
Bazin, André, 9, 187
BBC (British Broadcasting Corporation), 14,
56, 72, 73, 216, 217, 218, 238n.115
BBC Natural History Unit, 9, 11, 13, 37, 82,
169, 220; early years at, 73–76, 175, 211,
213, 214, 215, 231n.104; penetration of
American market by, 2, 76; productions

by, 1 2, 74–76, 81, 150, 160, 162, 177, 191,
214, 216, 217, 218, 219, 221, 223n.5
Bear Country, 132, 133, 134, 213
Bear, The (*L'Ours*), 114, 137, 179, 204, 220,
221, 237nn.84, 91
Beaver Valley, 66, 67, 132, 212
Beckett, Samuel, 183
Beetlemania, 119
Bellamy, David, 237n.84
Below the Sahara, 57, 213
Berger, John, 6, 227n.2, 248n.11
Best Boy, 23
Bettelheim, Bruno 139
Beyond Bengal, 53
Big Cat Diary, 76, 238n.129
Big Chill, The, 161
Biography of a Grizzly, 147
biological determinism, 164
Birds of a Far-Off Sea, 154, 166, 171, 204
Birds of Britain, 73
Birdwatch, 76
birdwatching, 99–100
Birth of a Flower, The, 57
Birth of a Nation, 46, 116
Bitzer, G. W. "Billy," 46, 198, 199, 200
Black Beauty, 102
blue chip wildlife film, 14, 15, 20; contrasted
with other models, 73, 187, 188, 191;
Disney films as models for, 63, 124, 134;
elements of in old films, 117, 122, 125, 154,
155; inclusion/exclusion of tribal peoples,
15, 224n.30; scenes of predation in, 182;
suitability to HDTV, 188
Book of Nature, The, 58, 60, 63, 203
Bordwell, David, 32, 227n.96
Born Free, 125, 147, 216
Born to Run, 150
Borneo, 49
Boswall, Jeffery, 11–12, 76, 216, 217, 225n.62,
238n.115, 243n.52
Bring 'em Back Alive, 54, 208, 229n.52
British Film Institute, 57
Brock the Badger, 118
Brock, Stan, 56, 72
Brownlow, Kevin, 21, 50, 51, 208, 228n.24,
229n.42
Buck Staghorn's Animal Bites, 73
Buck, Frank, 54–56, 60, 63, 186, 208, 210,
211, 229n.52
Buena Vista (Disney subsidiary), 68, 72, 146,
147, 221

Bunuel, Luis, 29
Burnford, Sheila, 138, 215
Burroughs, John, 100–102, 108, 109, 111, 141, 178–79, 183, 198
Burrud, Bill, 72, 213, 216, 218, 220
Buxton, Aubrey, 76, 80, 215

C-SPAN, 4, 13, 182
Call of the Wild, 154
Call of the Yukon, 125
Camera Trails in Africa, 209
Cameron, J, 41
Campbell, Joseph, 130, 136, 144
Captain Kleinschmidt's Arctic Hunt, 46, 203
Carey, Harry Sr., 123
Carpenter, C. R. 155, 211
Carrighar, Sally, 147, 216
Carroll, Noël, 224nn.39, 43, 233nn.4, 5
Carson, Rachel, 69, 90, 91, 180, 212, 234n.26
Caughey, John, 30, 226n.81
Cawelti, John, 20, 127, 130, 241n.13
CBC (Canadian Broadcasting Company), 22, 85, 215, 218, 219
CBS television network, 80, 150, 157, 175, 213, 214, 216, 221, 243n.67
Ceremony, 169, 170, 171
Chambers, Whittaker, 141, 206, 242n.41
Chandler, Raymond, 128
Chang, 119–20, 123, 203, 206
Characteristics of Gibbon Behavior, 155, 211
Charlie the Lonesome Cougar, 133, 148, 216, 218
chase pictures, 45–47
Chasing a Sea Lion in the Arctic, 46
Cheese Mites, 57, 198
Cheetah, 126, 243n.66
Cheetah Family, A, 163, 177
Chico, the Misunderstood Coyote, 72, 147, 215
Christian ornithology, 99, 100, 128, 166
Chronique d'un été, 27
Cinderella, 132, 242n.28
cinéma vérité, 22
Cinematograph and Natural Science, The, 202
Circulation of Blood in a Frog, The, 57
Clark, Barry, 93
close-ups: as dramatic intensifiers, 1, 3, 61, 116, 119, 183, 188, 226n.91; as elements in narrative construction, 31–32, 116; in creating individual animal characters, 29; in early wildlife films, 28, 115, 116, 117, 118, 119–20, 121, 122, 154, 206; in promoting

emotional involvement, 29–32, 116, 153; questionable or misleading uses of, 8, 12, 17, 24, 32, 48, 118,
Cockerell, T. D. A., 42, 210
codes and conventions (of film and television), 4, 11, 12, 25, 37, 126, 152, 224n.18, 246n.36
commercial pressures on content, 2, 6, 20, 38, 44, 45, 64, 80, 82, 84, 85, 96, 112, 175, 183, 191, 192
composite characters, 29, 43, 106–7, 109, 237n.98
composite events, 10, 14, 24, 25, 32, 88
concentration of wildlife film industry, 82, 185, 187, 248n.2
Congo Pictures, 53, 208
Congorilla, 49, 53, 207, 208
Cooper, Merian C., 119, 120, 206
Cooper, Susan, 101
coproduction, 82, 185, 186, 190
Corporation for Public Broadcasting, 86
Cousteau Society, 22
Cousteau, Jacques-Yves, 186, 212, 216, 221, 229n.35
Crocodile Hunter, 56, 72
Crocodile Territory, 164
Crowther, Bosley, 67, 213
Cruel Camera, 85, 219, 226n.79
cruelty to animals, 45, 55, 63, 68, 86, 99, 102, 200, 208, 210, 219, 226n.79, 240n.6, 245n.16. *See also* disposable subjects
cuckooism, 245n.19
Curtis, Edward, 229n.62
Curwood, James Oliver, 114–16, 124–25, 137–39, 141, 147, 158, 179, 204, 205, 206, 215, 217, 237n.84, 238nn.116, 118,121, 123

Dahmer, Jeffrey, 161, 145n.17
Daily Dozen at the Zoo, 59, 207
Darwin, Charles, 34, 35, 98, 99, 100, 135, 233n.5, 234n.24, 235n.50, 52, 55, 57; 236n.59
Darwin, Erasmus, 98
Darwinism, 33, 36, 60, 96, 97, 99, 103, 105–7, 135, 138, 163–64, 182–83, 230n.80, 236n.58, 59; 245n.14
Dassan, 54, 60, 63, 166, 171–73, 179, 183, 207, 231n.106
David, Dr. A., 47, 200
DaVinna, Clyde, 123, 208, 239n.141, 142
Dawn, Norman O., 116

Dead Birds, 22

Deadly Crocodiles, 56

Deadly Encounters, 191

death (depictions of), 4, 9, 19, 23, 36, 40, 42–43, 45–48, 52, 55–56, 58, 67–68, 80, 105, 113, 122, 136–37, 139, 141–42, 144, 152, 153, 160, 164, 173, 181–84, 189, 195, 196, 198, 199, 201, 203, 206, 207, 208. *See also* disposable subjects

Delemere, Lord, 43, 197

Denis, Armand, 55, 56, 57, 69, 186, 209, 210, 212, 213, 229n.56

Denver Post, The, 86, 87

DeRoos, Robert, 68

Description of Three Hundred Animals, A, 89

Devil Tiger, 53

Devillier-Donegan, 82

Di Di's Story, 121

Dialectics of Nature, 98

direct cinema, 22, 25, 27, 49

Discovery Channel, 14, 82, 150, 219, 221, 222, 223n.5

Disney, Roy, 63, 134

Disney, Roy, Jr., 29

Disney, Walt, 22, 53, 59, 60, 63–67, 69, 72, 89, 93, 101, 105, 118, 124, 133, 142–43, 145, 165, 186

Disney studio and productions, 13, 37, 59, 60, 62–72, 80–82, 103, 115, 118, 121, 123–25, 128, 131–41, 145–48, 150, 158, 173–75, 179, 180, 191, 207, 210, 211, 212, 213, 214, 215, 216, 218, 220, 221, 231nn.91, 104, 239n.133, 242n.28. See also *Bambi* (film); True Life Adventures

Disneyland series, 70, 213

disposable subjects, 42, 44, 45, 46, 47, 58, 60, 182, 196, 198, 203, 228n.17, 26. *See also* cruelty to animals; death

Ditmars, Raymond, 57, 58, 59, 60, 61, 63, 67, 118, 119, 143, 154, 186, 203, 204, 208, 230n.66

Divided World, A, 212

docudramas, 27, 28, 146

docu-soaps, 73, 76

documentary: differences from wildlife film, 13, 15, 20–28, 29, 38, 42, 46, 50, 57, 59, 61, 62, 66, 84, 88, 118, 119–20, 145, 146, 156, 188, 230n.83; early use of the term, 57, 202, 229n.62; exemption from formal or aesthetic debate, 12; manipulations in, 10, 233n.11; similarities to wildlife film,

10, 12, 22, 45, 72, 88, 146, 150, 155, 215, 216, 225n.44 (*see also* television science documentary); socially conscious uses of, 15, 21, 23, 42, 225n.61 (*see also* Grierson, John)

Donaldson, Leonard, 57, 202

Dorfmann, Ariel, 140, 243n.51

Downer, John, 183, 219, 220

dramatic (narrative) conventions, 1, 3, 5, 8, 9, 12, 14–16, 21, 25, 27, 28, 31, 33, 34, 152–53

Dressing for Dinner, 34, 183

Duck, Donald, 67

Dugmore, A. R. 166, 202, 205, 206

Dumbo, 62, 135, 136, 137, 138, 140, 144, 146

Dyer, Richard, 5, 225n.52

Eastman, George, 52

Edison films, 43, 45, 154, 196, 197, 198, 199, 204

Edison, Thomas, 57, 109, 154, 203

education (of animals in film). *See* animal education

educational use of film, 21, 37, 46, 58, 59, 61, 62, 65, 66, 68, 94, 125, 181, 202, 203. *See also* scientific-educational films

Eisenstein, Sergei, 163

Electrocuting an Elephant, 45, 113, 181, 198, 199, 228n.20

Eliot, Marc, 65

Emperor Penguins, 166, 214

Empire, 7

Enchanted Isles, 76, 216

Encyclopædia Britannica, 68, 148

Engels, Frederick, 98, 235n.53

Eternal Triangle, The, 116

ethics. *See* audiences, filmmakers' obligations to

ethnographic film, 22, 24–25, 236n.74

Eustace, Harry, 49

Everson, William K. 119, 120, 122

Everybody's Magazine, 111, 200

factual re-creations, 10

fairy tales, 92, 111, 136, 139, 241n.16

Falconeye, 178

family. *See* nuclear family

Family, 169, 170, 171, 180

Family That Lived with Elephants, The, 175, *176*, 218

"family values," 152, 157, 159, 173, 184

Fang and Claw, 54, 210
Fantasia, 132, 133, 134, 135
Farber, Manny, 67, 68
Federal Communications Commission
(FCC), 80, 85, 217
feeding films, 44, 197, 198, 199
Fell, John, 19
Field & Stream, 142, 242n.45
Field, Mary, 59, 61, 117–18, 186, 205, 209,
230n.74, 241n.11
5th Estate, The (CBC), 219, 233n.6
Fight Between Tarantula and Scorpion, 45, 198
Fighting Roosters, 45
film editing: as dramatic intensifier, 1–2, 6,
9, 27, 73, 113, 120–21, 237n.91; in nar-
rative construction, 9, 10, 18, 27–31, 38,
84, 108, 113, 116, 117; or misleading uses
of, 5, 6, 8, 9, 10, 17, 18, 24, 27, 28, 30–32,
51, 107, 118, 121, 169, 170, 189, 203, 208,
237n.91
financing of wildlife films, 7, 63–65, 76, 95,
96, 133, 185, 190, 203, 207, 208, 210
Finnegans Wake, 130
Fishers in the Family, 121, 128, 148
Flaherty, Robert, 123, 204, 229n.62,
239n.141
Flash, the Teenage Otter, 147, 216
folk tales, 62, 93, 95, 96, 128, 241n.16
Fonda, Henry, 76, 79, 217
Ford, Henry, 109
Forsythe, John, 72, 80
Fossey, Dian, 90
Fothergill, Alastair, 223n.3
Four Seasons, The, 143, 204
Four Years in Paradise, 51
Fowler, Jim, 56, 72, 215
Fox and the Hound, The, 150
Foxwatch, 76
Francis the talking mule, 237n.92
Franklin, Chester, 123, 124, 210
Franklin, Sidney, 124, 126, 142, 143, 209,
210, 243n.51
Fred Ott's Sneeze (a.k.a. *The Sneeze*), 19
Freud, Sigmund, 103, 134, 234n.31, 242n.46
Fromm, Erich, 136, 1377, 144, 242n.32
Frye, Northrop, 130, 136, 241n.13, 242n.31
full coverage, 32, 227n.97
Fun & Fancy Free, 132–33

G.I. Joe cartoon series, 20
Gardner, Robert, 22

Garmon, Linda, 23
Gay, Peter, 103
General History of Quadrupeds, A, 89
genre(s): of film and television, 5, 38, 62, 88,
156, 162, 182; wildlife film as, 2, 4, 20, 37–
38, 46, 49, 56, 62, 69–70, 85, 88, 96, 119,
120, 125, 131, 153, 156, 171, 207, 209
Gilmour, Dione, 15
Girl of the Limberlost, A, 237n.84
Glacier Fox, The, 148
Glasgow Media Group, 234n.18, 247n.48
Glass, Philip, 2
Godard, Jean-Luc, 238n.121
Goethe, Johann Wolfgang von, 98
Goldberg, Robert, 243n.68
Goodall, Jane, 25, 72, 90, 175, 177, 183, 217,
227n.107, 247n.50
Gould, Stephen Jay, 90
Grass, 119, 123, 203
Great Adventure, The, 125
Great Panda Adventure, The, 126, 243n.66
Great Train Robbery, The, 19, 45, 108
Green Umbrella Ltd., 185, 220, 221
Greene, Lorne, 72
Grierson, John, 15, 21, 22, 23, 42, 59,
225n.61, 229n.62, 230n.72, 233n.11. *See
also* documentary, socially conscious
uses of
Griffith, D. W., 13, 46, 114
Griffith, Richard, 119
Grinnell, George Bird, 99
Grizzly King, The, 114, 124, 137, 158, 179, 204,
237n.84, 238n.118
Gross, Larry, 245n.21
Grzimek, Bernhard, 186, 214, 215
Guillemots, 154
Gull!, 61–62, 211, 237n.91
Gypsy Colt, The, 125, 147

Haraway, Donna, 233n.5
Hass, Hans, 61, 186, 211, 212, 214
Hawkins, Desmond, 73, *74*, 211, 222
Heine, Heinrich, 105
Hellstrom Chronicles, The, 119
heroes (animals as), 97, 105, 116, 127, 129,
131, 135–36, 148, 162–63, 168
heroic narratives, 127, 130–31, 136, 151, 163,
241n.10
Hibler, Winston, 67, 133, 145, 146, 160, 173,
179, 215, 217, 244n.13

high-definition television (HDTV), 185–86, 190

Historie of Foure-Footed Beastes, The, 89

Hitchcock, Alfred, 162

Hobbes, Thomas, 92, 98

Hollywood ("classical") film style, 8, 12–14, 17–18, 29, 31–32, 49, 68, 72, 84, 118, 119, 122, 128, 175, 191

Homeward Bound, 126, 138, 147, 237n.92

Homeward Bound II, 138

Hopkins, Anthony, 34

How to Read Donald Duck, 140

Hoyt, Vance Joseph, 123, 124, 210

Hughes, David and Carol, 26

Hughes, Howard, 63

humanizing animals, 72, 92–93, 103–4, 106, 109, 114, 135, 142, 173. *See also* anthropomorphism; morality

Hunters, The, 22

hunting (morality of), 242n.45, 47

Hunting Big Game in Africa (a.k.a. *Roosevelt in Africa*, 1909), 46, 201, 238n.125

Hunting the White Bear (a.k.a. *Une chasse à l'ours blanc*, 1903), 45, 113

Huxley, Julian, 65, 155, 165, 171, 209, 210, 227n.98

Huxley, Thomas, 235n.57

Ichabod and Mr. Toad, 132

identification. *See* audiences, emotional involvement of

IMAX (large format process), 182, 185, 188, 221, 222, 248n.7

Imperato, Pascal and Eleanor, 50

In Birdland, 45, 47, 154, 200

Incredible Flight of the Snow Geese, The, 78, 218

Incredible Journey, The (1961 novel), 138, 147, 215

Incredible Journey, The (1963 film), 128, 133, 147, 150, 215, 242n.34

Inflight Movie, 166

Ingagi, 53, 208

international style, 82, 185

International Wildlife Film Festival (IWFF), 38, 218

Irwin, Steve, 56

Island of the Penguins, 173

ITV, 14, 76, 215

J. Walter Thompson Co., 79, 175, 218

Jacare, Killer of the Amazon, 56

Jackson Hole Wildlife Film Festival, 38, 220, 222

Jacobs, Lewis, 21

James, Henry, 102

Jaws and Claws, 73

Jenkins, Alan, 89

Jensen, Joli, 234n.25

Johnson, Martin and Osa: ethnocentric attitudes, 22, 51; filmmaking style and skills, 49–51, 53, 56, 63, 116–17, 119, 121, 154, 204, 205, 207, 208, 229n.42, 245n.13; transition to sound, 53, 186, 206, 208, 229n.50; use of staged events, 49–50, 51–52, 206

Johnston, Ollie, 124, 133, 141, 144

Jones, Buffalo, 48, 49, 202

Jones, Peter, 220

Jonkel, Charles, 240n.147.

Joubert, Dereck and Beverly, 26

Journey of Natty Gann, The, 243n.66

Jungle Adventures, 49, 204

Jungle Book, The 103

Jungle Cat, 71, 133, 146, 160, 168, 180, 215

Jungle Cavalcade, 56, 211

Kael, Pauline, 144

Kali the Lion, 150

Kane, Dennis B. 175

Kapital, Das, 98

Kaplan, E. Ann, 225n.45

Kazan, 154, 114, 204, 238n.125

Kearton, Cherry: as late Victorian, 238n.116; attempts at comedy, 54, 60, 67, 171–72, 183, 207, 231n.106; compared to Rainey, 47–48; descent into nature-faking, 112–13, 171–74, 179, 209; early achievements, 43–44, 47, 186, 196, 197; filming Roosevelt, 48–49, 200–201, 229n.34; working methods, 47–48, 54, 110, 122, 174, 228n.26; recognition and tributes, 22, 47, 112, 113, 201, 202, 238n.115

Kearton, Richard, 40, 43, 110, 196, 197, 200

Kein Platz für wilde Tiere, 214

Kellert, Stephen, 234n.18

Kenworthy, Paul, 137, 145

Khmer Rouge, 160

Kimball, Ward, 136

King of the Grizzlies, 133, 147, 217

King of the Sierras, 125

King, Simon, 238n.129

King, Thomas Starr, 101
Kipling, Rudyard, 103, 106, 111
Klein, Melanie, 242n.38
Kleinschmidt, "Captain" Frank E., 46, 154, 186, 202, 228n.24
Korda, Alexander, 155, 209
Koster & Bial's Music Hall, 43, 197
Kraft Foods, 175
Kratt's Creatures, 73
Kuehl, Jerry, 28

L'Aventura, 162
Lady MacKenzie's Big Game Pictures (a.k.a. *Heart of Africa*, 1915), 49, 203
Landis, Bob, 243n.68
Lassie (television series), 116, 128
Lassie Come Home, 116, 125, 147
Lassoing Wild Animals, 48, 49, 202
Last Wolves of Ethiopia, 150, 158, 163, 243n.68
Leacock, Richard, 25, 26
Leakey and Lewin, 34, 237n.95
Leakey, Richard, 90
Legend of Lobo, The, 133, 147, 215
Leopard Son, The, 150, 182, 221
Leopard That Changed Its Spots, The, 78, 79, 128, 148
Lévi-Strauss, Claude, 130, 241n.15, 16, 17
Liers, Emile, 147, 216
life-cycle storyline model, 143–44, 148, 174, 201, 203, 204, 243n.52
Life of an American Fireman, The, 45, 108
Life of Birds, The, 190
Life on Earth, 81, 190, 218
Lifesense, 235n.49
Lincoln Park Zoo, 70
Lion King, The, 135, 150, 220, 243n.55
Lion Queen, The, 167
Lion: King of Beasts, 167
Lions and Hyenas: Eternal Enemies, 26
Lions of the African Night, 26
Listener, The, 6
literary naturalists, 62, 89, 101–2, 108, 114
Little Fox, The, 150
Liversedge, Tim, 101
Living Desert, The, 21, 67, 69, 132, 137, 213
Living Europe, 185, 221
Living Free, 125, 147
Living Planet, The, 31, 219
Living Planet Report (World Wildlife Fund), 224n.36
Lobo, King of the Currumpaw, 147, 215

locomotion studies, 19, 42, 64, 196, 228n.9. *See also* Muybridge; slow-motion
Lodge, R. B., 43
London, Jack, 103, 108, 206
Long, William J., 103–4, 108–11, 178, 179, 238n.116
Look, 73
Lopez, Barry, 92
Lords of the Everglades, 35, 150
Lorentz, Pare, 230n.78
Lorenz, Konrad, 90, 157, 210, 213, 246n.39, 247n.56
Lumière, Louis, 13
Lyell, Charles, 98
Lyotard, Jean-François, 233n.5

MacDougall, David, 9, 24
Making Wildlife Movies, 11, 68, 241n.24
Malthus, Thomas, 34, 98, 235n.55
Maltin, Leonard, 136
Man Who Loved Bears, The, 148, 218
Marey, Etienne-Jules, 41, 42, 43, 118, 196, 228n.13
Marsh, George Perkins, 101
Marshall, John, 22
Marx, Karl, 98
Mattelart, Armand, 140, 243n.51
Matto Grosso, 53
May, Rollo, 240n.4
Maysles brothers, 26
McCarten John, 68
McHugh, Tom, 174, 231n.100
Mead, Margaret, 23
mean world syndrome, 5, 223n.5
media "effects," 6, 20, 97, 192, 232n.155
Meerkat Family Saga, A, 150, 157
Meier, Don, 70, 72, 212, 213, 215
Méliès, George, 13
Melody Time, 132, 133
Memphis Belle, 63
MGM, 123, 124, 139, 208, 209, 210, 211, 229n.52, 239n.144
Microcosmos, 119
Mighetto, Lisa, 103
Miles, Hugh, 31, 238n.129
Mills, Stephen, 10, 14, 16, 33, 223n.10, 225n.36
Milotte, Al and Elma, 64, 66, 212, 214
Miss Jane Goodall and the Wild Chimpanzees, 72, 216
Moana, 123, 229n.62

monogamy (among animals), 135, 157, 168, 170–71, 173, 244n.4

Moose Hunt in New Brunswick, 46, 199

morality (projected onto nature), 92, 93, 99, 100, 105, 106, 128, 134, 15–23, 155–57, 159, 160–62, 164–66, 172, 174, 180–81, 190, 192, 225n.64, 236n.67, 245n.16

Morning in America, 170

Morris, Johnny, 89

Motion Picture Academy, 64

Mototo, 172

Mountain Gorilla: A Shattered Kingdom, 121, 184

Mouse, Mickey, 136, 144, 239n.133, 242n.32

Moving Picture World, 46, 58, 202, 228n.24, 230n.62, 238n.113

Mowat, Farley, 240n.147

Mozu, the Snow Monkey, 121, 150, 163

Mr. Delaware and the Boxing Kangaroo, 43, 44, 196

Mr. Ed (series), 237n.92

MTV, 6, 13, 20, 72

Muir, John, 109, 110

Museum of Modern Art Film Library, 119

music: as intensifier of content, 1, 8, 43, 67, 153, 237n.91; images set to, 2, 3, 17, 59, 121, 191, 207, 213; ethnic, 8, 12; comical uses of, 59–60, 66–67; wall-to-wall, 79–80

Muybridge, Eadweard, 19, 41–43, 118, 182, 195, 196, 228n.13

myth(s), 62, 92–93, 95–96, 128–30, 134–36, 138, 140, 144, 148, 151, 174, 207, 240n.4, 241n.10, 241n.17, 242n.31, 243n.55. *See also* heroic narratives; narrative formula; traditional narratives

mythic time, 15, 20

Nanook of the North, 204, 228n.17

narration. *See* voice-over narration

narrative formula(s), 4–5, 9, 13, 20, 61, 80–81, 84, 90, 95, 96, 115, 127–30, 136–38, 147–48, 150, 157, 232n.123, 240n.4, 243n.55; Disney, 64, 66–69, 78, 80, 132–33, 136–37, 140, 144, 147, 232n.122, 244n.71; Martin and Osa Johnson, 50; tyranny of (in media industries), 69, 78, 80

National Geographic: film and television productions, 35, 72, 150, 175, 191, 216; *Explorer* series, 82, 177, 219, 222, 243n.68, 244n.71; magazine, 64, 232n.130; Society, 72, 215; television division, 19, 220; cable television channel, 221

National Wildlife Federation, 22

Native Lion Hunt, 47, 48

Natural History (magazine), 50

Natural History of Beasts, The, 90

natural history science: fictionalizing of, 11, 88–89, 94, 96–97, 102–3, 105–6, 109–11, 131, 143–44, 150; formal study of, 41, 50, 89, 93, 98, 100, 111, 122, 202; popularization of, 1, 40, 44, 46, 48–89, 53, 57, 58–62, 68, 70, 76, 88–91, 96, 98, 99–102, 105–6, 111, 118, 129, 131, 143, 145, 152, 155, 161, 168–69, 232n.147; visual representation in, 39, 196

Natural World, The, 76, 219

"naturalist" (definitions and uses of term), 62, 66, 100, 101, 102, 111, 231n.100, 236n.76

Naturalist, The, 73

Nature (PBS series), 81, 150, 163, 219, 221, 244n.71

nature faking: in literature, 97, 108–12, 114, 172–73, 178–79, 198, 200, 209; film, 43, 54, 85–88, 112–13, 120, 173–74, 205, 208

Nature of Things, The (CBC series), 22, 215, 218

Nature's Assassins, 160, 183

Nature's Half Acre, 135, 212

Nature's Nightmares, 191

NBC television network, 70, 72, 80, 175, 212, 215

Never Cry Wolf, 126, 240n.147

New Chimpanzees, The, 175

New York State Board of Censors, 174

New York Times, 48, 67, 203, 230n.83, 238n.109

New York Zoological Park (Bronx Zoo), 58

New Yorker, The, 68

Newsweek, 67

niche (media) markets, 72, 186, 187

Nichols, Bill, 12, 17

Nikki, Wild Dog of the North, 115, 133, 147, 158, 215

90° South, 48, 228n.33

Niok, 146, 148, 150, 214

Nippon TV, 148, 150

Noble, G. K., 61, 155, 211

Nomads of the North, 115–17, 121, 139, 146, 154, 158, 204, 215

North American Review, 110

"northern" plot type, 238n.123
Nova, 22
Novak, Barbara, 15, 236n.59
nuclear family (projected onto nature), 18, 135, 153, 166, 172. *See also* anthropomorphism; morality

object relations theory (British school of), 242n.38
observational cinema, 22, 25
Old Man Muskrat, 148
Olympic Elk, The, 132
On Safari, 214, 229n.56
On the Origin of Species, 98, 235n.50, 52
One Day at Teton Marsh, 147, 216
orphan motif, 79, 115, 123, 137, 139–40, 141, 144, 147, 148, 158, 159, 204, 205, 208, 212, 214, 218, 243n.66
Orphans of the North, 125
Outside magazine, 6
Oxford Scientific Films, 13, 80, 119, 216, 221

Page, George, 72, 81, 121, 219
Palace Theater, London, 45
Palmer, Ernest, 48
Panda's Story, A, 148
para-proxemics, 226n.80. *See also* teaming
para-social relationships, 29, 226n.80
Paramount Studios, 119, 123, 208, 239n.144
Parer, David, 31
Parrots: Look Who's Talking, 162
Parsons, Christopher, 9, 11, 37, 241n.24, 243n.52
Partridge Films, 83, 94, 150, 218, 219, 221, 233n.10, 248n.2
Pathé Frères, 45
Paul J. Rainey's African Hunt, 47, 202, 203
Paul, Robert, 44, 197
PBS, 14, 22, 81, 86, 150, 163, 175, 219, 221, 234n.24, 244n.71
Pearl, Harold, 137
Peas and Cues, 59, 208
Pennebaker, D. A., 26
People of the Forest, 25, 121
Perkins, Marlin, 70, *71*, 72, 89, 211, 212, 213, 215, 219
Perri, 29, 133, 145–47
Peter Pan, 132
Peterson's Guides, 39
Philadelphia Zoological Garden, 19, 41, 42
Physiologus, The, 89, 90, 92

Pike, Oliver, 42, 43, 45, 47, 186, 196, 200, 202, 204, 228n.21
Pinocchio, 132
Pirsch unter Wasser, 61
Plage, Dieter, *26*, 78, 218, 220
Playtime at the Zoo, 59, 207
Pliny, 89, 91
point-of-view, 28, 96, 97, 103, 105, 114, 116, 153, 226nn.91, 92, 94, 235n.49
Pol Pot, 160
Polar Bear Hunt, 46
Ponting, Herbert, 48
Porter, Edwin S., 45, 46, 108, 113, 199
Porter, Gene Stratton, 103, 110, 111, 237nn.84, 88
predation (portrayals of), 9, 15, 34, 35, 81, 100, 104–6, 128, 138, 153, 159–61, 177, 180, 182–84, 200, 208, 226n.79
presenters, presenter-led programs, 8, 37, 72, 76, 80, 81, 162, 207, 215, 218, 221
Pribiloff Islands, 134
prime-time television (U.S.), 4, 13, 80, 81, 102, 153, 177, 217
Private Life of Plants, The, 191
Private Life of the Gannet, The, 61, 65, 155, 166, 171, 172, 209, 210
Private Life of the Kingfisher, The, 166, 216
Private Lives series, 76, 166, 217
production code, 244n.3
profitability of wildlife films, 2, 6, 38, 44, 45, 63–65, 85, 96, 192, 217, 219, 222, 228n.30
Propp, Vladimir, 128, 240nn.1, 4, 241n.8
proxemic zones, 30, 226n.83, 244n.1
Psycho, 162
Puma, Lion of the Andes, 31, 238n.129
Pygmy Chimpanzee: The Last Great Ape, 177

Quaker Oats, 79
Queen of Beasts, 167

Raglan, Lord, 92, 240n.4, 241n.16
Rainey, Paul J., 48, 50, 56, 154, 186, 201, 202, 203, 228n.30
Rainey's African Hunt, 48
Rango, 120–23, 145, 155, 208
Rank, Otto, 150, 241n.10, 246n.35
ratings. *See* TV ratings
Ray, Robert, 18
Reagan, Ronald, 170, 237n.84
realism, 7, 13, 14, 85, 104, 187, 188, 225n.54, 233n.4, 248n.4

Red Queen, The, 245n.15
Reggio, Godfrey, 2, 237n.91
Reindeer Time, 61, 125
Reluctant Dragon, The, 63, 132, 133
Renaldo, Duncan, 123
Reptiles of the World, 58
reproductive value (of individual to species),
   159–60, 244n.112
Re(y)nard the Fox, 91
Ridley, Matt, 34, 227n.98, 245n.15
Rin Tin Tin, 116, 128, 238n.126
River, The, 230n.78
RKO Studios/Distribution, 56, 63, 64, 69,
   208, 212, 213
Roberts, Charles G. D., 103–6, 108, 110–11,
   122, 138, 141, 183, 238n.109, 238n.116
Roosevelt in Africa. See *Hunting Big Game in
   Africa*
Roosevelt, Theodore, 46, 48, 49, 101, 109,
   111, 112, 113, 178, 200, 201, 203, 229n.34,
   238n.112
Root, Alan, 76, *77, 86, 87,* 101, 215, 216,
   233n.10, 248n.7
Root, Joan, *77, 87*
Rosenberg, Michael, 94, 96, 218
Rotha, Paul, 21
Rouch, Jean, 27, 226n.74
Rough Sea at Dover, 43, 44, 197
Rush, the Fallow Deer, 150

safari film, 46, 62, 63, 114, 125, 126, 153,
   209, 210, 212, 213 229n.52; rise of, 46–49,
   113, 127; decline and decadence, 53–57;
   rebirth on television, 70; vs. expeditionary
   documentary, 48
Safari to Adventure, 232n.154
Sagan, Carl, 90, 234n.24
Salmon: Against the Tides, 223n.5
Salten, Felix (Siegmund Salzmann) 124,
   141–43, 145, 173, 205, 209, 214
Saludos Amigos, 133
Savage Splendor, 212
Scenes in Massua, 47
Schickel, Richard, 65, 68, 140, 146, 242n.28
Schindler's List, 163
Schoedsack, Ernest B., 119–22, 203, 206,
   208
Scholes, Robert, 19, 225n.50
Scholey, Keith, 248n.11
School of the Woods, 178
Scientific American, 50, 60, 209

scientific-educational films, 46, 57 59, 62,
   144
Scott, Jonathon, 238n.129
Scott, Peter, 73, 76, 89, 213, 220
Screen, 17, 18, 224n.42
Sea Around Us, The, 69, 180
Sea Lions' Home, The, 44, 113, 197
Seal and Walrus Hunting, 46
Seal Island, 35, 63–64, 66, 132, 134, 140, 145,
   173, 179, 212
Sears, Ted, 132, 133
Secrets of Life (Disney), 132, 133, 134, 168,
   214
Secrets of Life (Field and Smith series), 119,
   209, 210, 231n.114
Secrets of Nature series, 59, 62–63, 117–
   19, 155, 205, 207, 208, 209, 230n.74,
   231nn.91, 104, 239n.133
Secrets of the African Baobab Tree, 166
Secrets of the Wild Child, 23
Selig, "Col.", 46, 47, 56, 154, 201, 204
separation-initiation-return theme, 130, 136,
   137, 138–40, 146, 147, 148, 150, 165
Sequoia, 123, 124, 139, 145, 146, 155, 210,
   239n.142, 144
Serengeti Diary, 238n.129
Serling, Rod, 72
Seton, Ernest Thompson, 104–11, 131, 138,
   141, 164, 167, 183, 238n116
Sewell, Anna, 102
Sharpsteen, Ben, 132
Shiras, George III, 43, 197, 198
Sielmann, Heinz, 74, 166, 186, 213, 214, 217,
   218, 219, 246n.26
Silent Spring, 90–91
Silly Symphonies series, 142
Simba, 49, 51, 53, 206, 229n.50, 245n.13
Sinyard, Neil, 66
Sklar, Robert, 19, 45
Sleeping Beauty, 132, 133
slow-motion, 8, 10, 11, 12, 42, 62
Smart, Keenan, 247n.60
Smith, Percy, 57, 59, 61, 117, 118, 186, 201,
   202, 205, 209
Smoky, 125
Snow White, 132, 133, 142
Snow, Michael, 7
So Dear to My Heart, 133
Social Behavior of Rhesus Monkeys, 155, 211
Social Behavior of the Laughing Gull, The, 61,
   155, 211

social Darwinism, 34, 98, 156
Song of the Cardinal, The, 237n.88
Song of the South, 63, 133
sound (use of in films), 12, 24, 27, 28, 32, 52–55, 59, 60, 62, 66, 70, 80, 81, 107, 113, 116, 118, 120, 123, 172, 187, 189, 207, 208, 210, 212, 226n.95, 227n.96, 229nn.50, 56, 237n.92, 248n.4
Spencer, Herbert, 98
staged events, 9, 10, 14, 19, 25, 33, 44–47, 49, 52, 54–56, 58, 60, 84–87, 112, 113, 116, 118, 120, 122, 154, 169, 18, 182, 190, 191, 196, 197, 198, 199, 200, 201, 205, 206, 208, 209, 210, 228n.23
Stalking and Shooting Caribou, Newfoundland, 200
Stanford, Leland, 41, 195, 196
Steamboat Willie, 239n.133
Steinhart, Peter, 81, 93, 232n.155, 247n.59
Story of Peter the Raven, The, 118
Stouffer, Marty, 10, 33, 42, 69, 72, 80, 81, 82, 86, 87, 94, 95, 102, 121, 128, 131, 137, 148, 175, 182, 218, 219, 220, 221, 224n.16
Strength and Agility of Insects, The, 57, 58, 202
Sucksdorff, Arne, 61, 62, 63, 125, 145, 211, 212, 213, 230n.83, 237n.91
Summer's Tale, A, 61
Supernatural, 183
Supersense, 235n.49
Survival, 76
Survival Anglia, 13, 76, 78–80, 83, 128, 148, 175, 215, 216, 217, 218, 219, 221, 248n.2
survival fitness (of species), 33, 34, 35, 227nn.99, 100, 230n.80
Sutherland, Donald, 25
symbolic annihilation, 20, 165, 245n.21

Taku, 125
Tale of the Pregnant Male, The, 168
Tale of Two Critters, A, 148
talking animals, 91, 104, 124, 237n.92
Taming the Jungle, 53
Tarzan the Ape Man, 123
TBS, 82, 177, 219, 222
teaming, 244n.1. *See also* para-proxemics; para-social relations
Technique of Wildlife Cinematography, 37
television science documentary. *See* documentary
Ten Deadliest Snakes, The, 56
Terminator 2, 29

Terrier vs. Wildcat, 45, 200
Thalberg, Irving, 124
That Obscure Object of Desire, 29
Thomas, Frank, 124, 133, 141, 144
Thomas, Lewis, 90
Thomas, Lowell, 53
Thoreau, Henry David, 101, 102
Thorpe, Jim, 116, 204
Three Caballeros, The, 63, 132, 133
3 Men and a Baby, 29
Time-Life, 1, 2, 160, 183, 218
Time-Warner, 83
Titticut Follies, 23
Toothwalkers, 178
Topsy. See *Electrocuting an Elephant*
Toto's Wife, 172
T.R. in Africa, 47, 48
Trader Horn, 123, 208, 229n.52, 239nn.141, 143
traditional narratives, 92, 94–96, 128–30, 135–40, 143, 144, 240n.4, 241n.8
Trailing African Wild Animals, 49, 52, 205
Trials of Life, 1, 190, 220, 223n.1
True Life Adventures: as film hybrids, 62–63, 65–66; compared to ethnographic films, 22; on other wildlife filmmakers, 69, 76, 78, 137, 147–48, 150; portrayals of nature and wildlife, 35, 59, 66–68, 105, 135, 140, 142–43, 145, 167–69, 173, 175, 179–80; profitability of, 63–64; relationship to cartoons, 132–35, 137, 140–41; reviews and assessments of, 21, 67–68, 105; story and character formulas, 59, 62–64, 66, 67, 69, 78, 79, 80, 131–35, 137, 140, 143, 145, 147–48, 150, 158, 232n.122. *See also* Disney studio and productions
Tundra, 125
TV ratings, 68, 80, 81, 95, 96, 105, 153, 157, 192, 217, 219
Two in the Bush, 233n.10
tyranny of formula. *See* narrative formula

Ubangi, 53, 208
UFA, 204, 231n.104
Ultimate Guide: Horses, 164, 174
Ultimate Guide series, 177
Under the Red Sea, 69
University of Pennsylvania, 41, 196
Unseen World series, 57, 118
Untamed Africa, 53
Urban, Charles, 57, 198, 199, 201

Van Dyke, W. S. "Woody," 123, 208, 239n.141
Van Lawick, Hugo, 25, 72, 94, 150, 216, 217, 221, 227n.107, 238n.129
Vanishing Prairie, The, 67–69, 132, 137, 174, 213
Variety, 67
Venice film festival, 69
viewers. *See* audiences
violent content, 34, 44, 45, 47, 60, 67, 68, 105, 182, 183–84, 220
voice-over narration, 2, 8, 25, 27, 29, 67, 72, 81, 104, 113, 115, 121, 122, 126, 153, 154, 168, 170, 188, 216, 217

Wahoo Bobcat, The, 147
Wallace, Alfred Russell, 98, 245n.14, 247n.61
Walt Disney's Wonderful World of Color, 72, 215
Wapi the Walrus, 115, 204
Warham, John, 37
Warhol, Andy, 7
Warner Bros. studios, 209, 238n.125. *See also* Time-Warner
Warshow, Robert, 5, 7
Water Birds, 35, 132, 212
Wavelength, 7
Weismuller, Johnny, 123
Welles, Orson, 216
White Fang, 154
White Shadows in the South Seas, 239n.141
White Wilderness, 65, 132–33, 146
Whitman, Walt, 109
Wild America, 81, 86, 148, 219, 220, 221
Wild Animals I Have Known, 106
Wild Birds in their Haunts, 154
Wild Cargo, 54, 209, 229n.56
Wild Discovery, 223n.5
Wild Dogs of Africa, 150
Wild Fathers, 168
Wild Kingdom, 9, 56, 72, 80, 215, 219
Wild Survivors, 238n.129
Wild Things!, 73
Wild, Wild World of Animals, 232n.154
Wilderness Society, The, 22
Wildlife Emergency, 73

Wildlife on One, 76
Wildscreen, 38, 219, 222, 246n.37
Willock, 76, 78–79, 80, 148, 215, 217, 232n.147
Wilson, Alexander, 40
Wilson, E. O., 90
Winston, Brian, 26, 225n.44, 229n.62, 233n.11
Wiseman, Frederick, 23, 26
With Eustace in Africa, 49
With Roosevelt in Africa, 47
Wohl, Ira, 23
Wolf (a.k.a. *Wild Wolves*), 177
Wolf Hunt, 6, 113, 200
Women in Film Noir, 225n.45
Woodard, Stacy, 60, 61, 118, 119, 209, 230n.78, 80, 239n.134
Woodpeckers (a.k.a. *Carpenters of the Forest*, 1954), 75, 166, 213–14
Woody Woodchuck's Adventure, 148
Woolfe, Bruce, 59, 204, 205, 209
World About Us, The, 76, 216
World of Jacques Cousteau, The, 72
World of Survival, The, 80, 217
World of the Beaver, The, 76, 78, 79, 148, 149, 217
World Wildlife Fund, 2, 224n.36
Wright, Basil, 21, 67
Wright, Ralph, 145
Wright, Will, 129, 240n.1, 241n.8
Wyler, William, 63

Year of the Jackal, 150
Yearling, The, 124
Yellowstone Cubs, 121, 128, 147, 216
Yellowstone National Park, 109, 134, 198
Yellowstone, Realm of the Coyote, 150, 243n.68

Zanuck, Darryl F., 238n.126
Zooparade, 70, 212, 213
zoos (animals in), 6, 19, 40, 41, 42, 44, 59, 70, 72, 153, 196, 197, 199, 207, 211, 215, 230n.74
Zukor, Adolph, 48

Acknowledgments

During the course of researching and writing this book, I have enjoyed the camaraderie, support, and tolerance of a number of people in the wildlife and natural history film industry. Among those with whom I have had revealing conversations and correspondence, whom I have pumped for information, whose brains I have picked, who have allowed me to bounce ideas off them, who have shared with me their thoughts, insights, perspectives, arguments, experiences, stories, and memories, as well as, in some cases, books, photographs, clippings, tapes, and other documents, thanks go (alphabetically) to: Andrew Anderson, Allison Argo, Timothy Barksdale, Des and Jen Bartlett, Richard Brock, Cindy Buxton, Barry Clark, John Francis, Hugh Gardner, Dodo Humphreys, Albert Karvonen, Peter Jones, Dereck Joubert, Bo Landin, Bob Landis, Mike Linley, William Long, Sean Morris, Cathe Neukum, Barry Paine, Christopher Palmer, Christopher Parsons, Tony Phillips, Petra Regent, Alan Root, Rick Rosenthal, Kip Spidell, Harold Tichenor, Nick Upton, and Daniel Zatz—to name a few.

None has been a greater resource and ally, however, than Jeffrey Boswall. Over the years he has been a wellspring of research materials, information, and insights, as well as contacts, introductions, and opportunities. He has been a supportive colleague, a prolific correspondent, and a good and loyal friend. This book would not have come about without his help and prodding, as well as his steadfast intellectual and moral support.

In many more hours of conversation, I have also profited from the scientific knowledge of Rolf Johnson, Charles Jonkel, Nicholas Smith-Sebasto, and especially Wiltraud Engländer, who read and critiqued drafts of several chapters. I am also grateful to Robert G. Dickson, Dagmar Hilfert, Bienvenido León, Gaby Lingke, Thomas Nørfelt, Sasha Norris, Greg Philo, and Uwe Schmidt, who all shared with me the fruits of their various scholarly labors and researches.

Thanks also go to Allison Aitken, of Survival Anglia, for some of the photographs used in this book; to Judi Hoffman, formerly of the Library of

Congress Motion Picture Division, who helped me get the most out of my research time there; to Mary Plage, for the facts on Dieter; to Tom Veltre, of the Wildlife Conservation Society, at the Bronx Zoo, for valuable research materials; and to Amy Hetzler, Jen Thomas, and Heather Thoma, of the International Wildlife Film Festival in Missoula, Montana, who have cheerfully aided and supported my efforts in a thousand ways.

Since the time when I first began taking a serious look at wildlife films, I have also been aided and supported in my efforts by Larry Gross and Paul Messaris, of the University of Pennsylvania's Annenberg School for Communication, where I was privileged to study. Both saw the potential in the subject and helped me develop it, and over the years have continued to provide both resources and inspiration. I hope this book will serve as a down payment on my debts to them.

Patricia Smith, of the University of Pennsylvania Press, has been an enthusiastic ally and a sharp-eyed but gentle critic, and has nudged me in all the right directions. For her skillful assistance, her help in getting over the bureaucratic hurdles, and for her patience with my slow writing, I am sincerely grateful.